D0044035

LIBERALISM IN GERMANY

Liberalism in Germany

DIETER LANGEWIESCHE

Translated by Christiane Banerji

Princeton University Press
Princeton, New Jersey

English translation copyright © 2000 Macmillan Press Ltd

Published in German as *Liberalismus in Deutschland* © Suhrkamp Verlag Frankfurt am Main 1988

Published in the United States and Canada by
PRINCETON UNIVERSITY PRESS
41 William Street, Princeton, New Jersey 08540

The publication of this work has been sponsored by Inter Nationes, Bonn.

First published in English 2000 by
MACMILLAN PRESS LTD
Houndmills, Basingstoke, Hampshire RG21 6XS
and London
Companies and representatives
throughout the world

Library of Congress Catalog Card Number: 99–63007
ISBN 0–691–01031–5 hardcover
ISBN 0–691–01032–3 paperback

This book is printed on paper suitable for recycling and made from fully managed and sustained forest sources.

http://pup.princeton.edu

Printed in Hong Kong

10   9   8   7   6   5   4   3   2   1

Contents

List of Tables

Foreword

John Breuilly

Originally published in 1988 Dieter Langewiesche's study of liberalism in Germany has established itself as a concise and authoritative treatment of the subject. It is an important complement to the earlier book by James Sheehan,* able to take into account recent research, especially on the role of individual German states, the local roots of liberalism, the links between liberalism and its social bases of support (especially from bourgeois groups), and the forms of political organization adopted by liberals.

Liberalism is frequently treated in Germany as a failure, as a pale shadow of more vigorous liberal movements in other countries, especially in Britain and the USA. Alternatively, German liberalism is attributed with special qualities which rather cut off its study from any comparative understanding. Langewiesche's title makes it clear that he is studying liberalism *in* Germany rather than a special form of German liberalism. He argues for the centrality of liberal politics and ideas in modern German history, and he demonstrates that failure (if, perhaps, by that we mean the failure to establish a stable form of parliamentary government until the 1950s) does not mean weakness or marginality.

An especial strength of Langewiesche's study is the manner in which he relates political values, action and organization by paying close attention to the institutional framework within which a liberal political movement takes shape. The initial emphasis is upon the development of liberalism as an oppositional politics in

---

* James Sheehan, *German Liberalism in the Nineteenth Century* (Chicago: Humanities Press, 1978; 2nd edn 1995).

the years after 1815. Langewiesche is well aware of earlier intellectual roots of liberalism in the Enlightenment and of the liberal
values of reforming princes and officials. Nevertheless, bureaucratic liberalism had a limited impact and even where it was
significant, it soon found itself running out of steam or into insup-
erable obstacles after 1815. That type of aristocratic liberalism
that played so important a role in Britain with the Whigs was of
marginal significance in Germany. Instead, liberalism developed
primarily as movements of opposition seeking to place legal
restraints upon princely rule. Due attention is paid to the social
and economic values of liberals but Langewiesche makes clear
the central place of constitutionalism for early German liberals.

This in turn made the state–liberalism relationship crucial.
Pre-1848 liberalism was oriented to the individual state, indeed
even to provinces or regions within states, and only with difficulty developed either a national programme or connections.
Langewiesche brings out a key dilemma for such liberals: they
demanded political rights and yet without such rights it was
difficult for them to establish firm political organization, and that
in turn made it impossible to construct detailed programmes
or to cultivate particular social constituencies. Liberalism needs
the institutional framework it demands in order to advance as a
political movement. However, the very processes which led to
the desired constitutional framework within which a liberal
politics could be effectively organized created new crises for
liberals and consequent shifts in their values.

The 1848 revolution was the first of these crises. Langewiesche
persuasively rejects any notion of a liberal 'betrayal'. Liberals had
never sought a revolution and understandably were concerned
to bring it to an end as quickly as possible, especially when it
threatened to take directions which ran directly counter to their
values. This quickly divided liberals from those who wished to
prolong the political breakdown, either to press more radical
political ends or to entrench a concern for 'social rights' into constitutions. The problem then was how liberals adjusted to the
successful counter-revolution.* Langewiesche notes how important it was that Prussia retained a constitutional framework after
1848 whereas Austria, even when implementing reforms, did so

* For a fuller account of the revolution see the book by Wolfram Siemann in the
same series as this book: *The German Revolution of 1848–49* (Basingstoke:
Macmillan, 1998).

within a bureaucratic and absolutist system. The pro-Prussian turn in liberalism can therefore be interpreted not as opportunism or a capitulation to state power but in part as a response to this major difference. Furthermore, Langewiesche brings out the idealism even of those liberals who preached *Realpolitik*, an argument which made sense only if one firmly believed in progress and that history was on one's side. Langewiesche points up the continuing liberal opposition to the Prussian government and especially to Bismarck from 1862 until 1867. What is also valuable in this account is the continuing attention to the politics of liberalism in the 'third Germany' of the medium-sized states and the way in which it also acquired a popular and cultural base in middling strata within Protestant circles.

Langewiesche argues that this idealist element continued in the National Liberal acceptance of Bismarck's unification, an idealism which expressed itself in the energetic pursuit of liberal reforms between 1867 and 1871. Yet by now the tensions which have been interpreted by other historians mainly in terms of a transition from opposition to power, from principle to pragmatism, and from liberal nationalism to right-wing nationalism, are seen in a very specific way by Langewiesche. He has argued elsewhere that in Germany democratization (i.e., the granting of universal manhood suffrage for national parliamentary elections) preceded parliamentarization (i.e., the transfer of sovereignty to parliament). Liberals confronted the twin problems that they could not secure power through control of parliament and yet at the same time confronted challenges from non-liberal movements – above all, those associated with Catholic and labour interests – which threatened to undermine their domination of oppositional politics.

The result, as Langewiesche clearly shows, was a fragmentation of liberalism in both organizational and value terms. Some liberals shifted to an authoritarian emphasis upon their national and cultural values in order to justify supporting the state in attacks on socialists, Catholics and other opponents. Other liberals concentrated upon social and economic reforms, often achieved through control of particular urban or even state governments elected on undemocratic franchises. Yet others took refuge in a stubborn constitutionalist opposition to the existing state. New developments – for example, the pursuit of empire after 1890 – would be adopted by some liberals.

xii FOREWORD

However, Langewiesche also demolishes the idea of any precipitate decline or failure of liberalism after 1871. Such a judgement is in part a product of the sheer domination of liberalism over oppositional politics before 1871; once it ceased to dominate, some historians have been quick to write it off. Langewiesche points to the political strengths of not being focused on one party, social group or programme, as was the case with most non-liberal politics. It meant that the family of liberal movements could continue to attract a diverse and large amount of support.

The focus of this present book is on political movements, values and organizations At the same time, supported by well-chosen collections of statistics, Langewiesche demonstrates the shifting social bases of liberalism and connects political values to more general cultural values.

The section dealing with the period after 1918 inevitably has something of a postscript quality. Liberalism found it difficult to survive in most countries during the bleak inter-war period, but Langewiesche brings out well the way in which the earlier tendency to divide by interests and to compensate for this with rather grandiose claims to represent national values reached its apotheosis in the last years of the Weimar Republic. It was especially voters from the middling strata of Protestant regions – the core of liberal support in earlier decades – who displayed this fluctuating conduct, a conduct which led to the victory of the National Socialist party with its extreme nationalist claims but also characterized by chaotic and faction-ridden organization.

In the post-1945 period Langewiesche's central point is to contrast the *general* commitment to a liberal framework for politics in West Germany – signalled by the socialist surrender of a marxist programme and the Christian Democrat disavowal of confessional positions – with the rather curious transformation of the Free Democratic Party from rather illiberal beginnings to a small centrist party with liberal pretensions and a capacity to figure in coalitions with either of the major parties. The message seems clear: liberalism is secure when it is entrenched in the major institutions of state and society and in the values of all major parties rather than when it is a crusading political concern confined to just a few of the major social groups.

October 1998

Preface

In principle, liberalism is a perfectly clear and simple orientation for political action: it is about doing everything possible to increase the individual's chances in life. The more people there are with more chances in life, the more liberal a society is.

Ralf Dahrendorf's definition[1] is certainly consistent with the history of liberalism. Whether the reverse is true, however, is another matter. To say that is not to criticize liberalism, but to describe the long and often sorry path which has been trodden since the end of the eighteenth century; a path which during some phases has been marked clearly, and in others less so or hardly at all, by liberal ideas about the state, society and culture. These ideas, and the attempts made to use them to shape individual lives and environments, have never been applied in any consistent fashion. Indeed, as society became more complex, the variety of ideas also increased. Nevertheless, it is possible to identify some continuous threads. It may be appropriate to begin by outlining them in broad terms.

Social liberalism has always existed, even if this point is usually disputed. It was this, and not economic liberalism, that came first. German early liberalism did not focus on the legal and constitutional state 'alone'; it thought in social terms too. The aim of the early liberal utopia of a *klassenlose Bürgergesellschaft* (classless society of citizens) was a situation in which everyone would enjoy a secure livelihood without extreme differences in wealth, which were regarded as intolerable in the 'civil society' liberals aspired to. This Utopia was drawn from pre-industrial, urban middle-class conditions. When these conditions finally disappeared in

Germany around the mid-nineteenth century, it became necessary to redefine 'social liberalism'. In the absence of models this
was no easy task, but it was attempted nevertheless. But it was
not Friedrich Naumann and those few people who shared his
views at the end of the nineteenth century who made the first
attempts. The main line of tradition in German social liberalism
continued in the towns after the middle of the century. Little is
known of this subject, and this present volume can provide only
a provisional outline of it. This municipal social liberalism began
in the first half of the nineteenth century, but waned during the
Weimar Republic, when the 'welfare state' was developed along
centralist lines. Social liberal trends were reinforced and successfully continued in the Federal Republic. In the process, party
liberalism lost its formerly strong municipal anchor – an indication of the general decline in its importance. Today, the social
welfare programmes of the municipalities are no longer determined by liberals, and the history of municipal liberalism, which
was always a social welfare liberalism, has come to an end. This
is true at least of party liberalism. Liberalism continues in the
municipalities today without the liberal parties.

Economic liberalism is younger than social liberalism, at least
as a main liberal strand. It first acquired the status of a main
strand in the era of the *Reichsgründung*, or foundation of the
Empire. Of course, calls had been heard to free the economy
from shackles of all kinds before that time too, and some of
them had come from liberals. But it was not by such calls that
the liberal could be identified. Political and economic liberalism
only merged when the battle for national economic territory
became a vehicle for liberal nation-state policy. In the thinking
of many liberals, political and economic liberalism then fused
to the extent that the agreement of liberals to the introduction
of the German protective tariff policy at the end of the 1870s
appeared to be a departure from liberalism. After this decisive point, political liberalism was not able to coexist so easily
with economic liberalism, whose importance grew with the
liberal parties of the Kaiserreich. But they did not become
economic parties. That would not have corresponded to their
bürgerlich middle-class self-image. Their desire to assert themselves in the elections would also have militated against a transformation of that kind. Their major problem was rather: 'What
does *bürgerlich* mean?'

This question has accompanied liberals from the start. But
only around the mid-nineteenth century did it become the issue
which led to the decline of political liberalism from the national
constitutional movement to a majority party, and finally to a
niche party between the two major players. The problem had
hardly existed before the middle of the century. The liberal
image of the citizen contained a promise and a task for all: this
status would be accessible to everyone through their own economic, cultural and political efforts. Anyone who had not yet
achieved this state of full civic independence was not regarded as
a full citizen. This ideal of the citizen, who was responsible for
himself and therefore also able to assume political responsibility
for others, emerged as a promise for the future of great unifying
force. From the second half of the nineteenth century onwards,
however, it began to decline until it represented only the ballast
of tradition for the liberal parties. Liberals continued to participate in the 'Staatsbürgergesellschaft' project which aimed at a
future society of citizens of the state, but the liberal parties no
longer steered events. Free enterprise, which they hailed as a
guarantor of progress, restricted their opportunities in the political market, where others were making more attractive offers.
This was true above all of the most pressing task: the social
fulfilment of citizens' rights. Municipal social liberalism did not
do this. It improved social provision for all, but surrounded
them with the walls of undemocratic institutions; walls which in
the Kaiserreich were nowhere higher than in the municipalities.

The central liberal principle of the citizen as the core of the
state and of society lost its political competitive edge when, in the
second half of the nineteenth century, the middle classes of
industrial society began to fragment into countless social, economic and cultural groupings, with an extremely wide range of
interests. Ever since then the liberal parties have searched in vain
for a conceptual binding force with which this multitude of
interests and the conflicts between them might be reconciled in a
common policy. Understandably, liberals thought they had
found a binding force of this kind in the idea of the nation and
the nation-state. The great calls for emancipation in the nineteenth century came together in the idea of the nation, which was
largely formulated by liberals. They were also at the forefront of
the national movement, which may not itself have created the
German nation-state of 1871, but which certainly facilitated its

creation. After the foundation of the nation-state, the idea of the nation by no means lost its comprehensive social unifying force, but it did forfeit its liberal colouring.

Thus, the prevailing imperialist mood in Wilhelmine Germany, which demanded its 'place in the sun', benefited not the liberal parties but the new nationalist mass associations, for whom liberal values counted for nothing. The fact that political liberalism was nevertheless unable to see any binding force other than nationalism, which slipped from the grasp of its leadership, doubly weakened the liberal parties. In the vain hope of being able to influence nationalism, they followed it on its path to the right. And in doing so, they came into conflict with the central value of their political and social model: a liberal society of citizens of the state. Under the extremely difficult conditions of the Weimar Republic, this conflict between national and liberal aims, between the nation-state and the liberal constitutional state, reached its climax. It represented a bitter end for the liberal parties: they had played a major role in forming the basis of the parliamentary republic of 1919; with brief interruptions they were involved in Reich governments until 1932; and yet they still ended as inconsequential splinter groups, avoided by the very 'middle-class' centre which the liberals had once hoped would expand to form society itself and represent the basis of a liberal state. After 1945, too, German party liberalism retained its focus on the nation-state in the form which had emerged in 1871. Only in the *neue Ostpolitik* of the 1960s did this continuity come to an end. Since political liberalism had rightly seen itself as the representative of the national movement and the nation-state of 1871, this legacy was particularly hard to bear.

This introductory sketch is intended to show that there are many paths from the history of German liberalism to the present day. But they do not all lead to one party. The central ideas of historical liberalism are now common property, and in the Federal Republic they have been adopted as constitutional norms. This is true of the core liberal demands for a legal and constitutional state and for the opportunity for all citizens of the state to participate in state decision-making processes. However, liberalism has never developed similarly uniform concepts for the economic and social spheres and for everyday conduct. Preferences existed, but only within the framework of a broad spectrum of ideas. This made the liberals flexible and innovative.

Political liberalism's range narrowed after the second half of the nineteenth century, when it was no longer able to compete with other parties in important areas. This was true of the pressing problems of reforming the social order and the search for a way out of a politically divided class society. It was also true of the attempt to make the religious dividing line more porous on a political level. Liberalism suffered one of its gravest defeats on this issue. The liberal parties remained Protestant, yet ever fewer Protestants declared their support for a liberal party.

Conceived as a blend of political, social and cultural models, and as an organized pressure group or association, liberalism has left its mark on German society and its institutions in an extraordinary variety of ways. The central objective of a society which advances towards creating more chances in life for each individual is not considered outmoded. The paths leading to that point cannot, however, be read from the history of liberalism alone. But it may be useful to identify them – even if some of them proved to be wrong tracks.

Preface to the English Edition

Since 1988, when the German edition of this book was first published, the picture of German liberalism drawn by historical scholarship has not changed in any important respect. Many details have been researched more precisely but that has not altered the broad outlines.

This study was the first to be based on a notion that has since gained wide acceptance, i.e., that the history of German liberalism cannot be properly assessed if it is considered only on the level of the nation-state. The federal pattern of German history has also played a profound role in shaping liberalism, which served its apprenticeship in the commonwealths of the German Confederation (1815–66), and reached the height of its power in the states of the Empire (1871–1918). While that has been studied more precisely in the meantime,[1] it is only recently that historical scholarship has begun to consider the significant role played by the liberals in the cities up to 1918. It is here that we can expect new and pathbreaking results, as recent studies of the urban middle-class demonstrate.[2] After the First World War, the tradition of strong municipal liberalism in Germany came to an end,[3] and this was one of the most profound turning points in its development.

In the last decade, there has also been a very lively study of middle-class culture in Germany and in the European context,[4] but so far it has contributed little to the history of liberalism. This is surprising, since liberalism was always seen as a representative of the middle class and its culture. Nor do the latest studies clearly show whether 'middle-class culture' established a special proximity to liberalism. A work comparable to Hans H. Gerth's 1935 study, which substantiated the symbiosis of liberal thought and 'middle-class intelligence' with their common affinity for the new in the period of 1800, has not yet been written for this later period.[5] Therefore, we do not yet know if and to what extent middle-class culture as a particular life-style[6] was determined by liberal norms and whether the middle-class catalogue of virtues shaped in the eighteenth century made society receptive to liberal ideas.[7] Whether 'middle-class virtues' meant something different for a liberal citizen than for a conservative one, whether liberalism was 'only' a political party with a more or less open political and social worldview, or whether it also influenced middle-class norms and general life-style, have not yet been examined either. Therefore, work on German liberalism and the new studies of middle-class culture stand side by side, but are not yet connected to one another. Future scholarship must bridge this gap if it is to determine whether the basis for the enormous flexibility of liberalism in Germany, and in Europe in general, in adapting to the most diverse social and political relations may be precisely that liberals did not want to impose strict principles on social life. Herman Lübbe sees the liberating power of liberal philosophy in this lack of principles, which allowed it to triumph over its opponents who remained loyal to their principles: 'Liberalism is the system of a principled taboo against endowing the great truths that establish an orientation in life with an obligation of political recognition.'[8] Whether these timeless philosophical maxims did indeed permeate historical liberalism and determine its relations to middle-class norms of behaviour still awaits study.

November 1988   DIETER LANGEWIESCHE

Notes

1. See Konrad Jarausch and Larry Eugene Jones (eds), *In Search of a Liberal Germany: Studies in the History of German Liberalism from 1789 to the Present* (New York and Oxford, 1990); Lothar Gall and Dieter Langewiesche (eds), *Liberalismus und Region: Zur Geschichte des deutschen Liberalismus im 19. Jahrhundert* (Munich, 1995, Historische Zeitschrift, vol. 19).
2. See the research report that presents the collected new literature on German liberalism and the middle class from the late eighteenth century to the present, in Lothar Gall (ed.), *Bürgertum und bürgerlich-liberale Bewegung in Mitteleuropa seit dem 18. Jahrhundert* (Munich, 1997; Historische Zeitschrift, vol. 17).

3. Larry Eugene Jones, *German Liberalism and the Dissolution of the Weimar Party System, 1918–1933* (Chapel Hill and London, 1988) is now of fundamental importance for an understanding of liberalism in the Weimar Republic.
4. Gall (ed.), *Bürgertum und bürgerliche-liberale Bewegung*.
5. Hans H. Gerth, *Bürgerliche Intelligenz um 1800: Zur Soziologie des deutschen Frühliberalismus*, with a foreword and supplementary bibliography by Ulrich Herrman, *Kritische Studien zur Geschichtswissenschaft*, vol. 19 (Göttingen, 1976; first published in Frankfurt, 1935).
6. See, especially, M. Rainer Lepsius, 'Zur Soziologie des Bürgertums und der Bürgerlichkeit', in Jürgen Kocka (ed.), *Bürger und Bürgerlichkeit im 19. Jahrhundert* (Göttingen, 1987) pp. 79–100; M. Rainer Lepsius, 'Das Bildungsbürgertum als ständische Vergesellschaftung', in Lepsius (ed.), *Bildungsbürgertum im 19. Jahrhundert*, part III (Stuttgart, 1992) pp. 9–18. An excellent survey in an historical perspective is to be found in Georg Bollenbeck, *Bildung und Kultur: Glanz und Elend eines deutschen Deutungsmusters* (Frankfurt a. M. and Leipzig, 1994).
7. See the introduction in Dieter Langewiesche (ed.), *Liberalismus im 19. Jahrhundert: Deutschland im europäischen Vergleich, Kritische Studien zur Geschichtswissenschaft*, vol. 79 (Göttingen, 1988) pp. 11–19; Langewiesche, 'Liberalism and the Middle Classes in Nineteenth-Century Europe: A Comparative Study', in Jürgen Kocka and Allen Mitchell (eds), *Bourgeois Society in Nineteenth-Century Europe* (Oxford, 1993) pp. 40–69.
8. Hermann Lübbe, *Fortschrittsreaktionen: Über konservative und destruktive Modernität* (Cologne, 1987) p. 43.

Acknowledgements

Many people have supported me in the preparation of this volume. Without Hans-Ulrich Wehler it would never have been written at all. He persuaded me to start it, and then helpfully insisted that I finish. Friedrich Lenger offered advice and criticism on the entire manuscript and Beryl Wichmann typed it. Birgit Czernotzky, Michael Obergfell, Thomas Penka, Annette Roth and Edda Salzmann helped to locate the literature and checked countless details. I would like to express my thanks to all of them.

List of Abbreviations

ADAV	Allgemeiner Deutscher Arbeiterverein (General German Workers' Association)
AH	Abgeordnetenhaus (House of Deputies)
BDI	Bund der Industriellen (League of Industrialists)
BdL	Bund der Landwirte (Agrarian League)
BVP	Bayerische Volkspartei (Bavarian People's Party)
CDU	Christlich-Demokratische Union (Christian Democratic Union)
CSU	Christlich-Soziale Union (Christian Social Union)
CVDI	Centralverband Deutscher Industrieller (Central Association of German Industrialists)
DDP	Deutsche Demokratische Partei (German Democratic Party)
DHV	Deutschnationaler Handlungsgehilfen-Verband (German National Association of Commercial Employees)
DNVP	Deutschnationale Volkspartei (German National People's Party)
DVP	Deutsche Volkspartei (German People's Party)
FDP	Freie Demokratische Partei (Free Democratic Party)
FK	Freikonservative (Free Conservatives)
K	Konservative (Conservatives)
KPD	Kommunistische Partei Deutschlands (Communist Party of Germany)
LL	Linksliberale (Left Liberals)
NL	Nationalliberale (National Liberals)
NSDAP	Nationalsozialistische Deutsche Arbeiterpartei (National Socialist German Workers' Party)

SDAP	Sozialdemokratische Arbeiterpartei (Social Democratic Workers' Party)
SPD	Sozialdemokratische Partei Deutschlands (German Social Democratic Party)
USDP	Unabhängige Sozialdemokratische Partei Deutschlands (Independent German Social Democratic Party)
Z	Zentrum (Centre Party)

1 Early Liberalism and 'Middle-Class Society'

Early Liberalism as a Political Constitutional Movement

When did early liberalism begin in Germany? This simple question is hard to answer clearly. It depends on one's definition of 'liberal', and any definition is controversial, even amongst historians. If early liberalism is defined as a *political movement*, whose aim was to implement the legal and constitutional state, to safeguard the individual from the state, but also to enable that individual to participate in the state, then early liberalism began around 1815. It was then that hopes began to fade that the liberal society of citizens of the state would emerge directly from state reforms. For as the states of the German Confederation created in 1815 were able to demonstrate to the public within a few short years, the great reforms of Prussia and the Confederation of the Rhine could certainly be combined with political reaction. Indeed, political 'liberalization' was by no means an inevitable consequence of 'the modernization' of the state, society and the economy. Not even the existence of constitutions and parliamentary institutions could guarantee that, though they did pave the way for it. The south German constitutional states had legislatures which provided the emerging 'civil' society, enmeshed in its *ständisch* traditions, with a place in the state. These states consequently became the most important training ground for German early liberalism. It was here that it 'underwent its constitutional apprenticeship',[1] until the unrest and reforms which followed the French July Revolution of 1830 opened up new opportunities for activity in the north German *Mittelstaaten* too.

1

The restorative paralysis of the political system after 1815 taught early liberals in Germany that the 'political emancipation of society' must precede 'all future reforms'.[2] The opportunities for the participation of citizens in the state, from the municipal to the highest decision-making level, therefore had to be enshrined in a constitutional and legal framework. Individual reforms had to be linked so that they never lost sight of the lodestars of liberal politics. Under the heading 'Liberal, Liberalismus' (Liberal, Liberalism) in the Rotteck–Welcker *Staatslexikon* (vol. 9, 1840), these lodestars were defined as 'maturity', 'independent thought' and 'independent action', based on the 'principles of rational law'. In this 'fundamental work on the liberalism of the *Vormärz* period' (F. Schnabel), Paul Achatius Pfizer described basic convictions which were not automatically fulfilled as concomitant phenomena of state reform policy, but which had to be pushed through against it. This conflict between bureaucratic state modernization and liberal modernization, reinforced by the unfulfilled liberal hopes of a nation-state, led after 1815 to early liberalism's development into a political movement. Although it never abandoned its desire for compromise, this movement now voiced its core constitutional and political demands to the state rulers in an increasingly forceful manner.

If we define German early liberalism as an oppositional political constitutional movement between 1815 and 1848, we should not overlook the debt which early liberal models owed to the eighteenth century; to the '*ständisch* freedoms' of the Holy Roman Empire; to Enlightened Absolutism; and above all to the Enlightenment. 'The most important demands of the liberal era had already been formulated before 1815 in Germany.' Fritz Valjavec's belief has become one of the commonplaces of research into liberalism,[3] yet his pioneering work of 1951 has not yet stimulated further research. Valjavec regarded liberalism as an already pre-revolutionary 'current' which emerged around 1770, ahead of the conservative and democratic 'currents' which formed as a result of the critical analysis of liberalism. But although recent research has thrown light on the beginnings of conservatism and of the democrats ('Jacobins'), the development of early liberal thought in the final years of the eighteenth century has remained largely in the dark.[4] This may be because 'liberalism', as a term for a political alignment, only became fully current amongst the German public around 1830, and so the early representatives of liberal thought did not yet have at their disposal the term 'liberal' as a distinguishing political criterion.[5] This lack of etymological clarity reflects the difficulties in making clear distinctions between early liberal, early conservative and early democratic currents, not least because individual representatives of these alignments repeatedly changed their positions under the impact of the French Revolution and of post-revolutionary developments.

Even Valjavec stressed that it was only after 1815, after the beginning of the 'restoration' in Germany, that the 'full and conscious distinction was made between the legitimist absolute and the liberal middle-class principle', when it became clear 'that both parties wanted fundamentally different things' (Valjavec, p. 413). The history of terminology over the ensuing decades reflects this basic distinction after 1815. None the less, it should be noted that the early liberals' core demands had been formulated before the creation of the liberal constitutional movement and before the new meaning of the word 'liberal' emerged. These demands date back to the period before the French Revolution, which defined the fronts more sharply in Germany, too, but which did not create them.[6]

Some examples of precedents for early liberalism in the 'Enlightened' thought of the eighteenth century might be useful here. August Ludwig von Schlözer (1735–1809), whom Valjavec called 'the forefather of German liberalism' (p. 99), demanded that the monarch be bound to the principles of the rule of law so that the subject would be guaranteed 'original human and municipal rights' and 'total freedom in his actions'. He also argued for a representative body with two chambers, one of which should be elected. He called for public involvement in the state by means of a free press and petitions, and for the individual's right 'to think aloud'. Schlözer's position on two fronts – against the absolutism of the princes and against the democrats – and his plea for 'reforms but not revolutions', mirror the fundamental positions of the future early liberal movement, just as they reflect the desire for reform on the part of those contemporaries who shared his views. This is also true of his criticism of the aristocracy, a core element of early liberal thought, and of his demand for legal equality without blurring the 'inequality of rank and of the circumstances of fortune' which 'is based on the natural rights of the individual, on the differences between ability and talent and on the needs of civil society' (Peter Villaume, 1794). Legal equality and material inequality were not regarded as incompatible. It is only when the two are taken together, wrote the Schleswig-Holstein political journalist August Hennings in 1792, that we get 'civic freedom'; for the 'true civic order' recognizes the 'inequality which stems' from birth, income and 'the inner development of the forces of the soul', but 'the freedom must exist everywhere' to enable the 'continual development ... of the entire human race' to take place. He was against privilege, but in favour of protecting earned property, otherwise every 'generation' would have to 'dissolve the bonds of society and create a new one'.[7]

Liberal models of the early nineteenth century were permeated by these ideas from the German Late Enlightenment period. It is difficult to shed light on the fluid transitions between them, yet since Valjavec no serious attempt has been made to do so. For Valjavec the decisive difference between the two lay in the liberals' 'primarily political interests', and in their 'addressing of the concrete political situation' (p. 28), which the Enlightenment had mapped out in advance.

Bureaucratic Liberalism

The advantage of defining early liberalism as a constitutional movement is the selectivity of the definition. In doing so, we can exclude all 'liberalizing trends in sub-spheres, in economic life, in social relations, in the cultural and church context' (L. Gall), whose major aim was not the co-operation and shared responsibility of state citizens in a representative constitutional state. The middle-class liberal desire for the political emancipation of the citizen is thus clearly distinguished from the great bureaucratic reforms of around 1800. Yet these are also often referred to as 'liberal' because they 'liberalized', in the sense that they eliminated or curtailed *ständisch* and feudal ties, and restricted the traditional intermediate powers between the state and the subject. This broad understanding of the word 'liberal' gives rise to major problems in placing individual reforms and reformers in political categories. Thus, for example, whilst one person regards Freiherr vom Stein as a 'conservative innovator against the Enlightenment and rationalism, against the "idea of 1789" and economic liberalism' (B. Vogel), others hail him as 'the most significant example of *ständisch* liberalism in the Germany of the

turn of the century'. For 'the real criterion of party membership' – of liberalism – 'was energy for reform and desire for
innovation, in contrast to an adherence to traditional conditions'.
It did not 'originate in rationalist natural rights, or the historical
ständisch spirit' (H. Heffter).

Even if we do not accept this definition of 'liberal' as a collective term for desire for any kind of reform, it is impossible to
overlook the significance of bureaucratic reforms for the liberal
constitutional movement. Thus, the 'bureaucratic liberalism' of
the reform era in Prussia and in the southern German states has
with good reason been described as the link between Enlightened Absolutism and constitutional liberalism. The clear assignment of bureaucratic liberalism to one of these poles 'would
artificially sever the obvious links between the German reforming states of the late eighteenth and early nineteenth century'
and the numerous varieties of constitutionalist liberalism (K.-G.
Faber). The 'revolution before the revolution' (K. von Raumer),
Enlightened Absolutism and the Enlightenment, had prepared
the ground for the reform phase at the beginning of the
nineteenth century, but it was not until this 'revolution from
above' that the frontiers of traditional society in Germany were
shattered and the 'breakthrough of the middle classes' (E. Weis)
inaugurated. This had a profound impact on German liberalism,
and created a basis for its faith in the state's ability to reform, a
faith which may have been increasingly tested, but which also
proved to be resilient. The eagerness with which all liberals tried
to avoid a revolutionary break with the state authorities in 1848
(see Chapter 2) is impressive testimony to the liberal faith in the
state, which would be incomprehensible without the experiences
of the reform era. The reforming bureaucracy was one of the
'forerunners of middle-class liberalism' (Faber).[8] The two con-
verged in many demands, but diverged too on central issues.
A brief examination should be made here of the many tensions
between the two, which increased in intensity after the restorative changes around 1819; the Karlsbad Decrees were a milestone
throughout Germany in this respect.

The reform phase which began in 1800 drove forward the
development of modern state rule to an unprecedented degree.
A new concept of the state emerged. The state which now
developed – a modern state, indifferent to religious matters –
insisted that public power should lie entirely in its hands. It took

action on the numerous multi-tiered rural, *ständisch* and feudal rights which had evolved historically, and those who had enjoyed these rights now found themselves subject to a process of legal standardization, which forced them to accept a new concept of 'civil society'. This radical change was triggered externally by the export of French revolutionary ideas in the wake of Napoleonic hegemony in Continental Europe. It was carried out by reformers in the state bureaucracy, which regarded itself as the 'general estate', 'which made the general interests of the social situation' its business, and whose 'private interests were satisfied in its work for the general good'.

This definition by Hegel (*Philosophy of Right*, 1821, paragraph 205) corresponded to the German bureaucracy's self-image and to its social position. It was part of state rule, it formulated and implemented its aims and it stood apart from the feudal system of estates. The bureaucracy's isolation from the estates, its academic education, and its model of individuals rising through achievement rather than origins created a 'style of thought' (H. H. Gerth), which united civil servants and middle-class intellectuals against a society in which individuals were privileged by rank or birth. It is a feature of the relative backwardness in development of German society, compared with that in England and France, that the programmatic drafts outlining the future society of citizens of the state were not produced by the middle classes of the towns, who had adapted to the system of estates and who defended their own privileges, nor by a 'bourgeoisie' which did not yet exist in Germany, but by a non-*ständisch* intelligentsia. The bureaucracy was the only social group which could effectively attempt to put them into practice, since 'in pre-constitutional times it was the only group' which practised 'politics as a profession' (B. Vogel), and which could translate politics into state action. For this reason, the 'liberal civil service became one of the strongest unifying factors of German early liberalism' (Gerth).[9] The conditions of a society unshattered by revolution, still extensively obedient to tradition, made the civil servant, who was unplaced in the system of estates and capable of political action, the model citizen of the state.

In reality, however, the picture was not quite as clear as this might suggest. The 'revolution' of the bureaucracy not only remained a mere skeleton, but even where there were common threads, it conformed only to a very limited degree to the aims of the liberal constitutional movement. Desire for reform did not yet make the reforming, liberalizing wing of the civil service a permanent partner for the liberal movement. Whereas the movement's central aim was a constitution which safeguarded the rights of the individual and his participatory rights, the bureaucratic reformers focused primarily on the state which was able to act, and not on the participation of citizens in that state.

In *Prussia* almost all reforming civil servants agreed that a 'voice of the nation' which could be heard and shared in did not yet exist. As the Prussian finance minister and future minister of education and the arts, Karl von Altenstein (1817–38), said in 1808, 'what was heard was idle gossip or the one-sided, limited opinion of the individual, determined by private interests'. Gottlob J. Christian Kunth was one of the most important Prussian economic experts and a staunch supporter of freedom of trade and enterprise. He expressed in even clearer terms the reforming civil servants' lack of faith in 'society's' ability to form opinions of its own: 'It is true to say that people here (and by that I mean those who are not involved in public administration) live a kind of civic death.'[10] Creating a popular representative body would have implied the renunciation of radical reforms, given society's resistance to the abolition of privilege. It was for this reason that the guiding principle of the Prussian reforming bureaucracy was first reform, and then a constitution and national representation. It was unable to see its strategy through to the end, however. Bureaucratic liberalism increasingly lost its room for manoeuvre after the Wars of Liberation. The Karlsbad Decrees of 1819 not only served to tame the political public, but also to discipline the liberal wing of the civil service. Although it was liberal motives that initially delayed the keeping of the constitutional promises of 1810 and 1815, the 'return to bureaucratic absolutism' after 1815 ended the short 'decade of liberal politics in Prussia'.[11] The Prussian state liberalized economic society, but it did not open it up to make a society of citizens of the state with a constitution and with the opportunity to participate in parliament at state level. So although it freed its 'subjects from their regional *ständisch* ties', they became not 'free citizens' but 'administered' citizens.[12] There can be no doubt that this impeded and delayed the creation of a liberal movement in Prussia. But at the same time, during its brief phase of effectiveness, Prussian bureaucratic liberalism created the prerequisites for the constitutionalist liberalism which from the 1830s onwards began to issue ever more frequent and urgent reminders regarding the constitution that it was still waiting for as the final stage of bureaucratic reform.

The *southern German states* took a different path in the reform era, in which the economic order was liberalized to a lesser degree than in Prussia, but in which political liberalism was offered more favourable opportunities for development. Here, too, the reforms came from the state rather than from society. In contrast to Prussia, however, they were buttressed by the creation of legislatures and constitutions, with which the monarchs sought to form a unified state by integrating the territorial gains they had aimed for in the era of the Confederation of the Rhine, and which they had secured at the Congress of Vienna. In this they were successful. But even here, in this specifically southern German mix of bureaucratic and 'parliamentary representative integration' (E. R. Huber) in the new states which had emerged from the Holy Roman Empire and Napoleon's reorganizations, it was the bureaucracy which determined the political course. Even in Baden, regarded as a model liberal state, parliamentary liberalism was never directly involved in central political decisions. At best, liberal deputies could hope that at least some of their ideas would be 'represented by the left wing of the enlightened bureaucracy, by the so-called privy councillor liberalism within the government camp'.[13]

In contrast to Prussia, the era of Badenese liberalism lasted until the 1830s, when a series of reforms were implemented under interior minister Ludwig Winter and his permanent secretary Nebenius. Laws on the press and on the right to assemble were liberalized, as was local government. The conditions for the dissolution of feudal tenure and tithes were created and the judicial system was reformed (public and oral hearings). Co-operation between bureaucratic and constitution-alist liberalism did not break down until the new Blittersdorff government (1835), whose authoritarian policies included the disciplining of liberal civil servant deputies.

With its reforms in the southern German states and in Prussia, the enlightened authoritarian state had begun a course which went beyond the limits of reform, which as a rule even liberal civil servants were reluctant to cross. The criticism of the bureau-cracy, which increased during the thirties, documents the break between bureaucratic modernization, which was compatible with political illiberality, and the liberal public, which now began to emerge more self-consciously, and which had gained in extent and social breadth. It used its own wider structural demands to counter the 'tendency to patronize the people, to try to make them happy' (Gall), which linked bureaucratic 'privy councillor liberalism' to Enlightened Absolutism.[14] One might say that civil servant liberalism followed the same path as the liberal movement for a time, and that its reforms unwittingly created favourable conditions for the development of the movement – conditions which in Germany could only be created 'from above' by the state, given the 'incomplete formation of the middle class'.[15] The extent to which constitutionalist liberalism drew strength from state reforms is revealed in an examination of the *Habsburg Monarchy*, which did not participate in the reform era at the beginning of the nineteenth century. Together with the problems arising from the multiplicity of nations under Habsburg rule, this was a major factor in the retarded development of liberalism in the Austrian state.[16]

Political and Social Models of the Liberal Movement

Core Political Demands

'The future is progress towards freedom and reason: that, beyond anything that can be proved, is the true belief of liberalism.'[17] It was a belief in its own mission within a process of progress which was perceived as unstoppable. As Pfizer wrote in the article from the Rotteck–Welcker *Staatslexikon* referred to above (vol. 9, 1840), liberalism is 'nothing other ... than the transition, which becomes necessary at a certain level of human development, from the natural state to the *Rechtsstaat*', the state founded on the rule of law. Even if 'institutions and laws sometimes strive to go backwards', the 'ideas of reasonable law are always rekindled again and again. ... For freedom has now become a necessity, and no human power can hope to stifle those earth-shattering ideas which will find their way across all obstacles, over all barriers placed in their way until their course, which has been outlined by a higher hand, is complete.'

For liberals, the state which would house the society of the future, a society based on the principles of reason and freedom, was not the republic, but the *constitutional monarchy*. This is the central difference between liberals and democrats, who could be distinguished for the first time from the thirties onwards, and then even more clearly in the pre-revolutionary decade.[18] This process of separation peaked during the 1848–9 revolution (see Chapter 2), although it had begun well before that. A constitutional monarchy implied, as Pfizer wrote in 1840, the rejection of the 'most rampant radicalism', as well as the 'affected idolatry of the existing order, or of what has already died out'. As Karl von Rotteck wrote in the Foreword to the *Staatslexikon*, it meant 'establishing the proper terms of peace between reasonable and historical law', in order to achieve 'the most perfect form of state, given our historical conditions'. As an indispensable basis and guarantor of the 'idea of the true state' (C. T. Welcker), the liberals demanded a constitution which would preclude 'all despotism from above' and below, and which would establish 'the *bürgerlich* situation on the fixed and immutable law of morality' (K. H. L. Pölitz).

The political credo of German early liberalism was not freedom from the state, but freedom in and in relation to the state.

> Accordingly [Rotteck wrote], the constitutional system means that everyone enjoys the same rights of participation in the good deeds of the commonwealth, the same [legal and judicial] guarantees of personal freedom and of lawful property-ownership and the acquisition of wealth, that all those who are able are called to take up office, and in turn that everyone is subject to the same obligations by the law.[19]

Without a constitution, Rotteck wrote as early as 1818, a people was 'not a people in the pure sense of the word', but would remain always a mere 'sum of subjects'.[20]

The liberal idea of a state founded on the rule of law was aimed at political change whilst retaining what had evolved historically; it was a desire not for a revolutionary break, but for a 'kind of internal political pacifism'.[21] This ruled out combative action. Nevertheless, it did achieve a degree of success. But most of its achievements are concealed by the term 'restoration' which is commonly used to describe the period between the Vienna Congress and the revolution of 1848–9. These achievements included the *Grundrechte* or Basic Rights, which, like the constitutions, had been granted after careful bureaucratic calculation, but which then even 'before 1848 [became] a carefully calculated means by which the liberal parties of the chambers[22] could measure government policy against constitutional principles, and by which they were able to effect a limited degree of influence on them. At the centre of the lists of Basic Rights, and of liberal demands for basic rights, were the rights of the individual; above all, freedom of conscience and religion, the security of the individual and of property. There were also rights which, though they remained vulnerable, enabled a public to emerge which was able to organize and use its arguments to influence state policy. *Freedom of the press* was a core liberal demand; it was indispensable if the representative system was going to be able to function, and a vital component of that system. As Welcker said in 1830, only a free press could replace the direct participation of citizens in 'legislation, government and the courts'. Only this could break the despotism of the German 'civil servant pashas' to the advantage of everyone, including the monarchs, and pave the way for the unity of Germany as a 'source of common German national culture'. In short, without freedom of the press, there could be no freedom for the citizen of the state, and no hope of overcoming 'the estrangement of the fraternal German tribes'.[23]

The right to free association was no less important to liberals. For them, the *Verein* or association was the central form of the new post-*ständisch* 'civil society' which was free of bureaucratic patronization. After the dissolution of *ständisch*-corporate bonds, the association provided opportunities for creating new, freely chosen rules and the means by which the urgent social, economic and cultural problems of the day might be resolved.[24]

The Basic Rights were violated and curtailed by the individual states and by the German Confederation, yet even during the 'restoration' period they were always more than a worthless piece of paper. Again and again they were used by liberal deputies to draw attention to the way in which authoritarian power restricted the principle of the state founded on the rule of law. Reference to the Basic Rights was used to demand the abolition of feudal and seigneurial dues as well as the equality of all citizens in the payment of state and local taxes. It was used to demand public education, protection of the privacy of the postal system, the elimination of the administration of justice by the administration itself, and to demand compensation laws against damage to peasant property caused by hunting.

Equal *suffrage* for all men was not included in the liberal list of Basic Rights. (In the eyes of liberals, women were excluded from the society of state citizens with full political rights.) Liberals may have demanded equality before the law, but they did not seek 'the external equality of property and power'. Equality before the law, as Pfizer argues in his statement of basic principles in the *Staatslexikon* ('Liberal, Liberalism', vol. 9) is 'a world away' from 'despotic levelling out'. For liberals, establishing the 'particular will of the people' did not mean the 'general awarding of votes'. They therefore regarded suffrage restrictions as acceptable, and did not see them as a violation of the principle of equality before the law. Generally, they aimed at preventing 'rule by those without assets' by using moderate restrictions based on the payment of taxes, although they had no intention of excluding 'small or medium property owners' from suffrage. In the state 'the reliability of votes in no way' increases 'as it does in the private joint-stock company, with the number of shares' (Rotteck).

Although southern German liberals generally represented the perspective of the middle stratum in suffrage discussions, a more *bourgeois liberalism*, which favoured a more resolute tone, was represented by the Rhenish liberal David Hansemann: The 'true majority', he said, may have 'no other interest than that . . . of the majority by head count', but it was distinguished from them by the fact 'that its broader education afforded it greater insight, and its wealth gave it a greater interest in the existence of a solid, strong and good state government'.[25] On the issue of suffrage to the municipal representative bodies and to the chambers of commerce, Rhenish liberals also strongly defended their upper middle-class interests at the expense of the owners of smaller businesses.[26] In contrast to southern Germany, Rhenish liberalism no longer painted an ideal picture of a *bürgerlich* 'middle class' with roughly uniform political and economic interests. As early as the thirties and forties, economic development, which was further advanced in the Rhineland, had already begun to weaken the early liberal belief in the 'middle class' as the broad basis of the state and of society, which would guarantee political and social harmony. Yet these remained heralds of a development which only fully came to fruition after the middle of the century. Until 1848 the liberals' ability to undertake common political action increased, and the middle-class influence remained significant for the early liberal movement (cf. Chapter 1, pp. 34–8). The belief in an 'increasingly homogeneous middle class' (F. C. Dahlmann), into which more and more strata of society would be integrated, allowed the liberals to tolerate the political exclusion of the lower orders as but a transitional stage, and as an aid to education in the long term.

This faith in the power of the middle-classes to fuse and coalesce contradictory elements into the 'core of the population'[27] also determined the liberals' attitude to *Jewish Emancipation*. Not until the Imperial Constitution of 1848 was the full political and legal equality of Jews provided for. The German laws on Jews before 1848 were laws on education, rather than emancipation. Their guiding principle was the integration of Jews into middle-class society or, as it was graphically expressed in the Württemberg legislature in 1828, 'the de-Jewing of the Jew'.[28] Even liberals such as K. Steinacker, who called for Jewish equality before the law as a logical corollary of the 'constitutional principle', saw emancipation as a necessary prerequisite for the education of Jews as citizens (*Staatslexikon*, vol. 5, 1837).

There was no clear consensus amongst liberals on the concrete form that the *constitutional order* should take, or on the balance of political power between the institutions. The wide variety of views expressed corresponded to the variety of the forms of rule to which liberal ideas adhered, but which they also showed that they wanted to reform. That liberal aims for reform were based on a firm grasp of reality was revealed most clearly in the recognition of the constitutional monarchy and of the '*monarchic principle*'.[29] Monarchic power maintained a strong position in liberal theories and even more so in reality. The monarch had the state apparatus at his disposal – liberals did not dispute this; he enacted decrees; he represented the state abroad; he made decisions on war and peace; and appointed and dismissed ministers. But despite this wide-ranging authority, the power of the monarch was limited by the guarantees of freedom for citizens outlined above. That was the fundamental difference between a constitutional monarchy and an absolute monarchy. The constitution, even if it was sponsored 'from above', demythologized dynastic rule, and one of liberalism's major achievements is that it played both a theoretical and practical role in this progressive process of demythologizing. In this respect, the liberal constitutional movement clearly transcended civil servant liberalism, which went as far as the 'constitutionalization of the internal administration' (R. Koselleck), but which regarded the administration and not the representative organs as the core of the constitution. It was liberals in particular who questioned the self-image of the bureaucracy, which, they said, mistakenly 'identified its internal discussions as a kind of one-sided conversation on the part of the intelligentsia with public opinion itself'.[30] The liberal demand for the *separation of justice and administration*, for public and oral judicial hearings, and for trial by jury also conflicted with the bureaucracy's desire to act as the all-encompassing 'guardian of the people' by expanding administrative justice.[31]

The *parliamentary bodies* were some of the most powerful limitations on the 'monarchic principle' and the bureaucratic desire to rule and to patronize the populace. The core liberal demands included implementing parliamentary bodies wherever they did not yet exist at state level (Austria and Prussia) or extending their sphere of authority. However, the 'constitutional forms' already achieved inevitably remained 'fruitless without the essence of the representative system'. Pfizer's belief[32] – he preferred to see it as a description of the deeply illiberal state of affairs throughout Germany – was shared by all liberals. But it should come as no surprise to learn that they differed widely in their theoretical reasoning behind representative organs, and the sphere of authority they demanded for them. This was a reflection of the wide variety of German chambers and legislatures in existence, some of which continued to adhere to unbroken feudal traditions, and even where these had been broken, they pursued the *neuständisch* principle of the representation of 'property and education'.[33] Full popular representation on the legislatures, calculated according to the number of people in the population, was not part of the early liberal programme. Their ideas on suffrage testify to that in no uncertain terms. Dahlmann's readiness, influenced by the English situation, to protect the traditional and to allow 'justice to be done to inequality' was particularly pronounced. Yet even he did not use terms such as the *Stände* or *landständisch* to denote a continuation of old feudal principles: the old 'gulfs between the

Estates, which in former times people could hardly imagine would ever be overcome, no longer exist. There are few of those born to their station, and everywhere there is a culture of choice and profession.' But in the absence of a 'total reorganization of the German aristocratic sphere', he saw the need for an upper house, in which nobility by birth or office would be represented. Many liberals, not just those who looked to England, but francophiles too, agreed with him on this point; Rotteck, on the other hand, and most of the Rhenish liberals, who were usually divided on other issues, agreed on the rejection of a chamber of peers.[34]

At the centre of the liberal theory of representation and liberal practice were the elected *Abgeordnetenkammern* or Chambers of Deputies, where 'civil society' was to play a part in the business of state. Liberals believed that this could not be done without important tools, such as the right to approve taxes and participation in legislation, whose sphere they wanted to extend in order to put an end to the practice of issuing decrees. They also demanded the right to take the initiative in the formulation of laws. This was permitted for the first time in Germany in 1831 in the Constitution of the principality of Hesse, which also demanded for the first time that all civil servants and soldiers be sworn in on the constitution.

Even this constitution, which was produced under pressure of the threat of revolution, and which is regarded as the most liberal in the pre-revolutionary or *Vormärz* period in Germany, did not allow the Estates to participate in government. Nor was this one of the aims of German early liberals. 'The chambers should play a part in the formulation of legislation and should protect the law, but for this very reason they should not play a part in government or administration', declared Dahlmann. In 1819 in his influential work, *Ideen über Landstände* (Ideas on the Chambers), Rotteck defined a chamber as a 'committee ... which represents the people as a whole, united in a state, charged with exercising the rights of this people (or part of this people) in relation to the government'.[35] This *dualistic view of government and parliament* did not provide for the division of the deputies into government and opposition parties at all; parliament was to stand opposite the government as an institutionalized opposition. However, this strict division of roles between the acting government and parliament, which ascertains the 'true overall will' (Rotteck) in free debates, gradually weakened before 1848, both in theory and in practice. The beginnings of this weakening can be identified in Welcker's article 'Centrum der Deputirten-Kammer' in the *Staatslexikon* (vol. 3, 1836). Karl Salomo Zachariä and Robert von Mohl were the first in Germany to develop theories on the manner in which the *parliamentary system of government* would function, as an alternative to the dualistic view of the early constitutionalists. In a constitutional monarchy, wrote Zachariä, it is possible for 'first one then the other party to be the ministerial or the opposition party'. The government should join with the party 'which has the majority of votes in the second chamber'. The aim was parliamentary ministerial responsibility, while the dualistic view of the chambers halted at the legal responsibility of ministers. They could be indicted by parliament, but not relieved of their posts.

In practice too, especially after the July Revolution of 1830 in France, a limited degree of cooperation took place between government and deputies. This led to a split in parliamentary liberalism into a wing which was true to principles, which rejected the combination of government and representative body, and a wing which dismissed 'tarrying in opposition [as] a cosy martyrdom' (Pfizer), and decided to support the reforming forces in the bureacracy in order to be able to achieve limited successes.[36] Without this learning process it would never have been possible to practise the parliamentary method of government so quickly in the Frankfurt National Assembly of 1848–9.

The Early Liberal Social Model

Early liberals were dissatisfied with conditions in Germany, but they respected the existing order, and wanted to protect it as far as possible. 'Some people', said Dahlmann, 'live with their hump backs for eighty years: an operation would cost them their lives'. This image is relevant to early liberal ideas on politics, on the economy and on society. They sought to avoid dramatic interventions and revolutionary leaps in all areas. This meant that liberals were ill-suited to the role of prophets of industrialization programmes. Their social model was based on the German social structure, which remained agrarian and was characterized by small businesses. The society of the German states of the first half of the nineteenth century was coloured by small and medium-sized businesses and towns, most of whose inhabitants wanted to retain the stability that had traditionally been protected. They had no desire to launch themselves into an incalculable future. The early liberal idea of '*civil society*' was consistent with such feelings. Two concepts overlapped here. The first was the traditional Aristotelian concept, the '*societas civilis sive res republica*', which was open for development into a more modern legal, and to some extent more politically egalitarian, society of citizens of the state, but which on a social level remained strongly bound to traditional *ständisch* conditions. The other was a concept of 'civil society' which aimed for a modern economic society, freed from *ständisch* corporate ties. It was Hegel who developed this theory most clearly. It was pushed forward more energetically by the reforming bureaucracy than by the early liberals, who after 1815 saw in the 'English model' a warning, rather than an example to follow.[37]

The German early liberals' social and economic expectations of the future were overwhelmingly based 'on an environment which was pre-revolutionary in an economic, and at the same time political respect'. Their image of the future was that of 'a classless society of citizens "of moderate livelihoods"; a pre-industrial civil society formulated in retrospect, organized along guild and *ständisch* lines on a patriarchal basis'. Lothar Gall's description has been confirmed by a series of more recent studies.[38] Earlier works were also familiar with this viewpoint, although they might not have put it in such extreme terms. Many general analyses of liberalism, however, which tend to stereotype early liberalism as the midwife of modern industrial capitalism, have ignored this point of view.

Liberals were flexible in their views on how society might be formed. Some called for state intervention to retain the existing order, others for society to be adapted by means of reforms and state aid. *Laissez-faire* arguments were also put forward. But the main concern was always to find the best way of achieving the ideal of a middle-class civil society. The ideal itself was not questioned. It meant moderate happiness for many in a society 'of moderate livelihoods'. Early liberal theories on society subordinated everything else to this single aim.

The authors of the liberal *Staatslexikon*, for example, rejected any attempt to apply the idea of equality before the law to *property ownership* too. They did, however, reflect deeply on the issue of how the freedom to acquire property might be limited by means of a social contract. 'In principle', wrote W. Schulz in his article 'Communism' in 1846, there 'has never been an unconditional right to property in such a sense that the necessary aims of every member of society, and therefore of the state, could thereby be thwarted.' Rotteck's article 'Property' (1836) also raised questions on the 'limits of legal tolerance and the lack of political foresight in the recognition of property', in view of the threatened 'war of the unpropertied against the propertied'. The answers he gave did not provide concrete measures for tackling these issues, but in principle they were unambiguous: he was in favour of the 'safeguarding of property' – including inherited property – but against the privileging of manorial property; in favour of the consolidation of the position of the urban 'middle class'; and against the 'excessive accumulation of industrial or financial capital in individual hands, which strengthens the hated moneyed aristocracy and condemns the broad mass of the nation to be dependent for its livelihood and therefore its person on the goodwill, despotism, or egotistical self-interest of the large-scale property owner'.

In the opinion of German early liberals, freedom of the individual, that great liberal aim, inevitably led to the right to acquire property. Yet at the same time, this right had to be limited. In his *Lehrbuch des Vernunftrechts*, Rotteck therefore demanded *laws governing trade and industry* which would protect and strengthen the traditional by means of a process of careful liberalization. There should be free access to the guilds, but not 'unlimited freedom of enterprise', which would mean a 'war between everyone and everyone else'. And that would 'bring an end to calm domestic happiness, based on moderation, but also on the secure knowledge that one can feed oneself. ... The commercial class can be divided into cunning, happy and greedy entrepreneurs and constantly anxious working people, who are exposed to misery and who can never be happy.'[39]

This image of society represented an absolute rejection of the 'English conditions', of unrestrained *Manchester liberalism*, which enjoyed no support amongst the early liberals in Germany. They were no followers of Adam Smith, and even Smith's supporters amongst German economists were careful not to link their economic theories with political liberalism, which they rejected or regarded with scepticism. The doctrine of free trade was not described as 'liberalism', and only after the turn of the twentieth century were terms such as 'liberal' and 'economic individualism' linked. This is a reflection of the length of time it took in Germany for 'economic freedom' to become part of political liberalism.[40]

State intervention was not a taboo subject for the early liberals. In order to balance out the 'disparity between capital and labour', the Badenese liberal Karl Mathy demanded a tax reform which would eliminate unacceptable differences in property ownership and unburden the poorer orders. He also demanded increased rights to self-government for the municipalities, and a decentralized state administration which would limit the 'civil servant state'. He sought improvements in educational provision, above all for the lower strata of the population, and an active social policy. This included a reduction in working hours; sickness and invalidity insurance; and, most important of all, measures to create employment. Liberal social policy did not mean 'feeding the idle from convent soup kitchens' in the traditional manner, but 'creating work – the best kind of poor relief, which at the same time makes the poor intelligent, in contrast to the other way, which causes them to go under'.

Not all German early liberals went as far as Mathy by any means. But his two guiding principles were shared by all, although their ideas on the means by which they could be achieved differed: 'An increase in the productivity of the German economy and support for and the expansion of the *bürgerlicher Mittelstand*', whose 'middle class position' was more advantageous for society than that of the waged labourer. This would allow a 'more appropriate distribution of income throughout the population' than 'big entrepreneurs with many day labourers'.[41] The liberal Carl Theodor Kleinschmidt, for example, who worked for the Bavarian state civil service, believed that the continental late-comers should begin by understanding English industrialization, although he wanted to see this 'modern system of enrichment' socially restrained under the 'absolute authority of the state'.[42] However, most German early liberals believed that the state in the first instance should address the task of creating favourable legal frameworks. What was needed, Welcker said, was an 'essentially just, relatively equal distribution and protection of property for the heads of all households, according to legally proven need and legitimated by their contribution to the general culture. As far as possible, acquisition and injustices which result from profiteering should be eliminated'. All violations of the equal opportunity to earn money 'by means of private despotism and unfair public measures, by laws on inheritance and taxes, privileges etc.' were, he said, to be avoided.[43]

Liberals like Welcker were clearly convinced that a society of free individuals which was founded on reason and which excluded despotism and privilege, would inevitably limit material inequality so that the freedom of the individual was not jeopardized. This belief in a socially harmonious 'civil society' had a twofold aim: criticism of the old *ständisch*, feudal, privileged society; and criticism of the class-based society of industrial capitalism, which was already clearly evident in England, and which they saw emerging in Germany. As the *Vormärz* period came to an end, however, this two-pronged criticism was no longer shared by all liberals.

It was in *Rhenish liberalism* that the industrial capitalist model first, and most decisively, began to replace the middle-class model. David Hansemann went beyond the middle-class perspective of south and south-west German liberals when he called for the Prussian state to endorse the gravitational force of the new era; the *Mittelstand*, but a *Mittelstand* whose core was formed by 'reputable merchants and manufacturers'.[44] As early as the 1830s, and above all the 1840s, Rhenish liberals had set their sights on industry, which Gustav Mevissen hailed as the 'new social centre' and the 'true basis of the state'. 'Industry', he said, 'has grown to form the independent force at the centre of German life. ... Through the creation of this new social power at its heart, Germany is undeniably moving towards a new era, politically too; for where industry is strong as a force, so too is political power and freedom. Each mutually reinforces the other.' While Rotteck still believed in an 'ideal maximum' in the use of machinery, whose 'excessive proliferation' encourages 'the omnipotence of money',[45] Ludolf Camphausen saw the decline of the craft trades as a 'necessary evil', whose concomitant social phenomenon, the crisis in the cottage industries, was the 'pain' of an unavoidable period of transition.

This image of bourgeois Rhenish liberalism, which placed its faith in industrial capitalism, should not be over-emphasized, however. Even amongst Rhenish liberals, who were not blind socio-politically, but who rejected state interventionism, it was still possible to find 'those social ideals which call to mind the old liberal ideal of a classless society of citizens'. They still sometimes defined 'industry' as 'commercial industriousness' and 'the welfare of the whole', and their dislike 'of great factory towns and of the emergence of monopolistic economic power was, as ever, based on the model of a balance of forces between agriculture, trade and commerce' (E. Fehrenbach).

Nevertheless, we see here the beginnings of a liberalism which did not place its hopes in the 'yearning for a constitution', which Hansemann held before the liberals of south and south-west Germany, but in the new economic middle-class 'gravitational force' in the state and society. The 'gravitational force' called for a national economic sphere, which was already in evidence in the form of the *Zollverein* or Customs Union. This was to be accompanied by a *Zollparlament*, a Customs Parliament.[46] This was not only a reaction to the illiberal policies of the German Confederation, but also to the limitations of the reform policies of the individual states, whose scope for action was to be expanded in economic and constitutional terms. The liberal group around Rotteck had used the slogan 'freedom without unity is preferable to unity without freedom' to counter Pfizer's hope in the Customs Union as a 'champion and defender of the new Germany'. But attitudes began to reverse when sections of the liberals declared the *nation-state* to be the vehicle of the political liberalization and democratization which had failed in the individual states. The 'nation' could thus develop to form a guiding principle which engulfed liberalism. But this was not yet typical of early liberals. For them, the nation-state meant above all eliminating the restrictions on freedom which were imposed by the small states and the federal constitution: 'unity – positive, not mystical unity – is the almost undampened battle-cry of all spokesmen' (Heinrich von Gagern).[47]

The socio-political model of the future was the 'classless society of citizens' (Gall), but there was also a desire for a middle-class society which would have to remain a class society until all sections of society had been integrated into the *bürgerlich* 'middle class'. This early liberal Utopia only became an ideology which sought to defend the status quo when, from around the middle of the century onwards, it was overtaken by economic developments. The revolution of 1848–9 accelerated the change in models. Those who wished to assimilate liberalism to the conditions of the new industrial society were forced to look for new concepts of social order.

On one fundamental point, however, the early liberal model of the future abandoned the Utopia of a classless civil society, equal before the law: and this is a point which has so far been largely neglected by scholars. We refer here to *the position of women in society*. The society of citizens of the state was based on the community of heads of households, and they did not include women. Politically, women were regarded as dependent, and were therefore excluded from the most important right of political participation. 'Women's suffrage in Canada' wrote Dahlmann[48] 'will probably remain a bright exception'. Reconciling the fundamental legal inequality of women with the no less fundamental postulate of the equality of all human beings before the law, presented early liberal thinkers with some degree of difficulty. But they managed to 'overcome' it by means of their definition of marriage, which they regarded as the basis of a politically organized society: 'The state is the founding principle. The original family is the original state; each family, represented independently, is the state' (Dahlmann).[49] But it was not a constitutional state, like the one the liberals demanded of a political state. The liberal *Staatslexikon* regarded marriage as a contractual arrangement, yet the authors excluded marriage from the legal term 'contract'. For them, biological inequality took precedence over the legal principle of equality. Family law, wrote Rotteck, did not rest 'simply on the principles of social law. But rather, it is determined by other laws, sometimes mutually agreed contractual regulations, sometimes sentimental and moral laws, and sometimes simply by natural conditions.' These 'natural conditions' made it possible for the husband, as Welcker saw it, to have a 'freer and more wide-ranging effectiveness in the outside world', to enjoy 'supremacy of reason', and to 'be in charge of the family, the earning of money and the political and armed struggle'. 'Just as naturally', on the other hand, 'woman's greater weakness and softness, her predominant emotion and feelings are the basis of ... her greater capacity for tolerance and yielding.'[50] The 'natural' definition of the sexes therefore made the family the 'original cell' of the state; a private sphere in which, the liberals believed, the power of the head of the household could only be legally regulated to a limited degree. The 'overall will' (Rotteck) in a marriage was male and patriarchal, although it was nurtured by means of deep relationships between the members of the family, and was not despotic. This middle-class self-image, which the early liberals shared, is also reflected in the family portraits, which proliferated at no time in the nineteenth century as greatly as they did in the period between 1815 and 1848.[51]

The Organization and Social Profile of Early Liberalism

The attitude of German early liberals to organizations was inconsistent. Since the eighteenth century, the 'association' had played a key role in their attempts to organize 'civil society' in keeping with the times, and to resolve the ills of society. Their passion for associations, however, was also linked to the rejection of 'parties', which were regarded as reprehensible if they placed party spirit or minority interests above 'the true public interest'. Nevertheless, early liberals did form extra-parliamentary organizations and parliamentary parties, and learned how to use them to safeguard their political interests.

Parliamentary parties were formed in the Chambers of Deputies, where deputies increasingly acted together with the liberal press and the public. This is also true of the Prussian provincial diets, whose political profile increased during the forties. The publication of diet proceedings, guaranteed since 1841, played an important role here, as did the easing of censorship and the publication of newspapers such as the *Preußische Zeitung für Politik, Handel und Gewerbe*. The *Preußische Zeitung* may have been suppressed again after only a brief period of existence (1842–3), but nevertheless it strengthened Rhenish liberalism. However, in the absence of an overall state diet (before 1847), Prussian liberals' opportunities for political action remained restricted to individual regions.[52] This changed during the forties, as a result of the fundamental politicization of society, which was helped on its way by the press and the associations.

Association law did not permit overt political activity on the part of the *associations*, yet a 'civil society' was constituted within these organizations, which regulated its affairs independently. Heinrich von Gagern's election to the post of President of the

Agricultural Association for Rhine-Hesse in 1845 was regarded by Gagern himself, his like-minded friends and by the government as a triumph for the liberal public.[53] As Welcker explained in the article on 'Associations' in the *Staatslexikon* (vol. 1, 1845[2]), 'there was no clearly recognizable dividing line separating' political associations 'from the non-political'. The association movement was growing stronger all the time. In 1850, for example, Munich had at least 150 associations (and more than 3000 by around 1900). As society became more politicized, the association movement became instrumental in breaking down provincial political barriers and in extending the social spectrum of politically active population groups. This also had beneficial effects on the liberal movement.

The 'German Press and Fatherland Association', founded on 29 January 1832, marks a climax in the undisguised politicization of the population.[54] It acquired more than 5000 members and produced and disseminated large numbers of liberal writings. It organized popular festivals and mass rallies, of which the Hambach Festival of 1832 was the largest. The Prussian Association had its centre in the Bavarian Palatinate, but it also maintained branches in other German states. The Association highlights the great (and as yet barely researched) social unifying force of German early liberalism. Its members came from all branches of the economy, with the emphasis on the craft trades (*c.* 22 per cent) and merchant professions (*c.* 29 per cent). The opportunities for liberals to influence the Association are reflected in its social composition. In its core Palatinate territory, the *Kleinbürgertum* or lower middle-classes, represented 65 per cent of members, far exceeding the *Bildungsbürgertum* or educated middle class, which made up just 19 per cent of the membership. In the branch associations outside the Palatinate, on the other hand, the educated middle class dominated at almost 51 per cent. This also held true for the association's leadership. The educated middle class was still regarded as the 'natural' representative of civil society, which in the Press Association extended to farmhands and day labourers. Members of the educated middle class were 'available for office' and were the group most obviously able to adopt an overall national perspective. Another feature of early liberalism was that, although the leadership of the Press Association addressed the social privations of its wider membership at meetings and even took up traditional forms of 'popular protest' such as 'rough music'[55] punishment campaigns, it rejected revolutionary action and violence of any kind. It focused on mobilizing supporters using constitutional political demands. Thus, the Press Association is revealed to be a typical creature of middle-class liberal politics in the revolutionary unrest of 1830–2. The unrest was founded on social protest, but it was integrated within a constitutional political framework, and tamed by the middle-class spokesmen.

The positive developments of the early thirties could not be sustained under the impact of restorative federal policy, however, and the Press Association was disbanded in 1833. In the forties, the dams which the German governments had constructed in an attempt to hold back the politicization of society finally burst their banks. From now on the early liberal movement drew strength from the national excitement which followed the Franco-German crisis of 1840, and above all from the broad social base which the German *national movement* had now acquired. A number of factors contributed to these developments, including the advancing economic integration of the German states and improvements in communication (the press, improvements in literacy and the building of railways). The alliance of the national and liberal movements not only shifted the main emphases which had hitherto characterized the aims of early liberalism, it also extended the social base of the liberal movement, increased its organizational force and 'nationalized' it, in that contacts between liberals across individual state borders became closer and more durable. The many variations of German early liberalism, demonstrated in the literature with a confusing array of competing terms, did not disappear, but were balanced out. But something else was added too: the programmatic and organizational split of the political opposition into liberals and democrats. This was true of the highest level, the spokesmen, as well as of the broader movement.

Only in the forties did the *liberal élite* of the German states grow to form a group of people who shared their thoughts in the press and in correspondence between individuals, who saw each other frequently on their travels and who held meetings.[56] Only contact with like-minded Austrians remained weak. This increased communication reached a peak in 1846–7. From then on, links were maintained between liberals in Rhineland Prussia, East Prussia (with Königsberg as a centre) and the south or south west. A younger generation entered the leading liberal groups, as did representatives of the commercial middle class. The establishment of the *Deutsche Zeitung* in 1847 highlights the growth of early liberalism beyond the individual states, as well as its division into liberals and democrats. This newspaper enterprise was supported by the moderate constitutionalist wing of liberalism alone. The completion of this process of division during the *Vormärz* period was marked by the liberals' Heppenheim Meeting of 10 October 1847 and the democrats' Offenburg Meeting of 12 September of the same year. Thus, the middle-class parties of the year of the revolution were already formed before the revolution broke out.

A similar process can be identified in the political *mass movement*; amongst gymnasts and singers, for example.[57] Until the very eve of the revolution, the gymnastic and singing associations continued to evolve, broadly speaking, from organizations of the élite to mass organizations. Membership of gymnastic associations in 1847 is estimated at between 80 000 and 90 000. Singing associations are thought to have had at least 100 000 members. In the forties both these groups of associations began to communicate increasingly effectively in organized meetings, festivals and newspapers, and then extended their territorial range. Focal points were in south-west Germany and Saxony. Austria remained largely separate.

As membership grew, the social profile of the organizations changed. Men from all strata of the middle classes joined them, although the degree of importance of each stratum varied. Journeymen dominated the gymnastic associations of the forties, while master craftsmen dominated the singing associations. In marked contrast to the singing associations, the gymnastic associations were almost entirely devoid of the propertied middle-classes. Few statistics survive. As far as we can judge, educated middle-class professions were represented in both organizations, but were far less significant than the small commercial middle-class professions.

Liberal ideas were disseminated by singers and gymnasts, as their festival speeches and songs testify. Their diverging social profile, however, highlights a difference which is also mirrored in their political orientation. While the singers' movement took up and disseminated only liberal constitutionalist ideas, the gymnastic movement was also opened up to democratic aims. In the revolution of 1848–9, this led to a split into a liberal and a democratic gymnastic association.

Gymnastic and singing associations are just two examples of the broad organizational and social roots which the early liberal movement acquired as the *Vormärz* period came to an end. The religious opposition movements of the 'German Catholics' and the Protestant *Lichtfreunde* (Friends of the Light) also provided organizational support to the liberals and democrats. The *attempts to bring about internal church reforms* were also significant for early liberalism. 'The liberal movement enjoyed institutional support in the church, the vicarages and the synods.'[58] But it had its opponents too. None the less, 'church liberalism was the training ground for political liberalism' (R. Haym). *Catholicism*, on the other hand, closed itself to liberalism and vice versa. Three-class suffrage, which was introduced in the Rhine Province in 1845 and throughout Prussia in 1850, was suported by the Rhenish liberal middle classes, and hit the smaller, primarily Catholic, commercial traders hard. Here 'Ultramontanes' and liberals opposed each other as rival 'parties'. But 'liberal' and 'Catholic' did not always mean irreconcilable differences, as the Rhenish municipal elections show.[59] German early liberalism was undoubtedly a movement of Protestants at heart, both in terms of its spokesmen and in terms of its ideas, which aimed at individual autonomy. Whether this image changes if one examines the basis of *Vormärz* politics and political movements in the small towns, however, we do not know. Municipal freedom was part of the 'original stock' of early liberal demands, but liberalism at municipal level has not yet been sufficiently researched.[60]

2 Liberal Politics in the Revolution of 1848–9

Images of the Revolution: Limiting the Revolution

The revolution began with the triumph of liberalism. It is true that the sudden collapse of the old ruling order in March and April 1848 was brought about by the great popular movements in the towns and in the countryside, which extended far beyond the social and political catchment area of *Vormärz* liberalism. But liberals were the first to reap the benefits of the rapid success of this first revolutionary wave, whose aims and limitations they had helped to formulate. They achieved this through action on several levels.

Under the impact of the revolution, the rulers of most German states appointed so-called *Märzministerien* or March ministries, which were headed by prominent liberals. As the Badenese liberal Ludwig Häusser said as early as 1851, the fact that the dynasties 'were able quickly to defend themselves with the popular shield of liberal ministries played a key role in disarming the revolution at its most dangerous moment'.[1]

The policy of limiting the revolution began even as it broke out. Even the *Bundestag* or Federal Diet, the central institution of the German Confederation, pursued this strategy. Already at the beginning of March, for example, it allowed the federal states to introduce freedom of the press (3 March). Most importantly, it established a committee of seventeen 'generally trusted men', which was to prepare a 'revision of the federal constitution on a truly national basis, in keeping with the times'[2] (10 March).

28

Members of the committee included such prominent liberals as
Max von Gagern and Friedrich Daniel Bassermann, who acted as
chairmen, Friedrich Christoph Dahlmann, Sylvester Jordan,
Johann Gustav Droysen, Wilhelm Eduard Albrecht and Georg
Gottfried Gervinus. More so than the later Imperial Constitution, in which the liberals were forced to make concessions to
other political groupings, the draft Imperial Constitution[3] made
clear the limits of the course of reform with which they sought to
bring a rapid end to the revolutionarily enforced collapse of the
political ruling order, but which they wanted at the same time to
use to implement their aims for reform. A briefly formulated list
of Basic Rights, which focused entirely on central issues, was to
safeguard the rights and freedoms of the citizen of the state
down to the municipal level. The intention was to expand the
German Confederation by the inclusion of East and West Prussia, parts of the province of Posen and the Duchy of Schleswig.
It would be reformed to comprise an empire, organized on
federal state lines, whose area of authority was broadly enough
conceived to safeguard the nation-state as a military, economic,
legal and political unit, despite the continuing 'independence
of the individual German states' (paragraph 2). In the draft,
imperial power consisted of imperial authorities led by imperial
ministers, who were appointed by the Kaiser and were responsible to parliament. A hereditary emperor would lead the Reich.
Further central institutions would include an imperial court and
a bicameral Reichstag or Imperial Diet. The institutions of the
hereditary emperor and of the Upper House, to which delegates
from the individual states and the 'ruling princes' or their
representatives would belong (paragraph 12.1), highlight liberal
constitutionalist attempts to build a bridge to the dynastic federal
past in the construction of the state.

The 'Foreword' to this draft is instructive and outlines the
grounds for this bridge-building, to which liberal policies remained committed from the beginning of the revolution until its
violent end: 'It is not only the old habit of obedience which is
associated with our princes' houses – and this obedience cannot
simply be transferred to another authority – but in truth our
only opportunity to gradually unite this many-layered Germany,
with its many different forms; a unity which for greater reasons
we can no longer do without.' The 'one and indivisible republic
with a president at its helm', the Foreword read, would only be

achievable 'on a path sprayed with the blood of German citizens', for it was 'a myth which has only managed to find temporary credence in the unrest of the last few weeks, as if the value of their royal houses had suddenly vanished from the hearts of Germans'. Only the election of a hereditary imperial sovereign would make it possible for 'freedom and order to shake hands in reconciliation on German soil, and never let go of each other again'.

Liberal constitutionalists in the 'March cabinets' of March and April 1848 attempted, with the support of their like-minded friends, to reform the German Confederation into a federal nation-state with a constitution, with the agreement of the ruling dynasties. They failed for two reasons. On the one hand, the monarchs of Hanover, Bavaria, Austria and also Prussia resisted the reform 'from above'[4] – an early portent for the plan of a *kleindeutsch* nation-state under a Prussian hereditary Kaiser, to which the Frankfurt National Assembly finally committed itself in 1849. And, secondly, despite the intensive efforts of the liberal spokesmen, the German nation-state could not be created without reference to the revolutionary movement. In the spring of 1848 it had already advanced too far for this.

Liberal constitutionalists were forced to confront this in their second attempt, which also began in early March 1848, when they tried to present several *faits accomplis* before the election of the German constituent National Assembly. On 5 March fifty-one representatives of the middle-class national movement met in Heidelberg. They represented all political alignments, from moderate liberalism to the republican left. The meeting called on the governments to allow the election of a National Assembly, and appointed a Committee of Seven to work on suggestions for the Assembly. The fact that the fifty-one meeting in Heidelberg claimed only advisory functions for themselves and for the '*Vorparlament*' or Pre-Parliament to be established, was a 'clear victory for the moderates'.[5] Anything else would be the preserve of the National Assembly, the 'strong protective wall' around 'the entire German fatherland and the thrones'.[6] Still in March, before the National Parliament had even met, Heinrich and Max von Gagern went even further, attempting with the Bundestag Committee of Seventeen to have a provisional federal leader appointed by the rulers of the individual states, and to establish the essential features of constitutional order. But their attempt failed. A preliminary decision on central constitutional issues, and on the path which would lead to the nation-state, therefore had to be pronounced by the Pre-Parliament, which from 31 March to 3 April 1848 brought to the Paulskirche in Frankfurt 574 representatives of the German national movement, including the most prominent liberals and democrats.

One of the fundamental problems of the German revolution was already openly discussed in the pre-parliamentary debates. It was a problem which at an early stage split the middle-class revolutionary movement into two enemy camps; into liberals and democrats, who now opposed each other with growing mistrust as they waged a bitter dispute on the principle by which a new national constitutional order should be adopted: whether revolutionary 'law' should be invoked, or whether the agreement of the representatives of the traditional dynastic federal rulers should be sought.

In the Pre-Parliament the controversy was unleashed by a motion submitted by Gustav von Struve on behalf of the republican left. This clashed with the views of the liberals around Heinrich von Gagern, who wanted the Pre-Parliament to confirm the essential features of the federal constitution, which had been drafted by the Heidelberg Committee of Seven and had already been accepted by the Bundestag's Reform Committee. This would have fixed the scope for action of the individual states and future National Assembly. Struve's motion,[7] on the other hand, combined the widely accepted liberal *Märzforderungen* (the demands made during the March revolution), such as freedom of the press, public trial by jury, the freedom to associate and assemble, with Utopian demands such as 'the dissolution of the standing army of civil servants' in favour of a 'cheaper form of government', made up of 'freely elected men of the people'. A motion such as this was unacceptable to the moderate majority of the Pre-Parliament, for it could only have been implemented by means of a new revolutionary wave, which would have extinguished the individual states along with the dynasties. The proposers of the motion started from the premise (soon to be revealed as erroneous) that the 'long period of abject humiliation' which Germany had suffered, had 'dissolved all those bonds which until now have tied the German people to the so-called order of things'. They therefore demanded the appointment of an 'executive committee', which would 'prepare the great task of the re-establishment of

Germany' until a national parliament was elected. 'Re-establishment' would have meant the dissolution of the existing order. The motion proposed that Germany be organized into 'imperial districts', though 'with appropriate consideration of the conditions of the time'. Above all, however, Point 15 of the motion referred to the 'dissolution of the hereditary monarchy [*Einherrschaft*] and its replacement with freely elected parliaments, led by freely elected presidents, united in the federal constitution on the model of the North American free states'.

This radical republican programme stood no chance of success, given the majority in the Pre-Parliament. It did, however, give rise to an intense debate, which brought home to those gathered in Frankfurt, and to the German public as a whole, the connection between constitutional order and the 'social question', and in particular the most urgent of all unresolved problems: whether a constitution should be created only by a national parliament legitimated by the revolution, or whether it should be created by means of reforms, in agreement with the individual state dynasties. The Pre-Parliament refused to commit itself. Nevertheless, it decided the future course of the German revolution, in that it left the formation of the constitution 'solely' to the future National Assembly.

This compromise avoided the clear decision which the republicans around von Struve had wanted as much as the liberal constitutionalists around Heinrich von Gagern. But it favoured the policy of the 'legitimization' of the revolution sought by liberals and many democrats. The Committee of Fifty, which was appointed by the Pre-Parliament until the National Assembly met, also adopted the policy of limiting the revolution by parliamentary legitimization. This was a concession to the democrats, but one which primarily accommodated the liberals. It meant that the revolutionary central authority demanded by the republican left could be avoided, whether it be in the form of the Pre-Parliament transformed into a Convention, or of an Executive Committee.

The republican representative Friedrich Hecker called for the Pre-Parliament to become a permanent body, so that 'at this moment of the impotence and dissolution of the German Confederation and the German governments of the nation', it might stand as an 'overall guarantee' of the continuation of the revolution, and create a 'central point' against external political dangers. Yet moderate democrats such as Franz Raveaux had quite different expectations of the permanence of the Pre-Parliament. 'Peace must be re-established quickly, for the unrest has sown distrust in everyone', he said. Liberal constitutionalists such as Carl Theodor Welcker were even clearer about the tasks they envisaged for the permanent committee. It was to make contact with the 'Bundestag, which has now been reinforced with men of trust', to give the federal organ 'power and vigour' on two fronts: against the individual states, should they attempt to withdraw from the new nation-state order; and above all against the grassroots revolution. 'We live in a time of need, where the whole of society is on the point of collapse, and where disorder and anarchy threatens the land internally and externally.' The liberal political motto, adroitly formulated by Heinrich von Gagern, was 'order and unity' not 'revolutionary movements'. The permanent committee would 'instill' in the people 'a sense of trust', yet facilitate co-operation with the German Confederation, the only central authority available.[8]

This perspective corresponded to the tasks set by the Pre-Parliament. The committee was to 'independently advise the Bundesversammlung, whilst safeguarding the interests of the nation, and administering federal affairs until the constituent assembly is convened'.[9] With the resolutions of the Pre-Parliament, the liberals around Gagern had defended the cornerstone on which the revolutionary movements would break at an early stage: legitimization of the new by safeguarding legal continuity. This was achieved, even if the form of the federal monarchic nation-state was left to the future National Assembly to decide. But the liberals won only a partial victory in their war on two fronts, against 'revolution' and 'reaction'. The revolutionary movement was already harnessed in March/April 1848. The individual state dynasties and their governments, however, refused to commit themselves to a new constitutional order. They protected their room for manoeuvre and, inevitably, the more successful the liberal policy of limiting the revolution was, the more their scope for action grew.

Liberals were well aware of this fundamental problem of the German revolution. But they also believed they could resolve it. The ruling dynasties had, after all, paved the way for a nation-state constituted on liberal lines: they had appointed the 'March governments'; they had revoked reactionary decrees enacted by the Bundestag in the *Vormärz* period; and they had agreed to the election of a German National Assembly. A reform of the existing order therefore seemed possible without further uncontrollable revolutionary pressure.

Liberals were the loudest champions of the early harnessing of the revolution and its channelling into a reform movement. But it would be wrong to hold them alone responsible for it. 'Germany wants its dynasties, for they are the historical keystones of civilization and culture.'[10] This statement by a liberal supporter of the permanent establishment of the Pre-Parliament characterized the political models which held far into the ranks of moderate democrats. To 'smash the head of anarchy', and at the same time 'to refuse to tolerate reaction rearing its head anywhere in the German Reich' was also the basic position represented by men such as Raveaux for the moderate democrats in the Committee of Fifty.[11]

In this war on two fronts, whose objective was profound reform, combined with the safeguarding of legality and legal continuity, the liberal and democratic majority in the Pre-Parliament certainly did not conflict with the central aims of the extra-parliamentary March movement. For it, too, halted before the thrones everywhere. An attempt was made to rectify this in a second revolutionary wave in Baden in April 1848, which led to the first important test of strength between revolutionary republicans and those who wanted reforms to be implemented under the aegis of the traditional dynasties. The republicans around Hecker and Struve, who were defeated in the Pre-Parliament, tried in vain to use violence to push on the revolution against the reforming vote of the liberals and also of the majority of the democrats. They failed for two reasons. It rapidly became clear that the governments and the Bundesversammlung, with the co-operation of their liberal members, were prepared to deploy federal troops to counter the revolution, and the Badenese revolutionaries were forced to accept that their call to enforce a republic in the revolutionary battle enjoyed little support amongst the populace. Hecker and Struve became popular revolutionary heroes who fired the imaginations of many, yet inspired only very few to take action themselves. The failure of the Badenese April revolution was not only a demonstration of the strength of the governments and their liberal ministers. It also came close to a silent plebiscite on the part of the German public, which, by failing to support the Badenese revolutionaries, decided in favour of the course of reform desired by liberals and the moderate majority of democrats. The April revolution both reinforced and weakened the position of the forces for reform. Republican hopes for the revolution were dashed, yet the liberals increasingly focused their two-pronged attacks on anyone who refused to denounce the republican form of state on principle. Thus, even moderate democrats, who wanted to leave options open for a constitutional monarchy *and* a republic, as far as this could be achieved without bloodshed, now found themselves branded by the liberals as enemies, tarred with the brush of the 'republic'. This was interpreted as meaning civil war, anarchy, mob-rule, the decline of civilized behaviour and culture, and the collapse of all rational social order.[12] Already in the *Vormärz* period, the German liberals' concept of revolution, schooled in the French revolution of 1789, had regarded the republic as a transitional stage between *terreur* and the dictatorship of an individual.[13] They believed they could see these fears being constantly confirmed in the revolutionary events of 1848 in France, in the Badenese April revolution, and in every attempt to push forward the revolution.

The horrific visions of revolutionary chaos which the word 'republic' triggered in the minds of liberals restricted the room for manoeuvre which they regarded as acceptable in their policies for reform. Alexander Freiherr von Soiron, Chairman of the Committee of Fifty, and later member of the liberal 'Casino' parliamentary party in the Frankfurt National Assembly, declared on 26 April 1848 that the best way to avoid reaction was to 'use a firm hand to keep down anarchy and rebellion'; a conviction shared by all German liberals. He continued, 'I openly admit that we must be conservative regarding the position which the German people have won for themselves, in order to retain what we have and to make it possible to achieve even more; for anarchy will rob us of our rights and it will rob us of our freedoms and our civilized behaviour too, and God only knows what will become of us then.'[14]

The liberals thought they knew. For this reason, filled with a mixture of hope and visions of decline, they set about finding another path of reform between 'revolution' and 'reaction'. The following quotation highlights the predicament in which the liberals believed themselves to be, and on which they focused

their political activity during the two years of the revolution. It is
taken from a report by Otto Camphausen, describing the events
of the March revolution as experienced by himself and his
brother Ludolf, Minister President of the newly formed liberal
Prussian government from 29 March 1848 onwards.

> The terrible events threaten to wrench the old world from its
> hinges, and in Germany at least will bring about the total
> collapse of the existing order. They will make many rich
> people poor and poor people rich. Never in the history of the
> world has there been an era in which threats from all sides
> have mounted up in this way. Bravery and courage are
> required, even only to attempt to conquer them, but it would
> be ungodly to despair prematurely; one has to be strong and
> seek to create the foundation for a new edifice from the gen-
> eral destruction. A heavy burden rests on Ludolf's shoulders
> at the present time. To the best of my abilities, I will help him
> to bear it. Yesterday and the day before that, we cried quite a
> number of honest tears together, but we also made jokes no
> less frequently, and will, I hope, keep our spirits up. If after-
> wards a deluge comes, if it proves impossible to bury the wild
> stream of ghosts and build protective dams, then the new
> generation may assume the worries and cares of organization;
> retirement into a quiet private life remains an option for us.[15]

Liberals were by no means alone in their nightmare visions of the
'republic'. The social unrest which seeped into the politically
motivated March movement, and which played a key role in its
successes, also led large parts of the democratic middle classes to
believe in the direct threat of a social revolution on the part of
the 'mob'. The republic seemed to stand at its gateway. For
'republic' meant the elimination of the monarchy and therefore
the destruction of the mainstay of the existing ruling order. The
'republic' was also the central political demand of the lower
orders. So right from the beginning of the revolution, the
republican state was tarred with the brush of social collapse,
which German citizens saw in the February revolution in Paris,
and which they believed would befall them too with the social
revolts in German towns.

   Thus, for example, the arson attacks and machine wrecking
which took place in March 1848 in the Vienna suburbs, parallel

to the constitutionalist 'middle-class' revolution in the centre of Vienna, seemed to herald a 'proletarian' social revolution. This proletarian revolution irrevocably discredited the republican form of state in the eyes of reform-minded liberals, and even in the eyes of moderate middle-class democratic circles. A young middle-class Viennese woman, hoping for reform, noted in her diary that 'The republic now meant murder and robbery', 'destroying the palaces of the rich and collecting all the looted money in a national treasury etc.'[16] Viennese citizens responded to this social revolution with the formation of a National Guard, from which workers were excluded, and by demonstrating their loyalty to the Kaiser, whose portrait even decorated a barricade – the symbol of the 'legal revolution', for which liberals and even the moderate democratic majority strove.

The Württemberg democrat Adolph Schoder, who hoped that the revolution would lead to a parliamentary monarchy, judged matters no differently in a report to his constituency in April 1848: 'This is the republic which is preached by a number of the men who took part in the uprising in Baden and in revolutionary enterprises in other German states; the red republic, rejoiced in by good-for-nothings who have nothing left to lose, and who only have themselves to blame.' Hecker, he conceded, wanted the 'republic as the best form of state and not as a state of anarchy'. But 'at present, where the task is to re-establish peace and order' the republic would inevitably bring anarchy to Germany. That the republic offered 'no guarantee of the freedom and well-being of the citizen', 'is clearly demonstrated by the most recent events in France. And that it is possible, on the other hand, for freedom and wealth to thrive in a constitutional monarchy, is shown by the example of England, and to an even greater extent by that of Belgium.'[17]

Liberals and moderate democrats shared many views on the revolution and the republic. Nevertheless, it proved impossible to form a viable middle-class alliance for the purpose of reform. This was primarily because the two major middle-class reform camps (decided republicans formed only a minority in Germany in 1848–9) based the scope for action which they regarded as justifiable during the revolutionary years on their socio-political views of the world, and these were too divergent for an alliance to be possible. The chances and limitations of a compromise within the middle classes in favour of a common goal – reform of the ruling order in the individual states and their unification in a

German nation-state – had to be tested on the two central political levels of action in the years of the revolution: the parliamentary
and the increasingly better organized extra-parliamentary level.

Liberal Parliamentary Politics

The Bundestag, the governments of the individual states and the
approximately 80 per cent of adult males entitled to vote in the
elections entrusted the parliamentary decision on the form that
German unity should take to the Frankfurt National Assembly,
which met for the first time on 18 May 1848. But we should not
forget that the Prussian National Assembly in Berlin, the Austrian
Reichstag in Vienna and the chambers and legislatures of the
other German states also represented further parliamentary focal
points, whose significance should not be underestimated.[18] The
large numbers of petitions submitted to the chambers, a subject so
far neglected by research, reflect the extent to which the individual states were rooted in the consciousness of the populace,
alongside the national central authority in Frankfurt.

    The positions adopted by the liberal 'March ministries' in the
German states once again highlight the policy of legal continuity with which the liberals attempted to channel the revolution
into legal reform. In most states, chambers were initially called into
session according to *Vormärz*-era principles, with unequal suffrage
and numerous *ständisch* special representations which varied
widely from chamber to chamber. The Upper Chambers of the
privileged Estates remained. This continuity of *ständisch* representation by no means excluded the possibility of reform, but it
acted as a filter which moderated the demands of the popular
movement. This was one reason for the liberal-led governments'
extreme reticence when it came to reforming the chambers and
the constitutions of the individual states. People also wanted to
wait to see what the superior authority, the constituent German
National Assembly, would do. It was only after pressure from the
public and from left-wingers in the chambers that, from autumn
1848 onwards, new elections to the chambers of most German
states were held on the basis of new electoral laws. Even in those
places where constitutions were revised, the authority of the
legislatures remained 'largely unchanged'.[19] Whether it would

be possible to implement the rules of play of the parliamentary system on a permanent basis depended on the readiness of the ministries and the princes to act according to them, and ultimately on the success of the revolution. This had to be decided in Frankfurt and in Prussia and Austria, the most powerful of the individual states.

At the time of the elections to the Frankfurt National Assembly at the end of April and the beginning of May 1848, the organization of deputies into parties which represented a particular political alignment had not yet crystallized. Once the National Assembly met, however, this rapidly took place. As early as the beginning of June, parliamentary parties formed which developed functioning parliamentary working methods (although switching between parties was common), and of the total of 812 deputies who belonged to the Parliament (as a rule only around half of them were ever present at the same time), around a quarter to a third remained without any party ties at all. Constitutionalist liberals formed three parliamentary parties during the first year of the revolution, which together made up the largest and most influential bloc, the 'centre-right' (see Table 1): they were known as the 'Casino', the 'Landsberg' and the 'Augsburger Hof'', which represented the bridge between the liberal constitutionalists and the moderate democrats of the 'liberal left'. In this transitional zone between liberals and democrats, the dividing lines were blurred. This was also clear in the social profile of the parties.

As a rule, academically educated men made up around three-quarters of all liberal and democratic deputies. Their parliamentary parties can be distinguished by whether civil-servant or independent academics formed the major part within the educated middle-class bloc (Table 1). The proportion of independent professions increased the further to the left the party stood, while that of senior civil servants increased in the opposite direction. Only the 'right' deviated from this distribution pattern; in the 'Café Milani' the upper middle classes, the military and above all landed estate-owners were disproportionately represented at almost 30 per cent, although here too civil servants in state employment dominated at almost 49 per cent.

The usual assignment of individual parliamentary parties to larger political groupings also holds true for their social composition. On the 'left', comprised of the democratic 'Deutscher Hof' and the republican 'Donnersberg', the independent educated

Table 1 Strength and social composition of the parliamentary parties of the Frankfurt National Assembly (October 1848)

	Milani	Casino	Landsberg	Augs. Hof	Württ. Hof	Westend-hall	Deutscher Hof	Donners-berg	Independent	Total
Large landowners	8	8	1	3	3	2	2	0	11	48
%	21.6	6.7	2.7	7.1	7	4.9	3.6	–	7.2	6.6
Großbürgertum	3	5	1	2	1	2	1	1	4	20
%	8.1	2.5	2.7	4.8	2.4	4.9	1.8	2.1	2.6	3.5
Senior civil servants	18	80	23	20	15	22	17	17	78	290
%	48.7	67.2	62.2	47.6	36.6	53.6	30.3	36.2	51.0	50.6
Independent professions	4	12	5	12	16	13	22	23	32	139
%	10.8	10.1	13.5	28.5	39.0	31.7	39.3	48.9	20.9	24.3
Junior and middle-ranking civil servants	1	5	6	1	4	0	7	3	15	42
%	2.7	4.2	16.2	2.4	9.8	–	12.5	6.4	9.8	7.3

	'Right'		'Centre right'		'Centre left'			'Left'		Total
Kleinbürgertum	0	0	1	2	1	0	7	2	7	20
%	–	–	2.7	4.8	2.4	–	12.5	4.3	4.6	3.5
Military	3	5	0	1	0	0	0	0	2	11
%	8.1	4.2	–	2.4	–	–	–	–	1.3	1.9
No profession given	0	4	0	1	1	2	0	1	4	13
%	–	3.4	–	2.4	2.4	4.9	–	2.1	2.6	2.3
Total	37	119	37	42	41	41	56	47	153	573
%	6.4	20.7	6.5	7.3	7.2	7.2	9.8	8.2	26.7	100

Note: Großbürgertum: merchants, manufacturers; *senior civil servants:* includes clergymen and university teachers; *Kleinbürgertum:* tradesmen, craftsmen, farmers; *Deutscher Hof:* includes 'Nürnberger Hof'.

Source: G. Schilfert, *Sieg und Niederlage des demokratischen Wahlrechts in der deutschen Revolution 1848/49* (Berlin, 1952) p. 406; cf. M. Botzenhart, *Deutscher Parlamentarismus in der Revolutionszeit, 1848–1850* (Düsseldorf, 1977) p. 161.

middle class outweighed academically educated civil servants, while in the liberal-constitutionalist 'Casino' core grouping, and in the 'Landsberg' which split from it, civil-servant academics were by far the dominant group, representing two-thirds of all members. The transition zone between the 'left' and the constitutionalist liberals, not only with regard to their programme, but also in terms of their social composition, was marked by the moderate democrats, who joined together to form the 'Württemberger Hof' at the beginning of June. The 'Augsburger Hof' grouping which, with the 'Casino' and the 'Landsberg' formed the 'centre-right', split from the 'Württemberger Hof' together with the 'Westendhall' group in August and September 1848. Together with the 'Württemberger Hof' they formed the 'centre-left', maintaining links with the 'Deutscher Hof', which of all the left-wing groups was the one most open to compromise.

The formation of parliamentary parties was accelerated by the debates of June 1848 on the first fundamental decision to fall to the National Assembly: the form which the Provisional Central Power should take. The issue which had to be decided, even before the details of the Imperial Constitution could be debated, was whether a republican or monarchic form should be adopted. Fronts which had already characterized the Pre-Parliamentary debates emerged once more, although numerous attempts were made to reconcile differences. But these attempts were unable to prevent the deputies of the right and centre parties from linking any solution which involved a president to the republic, which 'would only be established on German soil by means of a bloody civil war and on the long path of anarchy', as Dahlmann put it.[20]

In vain did moderate democrats such as Wilhelm Jordan and Robert Blum call for the National Assembly to tame the impending anarchy – the 'impetuous ghost at work outside' – by appointing a republican head of state as a sign of hope: 'This will keep a rein on the lower orders – even now these reins lie within them, though they are entangled' (Jordan). Moderate democrats reaching into the ranks of the left-wing 'Deutscher Hof' group expected that the republic would secure the outcome and at the same time the end of the revolution. The revolution of the barricades, men like Jakob Venedy declared, had been necessary, but it had to be countered 'from this moment on', since 'it has led the ghost to victory'. This would only be possible when the 'spirit of the people' received its demand: the 'self-rule of the nation'. Otherwise, 'the revolution will strike again and again with the rabble-rousing fist of the masses'.

The democratic principle of re-establishing peace, law and order by 'bravely advancing as far as the final barrier' (Ludwig Simon) was unacceptable to liberals, who demanded 'that the revolution should finally be stilled'. Carl Theodor Welcker, member of the 'Casino' parliamentary party and of the important Constitutional Committee, clearly voiced the stance of liberals who believed that the republic would bring about a 'robber's society' in Germany.

> I have not received a mandate to tear governments from the throne, or to rob them of their dignity and honour in order further to open the maw of the revolution. My mandate says: use the legal basis of a constitutional situation to close off the unhappy road, the abyss of the revolution. Re-establish trust, mutual respect for the law, peace and calm, so that the businessman can once again enjoy wealth and freedom in his enterprises.

Heinrich von Gagern, leader of the liberal-constitutionalist 'Casino', finally succeeded on 24 June 1848 with his 'brave attempt', a motion which won a broad majority of 450 votes to 100, and so demonstrated the ability of liberal and democratic deputies to compromise; an ability which still existed, despite all the conflicts between them. Without the agreement of the individual state powers, which liberals had originally demanded, the National Assembly created the Provisional Central Power and elected the Austrian Archduke John as *Reichsverweser* or Imperial Regent, 'not because, but despite the fact that he is a prince'. It was not easy for the liberals to agree to this. 'It was a brave act', the 'Casino' liberal Carl Georg Beseler wrote to his wife,

> but despite the fact that I did not condone this pushing aside of the governments, it was probably the best way of achieving our goal quickly and safely, and of re-establishing faith in official power in Germany. People here are very happy about it; the factories immediately received new orders, stocks and shares are rising etc. God willing, our poor Germany can now breathe easily once more.[21]

Gagern's 'brave attempt' encountered the support of moderate
democrats since, with the imperial law of 28 June 1848, the
National Assembly on its own authority established the Central
Power, to which imperial ministers also belonged. Liberals could
breathe a sigh of relief, since the figure of the Imperial Regent
seemed to pave the way for a monarchic imperial sovereign.
It even seemed as if a bridge had been built between the rival
leadership demands of the two German supreme powers, for
liberals believed that there was an 'unspoken agreement' that
Prussian ministers would be placed at the side of the Austrian
Imperial Regent in important offices (foreign affairs and the
army).[22]

Controversy raged in the National Assembly about whether
the Assembly should be the sovereign authority, or whether the
agreement of the individual state powers should also be sought.
Nevertheless, all groups voted in favour of the law on the
formation of a government according to parliamentary majorities. Even the supporters of the monarchic sovereign did so.
Monarchy and parliamentarianism were regarded as reconcil-
able, and they acted according to this principle. The three
imperial ministries formed in 1848 – under Karl Fürst zu
Leiningen, Anton Ritter von Schmerling and Heinrich von
Gagern – emerged from the earliest negotiations of the liberal
and democratic parliamentary parties of the right and centre-
left, and they resigned when they lost the confidence of the
parliamentary majority.[23] Thus, the National Assembly, the
ministers and the Imperial Regent all acted according to the
rules of the parliamentary system of government, despite the
absence of a relevant constitutional framework. In the first
imperial cabinet, ministerial and under-secretarial positions were
occupied exclusively by members of the 'Casino' and 'Württemberger Hof' groupings. They also included three ministers who
did not have mandates as deputies. The government coalition
which led to the formation of the Gagern cabinet in December
1848, following the collapse of the Schmerling government's
großdeutsch-Austrian programme, was restricted to the right; to
the liberal 'Casino' and 'Landsberg' parties and the 'Augsburger
Hof', which had split from the 'Württemberger Hof'. Only when
the Prussian King Frederick William IV rejected the imperial
crown and Gagern's *kleindeutsch*-programme failed, leading to his
resignation on 9 May 1849, was a minority government formed

under Grävell, which included ministers without mandates as deputies, alongside members of the right-wing 'Milani' parliamentary party. Before that, in February 1849, the parliamentary parties had regrouped under the pressure of the *großdeutsch–kleindeutsch* conflict. The *Großdeutsche* left the liberal–constitutionalist 'Casino' and joined together in the 'Pariser Hof' group. On matters of domestic policy they formed single-issue alliances of convenience with the left which varied from case to case. The *Kleindeutsche* around Heinrich von Gagern formed the 'Weidenbusch' group which extended from the right to the centre-left, from the 'Casino' to some members of the 'Westendhall'. The 'Braunfels' group under Heinrich Simon represented a further alliance of liberals and democrats. The 'Weidenbusch' and 'Braunfels' finally agreed a compromise which brought work on the constitution to an end on 27 March 1849 with a slender majority of 267 votes to 263.

The liberals accepted the idea of universal suffrage. The democrats compromised on the issue of the Prussian hereditary imperial sovereign of the nation-state. Both compromises were hard to reach. Friedrich Theodor Vischer described the tortuous decision that the democrats' desire to preserve their work on the national constitution had forced them to make. 'I have fought a terrible battle inside me', in which finally 'I have perhaps not helped make the fellow [the Prussian hereditary emperor] but nor have I prevented it. I have allowed it to happen, just as our dear Lord allows evil to happen.'[24] In order that the constitution they had created might be pushed through the National Assembly, the liberals had to overcome their profound fears of the dangers of democratic suffrage. The 'many who have nothing are the worst voters. If only we could separate ourselves from every kind of aristocracy, though not from that of reason. That, as a rule, is linked to property ownership, and without it there can be no education.' This conviction, voiced by the independent liberal Friedrich Römer in the Constitutional Committee, was shared by deputies from the liberal middle ground and those on the right, whose position Ernst von Lasaulx expressed in stark terms: 'Allowing those without property to make decisions on the purses of the propertied is like making the goat the gardener.'[25] In his report for the 'Casino' liberals, Rudolf Haym saw matters no differently. The 'superstition of universal suffrage', he said, was 'a foreign tradition from the last century dragged into the German revolution of 1848', which benefited only the 'masses who are corruptible and desperate for a coup'. The liberal ideal was a moderate suffrage system based on the payment of taxes, which would prevent the 'aristocracy of riches' and the 'ochlocracy of the unpropertied masses', and which would 'safeguard the middle classes' dominant influence in the state' (Gagern).[26] They wanted the rise of the lower orders into the realm of citizens of the state, with full political rights, to be postponed for the future.

When the Prussian King rejected the title of emperor and the Imperial Constitution which had emerged from the liberal–democratic compromise failed, the liberals found themselves faced with a situation from which they could simply see no way out. They had come to the Assembly to create a German nation-state by parliamentary means, without a revolutionary break, and with the agreement of the individual state powers. The Prussian King's definitive refusal left them no option but renunciation and hope in the future. Effectively he had refused to bestow the dynastic consecration of legitimacy on the nation-state created by parliament. For a short time liberals like Welcker allowed themselves to be carried away in bellicose pathos, to storms of applause from the deputies: 'And if you want violence, a great nation will say: "Come over here then!"' But others immediately led the liberals back to a path more appropriate to the basic position they had held since the beginning of the revolution. Only legal means could be entertained, Minister Gagern stressed, otherwise it would be all too easy to 'break down the barriers' behind which revolutionary anarchy lay in wait.[27]

For most liberals, the battles to force the awkward princes to recognize the Imperial Constitution, which flared up in Germany in April 1849,[28] had already transgressed those 'barriers', which they had always defended and could not now cross without betraying their basic convictions. The 'campaign for the Imperial Constitution' was one factor which led to the uncontested resignation of the Gagern government, when on 10 May 1849 the Imperial Regent, not the National Assembly, withdrew his support for it and appointed the Grävell cabinet, whose programme of liquidating the revolution could only be pushed through against the will of the majority of the National Assembly. Some democrats and members of the republican left refused to simply acquiesce without resistance and met in Stuttgart on 6 June as a 'Rump Parliament'. Their intention was to bring an end to 'the legal revolution' (Raveaux) against the 'violation of the imperial peace on the part of the Prussians' (L. Simon). The liberals, however, submitted, in that they left the National Assembly. As the resignation statement of sixty-five 'Casino' members on 20 May 1849 declared, the only alternatives they could see were renouncing the implementation of the Imperial Constitution or 'breaking the last common and legal bond between all German governments and peoples, and spreading a civil war, whose beginnings have already shattered the foundations of the entire social order'. They chose renunciation as the lesser evil, and entrusted the care of the Constitution to the 'legal organs of the individual states and to the independent further development of the nation'.[29] This was entirely in keeping with their socio-political model, which had influenced all their policies in the revolutionary era, and which they had never publicly denied. To judge this attitude as a 'betrayal' is to judge liberals against non-liberal programmes of social change which were alien to them.

Liberals in the Extra-Parliamentary Revolutionary Movement[30]

The revolution saw the emergence, primarily in the towns, of a network of associations which played a key role in the formation of the political public. They created a kind of multi-party system which was divided into organizations of workers, republicans and democrats, liberals, political Catholics and conservatives. Some democrats and liberals initially organized together – in Württemberg, for example – whilst in Saxony, the state with the highest numbers of association members, democrats and liberals organized separately from the start. By the middle of the year of the revolution, the programmatic and organizational split was complete almost everywhere. Members of the liberal associations, which individually gave themselves very different names, came overwhelmingly from the upper middle and middle classes. Their social spectrum extended to journeymen and workers, but they were not represented on the executive committees. The educated middle class, which so dominated the Frankfurt National Assembly, also represented a high proportion of the

members of liberal associations, yet the lower middle classes and
the commercial middle class were also major participants. Thus,
in July 1848, of the 413 members of the main Stuttgart association of Württemberg liberals, around 35 per cent belonged to
the lower middle classes and almost 30 per cent were bankers,
manufacturers and above all merchants. Around 18 per cent
were civil servants employed by the state.[31]

Adherence to the principles of the 'constitutional monarchy' or
the 'republic' drew an even sharper line between liberals and
democrats in the network of extra-parliamentary organizations
than it did in the parliaments. The 'democratic monarchy' compromise formula suggested by moderate democrats, was unacceptable to most liberal associations. The democratic monarch
would have been a 'king without characteristics'. It was for this
reason that the liberals uncompromisingly rejected the 'republic
with a hereditary president' (Rudolf Virchow), for their major
concern was not the title. They wanted the monarch as a guarantor
of 'civil society' in exceptional circumstances: 'Call him what you
like, but don't take away his power ... he should have power, and
that is what we are trying to achieve with the hereditary monarchy',
was Ludwig Häusser's succinct description of the function which
the liberals intended for the monarch.[32]

The horrors of the republic were expressed by the liberal
associations and their publications in even more stark and drastic
terms than by the liberal deputies. France's development into a
social republic, whose defeat in June 1848 was welcomed with
a sigh of relief by German liberals, but also by moderate democrats, was regarded by liberals as a pointer to the inevitable
consequences of a republic in Germany too. A quotation from a
declaration by the Heidelberg Liberal Association in March 1849
is typical of the many similar nightmares which made the liberals
quake with fear in 1848–9 when they considered the republic
and its supporters:[33]

And the brand new Communist social republic – oh what a
wonderful sight it is! These Fourieresque educational estab-
lishments of urchins and pigs, these Proudhonic feeding
institutions of idle workers, and finally the June scenes in the
streets of Paris, where the red fighters fired poisoned bullets at
the citizens until that brute Cavaignac and his brutish soldiers
used case shot to mow them down! Yes, sirs, that was the great

turning point; from then on the world's eyes were opened to
the meaning of the *red republic*. ... Say, you sirs! Did perhaps
the idea of the social republic, the community of women and
property, come from us? Did we utter the words: property is
theft? Did we hold up the post coaches in the Badenese
Oberland, plunder the coffers and relieve the rich citizens of
Müllheim of their surplus property? Did we call to the people
at the meeting of proletarians in Rohrbach: Until now the rich
have eaten ham and you have fed the pigs; from now on they
shall feed the pigs and you will eat the ham? Or did we turn
the town hall chamber into a classroom for atheism and materialism, where Mr Feuerbach mocks the poor until they lose all
faith in God and robs their loose morality of its last prop? ... But
make no mistake. ... Even the heads of the Robespièrres [sic]
and the Dantons were not immune to the guillotine! Even you
will be in no doubt that your actions make your fellow citizens
poor, that you destroy commerce, trade, wealth and confidence.
The material wealth of a people flourishes only in the lap of
internal and external freedom, and under the protection of the
law. For as long as you undermine peace and law and order, and
threaten to erupt at any moment, every peaceful citizen will be
on his guard against you; business will falter, all confidence will
disappear, and the working class will be unable to earn a living.
Capital has not disappeared from the face of the earth; it is
simply lying fallow and will return to public circulation as soon as
the agitation and the communist tendencies stop.

A resilient alliance of liberal and democratic associations on
shared core demands was out of the question in the face of this
kind of caricature of the 'republic' as a magnifying glass of all the
fears which tortured liberal citizens. Some liberal deputies,
including Rudolf Haym, spoke of the 'justified battle of the
parties' and praised the Imperial Constitution as a 'symbol of
their reconcilability'. Democratic deputies such as Jakob Venedy
described the German people as not yet 'mature' enough for the
republic, and testified in word and deed to their rejection of a
'minority revolution'. Nevertheless, many 'nameless' liberals
refused to alter their views of democrats of all persuasions,
whom they divided at best into open and 'secret republicans'.[34]
    This deep-seated mistrust was one reason for the limited part
played by liberal associations in the campaign for the Imperial

Constitution. In May 1849 the *Nationaler Verein* (National Association), the umbrella organization of liberal associations, attempted to join with the democrats in support of the Imperial Constitutional movement. However, most other liberal associations ceased their activities in the final phase of the revolution, as did their representatives in the Frankfurt National Assembly.[35] This should come as no surprise. Liberal associations had always regarded supporting the National Assembly and its work as their most important duty. When this was abandoned by its liberal creators, following the loss of that vital component, the hereditary imperial sovereign, nothing remained for its organizations which could legitimize their co-operation in the campaign for the Imperial Constitution. They were also repelled by the enthusiastic participation of democratic and workers' associations. To constitutionalist liberals this was further confirmation of what they thought they had always known: that 'this time too, revolutionary radicalism' wanted 'only to fish in muddy waters' (Häusser). 'The "people" were using the constitution only as a visiting card, when in reality they were fighting for the republic.'[36]

There was another reason why liberals found it easy to allow their associations to decline, even before the beginning of the post-revolutionary era of reaction. Although the occasional liberal voice was heard which regarded permanent extra-parliamentary organizations as necessary for the formation of a political public, most liberals were suspicious of such organizations. When liberals formed associations, they did so with a bad conscience, and only as a defensive measure to prevent this sphere being left entirely to the competition – to the democrats in particular. Liberals took pains to remove from their associations any hint of a 'parallel and counter-parliament' – an intention which was ascribed to the democratic *Centralmärzverein* (Central March Association) by the liberal Stuttgart 'Fatherland Association', for example. Haym even called it a 'subversive association in the worst sense'.[37] With the Central March Association, the democrats formed the first German party with a modern colouring. It institutionalized the links between extra-parliamentary political associations and the 'Donnersberg', 'Deutscher Hof' and 'Westendhall' groupings, which assumed its leadership. Constitutionalist liberals created the National Association umbrella organization, which 144 associations had joined by April 1849,[38] but it did not unite parliamentary parties and associations. Deputies did not join it. This is a reflection of the liberals' 'reluctance to form parties', which could not theoretically resolve the dilemma they faced during the revolution, when they were forced to become a party in order to achieve aims which, as they saw it, transcended parties. They therefore experienced the decline in their 'enforced party status'[39] more as a relief than a loss.

Basic Liberal Positions in the Imperial Constitution

The work on the constitution, which was concluded with the election of the Kaiser on 28 March 1849, represented a compromise which its liberal and democratic creators were forced to make by the balance of power in Germany and Europe. This compromise ruled out or left open important issues which were fought over inside and outside the National Assembly. When the constitution was formulated, three great tasks stood in the foreground: the territorial extent of the German nation-state; the extent of the Basic Rights; and the distribution of power within the state.

A number of factors brought home to the deputies the *problems inherent in the drawing up of borders*: the competing demands of the various national movements; the objections of the European Great Powers – Russia, Britain and France – to an expansive German nation-state, which would have destroyed the 'European equilibrium'; and finally the refusal of the Habsburg monarchy to sacrifice the unity of its own state for that of Germany. By far the majority of all deputies, like the revolutionary movement as a whole, regarded the territory of the German Confederation as a kind of given situation, behind which that of the German nation-state must not be allowed to fall. When these territorial expectations encountered the resistance of other nationalities and states, the liberals of the 'centre-right' tended towards a concept of nationality which based German claims on that which had evolved historically, and which saw in every renunciation a betrayal of the German nation. The left and the 'centre-left', on the other hand, were dominated by a willingness to recognize the right of a people to self-determination as a basis for the future nation-state order. This led them to express sympathy for the demands for independence on the part of the Poles in Posen and of the Italians in South Tyrol.

The Schleswig-Holstein issue, however, saw a shift in this line, which could not be sharply defined between the parliamentary parties on matters of national politics. The left decisively rejected the Malmö Armistice, which it regarded as a betrayal of the revolution and a surrender of the primacy of the National Assembly. Liberals and the right finally decided to vote in favour of the Armistice, to avoid a test of strength with Prussia, which could only have been won at the risk of a new revolution. They believed their fears had been confirmed when unrest broke out, triggered by their compromise. Although constitutionalist liberals praised the suppression of these uprisings as a fine 'example of energy and consistency' (Beseler) on the part of the Frankfurt Central Power, they also recognized the dilemma to which the National Assembly had succumbed. 'Faith in the omnipotence of the Assembly', wrote Carl Georg Beseler, 'is largely on the wane.' In retrospect, Rudolf Haym ascertained that, 'the moment we felt free of the dangers of anarchy, we realized that we were not free of the cunning of diplomacy'.[40]

With these words Haym addressed the fundamental problem of the 'liberal politics of the centre' (Nipperdey). Recoiling from the 'recognition of that foolish principle of the sovereignty of the people,'[41] they tried to avoid the break with the traditional dynasties. Yet they could only hope for concessions from them while the revolution remained untamed. They were forced to confront this issue in the most urgent manner from November 1848 onwards, when the reinforced Austrian state leadership dashed all hopes of a greater German nation-state and of Gagern's emergency programme of a narrower (*kleindeutsch*) and wider (*großdeutsch*) federation. Liberals and democrats reacted with the regrouping outlined above, in order to enable a *kleindeutsch* nation-state to be formed, at least as an 'temporary emergency solution'.[42]

The Imperial Constitution did not reflect the European great powers' response to the territorial claims of the German national movement. Article I of the Constitution claimed the entire territory of the German Confederation for the nation-state, although special conditions were provided for 'as long as the German–Austrian lands do not join the federal state' (paragraph 87). No one can know whether the *kleindeutsch* nation-state would in the long run have been able to come to terms with the borders its creators were forced to accept in 1848–9. The failure of the revolution robbed it of the chance to test them out. Expansionist policies were not ruled out in the speeches by deputies from all factions, nor in the wording of the Imperial Constitution. However, in 1848-9 practice was more modest than rhetoric. With the election of a *kleindeutsch* head of state, the majority of moderate democrats and liberals proved their ability (though it was cloaked in wild imperial visions) to attempt to find a solution which could be reconciled with the interests of the European powers.

The *List of Basic Rights* of the Imperial Constitution, consisting of fourteen articles (paragraphs 131–89) above all safeguarded the freedoms, rights and private property of the individual from despotic state intervention. The list of Basic Rights was a 'classic expression of middle-class liberalism's understanding of the law' (K. G. Faber), not only in this respect, but also in what was omitted from it: basic social rights, for example, which were frequently demanded in the National Assembly and even more urgently in the extra-parliamentary movement, with often contradictory aims. The Pre-Parliament had also recommended to the future National Assembly a social extension of the Basic Rights which included the 'protection of work by means of institutions and measures which will protect those incapable of working from deprivation, measures which will create waged employment for those without income, and reconcile the constitution of the employment and factory sphere to the needs of the time'. Struve's radical democratic motion went further still in its demand for the 'elimination of the disparity between labour and capital'. However, even the Pre-Parliament President, Karl Mittermaier, a member of the 'centre-left' in the Paulskirche, warned his colleagues in his opening speech that they should be 'managers' even 'for that minority of the people who earn their bread miserably by the sweat of their brow, and who are demanding that the need for improved social conditions be finally satisfied'.[43]

The Workers' Commission, which was established by the Pre-Parliamentary Committee of Fifty and the Frankfurt National Assembly and its Economics Committee, discussed the opportunities for state intervention to regulate the social and economic spheres. The opinions represented by liberals varied. The only demand they rejected outright was that of the 'right to work', a concept which had been bound up in the fears surrounding the slogan 'red republic', particularly in the wake of the experiments with the 'national workshops' of the French 'second republic'.

For the urban lower classes in 1848, on the other hand, the 'right to work' had become the greatest symbol of hope, though their conceptions of what it actually meant differed widely.

Broadly speaking, it is possible to identify three basic liberal viewpoints in the debates on the social elements of the Basic Rights.[44] In the parliamentary parties of the 'centre-right', free trade and economic liberalism dominated, which demanded that the state 'leave matters to follow their natural course', as the 'Casino' liberal Merck described the *laissez-faire* principle. A second position, mainly represented by the centre-left, but also by deputies of other right-wing groupings, sought protectionist measures which would allow state intervention in order to protect, promote and make provision in the social and economic spheres. Thus, for example, protective tariffs were demanded externally, and customs unity internally.

Alongside these was a third variant, which was supported above all by the 'left', by deputies of the 'centre-left', and by republicans and moderate democrats in the extra-parliamentary revolutionary movement. They placed their hopes above all in universal, equal (male) suffrage as a central lever which would make the state capable of social, as well as political reform. In doing so, they postponed the 'solution of the social question' to the democratically constituted society of the future. But they also demanded more concrete immediate measures; above all the abolition of indirect taxation, which Bernhard Eisenstuck of the 'Deutscher Hof', for example, regarded as 'the main cause of the destruction of the social sphere of life'. But his resolute support for the simultaneous and equally important reorganization of the political and social order, so that the 'free people' would not 'be half-wasted away and half-starved at the very moment when it was to make use of this freedom', failed to win a majority in the National Assembly. Instead, the viewpoint of the Constitutional Committee, half of which was made up of 'Casino' liberals, won the day – the Basic Rights should not be expanded to include social elements: 'We will leave the development of our social conditions to the power and genius of our people.'[45]

We have already referred to the manner in which the creators of the constitution sought to regulate the third central problem of the constitutional order: the *distribution of power in the state*. Democratic demands such as universal equal male suffrage and merely a suspensory right of veto for the government in legislative procedures, joined with the aims of political liberalism, which removed a considerable degree of authority from the individual states and transferred it to the nation-state. Legal continuity with the dynastic federal past was protected, but none the less, the way was paved for a parliamentary monarchy.

When the Prussian King countered this great liberal–democratic constitution with the principle of dynastic legitimacy, German liberals had no option but to retreat from a battlefield which now belonged to the decisive forces on both sides, but which no longer had room for the political credo of the liberals – reform, not revolution. Gabriel Riesser was the Jewish Vice President of the National Assembly and embodiment of Jewish emancipatory hopes, whose fulfilment the Imperial Constitution promised. He described the lack of an escape route for the liberal politics of the centre in the final phase of the German revolution: after the 'declaration of bankruptcy on the part of the moderate majority of the Assembly', nothing remained but the 'sorry choice between the despotism of the princes and the so-called democrats'. 'I agree that under certain circumstances ... the victory of a despotic, even bloody reaction might be the lesser evil; but I dread the rule of a people which could be happy to see that victory.'[46]

3 Liberalism between the Revolution and the Reichsgründung

1849–58: The Decade of Reaction

The failure of the revolution marked the beginning of a period of rapid change, commonly referred to as 'the era of reaction'. Yet this term describes only *one* side of this phase in nineteenth-century German history: a period onto which, so far, the least light has been shed. Political life was coloured by repression and by the removal of the 'debris of March', as the Prussian staunch Conservative Leopold von Gerlach put it. Pre-revolutionary conditions did not return with the victorious authoritarian state, however. 'Reaction' did not mean 'restoration'. This was least of all the case in the sphere of *international and inter-state politics*. Many liberals regarded these areas as a lever which could be used to overcome the stagnation which had set in on national political issues, but a lever which they would not be able to set in motion alone. Even before the decade of the *Reichsgründung*, in the fifties, the political statements of *kleindeutsch* Prussian-oriented liberals in particular were filled with expressions of longing for a 'purifying' and 'strengthening' war. For them the German revolution did not end with the failure of the Frankfurt National Assembly and the campaign for the Imperial Constitution of 1849, but with the 'humiliation' of Olmütz in November/December 1850.

Hope in Prussia as 'realpolitik'?

In Olmütz hopes were dashed that the *kleindeutsch* nation-state, which the Prussian government was seeking in its *union project*, could be founded 'from above'.[1] On 28 May 1849, together with Saxony and Hanover, Prussia had put forward a draft constitution which came astonishingly close to the Frankfurt Imperial Constitution. The major differences between the two concerned the participation of the individual states in imperial government through the establishment of a College of Princes; an unlimited right of veto for the sovereign of the state; and the de-democratization of the elections to the *Volkshaus* by means of the three-class suffrage system. Whilst democrats firmly rejected the union project, liberals did not initially react as one. From 25 to 27 June 1849, their so-called *Spitzengarnitur*, made up of *Kleindeutsche* and supporters of a hereditary emperor, met in Gotha, where they decided, despite all their reservations regarding this 'enterprise with the most questionable prospects of success',[2] to take part in the elections to the Union Parliament in Erfurt. The 'Gotha party', as the *kleindeutsch* liberals subsequently became known, represented the majority in both chambers of the Erfurt parliament. They could be entirely satisfied with the government's draft of the Union Constitution: with the elimination of the merely suspensive right of veto for the imperial sovereign and the removal of democratic suffrage, it eliminated two aspects of the Frankfurt Imperial Constitution which the liberals had accepted only reluctantly.

These amendments, and the consolidation of the federal idea which they hoped would occur, also made it easier for south-west German liberals who did not want a nation-state under Prussian hegemony to agree to the union project. A series of motives were intertwined in their assent to the Union Constitution, including their hope that German economic power would be revitalized if the fragmentation of the state was overcome. But above all they believed that the Union Constitution would form a bulwark against both reaction and revolution. However, this war on two fronts was not waged in a balanced manner in their election campaign for the Erfurt Union Parliament. As in the revolutionary years of 1848–9, they continued to direct the force of their attack at the democrats, whose defence of the Frankfurt Imperial Constitution they still regarded as an attempt to 'dress up agitation for a revolution in a legal form'.[3]

After their experiences of the struggles for the Imperial Constitution in 1849, German liberals viewed their own creation, the Imperial Constitution, in a different light. Tarred with the brush of the social revolution, it had acquired the reputation of favouring 'anarchy' and 'the legally sanctioned rule of the masses', and many liberals now openly distanced themselves from the Constitution they themselves had created. They thought they could see two ways out. *Kleindeutsch* liberals sought refuge in the union project, which promised a Prussian-led nation-state with a constitutional order. This appeared to offer parliamentary participation to the middle classes, and at the same time to provide an effective filter against the alleged desire of the 'masses' for a social revolution. Austrian policies, on the other hand, meant that *großdeutsch* liberals could see no prospect of national unity imposed 'from above'. They were left with no option but to postpone their hopes for a nation-state to the future, and to focus on the readiness of the individual states to allow domestic reforms for the present time. As early as 1850, the union project came to nought, and domestic reform policies also rapidly dwindled to a disappointingly narrow path, even for the most moderate liberals. The individual states of the Confederation narrowed this path to varying degrees, however.

Prussia's renunciation of the union in the Treaty of Olmütz, which it signed on 29 November 1850 under pressure from Austria and Russia, was regarded by *kleindeutsch* liberals as a betrayal of Prussia's mission in German history. 'When Prussia bowed down before Austria, two hundred years of history was belied, the intellectual life of the nation back to the Reformation was denied, and the bright idea of Germany, in which Prussia has its strength and vocation, was pronounced dead.'[4] With these words at the end of 1851, Johann Gustav Droysen defined a view of history which would become a core element of middle-class Protestant belief in German progress. Although German liberalism did not surrender fully to this belief until the decade of the *Reichsgründung*, it was already formed in the fifties – in spite of the policies of Prussia, which was not yet doing what 'Borussianism' attributed to it as a historical task. Droysen was the first historian to describe this belief in the Prussian future of Germany. In his fourteen-volume *Geschichte der preußischen Politik* (History of Prussian Politics), published from 1855 onwards, he declared the Hohenzollerns to be partly conscious, partly blind tools of historical progress towards national unity and freedom. Like most liberals, he still regarded both as necessarily interwoven, despite the fact that as early as the fifties, voices were increasingly heard which elevated 'unity' to the central value.

Heinrich von Treitschke, later the eloquent harbinger of the Prussian–German powerful state, extolled any method which would rapidly lead to a nation-state – 'even if that should be despotism'. But even he regarded the unconditional pre-eminence of unity as only a transitional stage on the path to freedom, though he believed 'that when the genuinely national unity of our people has been achieved, any unnatural constitutional form could only be short-lived'.[5]

None the less, during the decade of reaction broad sections of German, and especially *kleindeutsch* liberalism, shifted their focus from domestic reform to national unification. This was associated with a process of rethinking in which the powerful state rose to become executor of the national unity which the middle classes had failed to achieve in 1848–9. For many liberals hopes for a powerful state included the acceptance, indeed the longing, for a war which would bring about unity – even a domestic war. 'What we need', wrote Treitschke, 'is a powerful, purely German state in which this particularist nonsense is forced to submit to a centralizing force.'

In 1849 Droysen retired from politics into his 'refuge; learning'. He continued to keep up with the events of the day, however, and commented on them in his historical works. He too was convinced of the non-viability of the German small and medium states: 'I also know that something is rotten in Prussia. But a stench is better than this paucity ... and the still-life of this Lilliputianism.' In his opinion, only Prussia was capable of bringing 'Germany together to form a paste, from which God only knows what further form would then emerge.'

> The era of the small states and the small European state system is over. In political life, as in manufacturing, only large mass structures will come to anything. ... Alongside the world powers of England, Russia, North America and China (which is reforming itself), the southern European and the Germanic races must either crumble or join together as a mass.[6]

Droysen's prophecies did not point forward to the imperialist liberalism of Wilhelmine Germany, but he did help to prepare the ground for the belief in Germany's world mission.

Already in the fifties, this belief in a mission included the close alliance of Prussian–German liberalism and Protestantism.

'Being German and being Protestant were regarded as synonymous',[7] as were education and Protestantism. When in 1854
Pope Pius IX announced the doctrine of the Immaculate Conception, Droysen described to his fellow historian and political
friend, Heinrich von Sybel, a view of the world which would be
shared by all Protestant liberals in the decade of the *Reichsgründung*. Catholicism was regarded as the embodiment of all
that was unscientific and un-German. 'Idolatry is here and suits
the rabble; the more our German governments try in their
wisdom to turn us all into rabble, the more prospects there are
for the Roman church. Without a war I can see no end to its
victories, but the dreadful gravity of a battle for life and death –
against the Russians or French, it's all the same to me – will make
us healthier.'[8]

The 'Borussian' belief in Prussia's historical 'German mission'
and the longing for a national war of unification assumed a
double function for the *kleindeutsch* liberals of the fifties. They
reworked their experiences of the revolution and they drew
hope for the future from the era of reaction, despite the fact that
the scope for active liberal politics was extremely limited. At the
centre of their thinking was their faith in the 'foreign pressures'
(Beseler), which would promote unity, and in the historically
'authenticated' Prussian desire for action on a national level,
which had only temporarily petered out. The 'people', on the
other hand, were ruled out for them as a significant political
group which could act independently. In 1853 Droysen voiced
the liberals' aversion to the 'masses' and their methods in graphic
terms. 'The people are but little or nothing. At best they are a
cloud of dust which fills the air and obscures the view until a light
rain returns all that has been thrown up to a thick, creamy
substance, which we usually refer to as mud. ... At any rate, "the
people" is not a form of address to which one might direct a
letter or a book. And that is always the most important thing.'[9]

Anything but an appeal to 'the people'. The liberals took this
warning from the events of the revolution, and again from Louis
Napoleon's *coup d'état* of 1851. Droysen perceptively analysed the
significance of Napoleon's autocratic rule for 'legitimate Europe'.
In the French empire, based on plebiscites, which denied the
monarch's divine right to rule, he saw the continuation of the
revolution of 1848 which was then transferred from the 'street to
the cabinets, from national to international law' by the European

powers themselves in the Crimean War (1854–6). The collapse of the conservative European alliance of Russia, Austria and Prussia, the shifting of the centre of power in Europe from Russia to Britain and France, the links between state power politics and social dynamics – Droysen found confirmations of all these trends, which he addressed again and again in his letters, in the Crimean War. He saw a 'terrible crisis of all European life' which would reform Europe as profoundly as the Napoleonic Era at the beginning of the century had done. 'Legitimacy will then be as cheap as blackberries.'[10]

Droysen's observations are but one example of the attempts of *kleindeutsch* liberals in the fifties to adapt to the new political and social conditions in the German Confederation and in Europe. Yet adaptation did not mean simply the sacrifice of old ideals. Distance from the 'masses' and internal and external co-operation with the monarchic state had always been part of the leitmotifs of liberal thought. Now, however, they were reinforced, and they increasingly eclipsed other principles. Nothing could be achieved on the level of national politics without links with state power. Liberals now used this belief to counter the 'mad notion' that 'the world could be reformed with cannons, which are loaded only with the *ideas* of law and truth'.[11]

Ludwig August von Rochau voiced this confidence in an alliance between the state power and middle-class liberals on national political issues. In his *Grundsätze der Realpolitik* (Principles of *Realpolitik*),[12] published in 1853 to widespread liberal acclaim, he examined German history in the light of the experiences of 1848, and devised perspectives of action for the future. His message for national liberalism was unmistakable: 'Only through the exercise of power is what is right appointed to rule.' This power had to be internal and external, for 'the strong cannot allow themselves to be ruled by the weak'. Those who failed to recognize this 'dynamic fundamental principle of state order' were building 'castles in the air' which would fade with 'right that was unable to defend itself' (p. 26f.). For this reason, Rochau believed, the German constitutional movement was doomed to failure. The movement would only have been able to create a viable constitutional state using revolutionary force. But, unlike in England and Belgium, this would not have restricted itself to a 'change in dynasty', but would have destroyed 'the monarchy, that is to say, the real basis of constitutionalism' (p. 129).

Thus, Rochau astutely defined one of the central problems of German liberalism in the revolutionary years of 1848–9. Unsuited as a constitutional party to enforce 'great changes in the state by violent means' (p. 129), it was forced to hope that the old powers would deprive themselves of their own power. And when it became clear that they would never willingly share power, the liberal supporters of the constitution had no option but to disappear 'silently from the Paulskirche, as customers leave a wine bar late at night' (p. 133).

Rochau not only offered German liberals a diagnosis of their impotence, he also gave them a perspective for the future at the side of the powerful nation-state. 'Constitutionalism' had failed in its attempt to seize power, but since it was rooted in the 'spirit of the century' (p. 129), it could not be destroyed. His comforting message to the *kleindeutsch* liberals was: undertake nothing single-handedly, but above all undertake nothing against the liberal middle classes.

He believed that the 'unresolved vital matter' (p. 175) between Prussia and Austria in the battle for Germany could only be resolved in the German 'national interest' (p. 163) by Prussia, at any rate only in alliance with the idea of unity: 'the great achievement of 1848, which cannot be reversed by violence or cleverness' (p. 68). A strong state *and* the 'national spirit' (p. 35 and elsewhere) had to merge together in order to create a united Germany, which would then be able to 'laugh in the face of any threat of war or revolution' (p. 191). This powerful civic state community, protected from external and internal threats, demanded insight on the part of the liberal constitutional movement into the 'incurable emptiness of constitutions' (p. 180) which were not built on power. Yet Rochau and his fellow thinkers did not see this as the capitulation of middle-class liberalism to the powerful national state. They put their faith instead in the silent power of the 'spirit of the age', in the 'opinion of the century which has consolidated to form certain principles, views and habits of understanding' (p. 33). In the long term, state politics could not be successfully pursued in opposition to 'civic consciousness, the idea of freedom, national feeling, and the idea of human equality' (p. 32), to these 'convictions of the people' which had shaped the *zeitgeist* (p. 34). Those post-revolutionary liberals who hoped for Prussia's national *Machttat* shared this conviction. Rochau's work reinforced their belief.

It also confirmed the liberal belief in the 'middle class' as the 'most indispensable and valuable substance for the German state edifice' (p. 141). Politics, wrote Rochau, can despise the doctrinarian, ignore the 'peasant class' and destroy the aristocracy, but it had to 'come to terms with the "middle class"' (p. 184): 'a permanent new political edifice' (p. 143) could never be established unless the middle class was won over. This certainty of the future, based on the belief in the superior social power of the 'middle class', bound post-revolutionary liberalism inextricably to its *Vormärz* roots, despite its experiences of impotence in 1848.

Liberals and the Politics of the Individual States: Austria, Prussia, Baden and Württemberg

Liberals reflected on the past in order to learn lessons for the future. But what did their present *political practice* look like? It is impossible to answer this in general terms. As before 1848, in the absence of a national parliament, liberal politics had once again to be primarily the politics of the individual states, and the opportunities for political involvement differed widely from state to state. They will be briefly examined here using the examples of Austria, Prussia, Baden and Württemberg.

Until 1848 the *Habsburg monarchy*,[13] the 'China of Europe' as some contemporaries called it, had with Russia formed the refuge of the restoration on the continent. The maintenance of the status quo was the basis of the Habsburg multi-ethnic empire, which was in danger of disintegrating if the territorial and political reorganization with which the European great powers had ended the era of the French revolution and Napoleonic rule at the Vienna Congress in 1815, was to be set in motion. The taming of the forces of the movement succeeded, but at great cost. The political standstill which was enforced under the repressive 'Metternich system' undermined the internal cohesion of the Habsburg monarchy. In the revolutionary years of 1848–9 it seemed to collapse under the onslaught of the national movements. The Habsburg monarchy managed to withstand this revolutionary shock thanks to Russian armed aid and the conflicts unleashed amongst its different nationalities. Enthusiastic state reforms were then carried out in the fifties, despite the fact that Austria reverted to a state without a constitution in 1851. After 1852 and the death of Minister President Schwarzenberg, Austrian neo-absolutism, entirely oriented towards the monarch, won the day. This neo-absolutist system was politically reactionary, but did not mark the beginning of a comprehensive counter-revolution. Instead, the fifties represent a significant period of reform in Austrian history, which only now caught up with the 'revolution from above' which Prussia had attempted to address at the beginning of the nineteenth century. Thus, the great agrarian reforms of 1848 were defended by the Austrian state leaders against the aristocracy. The state administration and the judicial system were reformed, as were the universities, the *Gymnasien* and the *Volksschulen*. The state bureaucracy also intervened in the economic sphere with liberalizing reforms.

But it was a social and economic liberalization, aimed against political liberalism, carried through by the state. It was founded on the army, the police and the Catholic Church, which grew out of its position of Josephinian state church with the Concordat of 1855, and became an institution with its own canon law and extensive authority in the state education sector. Attempts at liberal constitutionalist reform, and also aristocratic social restorative attempts were suppressed by an omnipotent state bureaucracy, which relegated 'the politically incapacitated society ... to the path of the private pursuit of economic profit'.[14] This course of politically illiberal social 'modernization' without a constitution finally failed in 1859, when Austria's inability to finance its Great Power policies was exposed in its failure in the Italian War. The capital markets refused to provide extra-constitutional state finance and neo-absolutism was faced with the ruins of a policy which sought in vain to introduce liberal economic reforms, in order to be able to prevent political liberalism. Political reforms had to be granted after all from 1859 onwards, but this did not narrow the gulf between the House of Habsburg and liberal nationalism in non-Austrian Germany; a gulf which had grown wider in the neo-absolutist era. Even before Austro-Prussian rivalry was decided on a military level in the war for Germany, Austria as a national force had already largely been ruled out of German liberalism's hopes for the future.

In national political terms, the beneficiary of Austrian policies was *Prussia*, which remained, or became once again after the brief revolutionary interlude, a 'monarchic civil servant and military state'[15] with a strong *Junker* and feudal colouring.

Prussia was the mainstay of political reaction and the backbone of the German *Polizeiverein* or 'police association'; an extremely effective secret pan-German instrument of surveillance.[16] And yet, unlike Austria, after the revolution Prussia remained a constitutional state with parliamentary representation. This played a key role in maintaining German liberals' belief in 'Prussia's historical vocation',[17] despite their disappointment in Prussian policies.

The imposed Prussian constitution of 15 December 1848 was subject to revisions from the start, and, given the nature of things, these could only be conservative. Examples of conservative revisions include the three-class suffrage system of 30 May 1849; the revised constitution of 31 January 1850; swearing the monarch in on the constitution, which came closer to the monarch distancing himself from the constitution in the spirit of the divine right to rule; the implementation laws of 1850–1, which restricted the Basic Rights; and the conversion of the First Chamber to a *Herrenhaus*, which was completed in 1854.[18] Liberals were no more able to prevent these measures than they could the budget regulations of the constitution, which failed to provide for a situation in which parliament and government could not agree.

Liberals in the chambers regarded the right to a tax boycott, which they called for in vain, as an emergency defensive measure against violations of the constitution, and not as an attempt to seize government power. They initially set their sights on a policy of parliament's indirect influence on the government:

> Of course the chambers should not want to rule directly themselves, but they should allow the mood of the state to sound out clearly over the government. It may not be possible to achieve a 'parliamentary government' always and everywhere, but parliamentary criticism is the first root of a free constitutional state, and the imperative herald of parliamentary rule which is its blossom.[19]

Liberal hopes in a Chamber of Deputies, from which 'the loud echo of the political and moral judgement of the people, of genuine overall public opinion' would ring out, were not fulfilled in Prussia. Political pressure, but also the general 'political fatigue of the reactionary period' (Heffter) which affected the middle classes in particular after the revolution, and which weakened the liberals, gradually turned the parliament into a mere branch of state administration. The 'bureaucratization' of the Chamber of Deputies peaked in the elections of 1855, when 61 per cent of its deputies were civil servants. Election turnout, on the other hand, reached a low ebb at 16 per cent. Already in the elections of 1852, the liberal opposition had had to manage without most of its central parliamentary figures who were no longer standing for election. They included L. Camphausen, Hansemann, Duncker, von Auerswald and Beckerath. In 1855 it won only 12 per cent of the 352 seats, while the government could count on a safe majority of at least 205 votes.[20]

Despite the limited opportunity for effective opposition, which was even further reinforced by the procedural rules of the parliament, the effects of the existence of a Prussian parliament should not be underestimated. Despite the reaction, Prussia remained a constitutional state, which revised its constitution using constitutional methods. Prussia also retained its overall state parliament, in which the conservative spectrum fanned out and came to terms with the post-revolutionary constitutional state. The democrats eliminated themselves when they boycotted the elections; their response to the imposition of three-class suffrage in 1849. Prussian democrats never fully recovered from this retreat from politics, which further reinforced the post-revolutionary flagging of political life. The democratic movement of the sixties was therefore primarily restricted to the German south. The liberals, on the other hand, who formed the left wing of the parliament after the July elections of 1849, were able at least to limit the electoral successes of the Conservatives and their power over the Chamber of Deputies, to some extent in co-operation with political Catholicism.[21]

Even in 1855, at the zenith of Conservative electoral success, they saw a glimmer of hope. The political lethargy of the middle-class public had by this time clearly passed its peak. For the low overall election turnout of around 16 per cent reflected conditions in the third class of the suffrage system in particular: only around 12.8 per cent of the approximately 2.3 million who were entitled to vote did so, while 27.2 per cent voted in the second class (401 098 voters) and 39.5 per cent in the first class (145 081). The *National-Zeitung* also stressed that 'the educated middle classes in particular have once again been gripped by an interest in politics, leaving the long years of indifference behind them. Their ranks are filled with the call to maintain the state order we have achieved.'[22] Vigorous election campaigns took place in the larger towns. The liberal opposition won seven of the nine seats in Berlin, and two of the three in Breslau.

Conservative victors also recognized that it would not be possible to repeat the electoral successes of 1855. The combined opposition, which ranged from the liberal 'left' to the right-wing liberal 'centre', to the Catholic parliamentary grouping, was working together on the most controversial problem of the legislative period: the change in the tax laws. And on the opposite side, the 'conservative adaptation of the liberal doctrine of con stitutionalism',[23] had already reached the point where the government's tax bill failed due to the votes of Conservatives, who, as Minister President Manteuffel complained, were trying to administer the state as if it were a manorial estate. The policy of preserving the constitution whilst simultaneously weakening it could obviously not be continued. The lack of unity amongst Conservatives, whose spectrum extended from the doctrinaire Ultras surrounding the Gerlachs, to the *Wochenblattpartei* around Moritz August von Bethmann Hollweg, made that impossible. When Crown Prince William became Regent in October 1858, the *kleindeutsch* liberals believed they were standing on the threshold of the re-birth of the 'true Prussia', which according to Haym was the only thing which could 'save Germany', 'if indeed it can be saved at all'.[24]

The Grand Duchy of *Baden* was more profoundly shaken by the events of 1848–9 than most other German states. It had been possible to put down the revolution there only after the military intervention of Prussia in 1849. Prussian troops also oversaw the beginnings of the reaction and the rebuilding of the army. 'The restoration of order in Baden by Prussia', the Prussian envoy reported to his King on 27 June 1850, had 'not only re-established basic discipline in the state', but had also made possible the 'rebirth of religious order in public life', which had 'been undermined by liberal constitutionalism for twenty to thirty years': 'Prussian bayonets have opened up the Temples of the Lord once more!'[25]

Despite this martial aid in the 're-establishment of the cross', the reaction in Baden was less profound than elsewhere, and during the period of reaction liberals in Baden found it easier to assert themselves than their friends in other states. There were a number of reasons for this. Baden did not have an aristocracy comparable to the Prussian *Junkers*, and unlike the civil servants in Austria and Prussia, Badenese civil servants were ill-suited as representatives of the core of reactionary policy. Badenese civil servants had been educated by liberal professors at the state universities of Freiburg and especially Heidelberg. Since the thirties, more and more men who supported the ideas of moderate liberalism had risen through the ranks of the state administration.

Even Prince Regent Frederick, who determined Badenese policy from 1852 onwards, had enjoyed an education which introduced him to middle-class liberal values. In Heidelberg he studied under the well-known liberal Ludwig Häusser. Through Häusser he met the leading personalities of south-German, Prussian–*kleindeutsch*-oriented liberalism. In Bonn he attended Dahlmann's lectures – an extremely unusual career for the son of a prince. When Frederick became Regent in 1852, he quickly toned down reactionary policies. This was made easier for him because his own experience had made him familiar with the moderate stance of liberals such as Häusser, who in the revolutionary years had disassociated themselves from the democrats, and had firmly condemned the radical concluding phase of the Badenese revolution, which seemed to disregard the throne.

Support of this kind from the Prince and in the state bureaucracy made it easier for Badenese liberals to withstand the decade of reaction than their counterparts in most other states of the German Confederation. Between 1850–1 and 1855–6, the liberal core of the Chamber of Deputies shrank from around thirty-two to fifteen (of a total of sixty-three seats in the Second Chamber), but on many issues 'almost double again' voted with them.[26]

Badenese liberals also managed to communicate effectively without a fixed parliamentary party and without extra-parliamentary associations. Candidates may have been chosen from amongst local notables, but in the fifties a unified leading stratum emerged at state level, which was centred on the legislature. Bonds had formed between members as a result of kinship, studies and professional connections. Its members knew each other personally, often from the *Korps Suevia* and the *Rupertia Freundschaften* which had been formed by liberal professors in Freiburg, and above all in Heidelberg. The resulting close ties between liberals made it possible in a small state such as Baden to dispense with a party organization. This is especially true of the younger generation which, after the revolution (when the old *Spitzengarnitur* had largely withdrawn from political life), was offered the chance at an unusually early stage to advance to the leadership of the liberal 'party'. August Lamey, reform minister in the seventies and Chamber President for many years, is one prominent personality amongst the thirty- to forty-year-olds, who left their political mark on Badenese liberalism for a long time after the revolution.

The liberal programme changed under their influence, as did their ideas on how this programme could be implemented politically. Even here, change did not mean a break with tradition. From the beginning, German liberal demands included increased self-government and administrative control. To a greater extent than in North German liberalism, in Baden these demands became more urgent during the *Nachmärz* or post-March-revolution period.[27] They were linked to the goal of extending the principle of self-government to the highest level of the state. The demand for political ministerial accountability went beyond the wishes of *Vormärz* liberalism, which had extended only as far as legal responsibility, with the right to indict ministers as the sharpest weapon.

Progress in the political life of Baden, however, only came as a result of the struggle between church and state, which culminated in November 1853, when the government ordered that every decree issued by the Freiburg Archbishop required the approval of a government commissioner. The battle intensified, clergymen were excluded from the administration of church assets, priests who had been appointed without government agreement had their salaries stopped, the Archbishop was placed under house arrest and troops were assembled against the rise of popular movements which seemed to be imminent. 'The real beneficiary was ... the liberal party.'[28] Although it did not identify directly with the demands of the church leaders, it did defend them in court and voiced the anger of the people of the Catholic Church in political and legal arguments. In Baden, as in Prussia, Catholicism and liberalism emerged as an opposition, loyal to the constitution, which joined together as soon as the government violated the constitution. As would soon be revealed, however, it was a unity which was held together only by a common opponent and not by shared basic convictions.

The political church movement led to the triumph of liberalism in Baden. The old government fell and the era of reaction
ended with a middle-class liberal government which took office
on 2 April 1860. It was led by Lamey, the liberal leader of the
opposition, 'elevated to the ministerial seat from the chamber
majority, taken from the ranks of the opposition and placed at the
helm, the first case of this kind to be experienced in Germany', as
a contemporary described the process.[29] As the Württemberg
envoy reported, Baden had 'joined the path which led to the
strictly parliamentary principle'. It was perhaps the beginning of
a 'very steep path', which he also believed the Prussia of the 'new
era' had joined.[30]

The success of the radical changes in Baden and their
durability was due not least to one man: Freiherr Franz von
Roggenbach. Born in Mannheim in 1825, he too had grown up
under the influence of the liberal Heidelberg professors. He
returned home in the mid-fifties, having left the Badenese state
service, and from then on secured an increasingly strong
influence over the young Grand Duke. Only the Grand Duke's
agreement could allow the liberals to acquire power. Roggenbach paved the way for them. His influence on Badenese
liberalism was great, above all in the sphere of national politics.
German liberals had – and this was no different in Baden – no
clear ideas on how the longed-for nation-state could be created.

> One of the most remarkable aspects of the history of German
> liberalism is that the middle-class administrative civil servants,
> jurists and merchants who represented it, hardly ever even
> attempted to dispute the aristocracy's ... monopoly in the area
> of foreign policy ... as they did so successfully in the area of
> domestic policy.[31]

They were waiting for an improvement in the national political
situation, and for external aid. In Roggenbach they found
someone to whom they could entrust themselves in foreign
policy and who determined Badenese government policy with
them between 1860 and 1865.

In *Württemberg*, the final example, the events of the years of the
reaction differ again from those in Austria, Prussia or Baden.[32]
The three constituent assemblies met in December 1849, when
the revolution had ended, and from March to July and October

to November 1850. In each case, democrats comprised around two-thirds of the deputies. In the first legislature of the decade of reaction, which met from 1851 to 1855, the democratic faction shrank to just eighteen, while the liberals doubled their numbers to around thirty-five of the seventy deputies elected. Like public life in general, parliament began to concentrate solely on domestic and above all economic issues, while national and constitutional matters took a back seat. This focus was also reflected in the deputies' professions.

Between 1851 and 1855 there were eight deputies from the commercial middle class, whose numbers had already increased from election to election in the three state assemblies. All the employers represented on the legislature joined the liberal parliamentary party, almost 23 per cent of which was made up of merchants and manufacturers. Senior teachers, professors and priests, the typical representatives of the educated middle class committed to national and constitutional politics, almost completely disappeared from the legislature in 1851 (1.2 per cent). In 1848–9 they had still represented 12.6 per cent, and in the three state assemblies they had comprised up to a quarter of all elected deputies. But the proportion of state and municipal civil servants rose to around 52 per cent. Although leading oppositionists had always been found amongst civil servant deputies, this was no longer true of the first post-revolutionary legislature. Eight democratic deputies, approximately 40 per cent of the parliamentary party, resigned from state employment in order to take up their seats. Amongst the liberals, whose ranks included eleven state and eight municipal civil servants, only one – August Ludwig Reyscher – regarded this step as necessary. This highlights the extremely moderate stance which the Württemberg liberals had adopted in the revolutionary years, and which they then continued with their 'tactic of reconciliation', as the liberal 'party organ', the *Württembergische Zeitung*, described their policy on 21 May 1851. This policy failed, as did that of the democrats, who devoted themselves to the uncompromising defence of the law in order to rescue the constitutional outcome of the revolution after it was over.

This joint failure – in March 1852 the Chamber of Deputies approved the repeal of the Basic Rights, helped by the votes of some of the liberals – laid the foundation for co-operation between liberals and democrats, who had been such bitter opponents during the revolution. This 'fusion of the parties' began with their successful joint resistance to the government's planned revision of municipal organization, which had been liberalized in 1849. In the elections to the legislature in 1855 this internal middle-class reconciliation paid off, and the political gulfs of the revolutionary years began to close. This was associated with the replacement of many of the deputies, which took place here on a similar scale to events in Baden. In 1855 half of all elected deputies (numbering 35) were entering the political arena for the first time, an arena to which prominent liberals and, above all, democrats no longer belonged. This did not have the effect of weakening the liberal–democratic parliamentary party, however.

Julius Hölder embodied the transformation which the Württemberg democrats and liberals were undergoing in the fifties, but he also represented the lines of continuity into the revolution and into the *Vormärz* period. Born into a conservative Württemberg civil servant family in Stuttgart in 1819, from 1837 onwards Hölder studied jurisprudence in Tübingen, where he joined the *Germania Burschenschaft*. The friendships he made there would later outlive even the most profound political conflicts. In 1841, filled with typical liberal–democratic middle-class ideas on reform, he joined the Württemberg state civil service. During the revolution, as a young man of barely thirty, he was promoted into the leading circle of the democrats. Although he remained part of this circle, he played a more secondary role when the liberal March minister G. H. Duvernoy made him *Regierungsrat* in the ministry of the interior. Hölder was regarded as a moderate amongst the already moderate Württemberg democrats. He sought to exploit the opportunities created by the revolution, but to translate them into firm policies of legality. This moderate position made him acceptable to liberals and democrats alike, when they united to form a joint opposition in 1855. Hölder now rose to become a great unifying figure in Württemberg liberalism, which now began to re-form, encompassing both democrats and liberals.

His career is typical of an important section of post-revolutionary liberalism in Germany, which has not yet been sufficiently researched, and which should not be rashly denounced as unprincipled '*realpolitik*', 'the loss of all ideals' or 'intellectual decline'. Hölder and his like-minded friends did not sacrifice old liberal values, but nor did they attempt to enforce them by returning to the *Vormärz* policy of 'opposition on principle'. The aim was co-operation with the government as far as possible, whilst avoiding 'a pig-headed loyalty to principles, which transcends the limits of reality', as the organ of the reunited liberal–democratic opposition declared in 1855.[33] As we have said, in Württemberg this policy failed in the attempt to defend a core element of liberal revolutionary policy, the Basic Rights, against the reaction in the German Confederation. It was not always unsuccessful, however. Laws governing local authorities and on the dissolution of agrarian burdens were essentially retained. In economic policy, too, this readiness to co-operate paid off.

The 'unfettered acquisitive civil society', the Tübingen philosophy lecturer Karl Christian Planck feared, would leave its mark on the state, but it would adapt to the bureaucratic authoritarian state.[34] This danger undoubtedly existed. Yet the Württemberg economic boom, the breakthrough of industrialization in the fifties, did not lead, as many had feared or hoped, to a depoliticized 'acquisitive civil society'. Academically educated people found it easier to find employment outside the state sector. Democrats and liberals took the opportunity to resign from state employment. This limited the extent of state reaction and allowed them confidently to continue their policy of limited co-operation with the state. Hölder is a good example of this. In 1853 he voluntarily left state employment to set up a practice as a lawyer, and to join the *Allgemeine Rentenanstalt* in Stuttgart, where he soon became full-time company lawyer. This gave the former civil servant independence from the Württemberg state, which he acted against as liberal–democratic party leader in the late fifties; prepared for conflict but at the same time capable of compromise. The upturn in the economy made it easier to adopt this stance, to do more than simply adapt to the economically liberal state and become depoliticized.

The fact that Württemberg liberals and democrats joined together in 1855 did not mean that they had committed themselves on issues of national politics. They had agreed on domestic policy. As was stated in a programmatic leading article in their organ on 1 January 1856, the 'future formation of the Fatherland as a whole' was to be left 'open'.[35] Like German liberalism in general during the decade of reaction, they had no plan for national politics and no opportunities to act anyway. This would have to wait until further progress was made on national politics after 1859, when a change began which would radically reform liberalism. However, this cannot simply be extended back into the decade of reaction, which, unfortunately, still remains dark in historiographical terms.

'Nachmärz' *Liberalism – A Summary*

The liberalism of the *Nachmärz* period was different. At a time of political repression and rapid economic and social change, liberals were forced to revise their experiences of the revolution and to adapt their guiding principles to these experiences and to their new scope for action. This was not easy. There was no national forum where discussions could take place, and the conditions under which they were able to practise politics varied from state to state. Little progress was being made in national politics, and what progress there was could certainly not be attributed to them, for they had no opportunity to effect progress of any kind. It is difficult to judge the many and various reactions of the liberals to the impenetrable situation in which they now had to find their way: disappointed by the revolution and fearful of the future. The aim of those who continued to be publicly engaged in politics – on the diets and chambers, in the press, in the municipal sphere or even in the state bureaucracy – was to defend what could be defended. Others withdrew into their professions. This sometimes meant depoliticization, but it did not necessarily have to mean that. Many members of the commercial middle class who concentrated solely on commercial life did so in the belief that, together with the state, which was willing to implement liberal economic reforms, they were building the economic basis of the future nation-state. What would happen later, if progress was ever made on the national question again, remained to be seen. But it was clear that their aim was co-operation with the state rather than conflict.

What has not yet been made clear, however, is the degree to which in the fifties the representatives of the up-and-coming commercial middle class used their economic position to represent their political interests to the state bureaucracy. They were not solely reliant on the diets and chambers here. The Rhenish commercial middle class, for example, had Chambers of Commerce at its disposal. In Cologne the Chamber remained a liberal bastion from which political desires and criticisms were voiced. These included the demand that the Prussian constitution should not be diluted, that cost-cutting reforms should be carried out in the army, and that industry should be granted a political position commensurate with its economic power. In the Cologne district council too, liberal constitutionalists asserted their supremacy, buttressed by the three-class suffrage system.[36]

The educated middle class had no such opportunity for influence, or if it did, it was to a far more limited degree. This probably contributed to the fact that it tended towards a policy of waiting, a policy of using other methods, in particular the methods of historiography: history as a political argument which worked slowly but profoundly. In Prussian history, Max Duncker said in December 1853, the historian should reveal to the public the 'seeds of a better world'. 'We should support these trends in the face of the materialism of the sciences and replace the fantastical idealism of philosophy, which filled and turned the heads of the young before 1848, with the real idealism of history.'[37]

For the Protestant liberal educated middle class, 'the real idealism of history' did not yet necessarily mean hope in Prussia's 'historical mission', although this was increasingly the case, above all amongst its intellectual spokesmen. Even then it didn't have to mean the rejection of liberal ideals and of opposition. Opposition remained possible – against the Prussia of the present in the name of the Prussia of the future, which they erroneously believed had been laid down in the past. As long as Prussia remained politically reactionary, German liberalism was protected from profound changes in its central ideas and from the need to commit itself. In retrospect, the enforced domestic political calm of the reactionary decade offered German liberalism the opportunity to slowly and hesitatingly correct and adapt its values and aims to a changed world, which could no longer be appropriately accommodated in early liberal models. The result of this necessary adaptation was not yet clear in the fifties. To post-revolutionary liberalism and to German history as a whole, the 'Borussian' path was not marked out as the only possible one.

'Unity' and 'Freedom'? Liberalism and the *Reichsgründung*

The 'New Era' and the New Mood for National Politics

A 'new era' began at the end of the fifties, not only in Prussia, to which the term is usually applied, but in other German states too. In 1859 in *Bavaria* King Maximilian II ('I want peace with my people and with the chambers')[38] used a change in government which paved the way for a series of liberalizing reforms to relax the conflict with the oppositional deputies. The legal emancipation of the Jews was completed, a new commercial law put into force, and the judicial system reformed in important spheres. Thus, social elements (factory police and child labour) were included in the police and criminal law, and the court constitution law realized an old liberal demand with the separation of justice and administration. The notary law removed from the state part of its jurisdiction in non-litigious matters.

The 'new era' achieved its greatest successes in *Baden*. Under the liberal Lamey–Roggenbach cabinet, which took office in April 1860, it became a field of domestic political experimentation, on which German liberalism was able to test out, and had to prove, its ability to govern. In no other German state were such profound reforms carried out over such a short period of time. The administrative reform formed their core. It eliminated the 'administrative system dictated entirely in the spirit of bureaucratic absolutism'[39] by decentralizing it. It abolished the central block of the state administration, and reinforced local self-government, above all through the creation of new district councils. Central liberal ideas were thus put into practice, as they were with the justice reforms concluded in 1864, and Baden was turned into a model liberal German state founded on the rule of law. Justice and administration were now completely separate, even at the lowest level. Civil and criminal trials were now oral and public, and even in minor criminal matters, laymen increasingly participated in the administration of justice. The police and criminal law of 1863 was intended to eradicate any form of police despotism, in that all state penal power was subordinated to the legal principle of *nulla poena sine lege*.

The implementation of the state founded on the rule of law realized old liberal goals which were now recognized by all social groups. But the simultaneous attempt to establish the equality of all citizens of the state did not run as smoothly, and in the long term encountered considerable resistance. The 'law on the equal legal civil status of the Israelites' of October 1862 was unanimously, or almost unanimously, passed by both chambers of the Badenese legislature. But because the views of the municipalities were also taken into account, Jews were to enjoy full municipal civil rights (poor relief and 'citizens' benefits') only after a transitional period of ten years.[40] The conflicts which could arise between the liberal model of the 'citizen of the state' and the 'citizen of a municipality' emerged even more clearly in the legal debates on freedom of trade, of movement and of marriage.[41] The government was unable to push its liberal revision of the marriage law through the legislature, and even the law passed in 1862, which retained restrictions on the marriage of citizens of a local authority to strangers to the locality, aroused controversy. This was particularly true in rural local authorities, where people feared that full freedom of marriage might lead to excessive demands on the poor relief system. Only in 1870 was full freedom of marriage introduced in Baden as a result of the legislation of the North German Confederation, which in 1868 passed the unrestricted freedom of marriage.

The laws on occupational freedom and freedom of movement, also passed in 1862, created further grounds in the countryside for complaint against liberal reformers. The trade ministry did obtain reports from those affected by such legislation, but it concentrated on those in the towns. And even there a large number of committees dominated by craftsmen pleaded not for full freedom of trade, but for a more careful reform of the guild system. All the same, most Badenese urban craftsmen saw little protection in existing guild regulations. They hoped, as Sattlermeister said, that 'freedom and courage would be of greater aid'.[42] This enforced reorienation in the craft trades was brought about by the acceleration of industrialization in Germany from the mid-nineteenth century onwards and was fostered by the healthy economy in the decade of the *Reichsgründung*. It allowed liberals – indeed forced them – to gradually surrender their traditional social model of a 'secure livelihood' for the 'middle-class citizen'. The political problems which arose for liberalism as a result will be examined below, as will the confrontation between liberalism and the state, and the conflict which emerged from education and church policies between liberalism and the

Catholic Church and political Catholicism, which was growing
stronger all the time.

These problems already weighed heavily on the Lamey–
Roggenbach government of the 'new era'. But this government
did not collapse until October 1865, when its clear failure on
issues of national policy was added to the conflict with Catholicism. Roggenbach's notion of a strong federalist *kleindeutsch*
nation-state led by Prussia, but 'with the direct participation in
federal power of the federal princes and the federal people',[43]
could not be realized with Bismarck. In the absence of realistic
alternatives, Roggenbach finally accepted Bismarck's policies.
Yet he was unable to win agreement for them from the Grand
Duke or from the majority of liberals. This would not change
until 1866.

So liberal hopes for a permanent 'new era' were dashed in
Baden too, both on a domestic and on a foreign political level. But
it had a profound effect and lasted longer here than in all other
German states. In particular it lasted longer than in Prussia,
where the constitutional conflict had already begun to undermine
the principle of the state founded on the rule of law at a time
in which it was still being developed in Baden. Symptomatic of the
Badenese development is the fact that it failed on account of Prussia, on account of Bismarck's Prussian–German policies. This is
true of German liberalism as a whole. In the decade of the *Reichsgründung* it split along the national political dividing line, as
liberals were forced to decide for or against the Prussian path to a
nation-state. What the 'Prussian path' meant, however, was hard
for contemporaries to establish. The issue was far too complex
for that.

The 'new era' seemed to herald the beginning of a liberal era
in *Prussia* too. In October 1858, when King Frederick William IV
became ill and Prince William took over as Regent, he replaced
the Manteuffel reaction ministry with a moderate conservative–
liberal ministry. The following month, he formulated a programme of government which Prussian liberals enthusiastically
welcomed as the 'victory of the constitution', since it promised
'the consolidation of civic freedom in Prussia' and above all 'the
rule of the law'.[44] Liberals certainly had grounds for optimism.
In November 1858 they became the strongest parliamentary
party in the House of Deputies, while the Conservatives fell back
to around one-fifth of the seats they had previously held. The

Regent's sensational programme ruled out any 'break with the past', but he did promise to lay 'a reforming hand' on the state and, most importantly of all, he closed with words in which the *kleindeutsch* liberals thought they could hear the voice of the new Prussia that they had been waiting for for so long:

> In Germany Prussia must use wise legislation to make moral conquests, by improving moral elements of all kinds and by keeping a firm grasp on unifying elements such as the Customs Union. . . . The world must know that Prussia is ready to protect the law everywhere. A strong, logical and, if necessary, energetic attitude in politics, coupled with wisdom and level-headedness must create political standing for Prussia and a position of power which it cannot achieve by means of its material power alone.[45]

Liberals were well aware of the vulnerability of this programme of 'moral conquests' in an autocratic state founded on the army, the bureaucracy and the *Junkers*. Their motto 'just don't push too hard' was aimed at preventing the Regent from falling back into the arms of the Conservatives.

> As far as possible, we must not shock or snub him. Those fellows from the 'Kreuzzeitung' are counting on us making mistakes like that and on 'monarchic instincts'. I mean that we should not help him into the saddle for a second time [as in 1848]. This government must not become a liberal experiment, it must become a solid liberal system. For this reason I ask you to practise moderation and moderation again, to the point of boredom.

Prussian liberals were not to blame for the fact that the policy recommended by Max Duncker could not be sustained. The 'new era' in Prussia was actively opposed from the start by a Conservative parliamentary party which, on the issue of military reform, found a way of separating the Regent (King William I after 1861) from his reform ministers and returning him to a position of confrontation with the liberals. They were unable to 'treat' the military reforms demanded by the King and his advisors as 'gently'[46] as would have been necessary to avoid constitutional conflict.

The fact that many liberals finally did 'gently' end the constitutional conflict does not mean that they could have avoided it
from the start. In 1866 their yielding won them a prize – the
North German Confederation – for which they were prepared to
sacrifice a great deal. But in 1861–2, the Prussian government
demanded unconditional capitulation. Liberals of all alignments
were not prepared to do this, but many of them let it be seen too
soon that success on national issues could move them to postpone
domestic political demands. 'Just don't start with a national
parliament!' implored Droysen to Duncker in June 1859.

This time we want first to create the power for ourselves which
we had to pretend we had in the figure of the stop-gap
Imperial Regent in 1849. If this power of Prussia is really first,
then it will be good enough to appoint the representatives of
the nation as and where it deems appropriate; it *constitutes* the
constitution. Every premature word on such matters is a
mistake and gives the enemies of Prussia, whose numbers are
legion, a helping hand.[47]

But the Prussia of the 'new era' had not yet joined this path of
power politics. In domestic politics it was a passing fancy which
had faded at the latest by 1861. In national politics it was not
even that. The Italian War of Unification of 1859 mobilized and
politicized the German public, but no national political decisions
were reached in the German Confederation.[48] Austria preferred
to renounce Lombardy rather than risk the military allied aid of
Prussia, which would inevitably have raised the question of
supremacy in Germany.

Like the German national movement as a whole, German
liberals did not react as one. Some were in favour of the 'whole of
Germany' coming together to help Austria as it came under pressure. Others believed that the favourable opportunity should be
exploited in order to secure Prussia's leadership in Germany.
But there were many nuances between these extremes, and they
changed frequently. The front which split the *national public and
the liberal movement* between this time and the *Reichsgründung*
had by no means crystallized in around 1860. Many changes in
fronts would still take place as progress was made on the
'German question'. Nevertheless, the flags had already been
raised in 1859.

Initially, only a very small section of liberals gathered around the *kleindeutsch* Prussians. Prussian politics seemed to them to be too undecided and leaderless, and the suggestions of the *kleindeutsch* wing of the liberals were not convincing enough. They all seemed to amount to the same thing: war! Many demanded a war, even their domestic political opponents, for the German public of 1859 had a variety of different expectations of a national war. Conservatives demanded the defence of the legitimate order and monarchic solidarity against Napoleon's 'Caesarism'. The left wanted to combat Napoleon as the representative of the counter-revolution. After the war many liberals, not just *großdeutsch* liberals, spoke out against French hegemony and in favour of domestic reforms in the German Confederation, while 'Borussian' liberals regarded the German war for Austria's northern Italian territories as an opportunity to weaken Austria's position in Germany. 'Austria forged to Italy' so that Prussia's room for manoeuvre could be extended, was Droysen's description of this policy, which – as his friend and fellow-thinker Haym admitted – would always be 'hard to make comprehensible to the Prussian public' in the 'artificiality' of the argument: 'a war not for Austria and yet, on the other hand, for Austria'. Haym was therefore clearly relieved when Austria unexpectedly accepted defeat in Italy. 'Austria's perfidy', he said, 'is too spectacular for us not to be able to win in Germany, as long as we proceed greatly and strongly enough': 'German parliament', 'total reform' and 'elimination of the Bundestag'.[49]

Numerous variations on this recipe were conceived by the national public and by *Großdeutsche* as well as *Kleindeutsche*. But only those in government were in a position to try them out. It was here that the dilemma of German liberals of all camps lay. They could formulate and organize their national interests, yet the system of government in the two German supreme powers, Austria and Prussia, denied them the opportunity to translate programmes into action at state level. This explains their hope in the 'great and tough man' (H. Baumgarten), who would 'Cavourize Germany'.[50]

The hoped-for alliance between the 'nation' and the 'state' on the Italian model was first presented as a possibility when the conflict between Prussia and Austria for leadership in Germany peaked in the Schleswig-Holstein crisis[51] from 1863 onwards, and when the rulers adopted the appeal to the nation as part of their political calculation. Before that point, from the national-political departure of 1859 onwards, German politics was a 'confusion of plans, actions and counteractions, irritations and vacillations'.[52] Only two concepts bore any relation to reality: the Austrian programme of 1863 and Bismarck's response to it.

Austria wanted to reinforce the authority of the German Confederation without destroying the basic federal order. The majority of the medium states agreed to some further federalist correctives, yet Bismarck allowed the reform project to fail on Prussian rejection. His rejection heralded a political strategy which Austria was unable to counter: the appeal to the nation and co-operation with parts of the national movement. Prussia demanded a national parliament, directly elected by the people, while the Austrian plan for the delegation of federal deputies did not go beyond the first and second chambers of the state parliaments.

In 1863 this Prussian appeal to the nation was no more than an offer which even 'Borussian' liberals did not take seriously, since it came from the conflict minister Bismarck, the 'dastardly player at the helm of the Prussian state' (H. Baumgarten), who was reactionary in terms of domestic policy.[53] But it was an offer with a future – in contrast to the Austrian reform plan. The Austrian plan was coordinated with the February constitution of 1861, which turned Austria into a liberalized constitutional state with considerable parliamentary rights. The constitution was aimed at courting the liberal public in Austria and in the non-Austrian part of the German Confederation; it also sought to secure the unity of the Habsburg monarchic state. Reforms in the German Confederation which were acceptable to Austria could therefore only be federalist, not nation-state or unitarian. This was the main reason that the liberal Austrian reforms had so little effect on German liberals outside Austria. A German nation-state could not be created with the Habsburg monarchy, and on the other hand, despite the constitutional conflict, many liberals placed their hopes in the liberalization of Prussia, the only German supreme power which was capable of sustaining the nation-state.

These different opportunities for the development of national politics in Austria and Prussia also determined the chances of success of the two largest political organizations which emerged from the national departure of 1859: the *Nationalverein* (National

Association) and the *Reformverein* (Reform Association).[54] Opponents of a *kleindeutsch*–Prussian nation-state from all political camps came together in the Reform Association, which was founded in October 1862. It was a negative *großdeutsch* alliance, ranging from left to right, which, even among the resolutely anti-Prussian liberal–democrats of Württemberg, could not rid itself of its reputation as an organization of reactionaries aimed at the prevention of a liberal nation-state.[55] Unlike the National Association, the Reform Association was unable to form personal links with existing liberal parties and the middle-class liberal national movement.

Founded in September 1859, the National Association was also an alliance of groups with very different ideas regarding the path to the nation-state and the form it should take. But this alliance remained within the parameters of the middle-class national movement. It was able to unite liberals and democrats by avoiding a programme of domestic policy. Johannes von Miquel gave the reason for this renunciation in 1860: 'We are members of an association which only prepares, which does not possess real power, which seeks only to educate the nation on an intellectual level, and which should place its hope in the future'; 'If circumstances show us the path, the rest will sort itself out.' Miquel's description of the National Association was an apt one. It had a policy of 'agitation and education', which helped 'get the German question moving again'.[56] It argued in favour of the *kleindeutsch* nation-state, although a small proportion of its members, above all southern German democrats, believed they could 'de-Borussify' the policies of the National Association.

The National Association began to flag in 1864. It lost its agitatory power when Prussia evaded the hopes of the *kleindeutsch* liberals. 'To be frank', wrote its chairman Rudolf von Bennigsen in November 1864, 'The outlook seems very bleak for a national movement for the moment and above all for the National Association': few 'connections with South Germany' remained, the 'bond with the majority of the population ... has not been so slack for years', a 'revolution [is] impossible and there are no prospects of a national initiative on the part of the Prussian government'. So what could they hope for? Like his fellow liberals, Bennigsen still believed in the silent power of progress – of political and economic progress. This was a long-term perspective which also included hopes in accelerated, though 'unpredictable European impulses'.[57]

Constitutional Conflict and the 'German Question', 1862–6

In Prussia the 'new era' gave rise to a monumental conflict on the principles of the political system.[58] Emerging from army reform plans, the necessity of which even liberals did not dispute, the argument extended to a budget conflict and finally to a constitutional conflict. The appointment of Bismarck as Minister President on 22 September 1862 as the final act against the liberal chamber majority which opposed the King's wishes, seemed to exclude all possibility of agreement. In the opinion of contemporaries – liberals and conservatives alike – the alternatives seemed to be monarchic or parliamentary rule; the military or the constitutional state.

Prussian liberals had not wanted this conflict. It was forced on them by the conservative opponents of the 'new era'. Under the pressure of the conflict, Prussian liberalism reformed. As early as 1860, liberal deputies had increasingly objected to the policies of the *Altliberale* (Old Liberals), who had tried in vain to tire conservative aggression with their tactic of 'moderation to the point of boredom'. February 1861 saw a first internal split in the liberal opposition, and finally on 6 June 1861 the *Deutsche Fortschritt-spartei* (Progress Party) was formally established. The aim of its programme was to counter conservative attempts to undermine the constitution with the demand for its liberal development, and it encompassed domestic and national-political aims.[59] The programme was silent on the issue of the path to the nation-state, and little was said on its form.

The Progress Party wanted the nation-state to be given a 'common German popular representative body', a 'strong central power in Prussia's hands', but it would have to be a liberalized Prussia, which would have to win the 'respect of the other German tribes' by 'the strict and logical implementation of the constitutional state founded on the rule of law'. Its aims for domestic political reform were clearly articulated. The security of the legal system should be achieved by means of 'genuinely independent judges', and self-government in local authority districts and the provinces should be strengthened. Improvements were called for in schools, as were a teaching law to guard against ministerial intervention, the equality of all religious faiths, the separation of canon and state marriage law and the revision of trade law, so that the 'economic forces of the state may ... be unfettered'. 'Great economies in the military budget in peace time' were demanded, although 'the Prussian people's complete fitness for active and armed service' should not be placed under threat. In concrete terms, this meant that the militia should continue to exist, male youths should receive pre-military training and the recruitment quota for the army should be raised, though the two-year period of service should not.

In order to achieve all this, the Progress Party demanded the 'profound reform' of the *Herrenhaus* and a law on 'ministerial accountability'. This amounted to the implementation of the parliamentary system of government, which only few Progress liberals expressly demanded, but which the majority believed would be the inevitable consequence of a consolidated and extended sphere of authority of the House of Deputies, and of the strict legal commitment to the constitution on the part of the forces of law and order.

The Progress Party received a glowing confirmation of this programme in the elections of November and December 1861. It immediately became the strongest party, while the conservatives fell back to the smallest (fourteen deputies). Altogether, the three liberal parliamentary parties held around two-thirds of all seats (cf. Chapter 3, pp. 102–20). The new Chamber of Deputies met for just short of two months. When it voted in favour of an itemization of the state budget, a move designed to prevent the government from circumventing parliament and continuing its army reform by redistributing state resources, it was dissolved in March 1862 by the king, who appointed a conservative government in place of the cabinet of the 'new era'. In the new elections the liberals, and above all the Progress Party, won an even higher share of the seats.

The conflict rapidly reached a climax. The king refused to agree to a compromise on army reform – a compromise which was even recommended by his ministers. The chambers, in which the liberals held almost three-quarters of all seats, then prepared to reject the entire state budget. 'Everyone here', reported Heinrich von Sybel, member of the liberal 'centre-left', 'feels that any discussion in the parliament could lead to a catastrophe, that the military debate before us necessarily calls into question the entire existence of the state, and that it could lead to a change in the throne, a *coup d'etat* or even a revolution'. The constitutional conflict was exaggerated to two basic alternatives: the introduction of the parliamentary system on the English and Belgian model; or monarchic rule, resting on the army as the basis of the state, which could not be touched by parliament. A profound change in political course, an end to the 'Prussian path' of only a limited development of the parliamentary system, seemed to be possible and seemed to justify the political tactics of the decided liberals. William I was ready to abdicate in order to leave to the Crown Prince the 'nullification of the King', as he described it.[60]

Instead of historical change, came Bismarck. For German liberalism and for the liberal permeation of political and social life in Germany, it was a change in course which might well be described as 'tragic' (Thomas Nipperdey).[61] Liberals were unable to influence this course, but they were subject to it; indeed they were more profoundly influenced by this than by all other events.

Initially, however, the already firm fronts were reinforced. Even those liberals who, if anything, regarded the Progress Party with scepticism, closed their minds to the 'enchantment of Bismarck's pretence of deliberate reconciliation'. The dreams of the Old Liberals, that they might be able to influence 'government trends by means of reserved agreement' had come to an end. 'For the time being we are *only* an opposition', declared Haym in December 1862, 'We have absolutely nothing in common with the present government and therefore stand on the same ground as those members of the Progress Party who have no specifically democratic principles, and no revolutionary ulterior motives.'[62]

The government left the liberals no other option. Government proceeded without a budget and the state was plagued with numerous repressive measures. This confirmed the liberals in their conviction that they were waging a 'war against absolutism and *Junkertum*', as Leopold von Hoverbeck, one of the founders of the Progress Party, put it in February 1863. This conviction was also voiced in an announcement of 22 May 1863, in which the Prussian House of Deputies demanded a change in the system shortly before its renewed break-up (27 May):

The House of Deputies no longer has the means of reaching an understanding with this ministry; it renounces all co-operation with present government policy. Any further negotiation can only reinforce our belief that there is a gulf between the advisors to the Crown and the state; a gulf which can only be filled by a change in personnel and even more by a change in the system.[63]

The new elections further reinforced the confrontation. On both sides of the political camp, it was the most decided parties who won. The conservatives trebled the seats they held from eleven to thirty-five and the liberals claimed around 70 per cent of all available seats, with a shift in favour of the Progress Party. The Old Liberal mediating grouping was completely wiped out (cf. Chapter 3, pp. 102–20).

The Progress Party's election programme was brief and to the point. Six demands were made: the reintroduction of freedom of the press, whose existence was threatened by the Press Decree of 1 June 1863; a law on ministerial accountability; no state expenditure without the approval of the House of Deputies; the reform of the *Herrenhaus*; an 'army on a traditional basis with a two-year period of service'; and a national 'parliament chosen in free national elections'.[64]

Just how these demands could be achieved was a controversial subject amongst liberals. The 'whole state must stand up and express its will', demanded Hermann Baumgarten, 'It seems to me and to us that until now the war in Prussia has been waged too gently. We should make those who despise people, the constitution, reason and law as if they were naughty boys, quake with fear. We have to arouse in them the real fear that one day they will be killed like mad dogs', even if 'fighting methods of this kind are certainly not to the taste of educated men'. Yet such radical words were not typical of German liberalism, not even in the era of the constitutional conflict. The fact that they were used by Baumgarten, whose extremely influential book just three years later justified liberal '*realpolitik*' at Bismarck's side, reflects the level of impotence such radical talk expressed. They had been victorious in the elections; they had received the approval of the population in other ways too; and they knew that the law and 'progress' were on their side. And yet still the Prussian state acted quite differently; it refused to fulfil the liberal and national mission with which the Prussian Progress Party was also filled. Sybel therefore immediately called his correspondent Baumgarten back to reality:

Our rulers have long since stopped quaking at the thought of announcements and deputations and the popular mood. ... Their only question is this: do we have money and reliable soldiers? They are terrified of every non-commissioned officer who reads the *Volkszeitung*, of every word in parliament which might attract soldiers, but not of anything else. The position they have adopted is quite correct; as long as the army holds, the people *cannot* need any material power. Their regime will last until the army has declared its support for the constitution, or until it is broken in a foreign war.[65]

Little research has been carried out into the Prussian liberals' political behaviour outside the parliament during the constitutional conflict. It is surely inadequate to point to the economic interests of the commercial middle class and Chamber of Commerce reports, and to conclude that the constitutional conflict did not affect 'the nerve centre of middle-class existence', since the middle classes used their desire for domestic political reform only as a means of satisfying economic and national-political aims.[66] Of course, some of the Prussian Chambers of Commerce did express themselves very negatively on the subject of the pre-eminence of political aims in liberal politics, and against the dominance of the educated middle class on the liberal executive committees. A report for 1862–3 from the Chamber of the district of Altena is a good example.[67] It hoped to see a 'peaceful resolution of the argument soon', but held the Progress liberals primarily responsible for the conflict. But it too argued for a two-year period of military service, at the same time calling for an army reform, which would strengthen the defence force in order to 'protect property from every attack', 'in consideration of our geographical position and national mission'.

It did not reject the 'so-called extension of the constitution', but it did decisively reject all demands for a 'parliamentary government'. The English 'parliament-government' was not a suitable model, for the extremely limited suffrage in England meant that parliament lay in the hands of three or four hundred families. Above all, England had a large number of men who were suited 'to the profession of statesman', who had wide experience of trade and industry.

While here the decisive tone is set primarily by the educated professional classes and men of academic learning, as have emerged in all German states, in the elections in England the demand is made above all for evidence of practical competence, experience of life and knowledge of human nature. This explains the unshakeable calm and conservative course of development of state life in that country. But unspeakable disaster would surely befall Prussia if the present majorities had to make urgent and essential decisions on the system of government.

The Chamber of Commerce report cited above addresses a problem which in many respects crossed the conflict-ridden relations between the German national movement, inside and outside Prussia: Prussian policy combined political reaction with economic liberalism. And it exploited Prussia's economic power against Austria in the sphere of national politics. Economically, the Habsburg monarchy could not afford a policy of free trade. This is where the Prussian government positioned its lever. In 1862 it signed a free trade treaty with France and until 1865 used the threat of dissolving the Customs Union to force the German small and medium states to agree to new Customs Union treaties under Prussian conditions. Thus, Austria left Germany in terms of trade policy. The Customs Union was reduced to a *Kleindeutschland* under Prussian hegemony, despite the fact that a decision on the form of the future nation-state had not yet been taken.[68]

Economic interests did not cause German liberals to become reconciled to the economically liberal, but politically still reactionary Prussian government during these trade battles between Prussia and Austria. This is true neither of Prussian liberals nor of those in other German states, where the Chambers of Commerce offered liberals no clear lines of approach into Customs Union policy. Many chambers in the medium states voiced only brief opinions in favour of or against the Prussian trade political diktat. And the process of separation, which took place at the same time in the south German states between liberals and democrats, did not cross over to the public debates which were triggered by trade policy. Even the staunch democrats of Württemberg did not allow trade policy to distract them from their fundamentally anti-Prussian position. Support for freedom of trade as the economic corollary of political liberalism, and thereby agreement to the Prussian Customs Union diktat, was accompanied by the firm rejection of the Prussian policy of reaction.[69]

This was the case in Prussia too. Many assented to Prussian trade policy without yielding on the question of the constitutional conflict. There is no other way to explain the many measures taken by oppositional civil servants (Parisius estimated them to number more than 1000); the election successes, above all of the Progress Party; and the continuing magnetic force of liberal opposition policy in the local authority districts.[70] This liberal policy has been called 'passive resistance' (T. Parent). It was no longer a retreat, as it had been in the decade of reaction. The 'new slogan of passive resistance' meant that 'the people must remain restless ... that is to say, always moving within the law, participating in everything, permanently guarding against reaction'.[71] Progress Party liberals in particular exploited many opportunities to achieve this. They had at their disposal a dense network of organizations (cf. Chapter 3, pp. 102–20). They organized popular rallies and solidarity addresses to the House of Deputies. They attempted, with varying degrees of success, to influence local institutions such as the town council assemblies or to politicize carnivals. And they held sway over a sizeable section of the press. The *Magdeburger Zeitung* estimated in December 1862 that the liberal press in Prussia enjoyed a daily circulation of around 250 000, whilst the conservative press reached 40 000 at the most. Periodicals, also dominated by liberals, should be added to this figure.[72]

'Passive resistance' did not imply defensive behaviour. They tried to hold their forces together and to subject the government to public pressure. But it was a limited pressure, not a revolutionary one. A revolutionary situation did not occur in the Germany of the sixties; and German liberals were no revolutionaries. On one occasion they did toy with the idea of a tax boycott; even such a moderate liberal as Sybel did so. But he immediately added, probably not without a degree of relief, that this thought was 'very much in the air'. But it was 'clear that, if this is to be effective, the high bourgeoisie must begin with it, and the matter needs to mature a little amongst them yet'. The liberals did not want to give them a helping hand. They had a different tactic, articulated by Hermann Schulze-Delitzsch in 1863: 'It is our job now to gather all liberal elements ever more firmly around us, to unite the property-owning classes ever more closely to us. It is the silent preparation for battle, but not its beginning.' But above all: 'Patience! We have been working for fifteen years and have not lost our stamina.' It was clear that he was deeply convinced of 'the victory of our case', despite the 'small matter of the imposition'.[73]

Liberals were filled with a certainty of the future. The 'small matter of the imposition' could not shake this certainty. Even this Prussia, Bennigsen said in 1864, would promote, albeit indirectly, 'the unity of Germany, just as it will the mighty industrial development which is soon to come, as long as the nation doesn't become despondent and *gradually* utilizes this power'. Karl Twesten, later a founder member of the National Liberal Party, put liberalism's belief in its own future in even clearer terms. 'The social order, however, creates the order of the state. The socially dominant classes must also directly become the ruling political classes.' The state may use 'organized power' to exercise 'a profound retrospective power over all circles of society', but at the end of the day, 'new views and social conditions inevitably create new forms of state'.[74]

The constitutional conflict united liberals across the wide spectrum of their political, social and economic views. They were forced together by a common opponent. From the end of 1863 onwards, however, this conflict began to ease when progress was made on the 'German question'. This overshadowed the constitutional conflict, finally ending it in 1866, or at least postponing it with a temporary compromise. Political and military developments from the Schleswig-Holstein crisis to the German war of 1866 cannot be examined here.[75] But we should ask how German liberals reacted to this new national and domestic political challenge with their changed room for manoeuvre and constraints on their actions.

When in November 1863 the Danish Reichstag decided a common constitution for Denmark and Schleswig, which amounted to the separation of the Duchy of Holstein and its incorporation into the Danish kingdom, a wave of indignation inspired by national feeling erupted amongst the German public. Large rallies were held, Schleswig-Holstein Committees were founded everywhere, and the National Association called for donations to be collected for a Schleswig-Holstein army – 'not disordered free corps!' On 21 December 1863 German deputies met at a conference in Frankfurt, where a permanent committee was established to steer the national movement. Most of its members belonged to the liberal National Association, but the movement transcended political camps. Conservatives, liberals and democrats all found common ground in the excitement provoked by the national feeling. A liberal described the general mood; 'A *new* era has dawned over Germany. Yes, truly, a new era, my friend! ... The warring parties have put their conflicts behind them so quickly; this mood is so united and decided, yes, I would say it is absolutely fearless. No government will be able to resist it.'[76]

But things turned out rather differently. Those who had not been overcome with enthusiasm had recognized the main problem from the start: the national movement demanded a German Schleswig-Holstein under the Augustenburg dynasty; but only the German states, and Prussia in particular, could turn this demand into reality. Prussia, however, was ruled by the powerful *Junker*, who had invoked a policy of 'blood and iron', but who now, when the nation demanded it of him, seemed unwilling to pursue this course against Denmark. Bismarck, said Georg von Bunsen, 'will do what he wants for the time being, that is to say, his worst'.

In the Prussian House of Deputies the beginning of December 1863 saw the first signs of the conflicts which would eventually lead to a split in German liberalism over the next few years. In a declaration supported by all liberals, the chamber called for the Prussian government to place itself at the helm of the national movement. This would inevitably have an effect on the constitutional conflict; as Twesten said, 'there is an old saying: he who has won does not have to account for himself'. A victory, he said, would decide the conflict and lend support to the conflict ministry. Twesten's position was clear: 'I would rather put up with the Bismarck ministry for a few more years than let the German state be lost.' But this certainly did not mean that Twesten had come to terms with the Bismarck government, which he regarded as a 'serious threat' and a 'misfortune for the Fatherland'. Yet some liberals had begun to reverse their view that the political path should lead first to 'freedom' and then to 'unity'. Safeguarding the 'national interest' began to take precedence over liberalizing the Prussian state, which Twesten described 'as still so healthy in its material and moral bases that it will outlive even a Bismarck ministry'. If it was prepared to pursue national politics in the Schleswig-Holstein conflict, he said, the House of Deputies should not deny Bismarck the financial means to do so.[77] The left-wingers around Benedikt Waldeck immediately formulated their counter-position: they were against all 'enthusiasm for German unity' if Germany and Prussia did not achieve 'internal freedom'.

Over the next three years, German liberalism split along this fault line, which was already clearly evident at the end of 1863.[78] We cannot analyse the details of the split here, and will focus only on broad developments. Since both German supreme powers distanced themselves from the national movement's pressure for a 'German' solution to the Schleswig-Holstein conflict, the national movement had no option but to bide its time. Its scope for action was limited to formulating plans and influencing the public. This is true of each of the three alignments into which the national movement, and with it liberalism, split: the *kleindeutsch* group, which, in spite of everything, still placed its hopes in Prussia; the *großdeutsch* group, which dwindled outside Prussia, above all in the south, but which knew it could rely on the support of sections of the public; and those who believed in a third way, between Prussia and Austria.

The degree to which an individual demanded domestic reform cannot be read from the national political option he chose. Compromises of all kinds were made, since everyone was looking for allies. 'Dirty' coalitions were not ruled out by the southern German democrats, whose strongest bastions were in Baden and Württemberg.[79] They were convinced that Prussia could not be democratized. '*Ceterum censeo Borussiam esse delendam*', in Ludwig Pfau's words. Only a Prussia dissected into its provinces would be acceptable for a democratic nation-state. Negative coalitions were not ruled out if they meant coming closer to their federalist ideal, modelled on Switzerland, and warding off Prussian hegemonic solutions. In October 1865 their Württemberg party organ called for them 'to gather all elements in preparation for battle ... the princes and the republicans, the whole army, from the socialists to the Ultramontanes'.[80]

Anti-Prussian democrats and liberals shared central aims for domestic reform with their pro-Prussian *kleindeutsch* rivals. All put their faith in the future – as long as the hegemony of Prussia, which was incapable of democracy, could be prevented. Everything else would sort itself out. The *kleindeutsch* liberals adopted the opposite approach. Convinced of the 'bankruptcy of particularism' (Theodor Mommsen), they believed that only a stronger

Prussian-led nation-state would allow 'unity' and 'freedom' to be combined. And they believed that both could be achieved simultaneously. Only very few wanted, like Treitschke, to 'wager everything, simply everything on unity'. Not until 1866, in the run-up to the German war, did some of the *kleindeutsch* liberals begin to change their views. An important role was played here by Bismarck's offer to the national movement of April 1866 – the reform of the German Confederation, which would be given a democratically elected parliament. They now regarded Bismarck as the wrong man with the right ideas. 'That this vital matter should be accomplished now, by these hands and in this way', Haym wrote in May 1866, 'brings with it countless moral, legal and political reservations.' These reservations would have to be overcome. 'We should not say: first secure the limits, then the freedom; nor should we say first the freedom and then the limits, but rather both at the same time, and at the same time the one by means of the other!' Only the war eliminated remaining doubts. Bismarck was now transformed from a 'frivolous *Junker*' to a national hero. Finally, Droysen rejoiced, the German nation had its 'Hercules . . . who would sweep clean the Augean stables which it had filthied'.

Not all *kleindeutsch* liberals judged matters in this way, however. Not all of them agreed with Baumgarten when he said, 'first a great state, then we'll have to bide our time for the rest'.[81] Forty-one deputies of the Progress parliamentary party voted against and thirty-four in favour of the Indemnity Law of 14 September 1866, which formally ended the constitutional conflict. Thirty-eight of the liberal 'centre-left' voted in favour and twenty-two against.[82] This was a measure of how differently Prussian liberals judged their chances of realizing their political aims with Bismarck in Prussia and in the North German Confederation. After October 1866, these differences led to a reorganization of Prussian and German liberalism, which led in turn to the foundation of the *Nationalliberale Partei*, the National Liberal Party. Whether the future would be on the side of the oppositional liberals, or on that of those who hoped to win Bismarck as their 'ally'[83] would only be decided by the domestic political reforms, in which all liberals hoped that the North German Confederation would be developed as the basis of the future nation-state.

Liberal Policies on the Path to the Nation-State, 1866–71

Views differed on the events of 1866: the Prussian military victory; the end of the German Confederation; the foundation of the partial nation-state; and Austria's exclusion from the German nation. Contemporaries saw them either as a kind of scientific experiment or, depending on the authority in which they placed more faith, a judgement from God.[84] But it was a judgement from a Protestant God: 'The triumph of the true German spirit over the false one, the spirit of 1517 and 1813', as Droysen extolled the events.

Those liberals who thought in similar terms, or who soberly regarded the North German Confederation as a step in the right direction, welcomed Baumgarten's 'Der deutsche Liberalismus: Eine Selbstkritik' (German Liberalism: A Self-Criticism), published in the *Preußische Jahrbücher* in November/December 1866, as the right words at the right time.[85] Baumgarten drew a historical picture in which the events of 1866 were described as a vital supplement to the Reformation, 'the Germans' last common undertaking in the sphere of active life' (p. 25), and which perceptively described the development of liberalism as pre-histories full of good intentions and unavoidable failures. 'It was not liberalism which was to blame, but the prevailing conditions' (p. 39). The 'dwarf's politics', which was inevitable in the small states, was bound to distort everything – the policies of the liberals and of the states – until they became 'more or less a caricature' (p. 40). The 'new era' in Baden had confirmed this once again. A small state could 'never, ever pursue real politics'. It could neither change the nation, nor could it put the 'parliamentary system' into practice (p. 102) – an encouraging message for those who believed that the liberal future was threatened at the side of the powerful *Junker*. Baumgarten's retrospective analysis led into a prognosis for the future, which drew instructions for present-day action from history. 'To be victorious in politics means coming to power' (p. 118). And Prussia had been victorious because it had not attempted to become a 'liberal model state', but had retained the 'elements of its state power': 'its serious discipline, its military severity and its aristocratic base' (p. 139). Opposing this now would return liberalism to the impotence of making plans. *'Liberalism must become capable of governing.*' Only then would it ever be able to hope to realize its own aims, one step at a time, by not transcending the limits of its power, so as not to 'lose all real power'. It would be better to 'do a little in government', Baumgarten said, than to 'make unlimited demands in opposition' (p. 149).

This widely read message described the hopes of the National Liberal Party, but not reality. The party did not succeed in joining the Prussian government, and in the North German Confederation all the parliamentarians' attempts to establish federal ministries failed.[86] This had been a declared aim of the National Liberals, whose founding programme of 12 June 1867 was a comprehensive account of the political principles and aims of the new party. As Hermann Oncken described it, it was 'not a party programme in the usual style, but more a memorandum', designed to convince themselves and written for an educated public, which they hoped to persuade with reasoned argument. Many National Liberals therefore found it hard to come to terms with the large numbers of citizens with full political rights which democratic male suffrage created. Democratic suffrage could become 'the strongest bulwark of freedom', their programme said, as long as the electorate votes 'truthfully'.[87] Their scepticism was unmistakable, but they agreed to it nevertheless. This agreement was by no means a foregone conclusion for the liberals, and later, in the wake of the the Social Democrats' electoral successes, many felt that a grave error had been made.

The National Liberal programme of 1867 did not bear the hallmarks of 'opportunists', as Oncken described those liberals who were prepared to compromise.[88] They demanded an extension of federal authority, not in order to strengthen the state, but to make it capable of reform. Although they supported Prussia's claim to lead the nation, they did not want to 'Borussify' the Confederation. On the contrary, the programme aimed to liberalize Prussia from within the new national centre. The Reichstag was to absorb the powers of the Prussian parliament and to set the pace of reform. For this reason, it would be necessary 'to complete' its budget law and to create responsible federal ministers. The catalogue of reforms for Prussia was wide-ranging and detailed. The reform of the *Herrenhaus* was top of the list, as the 'prerequisite for all reforms'. The programme took account of the fact that the constitutional conflict might flare up again. Its demands therefore included a return to an economical 'true peace-time budget for the army' as soon as possible. It also named 'the imperative condition' for co-operation with the government: that the government should give its unconditional agreement to abide by the law. The founding programme was not a document of the liberal worship of authority. It admitted that the constitution of the North German Confederation which came into force on 1 July 1867 was no more than an initial and incomplete step. As Bennigsen put it, it was a 'work which was in need of, but also capable of, improvement'.[89] In contrast to the majority of the Progress parliamentary party, the National Liberals accepted this part-payment because they believed that they could be sure of the future: 'Every step towards constitutional unity' was, as the present showed, 'at the same time a degree of progress in the sphere of freedom'.

What had the liberal deputies of the constituent Reichstag which was elected on 12 February 1867, achieved? What was the extent of their room for manoeuvre?[90]

The results of the elections were disappointing for the liberals, above all for the left, which won only nineteen seats (6.4 per cent). If we add to these the twenty-seven Old Liberals (9.1 per cent), who, on the evidence of their voting behaviour, ought really to be included with the conservatives, the liberals won 47.1 per cent of all seats. Thus, the results of the elections to the Prussian parliament in 1866, which had taken place the day after the battle of Königgrätz, and in which the liberals had fallen from around 70 to 49 per cent, did not remain an isolated setback. The euphoria of the Prussian military victory undoubtedly weakened support for the liberal opposition amongst the population, which remained largely passive during the debates of the constituent Reichstag. Only twenty-six petitions were submitted during this time, for example. There was no significant external pressure for reform and within the Reichstag itself the scope for action was extremely limited. The allied governments avoided involving the deputies in their constitutional disagreements, and the balance of power in the Reichstag placed clear limitations on any attempt to extend parliamentary rights.

The key role in the laborious amendment of the draft constitution which the governments had agreed, fell to the *Freikonservative Partei* (Free Conservatives), and above all to the National Liberals. As the votes showed, they would only be able to make changes if they were able to win over sections of the Conservatives or the Old Liberals, or of the left and the particularists. Under these circumstances, only compromises were possible. The draft constitution was amended to extend federal authority in particular, and to improve and safeguard the Reichstag's budget power. The military budget remained a significant exception. Initially, until 1871, a lump sum was decided for the military budget on the basis of a fixed peace-time army presence. A special federal law was envisaged for the subsequent period. The conflict between parliament and Crown on the constitutional position of the army was not resolved, but merely postponed.

The liberals failed in their attempt to create responsible federal ministers. Their sole achievement was that the Federal Chancellor – there were no federal ministers alongside him – would assume 'responsibility' for the 'orders and decrees of the *Bundespräsidium* (Article 17 of the Constitution). Whether this was a partial success or a defeat, which blocked the introduction of the parliamentary system in the North German Confederation and the Reich from the beginning, remains a controversial subject even today. The actors of the time could not have known the answer. One cannot judge their achievements only by what was made out of them later in the Kaiserreich. They themselves regarded the Constitution as a transitional one, which they wanted to extend in various directions. For different reasons, they accepted it by a large majority (230 votes to 53). No one in 1867 was arguing for a parliamentary system of government, not even Left Liberals. They wanted legally accountable federal ministers and the clear separation of responsibilities for government and parliament, not parliament's participation in government. Some National Liberals and Old Liberals had more detailed ideas of what a parliamentary system of government might mean, but they either did not demand it, or rejected it outright. As Miquel declared in his explanation of the National Liberal motion to create responsible federal ministers, they wanted political influence, not a 'party government' on the English model.[91]

Despite all the conflicts between Progress and National Liberals, they frequently voted together on important issues to allow the draft constitution to be improved in accordance with their ideas. The common ground they shared was obscured by the political journalism of both liberal camps, which emphasized only the issues that divided them. In terms of what they were able to push through, and what could be averted, the Constitution was a work of the liberal left, although a majority of them proceeded to vote against it (fifteen of nineteen members, two were ill), because the 'main principle' of the constitution, the responsible ministry, had not been included. They were able to act in this way because, as Waldeck said in his parliamentary party vote – they were convinced that the issue of 'the alliance and unity had been fully settled' and was not threatened 'in the least' by the rejection of the Constitution. The National Liberal mediating party[92] relieved them of the necessity of testing the seriousness of Bismarck's threats of allowing all efforts on the constitution and on unification to fail, if the Reichstag were to refuse to yield on the most important points.

North German liberals wanted to develop the constitution in two areas: in domestic and in national politics. The limits of their scope for action in both respects rapidly became clear. In terms of domestic politics, they achieved a great deal, but only where the question of power was not posed. No progress was made on the core issues of constitutional policy. But here, as Wilhelm Wehrenpfennig, editor of the *Preußische Jahrbücher*, wrote, 'the main focus of the entire development rested, not in the Reichstag, but in Bismarck'. The legislative achievements of the North German Confederation were impressive nevertheless. A number of laws were passed which liberalized the economy and society. Authoritarian state regulations were reduced and the freedom of the individual extended. The Reichstag and the Bundesrat acted together on this; the deputies, and above all the liberals, were the driving force. In practice, a 'parliamentarianism by agreement' took place, which was most successful where the Reichstag major-ity, organized by the National Liberals and the Free Conserva-tives, agreed with the Bundesrat and the Prussian bureaucracy. The result was not a 'pseudo-parliamentarianism ... but the division of the spheres of influence. The army, foreign policy, diplomacy and court and state offices remained in the hands of the monarchical governments. Trade and commerce, commu-nications and the law were assigned to parliament, as areas in which it could exercise more than merely a right to have a say.'[93]

Although the Reichstag set the pace of reform in domestic politics, which might have misled people as to the real distri-bution of power (the *Reichsgründung* subsequently corrected this assumption in no uncertain terms), the stagnation which had set in on national politics could not be overlooked. In retrospect many repressed this fact, and came to regard 1866 as a mere stage on the path to the *Reichsgründung*. The liberals drew strength from this hope and the National Liberals used it to justify their compliance towards Bismarck. As Miquel said, politics was not about being 'simply logical', but about being 'patriotic and not losing sight of the final goal'. In 1867 he still seemed very optimistic about being able to reach this 'final goal'. The *Mainlinie* of the time (the division of Germany into north and south along the river Main), was 'not the *Mainlinie* which we used to fear, the dividing line between Austria and Prussia'. Now it represented merely a 'stopping point for us, where we can take on board water and coal, and catch our breath, before resuming our journey'. When he took up these words again two years later, his demand seemed more urgent, his disappointment unmistakable: 'Whatever happens, we must have south Germany. We would have it already if the south German people possessed a true German spirit.'

Between the two statements lay the Customs Parliament elections of 1868. Bismarck and the *kleindeutsch* liberals wanted the Customs Union, which was restored in 1867, to push forward the process of political unification. An important role was ascribed to the Customs Parliament, which consisted of all 297 deputies of the North German Reichstag and 85 democratically elected south German deputies. But the Customs Parliament did not become a parliamentary signal for the German population's desire to unite as a nation. Instead, it highlighted the broad disinclination in the south for a German nation-state determined by Prussia. Its opponents won fifty-nine of the eighty-five south German seats. 'I believe', wrote the staunch unitarian Wehrenpfennig, at the time of the Customs Parliament elections, 'that for the time being, the revolution of 1866 has reached its goal. Before now, its power to transform extended only as far as the river Main. We must not pick the fruits before they are ripe, unless a storm tears them down and drops them into our laps.'[94]

This was to come. Nevertheless, the new Customs Union and the Customs Parliament by no means only represented the failure of the *kleindeutsch* liberals' national hopes. Their opponents were only able to act so decisively against all attempts to extend the authority of the Customs Parliament because the continued existence of the Customs Union had been safeguarded. Nor were they able to prevent the Customs Parliament from applying measures to further unify the *kleindeutsch* economic territory. None the less, the confidence of *kleindeutsch* liberals in the north and south, that the political *Mainlinie* would be broken down by peaceful progress under liberal leadership, and under the pressure of the 'nation', was clearly misplaced. Germany must not emerge from a process of 'conquering', Miquel demanded in 1869, it must not be based 'on military power, but on constitutional development'. Measured against these hopes, even the *kleindeutsch* liberals were amongst the losers of 1870, like their anti-Prussian opponents on the left and the right, even if they refused to admit it. They placed their hopes in the ability of the new Reich to develop, and so once again, as in 1867, they accepted a constitution which did not fulfil their wishes. Bennigsen encouraged his fellow National Liberal Party members on 9 December 1870, saying that a 'serious permanent resistance to the unanimous will of the German people is impossible'. But in saying this, he glossed over the fact that this 'unanimous will' did not actually exist. The south German liberals were forced to confront this fact, not least during the *Kulturkampf*, which was just beginning (cf. Chapter 4, pp. 199–206).

But initially the *kleindeutsch* liberals saw only the fulfilment of a dream, in which they had collaborated to the best of their abilities. The national movement which they represented was, in Hermann Oncken's view, 'the strongest missile for Bismarck's superior diplomacy too'. 'Of course', he added, 'to a greater extent than in 1866, in 1870 the men of the National Party were forced to accept that their role was only that of the chorus in the most sublime dramatic development in the fate of a nation.'[95] The way in which the Reich was founded, the way in which it emerged from wars, left the liberals no other choice. Only time would tell if they would be able to exchange the role of the chorus for that of the actors. The first Reichstag elections (1871) were not exactly a bad omen, but nor did they promise victory. The National Liberals became the strongest parliamentary party, with around a third of all seats, and together the liberals had a slim majority of about 52 per cent. This too reflects liberalism's limited scope for political action in the decade of the *Reichsgründung*.

*Pressure Groups and Social Images: The Formation of Parties,
Members and Voters*

The nineteenth century was the century of the association. An
association was created to represent almost every social interest,
and in the second half of the century more and more different
types of association were founded. The rise of political parties is
part of this process of differentiation. After an initial surge
during the 1848–9 revolution, from the end of the decade of
reaction onwards, parties once again became the focus of the
political representation of interests, and now remained there
permanently. Yet the parties did not have the monopoly on
organization. Large numbers of associations were also attempting to mobilize and steer the political public. It was in these
associations that the national movement of the era of the
Reichsgründung was formed. This was an important political
force, but one which is hard to understand in concrete terms. It
was a community of shared beliefs, represented by spokesmen in
the press and in the parliaments, which expressed itself in books,
in private letters and conversations, which appeared publicly at
countless meetings and festivals, and which found organizational
backing in the most wide and varying kinds of association. This
phenomenon has been neglected in research into the post-
revolutionary decades.[96] Liberalism was closely linked to the
many branches of the national movement. It gave it its political
strength, ensured its influence beyond the limited opportunities
for parliamentary participation, and reinforced its optimistic
view of the future in politically dark times, and during the
years of constitutional conflict.

The current state of research permits no more than a broad
outline of these organizations; we will focus on a few examples.
Since the 'new era' a Navy League (*Flottenverein*), supported by
the National Association, had collected contributions for the
expansion of the German fleet. The great Schiller Festivals of
1859, which were rather like popular festivals, offered the
liberals opportunities, of which they gladly took advantage, to
address a wider public, as did the Deputies' Festivals of 1863 and
1865, or the celebrations in memory of the Leipzig Battle of the
Nations and the Battle of Waterloo. There were also regional
celebrations; on the fiftieth anniversary of the Rheinland coming
under Prussian control, for example, or the Gauturn festival at

the end of August 1863 in Göttingen. As chairman of the Göttingen Male Gymnasts' Association, the liberal Miquel made the festival speech, in which he celebrated the gymnasts' associations as vital elements of the national movement, which were aimed not in a political, but in a non-partisan, patriotic manner 'against the spirit of the differences between the *Stände*'; 'a true national educational institution for good patriotic men', on whom the 'well-being and the hopes of the Fatherland' depended.[97]

Liberals used these great festivals and meetings as platforms from which to introduce their central ideas to a wider public. In the social associations they acquired a base which probably influenced the political climate no less than the spectacular events themselves. In Constance, for example, the 'Harmony' Song Association formed an 'outpost of liberalism', closely linked to the Workers' Education Association and the fire brigade, whose leadership lay almost entirely in the hands of liberals after 1862. Their organizational core was in the 'civic museum' and the 'Friday Circle'. After 1865, regular 'civic evenings' were held, where their developmental concepts for the region were publicly aired. However, they failed in their attempt to establish the Constance Theatre as a liberal educational facility, and to bring professors to the provinces to give lectures, financed by a 'joint-stock educational institution'. In 1866 the Constance liberals finally succeeded in putting up the mayor. Now, however, they had reached the limits of their ability to push through liberal policies, whose aim was 'progress' as opposed to 'tradition'. The planned abolition of common land, a vital institution for 300–400 families of small businessmen, gave rise to an opposition which combined with increasingly politicized Catholicism and forced liberalism onto the defensive. The local political public slipped from the liberals' grasp. It was no longer possible for liberals to permeate the many social associations which were still being formed, and to gear them towards a generally liberal urban public. At the end of the day, it was reported in the press in 1878, 'liberalism in Überlingen has left behind an enormous number of associations and a good deal of disunity'.[98]

As we have said, little research has been undertaken on the local organizational network into which liberalism was bound. We are somewhat better informed on the organizations which operated at individual state level, and across state borders. 1858 saw the first meeting of the 'Congress of German Economists', which later became an effective pressure group of German free traders, and which was closely linked to *kleindeutsch* liberalism in terms of its membership and programme.[99] The Congress began as a forum for the concerns of small- and medium-scale tradesmen; but from 1861, trade policy and issues of national politics came to the fore. After 1863 a broad spectrum of economic subjects was addressed. Congress liberals preceded political liberals in this abandonment of the middle-class perspective. The economic ideas of the Congress Liberals had a profound influence on political liberalism.

Contacts between economic and political liberalism were also reflected in the professional composition of the members of the Economic Congress. Typically, the educated middle class dominated, even in this economic organization. The wave of industrialization from the mid-nineteenth century onwards undoubtedly gave rise to a modern, commercial middle class in Germany, which was no longer solely comprised of small traders. Yet academics employed by the state or in independent professions continued to dominate the leading committees of the liberal organizations and the parliaments. In particular, they were able to unite diverging political, economic and cultural interests in the central value of the 'nation'. They defined the aims of the nation-state movement, although it encompassed far more than the academically educated class. It was for this reason that, wherever liberal and national ideas were formulated and prepared for public consumption, the educated middle class was more strongly represented than any other social group. Thus, it was speakers from the educated middle class in particular, who invoked the cultural unity of the nation as a basis for political unity at the great Schiller Celebrations of 1859.

The National Association enjoyed close personal links with liberal parliamentary parties, with the Congress of German Economists, and with the Protestant Conference or *Protestantentag*. Its leaders also came from the educated middle class. In many local groups, however, their numbers were exceeded by those of merchants and manufacturers. Craftsmen, too, were well represented. The Association, which had approximately 25 000 members at its peak in October 1862, was the largest mass political organization in the era of the *Reichsgründung*. Crossing the borders of the German individual states, though with its focus north of the *Mainlinie*, the National Association was a testament to the strong political and social unifying force of the national idea. Its social profile, however, also reflected the increasingly 'middle-class profile' of German liberalism.

The large organizations, which, like the German Press Association or the many gymnasts' associations, had acquired members from the lower edges of the middle classes, and from the lower classes, could still as a whole be included in the liberal community of shared ideas in the *Vormärz* period. During the 1848–9 revolution, however, and again and to a greater extent in the decade of the *Reichsgründung*, non-middle-class social circles announced their claim to political maturity. This is particularly true of urban workers, whose numbers were inevitably increasing massively with the advance of industrialization. The political public extended beyond the middle classes, yet this was reflected only to a small degree in liberal organizations. The 'middle-class profile' of post-revolutionary liberalism did not mean that it reduced its social catchment area in comparison to that of the *Vormärz* period. Rather, it was unable to keep pace with the expansion of the society of citizens of the state, and with the growing working class in particular. Liberalism had always been a middle-class movement. This social anchoring in the middle classes posed no threat to the liberal claim to represent all social interests, as long as the non-middle-class social circles supported liberalism. But with the increased politicization of all social strata in the era of the *Reichsgründung*, institutionalized by the universal male suffrage of the North German Confederation and then that of the Kaiserreich, the liberal claim to represent the whole of society was challenged more strongly than ever before.

The largest liberal organization, the National Association, did not meet this challenge; indeed, it was hardly even aware that it existed. On several occasions the General Assembly rejected requests for subscription concessions to enable workers to join. Even Schulze-Delitzsch, who attempted to whet the 'social conscience' of the liberals, was prepared only to recognize workers as 'honorary members', that is to say as protégés. 'My dear friend,' he attempted to advise a worker seeking membership,

You would serve the national issue far better if you would think first of your own material improvement, for our national issue is threatened by nothing as much as by the rise of the worker's *Stand*. If after that you still have something left over, we will welcome you with open arms. But think first of yourself and first establish a certain degree of wealth and improve your education. For what good are political rights if I do not have a certain modest degree of wealth?[100]

It was not that Schulze-Delitzsch rejected workers' demands to be recognized as state citizens with full political rights – on the contrary, he argued for democratic suffrage. But he believed that the full ability to act politically was linked to a certain degree of education and economic independence. This linked him to early liberalism, whose social model he carefully tried to assimilate to economic change. Liberals like Schulze-Delitzsch had no desire for a return to pre-industrial conditions. Nor was their ideal the unrestrained industrial society. Instead, they hoped for a 'clearly comprehensible, less industrialized society of small and medium concerns and co-operatives of all kinds'.[101]

Many population groups welcomed the idea of the co-operative, adapted to the ideal of a civil society, which would pave the way to economic independence for as many people as possible. But it was not an instrument with which workers could be immunized against socialist ideas or which could bind them to liberalism politically. From the beginning, the production co-operatives, which also formed the core of the visions of the future in Lassalle's General German Workers' Association, failed to fulfil the hopes that were placed in them, of offering an alternative to emerging industrial capitalism. The consumer associations, and above all the credit associations, of which there were around 1700 in 1875, enjoyed greater success.[102] The 815 credit associations for which exact statistics exist had around 418 000 members. The educated middle class dominated their committees, the wealthy middle class their membership. In 1870 workers represented only around 7 per cent of those members whose professions are known. The membership of the consumer associations included a higher proportion of 'lower classes' (c. two-thirds in 1870), and they came close to Schulze-Delitzsch's ideas, yet he was forced to admit that co-operatives were not the means by which the 'social question' could be resolved and workers won over to liberalism.

The co-operative idea waned in the liberal social models of the sixties, but was not replaced by a new, generally accepted idea. *One* conviction permeated liberalism as a whole in the era of the

Reichsgründung, however: that the future meant progress – political, economic and social progress – if only society could be freed from the state which took decisions on its behalf. This image of the future was based on a fundamental harmony between all strata, both within the middle classes and between the middle classes and the workers. As far as they thought deeply at all about the social interests of workers, liberals believed that 'enlightenment' in particular was needed before this could be achieved.

John Prince-Smith, one of the most resolute German free traders, was one of those who accepted the challenge that the emerging independent workers' movement posed to liberalism. Like the south German democrats, he saw the key to 'the solution of the worker's question' in a militia, which would lower unproductive state expenditure, and in improved education for all – the most important task assigned to the liberal state. The 'light of culture' must shine 'right into the deepest and innermost rooms of the social edifice', in order to create in workers the desire to elevate their way of life to the highest possible level. If that succeeded, Ferdinand Lassalle's 'iron law of wages' (according to which workers' wages would never permanently exceed 'the bare necessities of life for people who are customarily required to eke out an existence and reproduce') would be turned into the 'golden law of wages'. For what was meant by 'customarily' could change, could be trained in a different direction, in that the 'habits' of workers could be cultivated. The economic prerequisite for such changes was the rapid increase of capital which Prince-Smith believed would come 'as a result of new inventions and discoveries, or the expansion of economic freedom'.[103]

Even those liberals who did not share Prince-Smith's ambition to become an important economist, were filled with this optimism. It was rooted in the economic prosperity of the decade of the *Reichsgründung*, which the liberals furnished with a certainty of the future which made them largely blind to social deprivation, or which allowed them to believe that the elimination of such deprivation was only a matter of time and good intentions. Miquel was one of the most prominent liberal politicians who tried to court workers. He did not shy away from speaking at workers' meetings, although he had no concrete social programme to offer them, any more than his fellow liberals did. Miquel combined well-meaning advice, born of a paternalistic desire to transform workers into equal citizens, with the recognition of the strike as a collective bargaining tool. Even his language reflected this mix: he sometimes referred to the 'worker's *Stand*' and sometimes to the 'working class'. Ultimately, however, he placed his faith in the harmonizing force of economic and political progress. All that was necessary was to unleash it. 'Where does the interest of the workers' estate lie?', he asked an audience of around a thousand at an Osnabrück workers' meeting on 9 February 1867 in a speech on his election to the North German Reichstag. His answer was, 'In a great and powerful Fatherland. For when the whole is well, all its component parts are well too. It is therefore our duty to look after the whole.' 'A great, strong and powerful Germany must also have a powerful effect on trade and commerce. But where there is trade and commerce, there is also a need for workers, and wages are high'.

Miquel's speech united the economic and social promise of the nation-state in his reference to the 'gift' of full political citizenship to the workers; a gift which also brought certain responsibilities with it.

> My dear sirs! You are from the workers' estate, and you have won a precious right without doing anything at all to get it. Every man in the population now has an equal right to vote. ... Everyone in the population is equal. ... But these great rights are associated with great duties. No one receives a right without a duty. The duty consists in the worker's estate enlightening itself, so that it no longer just lives, but so that it develops its own conviction as to what is needed for its estate, for itself and above all for the Fatherland.

Miquel had no doubt that this 'duty' placed the workers in the care of liberalism, the party of progress. 'As long as the workers' *Stand* has been politically active, it has been in favour of progress. ... Work is synonymous with progress.'

In many of his speeches Miquel described his liberal vision of the future to his audiences as the nation-state: externally strong, internally equipped with a liberal constitution; a state which renounced authoritarian intervention in social and economic life. It was an image of society which aimed not at the industrial class, but at a politically liberal, socially harmonious society, which was

open to progress. In order to achieve this, he argued for freedom of enterprise, which, as in England, would lead to a situation
where 'craft, trade and factories compete peacefully alongside
each other, for each other and not against each other'. He argued
in favour of co-operatives, as far as they were based on the
principle of self-help, and was also in favour of freedom of
coalition, which, like free trade and the right to strike, was in
keeping with 'the spirit of progress'. Those who deprived the
workers of such things would, he said, tempt them to 'socialist
fantasies'. The freedom and the education of the citizen of the
state, he believed, were the most effective weapons against the
'false teachings which the Parisian workers of 1848 paid for with
their blood, and which are currently being preached again in
Germany by Lassalle and his consorts'.[104]

Not all liberals were in favour of such an extensive dismantling
of authoritarian barriers in the social and economic spheres.
Many regarded such barriers, not without pleasure, as protection in times of need. Yet more typical of the liberalism of the era
of the *Reichsgründung* was the hope that the 'magic solution' for
the 'modern sphinx', as Schulze-Delitzsch described the 'social
question', might be found in the 'humanity' which transcended
class. The

> solution with which modern society must address the question
> amounts to nothing less than complete humanity. It is the
> demand of the whole human race for all classes of human
> society, to help bring about a humane fate for the masses, so
> that they might participate in all great tasks of civilization,
> so that they might be led with us into battle, and help us decide
> the battles in the political, economic and humane spheres,
> which represent the substance of our time. Victory will not
> come to us until this is done. Humanity is the solution to the
> social question![105]

Such hopes, and the image of social harmony in which they
originate, cannot simply be dismissed as an ideology which veiled
the emerging capitalist class society. Like middle-class democrats,
liberals believed that it would be possible to bring workers and
the middle classes together in a coalition of interests. And in the
judgement of the liberal and democratic middle classes, their
prospects of success did not seem at all poor. In England, to

which the continental Europeans looked whenever they needed
an idea of the industrial society of the future, an independent
worker's party emerged much later than in Germany, namely at
the turn of the nineteenth and twentieth centuries. Even in
Germany (contemporaries had to force themselves to accept this)
it should be possible to win the workers over to the middle-class
political parties. Everything seemed to point to that. When political life began to change in the German states in around 1860,
and workers' associations were founded, they worked together
with liberals and democrats.[106]

This remained the case until 1863, when the *Allgemeiner
Deutscher Arbeiterverein* (ADAV), the General German Workers'
Association, was founded under the leadership of Ferdinand
Lassalle, although it had only 21 000 members at most before
1872. The majority of workers' associations continued to work
closely with democrats and liberals. Before the *Reichsgründung*,
two organizationally independent workers' parties had emerged:
the ADAV and the *Sozialdemokratische Arbeiterpartei* (SDAP), the
Social Democratic Workers' Party. But liberals and democrats
did not have to regard this as the final 'separation of proletarian
democracy from middle-class democracy' (G. Mayer). Together,
the two workers' parties had only around 30 000 members in
around 1871 and won only 3.2 per cent of all votes in the first
Reichstag elections (1871), which gave them two seats.

So the process of class formation was certainly not so far
advanced in political and organizational terms that the hopes of
liberals and democrats for a middle-class-proletarian 'alliance of
progress' became simply an ideological veneer, which masked
middle-class politics. A further indication of this is the development of the unions, which emerged independently from the
workers' parties in the sixties. In around 1870 they organized
some 2–3 per cent of all workers in industry and crafts, with at
most 78 000 members. Approximately 40 per cent of these were
members of the liberal *Gewerkvereine* or trade unions, which
remained as strong as the two socialist camps. And not only the
liberal 'Hirsch–Duncker trade unions' hoped that workers and
businessmen could go 'hand in hand', just as not only the liberal
unions remained open to 'small employers'.[107]

It should come as no surprise that in the era of the *Reichsgründung* so many liberals and democrats believed that they
could recruit workers to their political cause. Instead, we should

ask why German liberalism failed in this respect, in contrast to its English counterpart. The answers which have been given to this difficult question are clearly inadequate. German liberals, as John Breuilly stresses in one of the few comparative studies of the subject,[108] were not 'more bourgeois' than English liberals, and nor were they against reforms which would benefit the workers. The suffrage of the North German Confederation and the Kaiserreich was more democratic than that of England, and the right to coalition, liberalized even before the *Reichsgründung*, certainly did not place German unions in a worse position than their English equivalents. Why then were the liberals nevertheless unable to prevent the formation of workers' parties in Germany at such an early stage?

An important role must surely be attributed here to the tradition of reform in the German states. German society was used to accepting reforms from 'above'. This tradition of state reform lingered on in the 'state socialism' of the Lassalleans and in the workers' parties, which united in the Socialist Workers' Party of Germany in 1875. This was bound to reduce the chances of the liberals, who were pushing for a decrease in state control. In contrast to English politics, the German politics of the sixties was also profoundly influenced by the process of the formation of the nation-state. All controversial issues were related to the various ideas on the desirable paths to the nation-state, and acquired the status of issues of principle. Liberals and democrats were subject to the core question which eclipsed everything else. The Prussian–German *Reichsgründung* 'from above' therefore weakened the social unifying force of liberal and democratic parties and their social images. This must have played a major role in the fact that German workers were prepared at a much earlier stage than their English counterparts to found a class-based party which offered workers something new with which they could identify – something related to the nation-state and not to individual states, something which was not burdened by the fundamental controversies of the period of the battle for the nation-state. The formation of parties at an early stage was aided by democratic suffrage, which gave new parties better chances of survival than the English suffrage system. And, finally, the organizational weakness of the German unions in comparison to those of England may actually have favoured the early foundation of a workers' party. This might sound paradoxical, but workers who do not see their social interests represented by strong trade unions, will be more prepared to support their own workers' party, which will demand political payment of what cannot be pushed through by the unions.

However we weight individual factors, the fact remains that there were many reasons for the emergence of a workers' class party in Germany, rather than the rise of 'social liberalism' which also represented workers politically. These factors placed tight restrictions on the liberals' room for manoeuvre. It should be stressed that this loss of workers, irrevocable as it turned out, was by no means as clear to liberals and middle-class democrats in the sixties as observers have frequently assumed in retrospect.

Let us now turn to the *liberal and democratic parties*, their organization, their members and voters. We can focus only on a small sector, for despite all their links on the level of national politics, the parties remained dependent on the individual states as arenas where they could practise politics. It was here that they had to organize, to recruit members and voters, and only in the individual states did they find their parliamentary domain before 1867 (the North German Confederation) or before 1871.

Of particular importance for party politics as a whole was of course Prussia – the state to which all those who wanted to be effective at a national political level looked, either with expectation or rejection. Their stance on Prussian unification policy, on the Prussian claim to the national political leading role in Germany, influenced the party landscapes more strongly than any other factor. It also determined the process by which the middle classes split during the era of the *Reichsgründung*, though the development of the split varied from individual state to state.[109]

The National Association had still been able to embrace both democrats and liberals. But in 1863 a democratic opposition began to form against its Prussian–*kleindeutsch* orientation. Seeking a 'third way' between Prussia and Austria, the democrats emerged more forcefully than the liberals in their demands for domestic political reform, and made more concerted attempts to recruit workers. The democrats had their centre in Baden, Württemberg, Frankfurt and Saxony. Their attempts to unite failed, not least because of the extreme federalism of the Württembergers, who rejected the concept of national organization as an offence against the democratic spirit, which they hoped to introduce to Germany on the Swiss model. But there were other reasons for the failure too. They include above all the democrats' programme for national politics, which could neither be realized with the German governments, nor against them, and the varying social profile of the democratic organizations from state to state. The Württemberg *Volkspartei* (People's Party), which split from the democratic–liberal Progress Party in 1864, remained a predominantly lower-middle-class party, while the Saxon People's Party, founded in 1866, consisted primarily of craftsmen and workers. Under the leadership of August Bebel and Wilhelm Liebknecht, it joined the *Sozialdemokratische Arbeiterpartei* (Social-Democratic Workers' Party), while the Württemberg democrats attempted in vain to continue the co-operation and to some extent division of labour with the organized workers' movement.[110]

The German democrats did not succeed in amalgamating until 1869, when, after Austria had left Germany, their programme for national politics had been overtaken by events and their politics had been exhausted in their defensive actions against Prussia. In 1870–1 they joined the ranks of the defeated, who were never fully able to recover from this setback.

The democrats mark an important organizational innovation in the history of the middle-class parties. While for a long time the liberals remained attached to the model of the *Honoratiorenpartei*, or party of notables, which found it difficult to adapt to the conditions of the 'political mass market' (H. Rosenberg), the democratic parties began to develop into fixed, organized membership parties – with local associations, party meetings, state committees, a party press, regulated official channels and the delimitation of authority between extra-parliamentary associations and parliamentary factions. Under the conditions of the time, a membership party did not mean a mass party. Even in Württemberg, where the German democrats achieved their greatest successes before 1870, the People's Party had at most 4000 registered members in 1870 in the forty-three constituencies in which it had a local association. During the same period, the *Deutsche Partei* (German Party), as the National Liberals in Württemberg were called, had associations with around 2200 members in thirty-nine of the seventy constituencies. The German Party was an exceptionally well-organized liberal party; but it was a kind of enforced organization, driven forward by the more active democrats with whom it had to compete.

In Württemberg, too, with its particularly tightly organized parties, the political dividing lines inside and outside the legislature did not fully coincide. In parliament the split in the party, which took place in 1864, endured until the Customs Parliament elections of 1868, in which the liberal–democratic parliamentary party, which had previously been carefully maintained, finally collapsed. For the first time since the years of reaction, the legislature elections of the same year were held on the basis of universal and equal suffrage. From these elections twenty-two *Großdeutsche*, fourteen liberal and twenty-three democratic deputies emerged, who worked with the People's Party, but did not join their parliamentary party, and who were not organized outside parliament. The *großdeutsch* Catholics also gathered in this parliamentary grouping without a party sub-structure. In Württemberg, as in the other German states, Catholicism formed a bulwark in the era of the *Reichsgründung*, which became increasingly united against *kleindeutsch*–Protestant liberalism.

The same is true of Prussia, where the end of the constitutional battles and the foundation of the North German Confederation mark a profound break in the history of the parties between the revolution and the *Reichsgründung*.[111] With the end of the consti-tutional conflict, the bonds which had held the liberal opposition together, and which at times had even united liberals and Catholics against state policies, were dissolved. In contrast to the Württemberg liberals and democrats, the Prussian Progress Party, which was formed in 1861, and which united liberals and democrats, was a voters' and not a membership party. It did not issue membership cards or raise membership subscriptions, but financed its activities through donations. To some extent, the National Association, with which it enjoyed close personal links, represented a substitute for membership organization. Yet the Progress Party was not able to dispense with an organization entirely. It had a central election committee and provincial and local committees, onto which the main burden of election cam-paigns fell, and to which the entire organization was geared. In Berlin the democrats had formed additional organizations with the '*Volkstümliche Wahlverein*' (Popular Election Association) and the 'Committee of Liberal Craftsmen'. They demanded the elimination of the three-class suffrage system, while the Progress Party programme was silent on the matter.

During election periods, the Progress Party distributed leaf-lets. Most importantly, however, it could count on the support of a number of newspapers, whose editors and publishers had declared their support for the Party. They included the most widely circulated Berlin daily newspapers: the *Volks-Zeitung* (22 000), the *Vossische Zeitung* (13 000) and the *Nationalzeitung* (8500).

Already in 1861, the year in which it was founded, the Progress Party won 30 per cent of all seats in the Prussian House of Deputies. Only the National Liberals, who split in 1867, were able to replace the Progress Party as a stronger liberal parliamentary party. Together they provided more deputies than the conservatives, who had dwindled to form a splinter group in the era of the constitutional battles, but who formed the largest single parliamentary party between 1866 and 1870 (Table 2).

Liberals benefited from the Prussian three-class suffrage system. In 1863 their greatest rivals, the conservatives, needed on average across the state four times as many votes as the liberals to win a seat. This was not due to the class suffrage system alone, however. Liberals also profited from the fact that election turnout was higher in the towns than in the countryside. The liberals were also more likely to receive votes from electors from the first class, who made significantly more use of their entitlement to vote than the voters of the second, and especially of the third class, where turnout did not even reach 50 per cent of those of the first class.

Prosperous townspeople may have voted in disproportionate numbers for the liberals, but Prussian liberalism was not a party of rich town-dwellers. It is important to note that liberals achieved success in all three classes amongst primary voters and delegates, although there were differences from class to class. In the countryside in 1863 they were able to win more than a third of all votes on average. In four provinces they even won a majority. Election geography confirms this picture. The liberals, and only the liberals, won seats in all provinces, while the conservatives and Catholics did not manage to go beyond their few strongholds. Of all the parties, the liberals came closest to being an electable popular party for all social strata, although they were limited to the Protestant population. The shared aim of preventing the government from undermining the constitution did encourage liberals and Catholics to work together in

Table 2 Parliamentary parties in the Prussian House of Deputies, 1861–70

Parliamentary parties	1861		1862		1863		1866		1867		1870	
	No.	%	No.	%	No.	%	No.	%	No.	%	No.	%
Progress Party	104	29.5	133	37.8	141	40.1	95	27	48	11.1	49	11.3
National Liberals									99	22.9	123	28.5
Other Liberals	139	39.5	115	32.7	106	30.1	77	21.9	50	11.6	11	2.5
Conservatives	14	4	11	3.1	35	9.9	136	38.6	173	40	155	35.9
Catholic Party	54	15.3	28	7.9	26	7.4	15	4.3	–	–	58	13.4

Total Number: 352 = 100%   Number: 432 = 100%
(Remainder: Poles, independent)

Source: W. Gagel, *Die Wahlrechtsfrage in der Geschichte der deutschen Liberalen Partei, 1848–1918* (Düsseldorf, 1958) p. 176f.

elections, but it did not lead to the formation of permanent alliances. The more strongly the Catholic milieu was loyal to the Church (measured, for example, by its participation in pilgrimages), the more decisively it distanced itself from liberalism.[112]

Liberals were elected by all (Protestant) social groups, but not all social groups took part in the liberal organizations. This has not yet been fully researched. In 1865–6 in Aachen, for example, more than two-thirds of the liberal voters' organization was made up of members of the commercial and academically educated middle class – the situation was similar in other places. In contrast, the Catholic Constantia Association included a higher proportion of small traders. This is mirrored in the election results: the Catholic deputies' successes increased from the first to the third class, but for the liberals they ran in the opposite direction.

In terms of the social profile of their deputies, the liberal parliamentary parties differed less from others, though here, too, there were clearly significant variations (Table 3). Civil servants represented the largest professional group in the legislature elected in 1862, for which the most accurate figures are available. They were most strongly represented amongst the conservatives. Judges, who were less dependent on the government than administrative civil servants, dominated the opposition parliamentary parties. In its social composition, just as in its politics, the Progress parliamentary party was shown to be 'more left-wing' than the other liberal groupings: it had fewer administrative civil servants, more civil servants who were retired or given leave of absence, more non-civil-servant academics, and fewer agrarian professions and lords of the manor.

These data from Prussia cannot simply be transferred to other German states too. Civil servants certainly represented the highest proportion of deputies in all parliaments and chambers, but their political alignment seems to have depended strongly on the government course. In Bavaria, where the relationship between liberals and the government was not as strained as it was in Prussia, and where at the turn of 1866–7 Chlodwig von Hohenlohe-Schillingfürst, who may be regarded as a *kleindeutsch* liberal, assumed leadership of the government, more civil servants declared their support for the liberals than for the conservatives. Craft trades were more strongly represented in all the parliamentary parties of the Bavarian legislature, including the

Table 3 The Prussian House of Deputies, 1862: social composition

	Parliamentary groupings										
	Progress		Other Liberals		Polish		Catholic		Conservatives		Total
	No.	%	No.	%	No.	%	No.	%	No.	%	%
1. Civil Servants											
a. Municipal	7	5.2	8	5.3	–	–	–	–	–	–	4.3
b. Admin.	2	1.5	17	11.3	–	–	3	9.1	7	63.6	8.2
c. Judges	34	25.2	43	28.7	2	8.7	11	33.3	–	–	25.6
d. Retired, on leave	11	8.1	6	4	–	–	1	3	–	–	5.1
1(a)–(d)	54	40	74	49.3	2	8.7	15	45.4	7	63.6	43.2
2. Professors, Gymnasium teachers	6	4.4	4	2.7	–	–	3	9.1	–	–	3.7
3. Clergymen	1†	0.7	6*	4	5**	21.7	7**	21.2	–	–	5.4
4. Lawyers	12	8.9	4	2.7	–	–	–	–	–	–	4.5
5. Other non-civil servant academics	9	6.7	1	0.6	–	–	1	3	–	–	3.1
2–5	28	20.7	15	10	5	21.7	11	33.3	–	–	16.8

	No.	%	No.	%	No.	%	No.	%	No.	%	%
6. Agrarian professions	28	20.7	43	28.7	16	69.6	5	15.2	4	36.4	27.2
(of which *Rittergutsbesitzer*)	13	9.6	22	14.7	10	43.5	1	3	4	36.4	14.2
7. Craftsmen	3	2.2	2	1.3	—	—	—	—	—	—	1.4
8. Manufacturers	6	4.4	1	0.6	—	—	—	—	—	—	2
9. Merchants	7	5.2	7	4.7	—	—	—	—	—	—	4
10. Rentiers	6	4.4	5	3.3	—	—	1	3	—	—	3.4
11. Unknown	3	2.2	3	2	—	—	1	3	—	—	2
1–11	135	99.8	150	99.9	23	100	33	99.9	11	100	100
Prop. of parliamentary party		38.4		42.6		6.5		9.4		3.1	

* Protestant
† Non-denominational
** Catholic

Source: A. Hess, *Das Parlament, das Bismarck widerstrebte* (Cologne, 1964), pp. 65–7.

liberal parties, than in the Prussian or in the Württemberg Chamber of Deputies.[113]

Conditions in the Kingdom or (after 1866) the Prussian province of Hanover, were different again. Here, the liberal–democratic movement split three ways in 1866. For the most part, Left Liberals and liberal–conservative Old Liberals united with the Hanoverian opposition against Prussian annexation, while the National Liberal centre under Bennigsen's leadership, pursued *kleindeutsch* policies which supported the conversion of the North German Confederation into a liberalized nation-state. These state and national political dividing lines, sharpened by religious dividing lines, coincided with social divisions. The National Liberals enjoyed their greatest successes in Protestant areas, while Catholics voted against Prussia and against the National Liberals, which in this context meant voting for the 'Guelphic' opposition.[114] In Baden, too, liberals were forced to recognize the limits of their social unifying force and of their electability, when national politics and the 'social question' mobilized political Catholicism against liberalism. This will be examined below in the context of the *Kulturkampf* and its prehistory.

In summary then, in the decade of the *Reichsgründung*, the liberals of the German states formed extra-parliamentary organizations of varying degrees of effectiveness. Overwhelmingly, however, they took part in electoral campaigns but did not dispute the parliamentary parties' right to the leading political role. Liberal politics remained *Honoratiorenpolitik*, but it also claimed to represent the affairs of society as a whole. This was no mere ideology, which simply masked thoroughly bourgeois interest politics. Liberals of all alignments – factionalization and splits were typical of the history of liberal organizations from the start – saw themselves as popular parties, and in terms of the social composition of their voters, that is indeed what they were. Their focus, however, lay in the middle-class Protestant milieu. This defined a social spectrum whose lines they could not cross, and whose needs they were increasingly less able to fulfil.

4   The Nation-State, Industrial Society and Weltpolitik: Liberals in the German Kaiserreich

Social and Political Changes

The German Kaiserreich has many faces. Past and present judgements of it also vary, and sometimes contradict each other, depending on the stance of the observer. The Kaiserreich spans a period of great change, which demanded a high degree of adaptability from everyone; from individuals and institutions, and above all from the parties. Everyone was asked to co-operate in the central task of adapting the state and society to the dynamic changes taking place in all spheres, only some of which can be briefly outlined here.[1]

> How, by the Grace of God, did we deserve to experience such great and powerful things? And how will we live afterwards? The content of all our wishes and endeavours for twenty years has now been fulfilled in such a wonderful way! Where, at my time of life, am I going to be able to find a new content for the rest of my life?

Heinrich Sybel's sentiments, written to Hermann Baumgarten on 27 January 1871, were shared by many of those for whom the *kleindeutsch* nation-state had been more than just a political aim. In the *Reichsgründung* they saw the fulfillment of a promise which they believed had been laid down in German history. But not everyone saw it in this light. Even those who had geared their lives and their careers to this promise experienced doubts on the viability of the Reich, whose birth they had imagined in quite different terms. 'The new organization of the Holy Roman Empire', Gustav Freytag wrote in a letter in 1871, 'is an edifice so strangely full of holes, that even Prince Bismarck cannot live in it in the long term. And if there were to be a storm, this temporary building would be thrown about and utterly destroyed, as if it had never existed.'[2] In many respects the new nation-state was indeed 'incomplete' (T. Schieder) when it assumed life. The internal formation of the nation had not yet taken place. That this process would be beset by many complications was entirely predictable, given the large numbers of people who had been defeated, and whom the process of the foundation of the nation-state had disregarded, both on a foreign and domestic political level.

The new Reich saw itself as a nation-state. Yet it did not fully absorb the old imperial nation, and at the same time extended beyond the ethnic nation. German Austria was no longer part of the nation-state – people on both sides came to terms with this fact surprisingly quickly. With the annexed Alsace Lorraine, the Danes in Schleswig, the Poles, the Musurians, the Kashubs in the Prussian East and the Ruhr, the nation-state encompassed population groups who spoke different languages, and no one knew whether it would be possible to assimilate them politically and culturally. Even amongst the German-speaking majority, large groups lived side by side like foreigners. Catholics and socialists were stigmatized as 'enemies of the Reich', with the active support of liberals. The new anti-Semitism disputed the right of Germans of Jewish faith or origin to the equal state citizenship they had only just won. If a German nation was ever going to be created in the German nation-state, these fronts would have to be dismantled. This task was not yet complete, but nor had it failed, when an apparent social peace broke out with the First World War, which ended with the revolutionary overthrow of the Kaiserreich.

The internal formation of the nation, which had progressed despite continuing and difficult internal conflicts, is all the more remarkable since it occurred at a time of dramatic social change in the Kaiserreich. By the eve of the World War, Germany had evolved into one of the leading industrial nations of the world.

Her population had increased massively by around 58 per cent, in tandem with rapid urbanization and the creation of industrial conurbations – processes which were characterized by huge population shifts, by a social restructuring which saw a rise in the proportion of workers and employees, and by changing ways of life and standards of living. States and municipalities were forced to undertake new forms of social provision, which did not anticipate the welfare state of the future, but which certainly helped it come into being, and which improved everyone's chances in life. Individuals could count on an increased life expectancy, and everyone benefited from social and cultural improvements in living standards – though they varied from stratum to stratum. These developments were accompanied by a profound politicization, which finally permeated the whole of society. This is reflected in the increases in election turnout from 51 per cent to approximately 85 per cent between 1871 and the last two pre-war Reichstag elections. It is also seen in the rising numbers of pressure groups and organizations of all kinds and in the women's movement. Increasing politicization also meant increasing organization in many spheres of life, including the employment market. Those who wanted to assert their interests, and to protect them on an institutional level, were forced to organize. The 'political mass market' (H. Rosenberg) reached an unprecedented scale. An important role fell to the parties in this respect – in Reich and state politics, and increasingly in munici-pal politics too. Whether this fundamental politicization would mean more democratic opportunities of participation for all, had yet to be decided, not least by the parties: by their reactions to the new conditions, by their programmes, their organizations and their methods of pursuing politics in general.

The parties' chances of playing an active role in politics in this dramatically changed society largely depended on the extent to which they were able to determine government policy. These opportunities varied considerably from state to state and at Reich level. Liberals had failed to introduce imperial ministries in 1867 and again in 1871. This effectively blocked the introduction of the parliamentary system in Reich politics for a long time, and the parties were kept in the ante-chamber of power. This had a major influence on the German parties and their inclination to place party programmes above political compromise. But it would be wrong to stereotype them as philosophical associations with fixed principles, incapable of change. Hopeful of winning political influence, they showed a remarkable capacity for change. This was particularly true of the liberals. Scholars disagree on the extent to which they were able to influence the trend towards the introduction of the parliamentary system, which undoubtedly existed in Reich politics. The chances of implementing a parliamentary system of government, which Bismarck was determined to prevent, improved only when Germany demanded its 'place in the sun' alongside the great colonial powers. *Weltpolitik* then became the unintentional motor of the dynamics of domestic political change. This is one of the great burdens, whose effects can hardly be over-estimated, under which the German parties had to pursue politics in the Wilhelmine era.

Broadly speaking, society changed from an agrarian to an industrial state. Attempts failed to synchronize these radical economic and social changes with the democratization of politics and society, and with the introduction of the parliamentary system into state and imperial politics. This is hardly surprising. We do not have to interpret this failure as a 'German *Sonderweg*'. It is probably more true to say that in England – the yardstick against which contemporary German history is usually measured – the introduction of the parliamentary system succeeded because it could be achieved before the masses entered politics. In the German Kaiserreich, in contrast, both came at the same time. The fundamental politicization of society, with its democratizing effects, coincided with the, albeit restrained, attempt to introduce the parliamentary system to political rule. Both trends did not have to be mutually dependent by any means, or even mutually supportive. The existence of a highly politicized public in an industrial class society, which could voice its political demands by means of a number of channels of influence, above all by means of democratic male suffrage in the Reich, by no means encouraged the 'established' parties to fight decisively for the parliamentary system. Many people accepted with relief the fiction of a neutral state which floated above the parties and their interests, or balanced them out. This seemed a more comfortable and less dangerous image in a society whose parties were largely involved in pre-political milieux, which restricted their opportunities for action and their ability to compromise.[3]

Nevertheless, the political landscape changed to allow far greater chances of political participation for all. The parties and the many new mass organizations played a major role here. Even if these associations did not adopt the aim of daring to achieve democracy, the opportunities to take part in the formation of political opinion grew with the numbers of associations, and the available organizational spectrum became more open. But, it did not become pluralistic in the sense that a convinced Social Democrat, for instance, or a Catholic who was loyal to the Church, could work together with liberals at a political or any other level. Co-operation of this kind did exist, but it caused offence, and so did not exist for very long. Or it took place in the less exposed cultural or educational spheres. The capacity for pluralism of the great 'social moral milieu' (R. M. Lepsius), a capacity which was still very limited even at the end of the Kaiserreich, despite all the changes that had occurred, inevitably made the democratization of society and the introduction of the parliamentary system difficult. Possibly, there is an important difference here between developments in England and in Germany. How far the German liberals were ready and able to work towards a pluralism which transcended milieux, and to make use of the trends which worked in this direction, will be addressed below.

As little research has been carried out on this subject as has been undertaken on the influence of cultural processes on the 'liberal milieu', which had never been sharply defined, and had always been unstable. Above all during its Wilhelmine phase, the German Kaiserreich underwent profound cultural changes. The clearly differentiated cultural horizons which had formerly characterized society began to level out as a result of improved school education – illiteracy rates were now almost insignificant – the 'communications revolution', which was linked to the massive population shifts mentioned above, and as a result of urbanization and the explosion in disseminated reading matter (papers, periodicals and books). At the same time, however, representative culture and experimental culture diverged more strongly than ever before. The educated citizen, who had always been the liberal *par excellence*, sacrificed an important part of his social self-image and his sense of identity, when art increasingly began to be presented as that which artists called art, and not that which was immediately recognizable as art by the educated public. This disintegration of cultural homogeneity amongst the educated is one of the many radical changes which accompanied the German Kaiserreich on its path into 'the

Table 4 Proportion of votes (I), number of votes (II) and percentage of seats (III) in the Reichstag elections of 1871–1912 (I and III in %; II in millions)

		National Liberals	Left Liberals*	Liberals overall	Conservatives	Free Conservatives	Conservatives overall	Centre Party	Social Democs.	Election turnout/voters
1871	I	30.1	9.3	46.6	14.1	8.9	23.0	18.6	3.2	51.0
	II	1.17	0.36	1.81	0.55	0.35	0.90	0.72	0.12	3.90
	III	32.7	12.3	52.9	14.9	9.7	24.6	16.5	0.5	
1874	I	29.7	9.0	39.7	6.9	7.2	14.1	27.9	6.8	61.2
	II	1.54	0.47	2.07	0.36	0.38	0.74	1.45	0.35	5.22
	III	39.0	12.6	52.4	5.5	8.3	13.8	22.9	2.3	
1877	I	27.2	8.5	38.2	9.7	7.9	17.6	24.8	9.1	60.6
	II	1.47	0.46	2.07	0.53	0.43	0.96	1.34	0.49	5.42
	III	32.2	9.8	45.3	10.1	9.6	19.7	23.4	3.0	
1878	I	23.1	7.8	33.6	13.0	13.6	26.6	23.1	7.6	63.4
	II	1.33	0.45	1.94	0.75	0.79	1.54	1.33	0.44	5.78
	III	24.9	7.4	34.8	14.9	14.4	29.3	23.7	2.3	
1881	I	14.7	23.1	37.8	16.3	7.4	23.7	23.2	6.1	56.3
	II	0.75	1.18	1.93	0.83	0.38	1.21	1.18	0.31	5.12
	III	11.8	29.0	40.8	12.6	7.1	19.7	25.2	3.0	
1884	I	17.6	19.3	36.9	15.2	6.9	22.1	22.6	9.7	60.6
	II	1.00	1.09	2.09	0.86	0.39	1.25	1.28	0.55	5.68
	III	12.8	18.7	31.5	19.6	7.1	26.7	24.9	6.0	
1887	I	22.2	14.1	36.3	15.2	9.8	25.0	20.1	10.1	77.5
	II	1.68	1.06	2.74	1.15	0.74	1.89	1.52	0.76	7.57
	III	24.9	8.1	33.0	20.2	10.3	30.5	24.7	2.8	

Year										
1890	I	16.3	18.0	34.3	12.4	6.7	19.1	18.6	19.7	71.6
	II	1.18	1.31	2.49	0.90	0.48	1.38	1.34	1.43	7.27
	III	10.6	19.1	29.7	18.4	5.0	23.4	26.7	8.8	
1893	I	13.0	14.8	27.8	13.5	5.7	19.2	19.1	23.3	72.5
	II	1.00	1.09	2.09	1.04	0.44	1.48	1.47	1.79	7.70
	III	13.4	12.1	25.5	18.1	7.1	25.2	24.2	11.1	
1898	I	12.5	11.1	23.6	11.1	4.4	15.5	18.8	27.2	68.1
	II	0.97	0.86	1.83	0.86	0.34	1.20	1.46	2.11	7.79
	III	11.6	12.4	24.0	14.1	5.8	19.9	25.7	14.1	
1903	I	13.8	9.3	23.1	10.0	3.5	13.5	19.7	31.7	76.1
	II	1.31	0.88	2.19	0.95	0.33	1.28	1.88	3.01	9.53
	III	12.8	9.1	21.9	13.6	5.3	18.9	25.2	20.4	
1907	I	14.5	10.9	25.4	9.4	4.2	13.4	19.4	29.0	84.7
	II	1.64	1.23	2.87	1.06	0.47	1.53	2.18	3.26	11.30
	III	13.6	12.4	26.0	15.1	6.0	21.1	26.4	10.8	
1912	I	13.6	12.3	25.9	9.2	3.0	12.2	16.4	34.8	84.9
	II	1.66	1.50	3.16	1.13	0.37	1.49	2.00	4.25	12.26
	III	11.3	10.6	21.9	10.8	3.5	14.3	22.8	27.7	

* Left Liberals include the *Deutsche Volkspartei*. The column 'Liberals overall' also includes the *Liberale Reichspartei*, a party close to the National Liberals, which existed until the 4th Reichstag.

Source: G. A. Ritter and M. Niehuss, *Wahlgeschichtliches Arbeitsbuch* (Munich, 1980) pp. 38–42.

modern age'. No political grouping was more profoundly affected by this challenge than the liberal parties. For they had always seen themselves as the political representatives of cultural progress. When we talk about liberalism in the Kaiserreich, we are talking about an extremely complex subject, which had its centre in the liberal parties, on whom we will now focus, but was not restricted to them.

Parties, Voters, Members, Pressure Groups: The 'Liberal Milieu', 1871–1918

If one examines the elections to the Reichstag, the parliaments and the chambers, the history of liberalism in the Kaiserreich seems to be an almost continuous history of decline. In the first two elections, the liberal parties together won an absolute majority in the Reichstag, with 52 per cent of all seats. After that, their influence decreased. By the Wilhelmine era they represented less than a quarter of all deputies (Table 4). They suffered a similar loss of seats in a number of state parliaments. Between 1874 and 1913 in Prussia, for example, their share of seats fell from almost 57 per cent to around 25 per cent, and in Bavaria from almost a half to a fifth of all seats. They were better able to assert themselves in Saxony or Baden, although there too they suffered losses (Table 6).

The fact that there was a decline in the liberals' share of the vote, or in the number of seats they held, did not mean that absolute numbers of votes cast for liberals had decreased. On the contrary, in 1912 liberals received approximately 53 per cent more votes than they had in 1874,[4] which meant that they had roughly kept pace with population growth (58 per cent), and were not far behind the increase in those entitled to vote (69 per cent). But election turnout rose rapidly during the same period, increasing by 135 per cent. It is here that we see the effects of the above-mentioned fundamental politicization which took place during the Kaiserreich, and which benefited Social Democracy above all (Table 5). As the population and, more importantly, election turnout increased only the Social Democrats were able to increase their pool of voters. They were followed, after a large interval, by the conservatives, whose increased votes between 1874 and 1912 exceeded population growth by almost double,

Table 5 Population growth, rise in election turnout and in number of votes by party for the Reichstag elections of 1871–1912 (in %)

	Population growth	Election turnout	National Liberals	Left Liberals	Liberals overall	Conservatives	Free Conservatives	Conservatives overall	Centre Party	Social Democracy
1871–4	2	34	32	31	14	−34	9	−18	101	192
1874–7	4	4	−4	−2	0	47	13	30	−8	40
1877–8	1	7	−9	−2	−6	41	84	60	−1	−10
1878–81	3	−11	−44	162	0	11	−52	−21	−11	−29
1881–4	2	11	33	−8	8	4	3	3	8	77
1884–7	3	31	68	−3	31	34	90	51	19	38
1887–90	4	−4	−30	24	−9	−22	−35	−27	−12	88
1890–3	3	6	−15	−17	−16	16	−8	7	10	25
1893–8	7	1	−3	−21	−12	−17	−23	−19	0	18
1898–1903	8	22	35	2	20	10	−3	7	29	43
1903–7	6	19	25	40	31	12	42	19	16	8
1907–12	7	8	1	22	10	7	−21	−3	−8	30
1874–1912	58	135	8	219	53	213	−3	101*	38	1114

* 1871 or 1877–1912: 55% (in 1874 the Conservatives suffered their worst election results of the Kaiserreich).

Source: Table 4; G. Hohorst, J. Kocka and G. A. Ritter, *Sozialgeschichtliches Arbeitsbuch,* vol. 2 (Munich, 1975) 27f. (the average population for each year is given).

Table 6 Professions of National Liberal Deputies in the Reichstag and individual state *Landtage*, 1871–1914 (I), and in the Chambers of Deputies of Bavaria, 1881–1917 (II), Saxony, 1887–1917 (III), Württemberg, 1891–1917 (IV), Baden, 1871–1917 (V), Hesse, 1872–1917 (VI) and Prussia, 1867–1917 (VII)

	I		II		III		IV		V		VI		VII	
	No.	%	No.	%	No	%	No.	%	No.	%	No.	%	No.	%
1. Judicial officials	274	12.5	16	9.5	3	3	2	2.7	21	7.7	12	8.4	132	20.1
2. Administrative officials	261	12	11	6.5	1	1	9	12	45	16.5	17	12	87	13.2
3. Municipal officials	255	11.7	24	14.3	8	7.9	15	20	66	24.3	18	12.7	54	8.2
4. University profs.	71	3.2	2	1.2	1	1	3	4	6	2.2	1	0.7	22	3.3
5. Lawyers, notaries	175	8	4	2.4	7	6.9	3	4	17	6.2	18	12.7	46	7
6. Doctors	33	1.5	2	1.2	–	–	–	–	6	2.2	1	0.7	9	1.4
7. Writers	18	0.8	–	–	–	–	–	–	1	0.4	1	0.7	2	0.3
8. Clergymen	32	1.5	4	2.4	–	–	6	8	1	0.4	3	2.1	13	2

Table 6 continued.

	I No.	I %	II No.	II %	III No	III %	IV No.	IV %	V No.	V %	VI No.	VI %	VII No.	VII %
9. Teachers	63	2.9	10	6	4	4	–	–	9	3.3	5	3.5	18	2.7
10. Industrialists	253	11.6	18	10.7	36	35.6	7	9.3	25	9.2	13	9.2	55	8.4
11. Merchants	112	5.1	4	2.4	18	17.8	4	5.3	17	6.2	10	7.1	27	4.1
12. Traders, craftsmen	116	5.3	13	7.7	12	11.9	5	6.7	31	11.4	8	5.6	15	2.3
13. Employees	37	1.7	2	1.2	1	1	–	–	3	1.1	–	–	12	1.8
14. Assoc. employees	23	1.1	–	–	3	3	–	–	–	–	3	2.1	8	1.2
15. Farmers	345	15.8	42	25	5	4.9	11	14.7	11	4.1	25	17.6	127	19.3
16. Standesherren	29	1.3	7	4.2	–	–	7	9.3	–	–	1	0.7	5	0.8
17. No prof., retired officers, rentiers	85	3.9	9	5.3	2	2	3	4	13	4.8	6	4.2	26	3.9
18. Workers	2	0.1	–	–	–	–	–	–	–	–	–	–	–	–
Total: 1–18	2184	100	168	100	101	100	75	100	272	100	142	100	658	100

Source: H. Kalkoff (ed.), Nationalliberale Parlamentarier 1867–1917 des Reichstages und der Einzellandtage (Berlin, 1917) vol. XI, pp. 164, 273, 305, 339, 370, 406.

but who did not achieve an increase in election turnout. The Centre Party (*Zentrum*) was least successful in the battle for new voters. Not only did its growth, at 38 per cent, clearly lag behind that of the liberals (53 per cent), but, given the fact that the population and the degree of politicization had grown much faster than this figure, it amounted to a decline. Why is it then that contemporaries and historians alike nevertheless refer to the stability of the Centre Party and to the erosion of the liberal parties?

The Catholic population emerged fully mobilized into politics as early as the second Reichstag election (1874). More than 80 per cent of all Catholic voters cast their votes for the Centre Party, which now achieved its best result in the history of the Kaiserreich, in terms of its share of the vote (Table 4). Although the political binding force of the Catholic social milieu then began to decline, the Catholic church proved to be strong enough, despite all the conflicts of interests amongst its voters, to hold together the Centre Party as a party of Catholicism which transcended class-based or social strata. The remarkable stability of the Centre Party was also fostered by the electoral system, which rewarded parties with regional focuses and rural strongholds.

The liberal parties had no such mainstays on which they could rely. In contrast to the Centre Party and to the Social Democrats, they were not anchored in stable or still-growing ideologically bound and firmly established organizational 'social moral milieux'.[5] Protestantism was ill-suited to this. Its binding force declined to a greater degree than that of Catholicism under the pressure of secularizing forces. Politically it was open, above all to conservatism, but also to the imperialistic nationalism which developed during the Wilhelmine era in the mass organizations, which, in contrast to the national movement of the era of the *Reichsgründung*, was no longer the preserve of the liberal milieu. In comparison to the Centre Party and to the Social Democrats, but also to the conservatives, liberals were independent and sub-culturally homeless. Whilst this made them particularly open to new developments, it also meant that they were extremely vulnerable to them. Their voters shared no philosophy which could act as a shield to deflect the insecurity created by rapid social change. The Centre Party and the Social Democrats, on the other hand, imparted a certainty of the future which could be further reinforced if the present seemed more like a vale of tears.

The liberals' great vision of the future, on the other hand, had been fulfilled with the *Reichsgründung*. Their vision lived in the past, for national unity could only be invoked as a force which would guarantee progress while it was still being striven for. Once it had been achieved, new great aims were required. The programme of the liberal consolidation of the Imperial Constitution held only until 1878, when the liberals were forced to recognize that Reich politics was possible without them too. They now began the permanent search for new tasks which could foster unity. Their attempts to continue the *Kulturkampf*, and their turning to *Weltpolitik* were part of this. Yet liberals could not claim to be the sole representatives of these aims. Once the national idea had been fulfilled, all their ideas on the mobilization of society were unsuccessful.

The political sensitivity of liberal voters is revealed in the rapid changes from vote gain to vote loss in the Reichstag elections; in no other party were developments so inconsistent (Table 6). Without 'the armour of a philosophy', they reacted particularly sensitively to political change. This is also reflected in liberalism's fragmentation into a number of frequently short-lived parties (Fig. 1).

Liberal losses of seats in the Kaiserreich appear dramatic – as we have said, they declined from an absolute majority to around one-fifth of seats – but was support for liberalism amongst the population unstable? Was it damaged by the organizational splintering?

If the anchoring of parties in the society of the Kaiserreich is measured according to whether they were able to maintain or expand their share of the votes between 1871 and 1912, the liberals appear to be the most unstable of the parties. But this is an inappropriate, if frequently adopted yardstick. In the era of the *Reichsgründung* they had not simply been one party amongst many, but had embodied a movement with which all those who hoped for a *kleindeutsch* nation-state could identify. This went beyond convinced liberals. Liberalism had become synonymous with the national movement. During the first decade of the *Reichsgründung*, the liberal parties were still able to profit from this association. But as the full party spectrum of the Kaiserreich emerged for the first time in organizational and programmatic terms, the former front – for or against the foundation of a *kleindeutsch*-Prussian nation-state – gave way to other, more

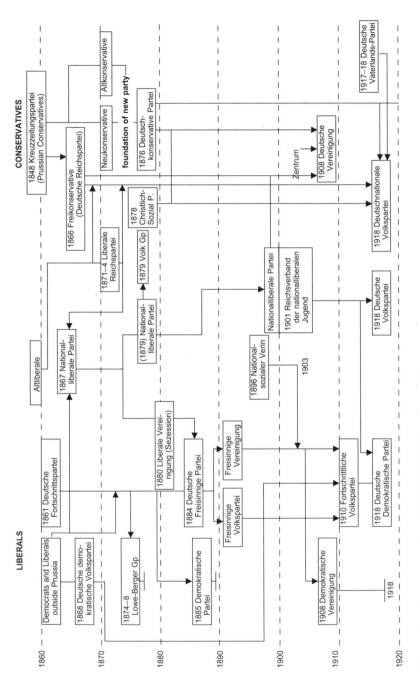

Figure 1 German parties, 1860–1920: Liberals and Conservatives

differentiated, fronts. This fanning out of the old front necessarily implied losses for liberalism, for it now declined from the
national movement to one party amongst many, and it had still not
found new aims to replace the great aim of the past. In this respect,
the losses suffered by the liberal parties in the post-1871 elections
signalled a process of normalization, which was completed towards
the end of the first decade after the *Reichsgründung*. Their share
of the vote levelled off at around a third by 1890, the end of the
Bismarck era and a central marker in the development of the
Kaiserreich. It is against this marker that the liberals' successes
and failures should be measured, not against the exceptional
results of the exceptional period around the *Reichsgründung*. By
1912 they had lost a further ten percentage points, the conservatives had lost slightly more and the Centre Party's share of the
vote had decreased by around 7 per cent during the same
period. Social Democracy had gained the same percentage share
of votes as was lost by the other large parties (Table 4).

If we take into account the exceptional situation in party
history during the formation of the nation-state, the line of
development of the liberal election results in the Kaiserreich is
put into perspective. Its decline was no steeper than that of the
other middle-class parties. The image of a dramatic decline in
the liberal pool of voters compared with the other parties only
arises if we observe it from the exaggerated and untenable
pedestal of the phase of the *Reichsgründung*. If we dispense with
this standpoint, the liberals proved to be surprisingly stable for
parties with no sub-culturally fixed 'camp', for their voting
numbers actually kept pace with population growth.

Liberalism's fragmentation into many political parties certainly
weakened its ability to assert itself in parliament and against the
leadership of the Reich. But it probably limited the erosion of
the liberal pool of voters. No studies exist on the shifting of voters
in the Kaiserreich – the available data would probably not allow
an analysis of this kind to be made[6] – but the data we do have
suggest that the party political fanning out of liberalism allowed
disaffected liberal floating voters to remain within the liberal
party spectrum. For frequent regroupings of the share of votes
were seen in this spectrum, but no decline in the relatively stable
overall circle of regular liberal voters.

When liberalism lost its exceptional position as the core of the
national movement during the so-called 'internal' or 'second

Reichsgründung' at the end of the seventies, and was forced to come to terms with the role of a normal party, it was the *Reichgründungspartei par excellence* which paid the greatest price. The National Liberals' share of the votes more than halved during the first decade of the Kaiserreich, whilst that of the Left Liberals more than doubled between 1874 and 1881. After that, the trend tended to level out the balance of power in liberalism as a whole – though large swings were seen from election to election (cf. Tables 4 and 6), which would certainly suggest that liberal floating voters remained within the liberal party spectrum.

If we compare the start and end points of election trends in the Kaiserreich, it is clear that it was the parties with clear and definite positions who won the battle for voters in the long term. This is true both of the liberals and of the conservatives. Whilst in 1874 and 1912, approximately similar numbers of votes were cast for National Liberals and Free Conservatives, votes cast for Left Liberals rose by 219 per cent and for the German Conservatives by 213 per cent. The liberal left wing and the conservative right therefore far exceeded the increases in election turnout (135 per cent) and in population growth (58 per cent) (cf. Tables 4 and 6).

Many different electoral systems and suffrage regulations existed at Reich, state and municipal level in the Kaiserreich.[7] As a rule of thumb, it is true to say that the lower the level, the smaller the degree of democratization was. Federalism therefore meant that citizens and parties did not have equal opportunities for political participation. The Social Democrats suffered most under these conditions, while the other large parties generally profited from it. This explains their reluctance to see the liberalization of suffrage in the states and the municipalities. This is also true of the liberals, even for the Left Liberals, whose support for a reform of the class suffrage system in the states, and above all in Prussia, was only half-hearted, and who did not include the issue of municipal suffrage in their list of reforms at all.[8] Unequal suffrage regulations created a decrease in democracy from the national to the municipal level. This played a significant role in the fact that, in contrast to England, workers in Germany only came to see the municipality as a sphere for political activity at a relatively late stage. From the beginning, the programmes and practice of the German socialist workers' movement focused on Reich politics. This helped the liberals, who were able to maintain their leading position in municipal politics for an especially long time,[9] but it damaged them in the sphere of Reich politics, where Social Democracy became their most bitter, and increasingly successful, rival for the urban voter. The parties which enjoyed the greatest success in the Reichstag elections were those with regional strongholds, preferably in the countryside, and those which were able to form alliances with other parties. There were two reasons for this. Firstly, the division into constituencies had not been adapted to population growth and urbanization. Secondly, the electoral system, according to which it was decided who had the absolute majority in a constituency, led to an increase in the number of 'run-off' elections, in which only those candidates with the highest numbers of votes took part. Those who were able to form alliances saw their chances of success improve.

Of all the parties, Social Democrats and National Liberals took part in 'run-off elections' most often between 1871 and 1912. But whilst the Social Democratic candidates won only 27.4 per cent of ballots, the National Liberals succeeded in 52.7 per cent of cases. The Left Liberals fared even better. They won 79.5 per cent of 'run-off' elections. Closely followed by the National Liberals, they were also most dependent on winning 'run-off' elections. The Centre Party was the least so. This is a reflection of the different degrees to which the social milieux in which the parties were anchored were 'closed', and the extent to which they had regional strongholds. Parties which were 'closed' in terms of milieu and region, were less dependent on 'run-off' elections than 'open' parties.

Once again it is clear that even during the Kaiserreich, the liberal parties and the Centre Party came closest to being popular parties which transcended all milieux. But in both cases this openness extended only as far as the frontier of religion – Catholicism remained closed to all non-Catholic parties – and the social range of liberalism decreased to the extent that Social Democracy grew. Whilst in 1890 the majority of 'run-off' elections had been between National Liberals and Left Liberals, by 1912 Social Democracy had become the liberals' keenest competitor for the urban voter.

Liberalism's relatively low attachment to a milieu also becomes clear when we break down the electoral successes of the great parties according to the commercial structure of the Reichstag constituencies and the size of the municipalities. In 1912 the conservatives won almost two-thirds of their seats in over-whelmingly agrarian constituencies, and the Social Democrats approximately 96 per cent of theirs in commercial–industrial constituencies. But the electoral success of the liberal parties depended to a lesser degree on commercial structure. This is also true of the size of the municipalities: the liberal parties' share of the votes was more equally distributed than others over all municipality sizes, although they too had their focal points. National Liberals saw their best results in Reichstag elections in the province of Hanover and in the Grand Duchies of Baden and Hesse. Left Liberals had their strongest bastions in cities such as Königsberg, Danzig, Stettin, Posen, Kiel, Hanover, Frankfurt and Strasbourg, but not in the cities of Saxony, Bavaria, Würt-temberg and Baden, where they came up against both the dominant Social Democrats and strong National Liberal parties. Before 1910, when Left Liberals united to form the *Fortschrittliche Volkspartei* (Progressive People's Party), they also had to compete with the small *Deutsche Volkspartei* (German People's Party). This Left-Liberal wing, to which the middle-class democratic move-ment which had been significant before the *Reichsgründung* had now dwindled, was able to assert itself only in the south, above all in Württemberg. But even at the peak of its success (1893), it had only eleven seats.

Although the Left Liberals had their main focus in cities, compared with the voters of non-liberal parties, their voters were more widely distributed throughout municipalities of all sizes. In Pomerania they were even able to assert themselves as the conservatives' major rivals in the countryside. In Mecklenburg-Schwerin, too, in the Reichstag elections of 1912 they won shares of the votes of between 20 and 40 per cent in the countryside and in small towns with populations of up to 10 000.

At Reich level, therefore, it is the liberals of all parties who could more readily be described as unifying parties – in terms of the social and geographical profile of their electorate and also in terms of the number of constituencies in which they fielded candidates. For one of the peculiarities of the Reichstag elections in the Kaiserreich is the fact that not all parties were represented by candidates in all constituencies. This meant that fundamentally different two-party constellations existed in many constituencies, which came together in the Reichstag in a multi-party system.[10] Only with the increasing politicization of the population, and with increasing party organization, did the number of competing parties increase in the constituencies. Even in 1912, the liberal parties as a group nominated candidates in more constituencies (447) than all other parties, followed by the Social Democrats (399) and the Centre Party (199). But their lead throughout the Reich had grown smaller since 1871 – a significant reflection of the fact that the liberals had lost their exceptional position in the era of the *Reichsgründung* as *the* party-political embodiment of the national movement. One reason for this loss – it is important to stress this again – was the normalization in political life. A multi-faceted party spectrum emerged in place of the politically diverse national blocs of the era of the *Reichsgründung*. How the liberals reacted to this in their political objectives will be examined below.

First, however, we will examine the professional composition of the parliamentary parties. Between 1871 and 1912, the National Liberals suffered heavy losses, and the Left Liberals considerable fluctuations, in the numbers of the Reichstag seats they held. This has already been described. These shifts coincided with a significant change in the professional make-up of the liberal parliamentary parties (Table 7). The proportion of civil servants decreased in all parties, with the exception of the Centre Party, but it was most striking in the liberal parties. Amongst civil servant deputies there was a clear party political division between administrative and judicial civil servants. Administrative civil servants tended to support the conservative parties, whilst the liberals, and indeed the Centre Party, had more judges in their ranks. The freelance professions, amongst whom lawyers always represented the majority, were also concentrated amongst the liberals, above all on their left wing.

The German Reichstag was an educated parliament. This is particularly true of the liberal parliamentary parties: more than 80 per cent of their members had attended a *Gymnasium*; almost two-thirds had studied at university; and almost a third held doctorates.[11] But amongst National and Left Liberals, the proportion of those who were employed in typical 'educated middle-class' professions decreased from approximately two-thirds in 1874 to around 50 per cent in 1912. This was linked to the overall decline in academics in the civil service outlined above. The proportion of members of independent professions rose. This shift, and the decline in the number of civil servant

Table 7 Reichstag Deputies: professions and parties, 1874–1912 (%)

	1874					1878					1884				
	NL	LL	FK	K	Z	NL	LL	FK	K	Z	NL	LL	FK	K	Z
1. Admin. officials	14.5	4.2	29.4	21.7	10.1	10.7	3	35	21.9	7.2	4	4.5	18.5	21.8	4.7
2. Judicial officials	14.5	12.5	5.9	–	16.2	16.1	9.1	6.7	4.7	17.5	10	7.5	–	3.8	16
3. Municipal admin.	6.6	6.2	–	–	1	4.5	3	3.3	–	–	12	3	–	–	–
1.–3.	35.6	22.9	35.3	21.7	27.3	31.3	15.1	45	26.6	24.7	26	15	18.5	25.6	20.7
4. Professors, *Gymnasium* teachers, archivists	11.2	10.4	2.9	–	8.1	8	21.2	1.7	–	8.2	12	6	3.7	–	5.7
5. Lawyers	12.5	16.7	–	–	5	8.9	21.2	–	1.6	6.2	2	16.4	–	1.3	5.7
6. Other indep. profs.	0.6	6.2	–	–	–	3.6	3	–	–	–	8	6	–	–	–
7. Clergymen	–	–	–	–	15.1	0.9	–	–	–	16.5	–	–	–	1.3	14.1
8. Writers, editors	2.6	8.3	–	–	1	0.9	6.1	–	–	2.1	2	7.5	–	2.6	0.9
4.–8.	26.9	41.6	2.9	–	29.2	22.3	51.5	1.7	1.6	33	24	35.9	3.7	5.2	26.4
9. Employers: indep. and managers	11.8	10.4	8.8	–	4	25.9	15.2	10	4.7	6.2	32	14.9	22.2	2.6	7.5
10. (a) *Rittergutsbesitzer*	10.5	10.4	38.2	69.6	19.2	3.6	3	30	59.4	19.6	2	4.5	48.1	51.3	20.7
(b) Other landowners	12.5	14.6	5.9	4.4	13.1	12.5	3	6.7	3.1	12.4	14	16.4	3.7	9	13.2
Mandates	152	51	34	21	91	98	29	60	59	93	50	67	28	78	99
Total cases	152	48	34	23	99	112	33	60	64	97	50	67	27	78	106

	1890					1903					1912				
	NL	LL	FK	K	Z	NL	LL	FK	K	Z	NL	LL	FK	K	Z
1. Admin. officials	4.8	6	30	17.8	3.7	6.2	–	16.7	11.5	5.9	8.9	–	15.4	4.4	3.3
2. Judicial officials	9.5	4.5	5	6.3	17.8	2.1	6.4	–	1.9	17.8	4.4	24	7.7	6.7	15.5
3. Muncipal admin.	4.8	6	–	–	3.7	4.2	3.2	5.5	–	1	2.2	2.4	–	2.2	–
1.–3.	19.1	16.5	35	24.5	25.2	12.5	9.6	22.2	13.4	24.7	15.5	4.8	23.1	13.3	18.8
4. Professors, *Gymnasium* teachers, archivists	4.8	8.9	–	–	4.7	6.2	6.4	11.1	–	3	6.7	9.8	7.7	–	7.8
5. Lawyers	4.8	10.4	–	2.7	4.7	4.2	16.1	–	1.9	7.9	20	29.3	7.7	2.2	6.7
6. Other indep. profs.	–	4.5	5	–	–	4.2	6.4	–	–	1	–	2.4	–	–	–
7. Clergymen	–	1.5	–	1.4	13.1	–	3.2	5.5	–	17.8	2.2	2.4	7.7	–	11.1
8. Writers, editors	2.4	7.5	–	1.4	0.9	2.4	12.9	–	–	4	4.4	7.3	–	2.2	3.3
4.–8.	12	32.8	5	5.5	23.4	17	45	16.6	1.9	33.7	33.3	51.2	23.1	4.4	28.9
9. Employers: indep. and managers	40.5	26.9	25	4.1	10.3	33.3	32.3	11.1	3.8	7.9	15.6	19.3	–	4.4	8.9
10. (a) *Rittergutsbesitzer*	9.5	1.5	30	47.9	17.8	12.5	–	27.7	50	4	6.7	2.4	7.7	53.3	5.5
(b) Other landowners	16.7	11.9	5	8.2	11.2	22.9	6.4	22.2	23.1	16.9	17.8	7.3	30.7	22.2	15.5
Mandates	41	64	20	71	106	50	31	18	52	100	44	42	13	45	88
Total cases	42	67	20	73	107	48	31	18	52	101	45	41	13	45	90

* LL = *Fortschrittspartei, Freisinnige Volkspartei, Freisinnige Vereinigung* and *Fortschrittliche Volkspartei.*

Source: W. Kremer, *Der soziale Aufbau der Parteien des Deutschen Reichstages von 1871–1918* (Emsdetten, 1934) pp. 4, 8, 13, 28, 46.

deputies, is also revealed in the increasing proportions of employers and senior employees in the liberal parliamentary parties. This reflects the increasing 'economization of politics', which is also expressed in the growing importance of pressure group organizations for political life and for the parties.[12] This trend should not be exaggerated, however. As we will see, although their representatives increasingly worked together with employers in the parliamentary parties and the party committees, the liberal parties did not become parliamentary agencies of economic associations.

In comparison to the history of the development of the Reichstag, that of the individual state parliaments has been neglected by scholars.[13] This is all the more regrettable since, despite the advancing 'nationalization' of politics, the individual states retained at least some of the traditions which had evolved historically, and they did so consciously. The tension between the relative importance of the Reich and the state is manifested in the rivalries between the cult of the Kaiser and the cult of the individual state ruler. Faith in the Kaiser was clearly the greater bond of loyalty, effective at mass level, but individual state traditions and loyalties had by no means disappeared.[14] The politics of the Kaiserreich had strong individual-state and regional colours. This is also true of the parties and of the parliamentary groupings. South German Social Democracy differed from its Prussian equivalent. Many south German liberals regarded their north German, and especially their Prussian counterparts, as doctrinaire. Many Württembergers, from the King to the liberals and democrats, also shared the belief that Württemberg was politically 'further advanced' than Prussia, and embodied a higher level 'of political culture'.[15]

An analysis of the professional composition of the parliamentary parties in the Reichstag and in the parliaments and chambers confirms the image of federal diversity, which must have influenced parties with less adherence to a particular milieu, as was the case with the liberals. As a rule, the proportion of employers was lower in the chambers and parliaments than in the Reichstag. Highly industrialized Saxony represented an exception amongst the large states. In the Wilhelmine era, industrialists, merchants and small businessmen made up two-thirds of the National Liberal parliamentary party in Saxony; a considerably higher proportion than in the Reichstag (cf. Tables 5 and 8).[16] In

Table 8   Deputies by parliamentary party in the Chambers of Deputies of some individual states

(a)   The Prussian House of Deputies

	1874		1883		1894		1904		1913	
	No.	%	No.	%	No.	%	No.	%	No.	%
National Liberals	174	40.5	69	15.9	90	20.8	77	17.8	73	16.5
Left Liberals	70	16.3	57	13.2	20	4.6	33	7.6	40	9.0
Free Conservs.	34	7.9	58	13.4	63	14.5	61	14.1	54	12.2
Conservatives	32	7.4	118	27.2	142	32.8	143	33	149	33.6
Centre	88	20.5	98	22.6	95	21.9	97	22.4	103	23.3
Poles	17	3.9	18	4.2	17	3.9	13	3	12	2.7
Others	15	3.5	15	3.5	6	1.4	9	2.1	12	2.7
Total	**430**	**100**	**433**	**100**	**433**	**100**	**433**	**100**	**443**	**100**

Source: B. Mann, *Handbuch für das preussische Abgeordnetenhaus, 1867–1918* (Düsseldorf, 1988).

(b)   The Bavarian *Landtag*

	1875		1881		1893		1905		1912	
	No.	%	No.	%	No.	%	No.	%	No.	%
Liberals	77	49.4	70	44.0	67	41.6	23	14.5	30	18.4
Volkspartei	–	–	–	–	1	0.6	2	1.3	–	–
Centre*	79	50.6	85	53.5	74	46.0	102	64.1	87	53.4
Conservatives	–	–	4	2.5	3	1.9	4	2.5	8	4.9
BBB, BdL†	–	–	–	–	9	5.6	16	10.1	8	4.9
Social Democrats	–	–	–	–	5	3.1	12	7.5	30	18.4
No Party	–	–	–	–	2	1.2	–	–	–	–
Total	**156**	**100**	**159**	**100**	**161**	**100**	**159**	**100**	**163**	**100**

*   Centre: Before 1887 *Bayerische Patriotenpartei*, (1881–7) joint party with the Conservatives.

†   BBB = *Bayerischer Bauernbund* (Bavarian Farmers' League), BdL = *Bund der Landwirte* (Agrarian League) (1912 includes 3 seats for the *Deutscher Bauernbund*, German Farmers' League).

Source: D. Thränhardt, *Wahlen und politische Strukturen in Bayern, 1848–1953* (Düsseldorf, 1973) p. 348.

Table 8 continued.

(c) The Saxon *Landtag*

	1873		1881		1893		1905		1909	
	No.	%	No.	%	No.	%	No.	%	No.	%
National Liberals	17	21.3	14	17.5	14	17.1	23	28.1	28	30.8
Liberals	20	25.0	2	2.5	–	–	1	1.2	–	–
Progress Party	5	6.3	15	18.7	8	9.8	–	–	–	–
Deutsch-freisinnige Partei	–	–	–	–	1	1.2	2	2.4	8	8.8
Conservatives	38	47.5	45	56.3	43	52.4	54	65.9	24	26.3
Social Democrats	–	–	4	5	14	17.1	1	1.2	25	27.5
Others	–	–	–	–	2	2.4	1	1.2	6	6.6
Total	**80**	**100**	**80**	**100**	**82**	**100**	**82**	**100**	**91**	**100**

Source: G. A. Ritter and M. Niehuss, *Wahlgeschichtliches Arbeitsbuch* (Munich, 1980) p. 172.

(d) The Hamburg *Bürgerschaft**

	1895		1904		1907		1910		1913	
	No.	%	No.	%	No.	%	No.	%	No.	%
Left	60	37.5	48	30	37	23.1	37	23.1	39	24.4
Centre Left	55	34.4	44	27.5	37	23.1	35	21.9	29	18.1
Right	45	28.1	52	32.5	43	26.9	38	23.7	40	25.0
United Liberals	–	–	–	–	23	14.4	29	18.1	30	18.7
Soc. Democrats	–	–	13	8.1	19	11.9	20	12.5	20	12.5
Total	**160**	**100**	**160**	**98.1**	**160**	**99.4**	**160**	**99.3**	**160**	**98.7**

* Parliamentary party described according to seating. The Left are closest to liberals. The United Liberals formed in opposition to the two-class suffrage system introduced in 1906.

Source: H. W. Eckardt, *Privilegien und Parlament* (Hamburg, 1980) p. 47.

contrast to the Reichstag, small employers determined the image of Saxony's Second Chamber. This is even more true of Bavaria, with its wide spectrum of economically independent men, who between 1887 and 1912 ranged from a miller and small merchant to two big businessmen, both of whom belonged to the liberal parliamentary party.[17]

Table 8 continued.

(e) **The Württemberg Chamber of Deputies**

Seats	1895		1900		1906		1912	
	No.	%	No.	%	No.	%	No.	%
National Liberals	13	18.6	11	15.7	13	14.1	10	10.9
Left Liberals	31	44.3	27	38.6	24	26.1	19	20.6
Conservatives	3	4.3	6	8.6	15	16.3	20	21.7
Centre	18	25.7	18	25.7	25	27.2	26	28.3
Social Democracy	2	2.9	5	7.1	15	16.3	17	18.5
Total	**67**	**95.8**	**67**	**95.7**	**92**	**100**	**92**	**100**

Votes (%)	1876	1882	1889	1895	1900	1906
National Liberals	57.5	57.5	63.9	24.0	19.6	14.5
Left Liberals	18.9	35.0	31.1	32.5	24.6	22.3
Conservatives	2.5		0.3	2.8	9.7	14.8
Centre	15.2			23.4	24.2	26.4
Social Democracy	1.3	1.4	4.3	10.9	18.7	21.8

Notes: Only the 70 elected deputies are recorded whose number rose to 92
following the electoral reforms of 1906. Of these, 69 were elected in direct
elections and 23 in proportional elections.

National Liberals = *Deutsche Partei*, 1876–89, including the *Landespartei* or
Mittelpartei, which was close to the government.

Left Liberals = *Volkspartei* and other left-wing parties.

Conservatives = 1900–6 including the Farmers' League.

Before 1895 classification according to party affiliation describes the political
alignment of many deputies only approximately. The Centre did not organize
as a party until 1894.

Source: Hunt, *People's Party,* p. 182; C. Große and C. Raith, *Beiträge zur Geschichte
und Statistik der Reichstags- und Landtagswahlen in Württemberg seit 1871*
(Stuttgart, 1912) p. 44.

The greater proximity of the individual state parliaments and
their parties to 'local' issues is also revealed in the high proportion of municipal civil servants. Whilst only small numbers of
them were represented in the liberal Reichstag parliamentary
parties, and these numbers were falling, as a rule there were
more municipal civil servants amongst the deputies of the state
parliaments than judicial and administrative civil servants put
together (cf. Tables 7 and 8).

Table 8 continued.

(f) *Landtag* Deputies in the Grand Duchy of Hesse by party, 1884–1908

	1884		1890		1897		1899		1902		1905		1908	
	No.	%	No.	%	No.	%	No.	%	No.	%	No.	%	No.	%
Nat. Libs.	39	78	30	60	22	44	20	40	17	34	18	36	20	40
*Freisinnig**	3	6	6	12	2	4	2	4	5*	10	3	6	3	6
Centre	7	14	5	10	7	14	7	14	7	14	7	14	8	16
Soc. Democracy	–	–	4	8	6	12	6	12	6	12	7	14	5	10
Hess. Bauernb.**	–	–	–	–	7	14	12	24	9	18	13	26	11	22
No party	1	2	5	10	6	12	3	6	6	12	2	4	3	6
Total	**50**	**100**	**50**	**100**	**50**	**100**	**50**	**100**	**50**	**100**	**50**	**100**	**50**	**100**

* Following complaints regarding the election, two *Freisinnig* deputies for Darmstadt resigned. Two National Liberal deputies were elected in their places, thus increasing their number from 17 to 19.

** Also *Hessische Volkspartei*. In 1897 under the name *Reformpartei* and in 1899 as the *Freie wirtschaftliche Vereinigung*. Deputies were elected by delegates for 6 years. Half of them were replaced every three years.

Source: Statistisches Handbuch für das Großherzogtum Hessen, ed. Großh; Hessische Zentralstelle für die Landesstatistik (Darmstadt, 1909) p. 293.

Table 8 continued.

(g) The Badenese Landtag

	1870	1873	1877	1881	1885	1889	1893	1897	1899	1901	1903
Nat Liberals	55	50	48	31	43	47	30	25	23	24	25
Freisinnig.				1		1	1	2	2	2	2
Democrats	1	3	3	5	5	1	4	5	5	5	6
Conservatives	1			3	1	1	2	2	2	1	
Centre	5	10	12	23	14	13	23	21	22	23	23
Soc. Democrats							3	5	7	6	6
Anti-semites								2	1	1	1
Others, no faction	1							1	1	1	1

Total = 63

Source: J. Thiel, *Die Großblockpolitik der Nationalliberalen Partei Badens, 1905–1914* (Stuttgart, 1976).

Table 8 continued.

(h) Kiel: proportions of the vote by party in *Landtag*, *Reichstag* and municipal elections, 1902–05

	Landtag elections 1903								*Reichstag elections 1903*		*Municipal elections**		
	Delegates in class												
	I		II		III		I–III				1902	1903	1904/5
Parties	No.	%	No.	%	No.	%	No.	%	No.	%	N	N	N
Nat. Liberals	154	33.5	469	32.0	1560	17.2	2183	19.8	4270	16.4			
Freisinnig. V'gung	24	5.2	75	5.1	218	2.4	317	2.9	4477	17.2			
Freisinnig. V'partei	203	44.2	397	27.1	185	2.0	785	7.1					
Conservatives	17	3.7	52	3.5	102	1.1	171	1.6					
Centre	–		–		–		–		518	2.0			
Soc. Democracy	6	1.3	231	15.8	5794	63.8	6031	54.8	16761	64.4	475 (24.2%)	189 (11.8%)	4640 (48.2%)
Others, unknown	55	12.0	242	16.5	1223	13.5	1520	13.8	17	0.1			
Total	**459**	**100**	**1466**	**100**	**9082**	**100**	**11007**	**100**	**26043**	**100.1**	**1964**	**1596**	**9620**

* The remaining votes fell to the middle-class candidates (primarily liberal in orientation). 1904/5: statistics for three elections are recorded.

Source: *Schriften des Vereins für Sozialpolitik,* vol. 118/2 (Leipzig, 1906) pp. 10, 24.

Prussia provides the best example of the degree to which the deputies of individual state parliaments had their roots in the municipalities (Table 9).[18] Left Liberal deputies increasingly had experience of urban local government. In 1913 this was true for almost half of them, and for more than a third of National Liberals. Figures for the Centre Party, and above all for the conservatives, were far lower. In contrast, local government in rural areas was the domain of both conservative parliamentary parties, at least a fifth of whom (in some legislative periods the figure was far higher) consisted of *Landräte* (the heads of a *Landkreis* or administrative district). Left Liberals enjoyed little support in the local governments of rural areas. More than a quarter of National Liberal deputies, on the other hand, were able to tap into this sphere of influence. Here, too, in contrast to the Left Liberals, the proportion of agricultural landowners was high (20 per cent in 1913), although they were unable to compete with their conservative parliamentary colleagues in this respect. The number of practising farmers was far lower than that of owners of agricultural estates in all parties, but the difference was more extreme amongst liberals than conservatives (cf. Tables 9 and 10). Although the ranks of the National Liberals in particular always included a high proportion of agricultural estate owners, civil servants and also a number of noblemen, during the course of the Kaiserreich the liberal parliamentary parties of the Prussian House of Deputies became 'more middle class': the proportion of independent men or senior employees in trade and commerce rose from 14 per cent to around a third amongst the Left Liberals and to a quarter amongst the National Liberals.

State federalism, deeply rooted in German history, also influenced the development of the German parties. This is particularly true of the liberal parties. As *the* parties of the *Reichsgründung*, their orientation was unitarian; for they hoped that the nation-state would provide a powerful impetus for reform. Their party structures, on the other hand, were weak. On an organizational level they essentially consisted of many individual state parties, which were held together on an institutional level by the Reichstag parliamentary parties, and on an ideological level by the central value 'nation-state'. The nation was the programmatic centre of liberalism as a party. Of all parties, it was the one which had the strongest Reich-wide presence in the elections. Yet nevertheless it was a party of *Honoratioren*, who had acquired

Table 9 Prussian House of Deputies, 1874–1913: local government officers, ownership of agricultural land, religious denomination, proportion of aristocrats

		1874		1883		1894		1904		1913	
		No.	%	No.	%	No.	%	No.	%	No.	%
Local Government											
Urban	LL	12	17	22	39	9	45	22	67	19	48
	NL	30	17	12	17	17	19	17	22	27	37
	FK	2	6	2	3	5	8	2	3	6	11
	K			2	2			5	3	8	5
	Z	11	12	10	10	11	12	14	14	20	19
	All	**55**	**13**	**49**	**11**	**43**	**10**	**62**	**14**	**88**	**20**
Rural	LL	6	9	10	17	1	5	2	6	3	8
	NL	22	5	15	22	24	27	24	31	19	26
	FK	14	41	31	53	35	56	35	57	34	63
	K	19	59	67	57	81	57	93	65	93	62
	Z	12	14	17	17	24	25	24	25	23	22
	All	**76**	**18**	**148**	**34**	**170**	**39**	**182**	**42**	**172**	**39**
Landräte	LL										
	NL	3	2	3	4	1	1	1	1	3	4
	FK	8	23	16	28	18	29	11	18	12	22
	K	14	44	43	36	34	24	28	20	31	21
	Z	3	3	3	3	2	2	2	2	2	2
	All	**29**	**7**	**68**	**16**	**57**	**13**	**42**	**10**	**48**	**11**

	C1	C2	C3	C4	C5	C6	C7	C8	C9	C10
Ownership of agricultural land										
LL	22	31	12	21	2	10	2	6	1	3
NL	42	24	26	38	31	34	19	25	15	20
FK	20	59	35	62	38	60	36	59	26	48
K	22	69	73	62	105	74	116	81	109	73
Z	30	34	28	29	30	32	27	28	30	29
All	**155**	**36**	**198**	**46**	**216**	**50**	**207**	**48**	**184**	**41**
Denomination Protestant										
LL	60	86	53	93	19	95	24	73	29	73
NL	153	88	64	93	86	96	76	99	71	97
FK	25	74	53	91	60	95	60	98	54	100
K	6	100	113	96	138	97	142	99	147	99
All	**281**	**65**	**297**	**69**	**311**	**72**	**311**	**72**	**306**	**69**
Population	65%	65%							62%	
Proportion of aristocrats										
LL	3	4	1	2	1	5	6	8	5	7
NL	10	6	13	19	8	9	11	18	13	24
FK	14	41	16	28	21	33	86	60	82	55
K	21	66	78	66	91	64	14	14	14	14
Z	24	27	23	23	19	20				
All	**93**	**22**	**148**	**34**	**147**	**34**	**125**	**29**	**119**	**27**

Source: Mann, *Handbuch für das preussische Abgeordnetenhaus.*

Table 10   The Prussian House of Deputies, 1874–1913: professional groups by parliamentary party

		1874		1883		1894		1904		1913	
		No.	%	No.	%	No.	%	No.	%	No.	%
1. Government and	LL	–	–	1	2	2	10	1	3	3	8
administrative	NL	15	9	5	7	5	6	12	16	13	18
civil servants	FC	8	23	18	31	23	36	10	16	8	15
	C	11	34	42	36	32	22	10	7	22	15
	Z	2	2	2	2	2	2	6	6	6	6
	HD	42	10	74	17	66	15	39	9	52	12
2. Judges	LL	16	23	9	16	3	15	3	9	–	–
	NL	48	28	11	16	10	11	14	18	13	18
	FC	4	12	3	5	3	5	3	5	4	7
	C	3	9	7	6	7	5	2	1	3	2
	Z	20	23	29	30	30	32	25	26	25	24
	HD	94	22	60	14	54	12	49	11	45	10
3. University,	LL	6	9	5	9	2	10	4	12	8	20
Gymnasium,	NL	15	9	4	6	5	6	4	5	5	7
Volksschule	FC	1	3	1	2	–	–	2	3	3	6
teachers,	C	–	–	5	4	4	3	5	3	10	7
clergy	Z	9	10	8	8	7	7	13	13	17	16
	HD	34	8	27	6	22	5	32	7	46	10
4. Independent	LL	7	10	4	7	4	20	6	18	8	20
professions	NL	12	7	2	3	8	9	4	5	6	8
	FC	–	–	2	3	–	–	2	3	4	7
	C	–	–	2	2	2	1	2	1	3	2
	Z	7	8	4	4	4	4	10	10	11	11
	HD	27	6	16	4	20	5	27	6	37	8
5. Trade,	LL	10	14	12	21	1	5	10	30	14	35
commerce,	NL	25	14	14	20	23	26	16	21	20	27
independent	FC	3	9	6	10	6	9	8	13	6	11
and senior	C	1	3	4	3	3	2	11	8	9	6
management	Z	9	10	8	8	11	12	7	7	9	9
	HD	49	11	44	10	48	11	55	13	60	13

Table 10   continued.

		1874		1883		1894		1904		1913	
		No.	%	No.	%	No.	%	No.	%	No.	%
6. *Farmers*	LL	18	26	12	21	–	–	1	3	–	–
	NL	33	19	14	20	21	23	11	14	5	7
	FC	13	38	21	36	20	32	27	44	15	28
	C	14	44	46	39	81	57	76	53	70	47
	Z	18	20	17	17	18	19	21	22	14	14
	HD	107	25	122	28	146	34	137	32	108	24
7. *Rentiers*	LL	13	19	11	19	8	40	8	24	7	17
pensioners,	NL	19	11	10	14	14	16	14	18	10	14
writers, quasi-	FC	1	3	1	2	3	5	7	11	12	22
professional	C	3	9	5	4	2	1	9	6	13	9
politicians	Z	16	18	22	22	18	19	11	11	17	16
	HD	56	13	55	13	47	11	56	13	69	16
House of	LL	70	16	57	13	20	5	33	8	40	9
Deputies	NL	174	40	69	16	90	21	77	18	73	16
Overall	FC	34	8	58	13	63	14	61	14	54	12
	C	32	7	118	27	142	33	143	33	149	34
	Z	88	20	98	23	95	22	97	22	103	23
	HD	430		433		433		433		433	

Notes: % = percentage of deputies in each parliamentary party or in the
House of Deputies (HD)
LL = Left Liberals; NL = National Liberals; FC = Free Conservatives;
C = Conservatives; Z = *Zentrum* (Centre Party); Remainder: others.

Source: Mann, *Handbuch für das preussische Abgeordnetenhaus.*

prominent positions in the municipalities and the states, where
they remained politically active. One of the most important
achievements of liberalism during the Kaiserreich is the fact that
it both retained this range and made remarkably successful
attempts to bridge it by around the end of the century. These
things were achieved despite, or perhaps because of liberalism's

weak party organization. When attempts are made to explain the decline in the significance of the liberal parties, this weakness is usually, and quite rightly, given as a factor. It may also have contributed to the fact that the liberals were more successful than the other parties in combining their focus on the nation-state with the recognition of federal autonomy. In doing so, they will have made it easier for large parts of the population who had envisaged the nation-state differently, to accept the new state. Little light has been shed on this achievement even by recent research on the Kaiserreich. The 'flash points of the Kaiserreich'[19] have been examined first, while we know far less about the by no means inevitable rapid integration of the many people who wanted a German nation-state, but not this one. The contribution of liberalism, and the liberal federal perspective to this process of reconciliation will now be addressed, using the example of Württemberg.

In the Kingdom of Württemberg two large political blocs had formed before the *Reichsgründung*; a pro-Prussian and an anti-Prussian bloc, whose cores were formed by the liberals and democrats respectively.[20] In the first decade of the Kaiserreich these blocs disintegrated, as did the organization of both large middle-class parties. The battles surrounding the *Reichsgründung* sapped the strength of the parties, but also caused the population's interest in politics to wane. High tension was followed by passivity. The Württemberg National Liberals (the *Deutsche Partei* or German Party) and the democrats (*Württembergische Volkspartei* or Württemberg People's Party), both of which had been moving towards organized membership parties before 1870, reverted to loose *Honoratiorenvereine*; the National Liberals to a greater degree than the democrats. In the German Party not even the leadership could say for certain whether the Reichstag candidates they supported would join the National Liberal parliamentary party or the Free Conservative *Deutsche Reichspartei*. The decision was left to the individual, and it was not unusual to belong to the National Liberal German Party in Württemberg, but to the Free Conservatives in the Reichstag. In the legislative chamber too after 1871 members of the German Party parliamentary party could not be clearly distinguished from the 'government party', which had no extra-parliamentary organization. Not even Julius Hölder, the unchallenged liberal party whip, knew the exact number of his parliamentary party colleagues.

The party leadership attempted to use this openness to the right to prevent the collapse of the National Liberal–Conservative *Reichsgründung* alliance. Openness of this kind facilitated co-operation with all those, including the government, who argued for the retention of proven Württemberg institutions, without rejecting the extension of Reich authority. Hölder, for example, spoke out against imperial intervention in the Württemberg municipal judicial system, in lawyers' regulations or in the special military position which remained in force. This federalism of above all strictly unitarian National Liberals helped to heal the deep wounds which had opened up during the bitter battles for the unification of the Reich. A tight National Liberal party organization which transcended states would probably have hindered this process.

The collapse of the democratic People's Party organization also made the search for new aims easier. Initially, the Württemberg democrats' uncompromising slogan had been: 'In the Reich against the Reich'. Later, too, they came down clearly in favour of federalism – one reason for their rejection of closer co-operation at Reich level with the German Progress Party, which they saw as too centralist. Yet the united front against this Reich, which was too Prussian, too militaristic and too centralist, and not democratic or federalist enough for them, was gradually eroded. As the organization was slowly revived after 1876, when it had not even been possible for the customary state meeting to take place on the traditional Feast of the Epiphany (6 January), it no longer represented the institutionalized hatred of Prussia. The decade-long political and organizational decline of the two great middle-class parties of Württemberg – the Centre Party did not form here until 1894 – had therefore helped them to adapt to the new conditions in the Reich and in Württemberg.

The liberals began as *Honoratiorenparteien* and remained so for a long time; to a greater degree than the other large parties.[21] A *Honoratiorenpartei* was one which was held together, not by a permanent organization, but by influential people, who were bound into a close-knit network of acquaintances, associations and committees of all kinds in the municipalities, the provinces and the individual states. Professional achievement qualified them for politics. They had to be both free to pursue politics and in a financial position to do so, although there were professional politicians amongst liberals too. They were not dependent party or association employees, but usually lawyers, for whom politics came with the job. A liberal politician had to be educated, and he had to be able to afford to pursue politics. His fellow party members and his electorate expected it of him. It helped to come from a well-known family; indeed it was not unusual for a political position to be 'inherited'. Gustav Böhm, for example, who emigrated to America as a disappointed 'forty-eighter', and who returned as a successful soap manufacturer, handed over the chairmanship of the National Liberal Party in Offenbach to his son. The son of the chairman of the Hessian National Liberals, Arthur Osann, a lawyer like his father, also succeeded his father in the post of chairman.

The Württemberg democrats' organizational structure was stronger than that of the liberals, but even in the People's Party the unchallenged leadership lay in the hands of a few men of great repute. Knowing them could help a political career. Friedrich Payer, son of a head porter at the University of Tübingen and Imperal Vice Chancellor from 1917 to 1918, was one of the young men who after the *Reichsgründung*, were promoted to the leadership of the Württemberg People's Party, groomed by the old triumvirate of Carl Mayer, Ludwig Pfau and Julius Haußmann. Payer's two sons, Friedrich and Conrad, lawyers like their father, grew into the leadership of the People's Party as a matter of course, more easily than Payer, who had first had to be 'adopted' – though he never lost the seniority which came as a result of his age and the fact that he had entered politics before them. As long as he remained politically active, Payer was granted chairmanship in all offices. After the First World War, Conrad Haußmann assumed this role[22] – a remarkable continuity in changing times, legitimized by personal authority, won by political achievement and trust, which resulted from the democratic tradition to which members and the leading circle commonly believed they belonged.

In the National Liberal Party the committee structure dominated until the beginning of the nineties. The committees, including the association executive committees where they existed, were generally only active in election periods. They put up the candidate, who sometimes did not even belong to the party. They concentrated on the indvidual: party membership would be sorted out later. Organization and 'party base' did not have to be questioned, for the National Liberals remained an 'association without sergeants and soldiers'[23] in the final two decades of the

Kaiserreich. This began to change, however, before the turn of the century. The nineties generally mark a watershed in the participation of the 'masses' in politics. With the large pressure group associations which now emerged, populist pressure on the parties also grew. Social Democracy, and the new agrarian and middle-class movements in particular, posed a challenge to the liberals, which forced them to create an organizational base to underpin the *Honoratiorenpartei*.

After the Anti-Socialist Law had lapsed (1890) the tightly organized Social Democrats won spectacular election victories. From 1890 onwards they consistently won more votes than any other party in the Reichstag elections, and after 1898 they beat all the liberal parties put together. Also important for the liberals were the anti-Semitic groups who with them were attempting to win over the *Mittelstand*, and who won 5.5 per cent of Reichstag seats in 1907, in some regions attracting even higher shares of the votes: 11.4 per cent in Berlin in 1898; in Hesse up to 15.9 per cent; and in the administrative district of Kassel after 1890 as much as 18–30 per cent.[24]

The *Bund der Landwirte* (Agrarian League) was a problematic 'partner' for the National Liberals in particular. In 1893, the year in which it was founded, it already had approximately 179 000 members. This figure had risen to 330 000 by 1913. Initial co-operation between the League and the National Liberals varied considerably from state to state and from region to region. By the end of the century, contacts in Hesse and Lower Saxony had become so close that the League represented a kind of substitute organization for the National Liberals. In the Hessian provinces both often shared the same local chairmen. The National Liberal *Honoratiorenpartei* of Hesse paid a high price for this organizational support: it now became even more strongly agrarian in the countryside too, since it lost the support of small traders and craftsmen. It also entered the line of fire of the *Mitteldeutscher Bauernverein* (Central German Farmers' Association). Founded in 1890, under the leadership of the Hessian 'Farmer King' Otto Böckel, it grew into a successful populist association, whose meetings were attended by up to 15 000 people. Its aggressive propaganda combined anti-Semitism with agitation against the 'rich' and democratic demands. Böckel had already issued the slogan 'Against the Junkers and the Jews' in 1887, framed by the democratic colours black, red and gold.[25]

As the organization of social interests amongst all strata of the population increased dramatically in the nineties, the conditions under which parties could pursue politics necessarily changed. Election campaigns became more lavish and expensive, and the parties also had to be represented in constituencies between elections. The National Liberals never developed into a membership party at Reich level, but even they tried to adapt to the trend of greater organization. The Young Liberals played a major role here. In 1907 they formed the *Nationalverein für das liberale Deutschland* (National Association for Liberal Germany).[26] They were unable to achieve their aim of reuniting the liberal splinter groups, revitalizing their programme and opening liberalism up to new social groups, but they strengthened the National Liberal organization and enlivened its discussions on how the dwindling social base of liberalism might be stabilized and expanded. In 1912, Young Liberals rejected the idea of founding local associations. Until that point they had only 1200 individual and a few corporate members. But their organization built bridges which crossed party boundaries in south German liberalism. The first chairman, Prof. Günther, was a member of the *Freisinnige Volkspartei* (Radical People's Party); his successor Freiherr Justus von Liebig was a member of the National Liberal Party. Public relations work was undertaken at general liberal level too. The Young Liberal National Association learned from the experiences of its political opponents. Like the Centre and Social Democracy, it organized educational courses, and above all developed a lively journalistic life. Under the leadership of its active General Secretary, Dr Wilhelm Ohr, lecturer in history at Tübingen University, three series were published which were envisaged as educational material for liberalism as a whole. Alongside the *Volksschriften des Nationalvereins für das liberale Deutschland* (Works of the National Association for a Liberal Germany; twelve brochures before 1912), ten volumes of the *Politische Handbücherei* (Political Reference Library) appeared, together with many studies on *Deutsches Parteiwesen* (German Political Parties). Together with the *Deutsch-Akademische Freibund* (or German Academic Free Association), founded in 1907 and closely linked to the National Association, he published a collection of *Dokumente liberaler Vergangenheit* (Documents of the Liberal Past; thirty-eight booklets before 1913).

The Young Liberals also provided the impetus which led to the at least formal surrender of the National Liberal Party's existence as an exclusive association of *Honoratioren*. In 1905 the party constitution was expanded by regulations, according to which every party supporter who was eligible to vote had also to be given the opportunity to become a member of the local association. Members were to elect its committee and even delegates to party conferences.

We do not know how many local associations existed. For this to be ascertained, all National Liberal regional parties would have to be examined. Even contemporaries had no clear overview. This only became possible when the statute of 1905 provided for reports to be sent from local organizations to the headquarters. As far as they were known to the headquarters, the number of associations rose from 940 in 1907 to 1870 in 1912 (1908–9: 1285, 1910: 1545, 1911: 1752, 1914–15: 2207), and membership numbers from around 200 000 in 1910 to 283 711 in 1914–15.[27] In 1912 around 11 per cent of all National Liberal voters were party members. In the party stronghold of Baden this figure was as high as 25 per cent. Certainly, these were not disappointing figures for a voters' party whose meagre organization had consisted for so long of a loose gathering of *Honoratiorenvereine* and which, despite all attempts at organization, remained more strongly influenced by *Honoratioren* than the non-liberal parties.

With a few exceptions, the social composition of the membership of the National Liberal associations is not known. No suitable sources exist. The professional composition of local and regional leading committees roughly corresponds to that of the parliamentary parties: the National Liberal Party represented education and property-ownership. There may have been differences in the individual states, but they will not have considerably altered this balance. In Baden, for example, between 1905 and 1913 almost half of the administrative civil servants amongst legislature candidates from all parties came from the National Liberal Party. In Baden being a member could still help a career in the civil service. In the two pre-war decades almost three-quarters of the Select Committee, the leading organ of the Badenese state organization, was made up of civil servants: above all of municipal civil servants (19–23 per cent), government civil servants (20–27 per cent), professors and teachers (13–23 per cent) and lawyers (14–16 per cent). In the association committees they represented 39 per cent, a far lower figure. Workers were rarely found on these committees. The National Liberal Party's official

statement that, in the Reich as a whole, approximately 12 per
cent (24 000) of their members were workers in around 1910, is
exaggerated, according to Thomas Nipperdey.[28] But we should
not dismiss this surprisingly high figure altogether, for the Left
Liberal Hirsch–Duncker trade unions organized around 100 000
members after the turn of the century after all, and the
wirtschaftsfriedlich associations (see below) even more. Whatever
the number of workers in the National Liberal associations was,
the liberals certainly reflected on how they might win over
workers for their organizations. However, the workers' voice
counted for little in the organizations.

Above the local associations were the state and provincial
organizations, which were always of great importance to the
Reich party. Their significance increased during the course of
the Kaiserreich because the National Liberals' search for new
aims and for a firm social base, and the different ways in which
this was attempted, reinforced centrifugal forces. This had a
beneficial effect on the regional parties, where conditions varied.
In Bavaria, for example, the liberals were largely represented in
state politics as a unit, whilst they campaigned separately in the
Reichstag elections, except in the primarily Catholic areas. In the
Protestant areas of Franconia, where a united front against
political Catholicism did not seem necessary, the liberals split into
National and Left Liberals as early as 1871.[29] Under these conditions, no tauter liberal organization could emerge in Bavaria,
in contrast to Baden and also to Württemberg and Hesse. It is
generally true to say that in the first instance, the increasing
degree of organization strengthened not the National Liberal
Party as a whole, but above all its regional parties.

The parliamentary parties of the Reichstag, the parliaments
and the chambers always belonged to the National Liberal leading
core. As early as 1870, it was expanded on a central level by a state
committee and an executive committee, which was replaced in
1873 by a Central Committee. But these committees were barely
visible. The Reichstag parliamentary party represented the
National Liberal Party as a whole, and organization was entirely
in the hands of individuals. They maintained contacts with the
state associations and the press and also owned the 'party organs':
Wehrenpfennig's *Nationalliberale Korrespondenz* represented the
right wing, Lasker's *Autographische Korrespondenz* the left wing.
With the great parliamentary party split, the Secession of 1880,

the situation became more complex, yet after the National Liberal victories in the cartel elections of 1887 these incipient organizational efforts began to flag. Only in the nineties did the central election committee grow from an organ of the Reichstag parliamentary party to form a Central Committee which, according to the statute of 1892, the first to be issued by the National Liberal Party, formally represented the party leadership.

The statute of 1905 then established the ratio of delegation for the state associations: for every 20 000 votes in the previous Reichstag election, there was to be one place on the Party Executive, which could also co-opt further people. The Central Committee elected an Executive Committee and three chairmen, of which the first was regarded as party whip. The Party Executive, which had an office with twelve employees in 1903 and seventeen by 1909, had informal opportunities to exercise influence, yet organization and agitation continued to be the province of the state parties, whose autonomy was not limited even by the party conferences. Formally, the party conference had been an institution of the National Liberal Party since 1892, but it had not had decision-making powers. The parliamentary party remained the central organ of leadership. It was here that politicians had to distinguish themselves if they wanted authority in the party. This was true at both Reich and state levels. Even in the relatively tightly organized Badenese party, important decisions were made in the parliamentary party and not in the party organization. The extensive independence of the state associations was vital if the many political alignments and social groups which made up the National Liberals were to be held together. This did not change in the four and a half decades between the *Reichsgründung* and the beginning of the First World War – a key reason for the National Liberals' inability to create a centralized organization with the hierarchically graduated formation of political opinion. This would not have suited this party or its clientele.

Many Left Liberal parties were founded, some of which were short-lived (see Fig. 1), but programmatically, organizationally, and in terms of personal links, three lines emerged, which in 1910 led into the *Fortschrittliche Volkspartei* (Progressive People's Party).[30] The main line led from the Progress Party to the *Deutsch-Freisinnige Partei* (German Radical Party) which was founded in 1884 when deputies who had split from the National Liberal Reichstag party in 1880 (the Secession) merged with the

Progress Party. This merger ended in 1893, when Left Liberalism collapsed on an organizational level. Under Eugen Richter, the Progress wing now formed the *Freisinnige Volkspartei* (Radical People's Party), in which the main Left Liberal line was continued, whilst the minority, dominated by the Secessionists, formed a subsidiary line calling itself the *Freisinnige Vereinigung* or Radical Union. In 1903 it absorbed the *Nationalsozialer Verein* (National Social Association), which had been founded in 1896. In 1908 the critics of the liberal–conservative bloc party split from it. Under the leadership of Theodor Barth, they went on to form the *Demokratische Vereinigung* (Democratic Alliance), which remained independent, even in 1910, when all other Left Liberal parties, including the German People's Party – another Left Liberal line restricted to southern Germany – united to form the Progressive People's Party. With the exception of the small, but intellectually extremely lively Democratic Alliance, which held until 1918, this brought to an end the organizational fragmentation of the Left Liberal–Democratic spectrum.

The German Progress Party founded local and election associations more rapidly than the National Liberals. This early organization on the model of the association system, which began as early as the 1870s (see Table 11), may have contributed to the cementing of the split in liberalism as a whole after the *Reichsgründung*. But this was by no means the case everywhere. We have already alluded to the fact that in Bavaria, for example, liberalism did not split, or at least not in all regions, because of the strength of political Catholicism. In Düsseldorf,[31] too, liberals remained united in the first decade of the Kaiserreich. This cohesion was probably made easier because they were initially supported by associations which were not expressly fixed in political terms, at least not in party-political terms. They included the Masonic Lodge, whose membership and committee included prominent liberals, and which retained its links with all liberal camps, even after local liberalism had split. Düsseldorf liberals were also rooted in the Old Catholics, in the veterans' associations and in the "Citizens' Shooting Club', which brought together a variety of liberal and national alignments and in 1874 split from the 'St Sebastian Shooting Club'. The German Association for the Rhine Province, founded on Sybel's initiative in 1874 to oppose 'Ultramontanism', also provided cohesion. In 1877 it had 7514 members in the administrative district of Düsseldorf.

Table 11 Left Liberal organizations in the Kaiserreich: associations and members

Year	Local associations (election associations)	Members	Subscribers to the 'Parlamentarische Korrespondenz' (members' publication)
(a) Deutsche Fortschrittspartei			
1877	17		1 859
1878	43		3 119
1879	40		5 503
1880	78		9 503
1881	110		19 154
1882			c. 20 000
1883			c. 12 000
(b) Deutsch-Freisinnige Partei			
1884	169*		c. 10 000
1886	210		c. 3 500
1893	418		
(c) Freisinnige Volkspartei			
1895/96	397		
(d) Freisinnige Vereinigung			
1902		c. 1 000	
1903		c. 3 000	together with the Nationalsozialer Verein
1907	60		
1909		9 494	
1910	150		
(e) Fortschrittliche Volkspartei			
1912	1581		151 713
1913			c. 120 000
1914			c. 140 000

* Matthes, p. 182, refers to 180 *Fortschritt* and 50 *Sezession* election associations when the merger took place.

Source: Nipperdey, *Organisation*, p. 176ff.; Steinbrecher, p. 115; *Lexikon zur Parteiengeschichte I*, pp. 623, 634, 657, 663; Simon, *Württembergische Demokraten*, p. 27; Theiner, *Liberalismus*, p. 202.

The profound crisis in liberalism towards the end of the seventies led to an organizational split in liberalism as a whole, in Düsseldorf too. Its focus, the Liberal Association, which had up to 500 members, completely collapsed in 1882, when its members supported different candidates in the Reichstag by-elections. Only in the municipal elections could overall liberal unity be maintained. The split had been heralded as early as 1876, when supporters of protective tariffs in Düsseldorf had founded a *Volkswirtschaftlicher Verein* (Economic Association) and above all in 1880, when Progress liberals had formed their own election association, which managed to win 37 per cent of all liberal votes for its candidate in the Reichstag elections of 1881. This Progress Party organization also reflects the extent to which local associations were independent, even in a relatively well-organized party: in 1884 the Düsseldorf branch of the Progress Party rejected a merger with the Secessionists to form the *Deutsch-Freisinnige Partei* (German Radical Party). Düsseldorf's Progress liberals continued to declare their support for the Progress Party programme of 1878 – a party which had ceased to exist. The development of the right wing of liberalism in Düsseldorf differed from that at Reich level. In 1882 an 'alliance of the centre parties' was formed, which extended from the National Liberals to the Free Conservatives, and which had almost 2000 members by the mid-eighties.

As the example of Düsseldorf makes clear, the already colourful picture provided by the liberal organizations would become even more so if we were to examine the local and regional situation in greater detail. Here, however, we will have to focus on the broad outlines, which do not adequately reflect the wide variety of developments.

In the second half of the seventies, the Progress Party developed its organization, enlivened by the discussions on the new programme of 1878 and by Eugen Richter, who rapidly rose to become a central figure in German Left Liberalism after the death of Hoverbeck in 1875. Richter was a controversial figure and was often challenged, but his uncompromising desire for leadership always won out.[32] Membership numbers for the Progress Party are not known – a measure of the degree of autonomy enjoyed by the associations, of the limited extent to which the organization was centralized and the degree to which the Progress Party was still a voters' party. In 1881 we can assume that it had around 20 000 members. That was the number of subscribers to the *Parlamentarische Korrespondenz*, which could only be ordered from the executive committee, since its purchasers were regarded as party members. After the merger with the Secessionists, the number of associations rose dramatically, while the circle of subscribers shrank. Whether this equates with a loss of members, we do not know. The number of votes which the German Radical Party of 1884 won before it was disbanded in the Reichstag elections, levelled out at around one million.

The Secessionists were a typical *Honoratiorenpartei*, consisting of Reichstag deputies without a fixed extra-parliamentary base. The merger with the Progress Party did not extend particularly deeply. The press remained separate. Alongside Richter's *Parlamentarische Korrespondenz* and his *Freisinnige Zeitung*, founded in 1885, Secessionist publications included Heinrich Rickert's *Deutsches Reichsblatt* and the *Liberale Korrespondenz*. Richter continued to issue his handbook for liberal voters on his own, and in many areas separate accounts were kept.

When in around 1890 the *Honoratioren* attempted to rehearse another uprising against Richter, whom they accused of demanding 'slavish obedience', they were once more forced to recognize the strength of his position. At the helm of the parliamentary party and the organization, and with the support of his press publications, he once again asserted his claim to leadership. When the German Radical Party finally collapsed in 1893, the majority of the associations remained with Richter's new Radical People's Party (see Table 11), whilst the Radical Union only acquired a stronger organizational base when it joined with the National Social Association (1903), which was organized into associations. The formation of opinion was more open and changeable here than in the Radical People's Party. It adopted a party statute in 1893 which provided for a graded, democratically legitimized decision-making procedure, with the Party Conference as the highest decision-making organ and a Central Committee as the leading authority. Yet these institutions were not particularly significant before Richter's death in 1906. Political leadership remained with the Berlin parliamentary party of the Reichstag and the Prussian parliament, so despite its democratic organizational statute, the Radical People's Party was led by a 'parliamentary oligarchy', in which Eugen Richter's 'authority' had become so entrenched that it had become 'more or less a dictatorship'.[33]

This fossilized structure broke down after the turn of the century, when efforts on the part of the Left Liberals to merge circumvented Richter. His death facilitated the Left Liberal merger to form the Radical People's Party, which had already taken place at local and regional level. Bülow's policies, which rested on a liberal–conservative bloc, seemed to offer the chance of a united Left Liberal party. This, coupled with disappointment over the failure of the bloc experiment (1909) accelerated merger negotiations and brought the new party into being. Even before 1912 it had approximately 1700 associations and in 1913 had approximately 120 000 members, some 8 per cent of its Reichstag voters of 1912 (see Table 11). The nineteen state or provincial organizations and the twenty-nine party secretaries, which the Radical People's Party already had in 1912, bear witness to the efforts made to build up an effective party organization. The sixty-seven delegate conferences which were held before that time testify to the lively internal party discussions.

Centralization remained limited. When candidates were put up, the constituency associations operated independently and in cases of conflict usually asserted themselves against the party leadership. This certainly made it difficult for the party to present a united front, but it enabled it to react flexibly to its voters, of whom the liberals could never be as sure as Social Democracy and the Centre Party.

In so far as women joined middle-class parties at all, they joined Left Liberal organizations. Before 1908, female party members are only found in states with liberal association practice, such as Hamburg (from 1903) and Baden (from 1904). After 1908, when the Imperial Association Law allowed women access to parties, leading feminists joined the Radical People's Party and the Democratic Alliance. The *Bundes Deutscher Frauenverein* (Federation of German Women's Associations) was the umbrella organization of middle-class women's associations, which organized almost 500 000 people in 1914. Its Select Committee was exclusively made up of members of the Progressive People's Party, which acquired a Central Committee at the end of 1910, as a representative organ of female party members. But we should not be misled by this organizational 'rapprochement': even Left Liberals ascribed little significance to the political equality of women. It was politically active women who approached the Left

Liberal parties, and not the other way around. After 1909, the National Liberals also accepted female party members.[34]

As for the membership numbers of the Left Liberal parties, little is known about the social profile of the associations. We have more information on the composition of the party conferences, but it allows only very limited extrapolations to be made on the membership structure of the local associations, which certainly extended further into the lower middle classes (see Table 12).

For parties like the liberals, in which voters rather than members were courted, and in which parliamentary parties formed the focus of the political leadership, the membership structure is anyway less informative on the question of the social range of the parties and their decision-making committees than the composition of the voters and deputies. These have already been examined above. We will turn now to the links between the liberal parties and the associations, which participated to such a great extent in the organization of social interests after the nineties, supporting the parties, but also competing with them.

The National Liberals, it may be said, were 'the "classical" party of the German commercial middle class', and the Left Liberal Radical Union was 'largely dominated by big business'. At the turn of the century, five of its thirteen Reichstag deputies were either close to the *Deutsche Bank* or members of it.[35] As we have seen, employers certainly represented a high proportion of the liberal parties, above all of their executive committees. Yet we cannot simply 'deduce' from this that they 'dominated' the liberal parties, although of course they also represented their interests in them. Liberal parties were middle-class Protestant integration parties in terms of their social profile and policies. If they wanted to be successful in the elections, they therefore had to be constantly balancing the very different interests of their middle-class clientele – a permanent problem for the liberals, which became all the more difficult, the more dramatically the 'middle classes' changed as a social group. Even the term 'commercial middle class' is far too broad to encompass definite interests. The liberals were constantly forced to confront the breadth of the spectrum that these frequently competing commercial middle-class aims encompassed. This is also reflected in the development of the commercial associations and their personal links with the parties (see Table 13).[36]

Table 12   Left Liberal organizations in the Kaiserreich: professions of members, association committees, party conference delegates

(a)   Progress Party: members of the election association, 6th Berlin Reichstag constituency, 1877–80, and of the association executives

	No.	1877 %	1878 %	1880 %	Executive 1880 %	1884 %
Manufacturers	11	9	7		18.1	14.9
Merchants	11	9	16	65*	18.1	22.7
Craftsmen	28	22	22		10.0	16.0
Civil servants, employees	19	15				
Others	31	25				
No details	25	20				
Total	**125**	**100**	**No. = c. 600**	**No. = 756**		

* Probably assistants in the main.

Source: G. Seeber, *Zwischen Bebel und Bismarck* (Berlin, 1965) pp. 101, 103.

The *Centralverband Deutscher Industrieller* (CVDI) or Central Association of German Industrialists was founded in 1876 as an association of protective tariff supporters. It grew into a broad industrial pressure group, which organized central and regional specialist associations, as well as chambers of commerce and professional co-operatives. As it expanded, the interests of its members became differentiated economically, socially and politically. The CVDI was therefore unable to commit itself clearly in party political terms. In the Reichstag and in the Prussian House of Deputies its members sat with the National Liberals and the conservative parties (Table 13). Although the CVDI had supported all middle-class parties in the Reichstag elections of 1907, in 1912 it supported only the Free Conservatives and the National Liberals. Forty-one of the 120 candidates who received financial aid from its election fund in 1912 were elected. After 1910 deputies from all middle-class parliamentary parties, including the Centre Party, were invited to its delegate meetings. Yet no more than sixteen ever came and in 1912 only eight attended.[37]

Table 12 continued.

(b) Party Conferences: Freisinnige Volkspartei and Freisinnige Vereinigung

	Freisinnige Volkspartei										Freisinnige Vereinigung 1893	
	1893		1897		1900		1902		1905			
	N	%	N	%	N	%	N	%	N	%	N	%
1. Employers, directors, company lawyers, Privatiers	152	47.5	111	47.8	61	44.2	70	47.6	98	48.0	79	37.4
2. Professors, teachers, indep. profs., engineers, journalists	111	34.7	79	34.1	51	37	51	34.7	53	26.0	89	42.2
3. Civil servants, employees, mayors	25	7.8	31	13.4	15	10.9	14	9.5	37	18.1	37	17.5
4. Farmers, landowners	14	4.4	5	2.1	2	1.4	4	2.7	9	4.4	–	–
5. Craftsmen	15	4.7	6	2.6	8	5.8	7	4.8	5	2.5	5	2.4
6. Workers	2	0.6	–	–	1	0.7	1	0.7	1	0.5	–	–
7. Others	1	0.3	–	–	–	–	–	–	1	0.5	1	0.5
Total	**320**	**100**	**232**	**100**	**138**	**100**	**147**	**100**	**204**	**100**	**211**	**100**

Source: Elm, *Fortschritt*, pp. 17, 26; Party Conference records (analysed by H. Meyer, *Die Stellung der Freisinnigen Volkspartei zur deutschen Kolonial- und Flottenpolitik, 1893–1907* (Staatsexamen Dissertation, Hamburg, 1984).

Table 12 continued

(c) Party conferences: National Social Association

	1896		1897		1898		1899		1900	1901		1902		1903	
	N	%	N	%	N	%	N	%	N = %	N	%	N	%	N	%
1. Clergy	42	36.2	17	16.7	21	22.6	21	18.6	10	14	11.6	17	11.0	9	4.8
2. Professors*	24	20.7	21	20.6	17	18.3	26	23.0	22	33	27.3	40	25.8	65	34.9
3. Teachers	5	4.3	25	24.5	19	20.4	20	17.7	18	22	18.2	46	29.7	38	20.4
4. Craftsmen, merchants, employees, junior civil servants	24	20.7	26	25.5	27	29.0	36	31.9	40	39	32.2	45	29.0	54	29.0
5. Manufacturers	3	2.6	2	2.0	2	2.1	3	2.6	3	3	2.5	–	–	3	1.6
6. Farmers	3	2.6	3	2.9	3	3.2	–	–	–	1	0.8	1	0.6	1	0.5
7. Workers	8	6.9	5	4.9	2	2.1	2	1.8	5	5	4.1	3	1.9	7	3.8
8. Others**	7	6.0	3	2.9	2	2.1	5	4.4	2	4	3.3	3	1.9	9	4.8
Total	**116**	**100**	**102**	**100**	**93**	**99.8**	**113**	**100**	**100**	**121**	**100**	**155**	**99.9**	**186**	**99.8**

* Primarily professors, but also including other academic professions.
** Primarily, and after 1897 exclusively, students.

Source: Düding, *Verein*, pp. 146–8; cf. Elm, *Fortschritt*, p. 27 (Elm divides groups 4 and 5 differently: he puts the higher figure under 5, while Düding groups the majority of commercial professions with the *Kleinbürgertum*, no. 4).

Table 13 Personal links between the parties and the pressure groups and associations

(a) **Members of the Reichstag in the Centralverband Deutscher Industrieller (CVDI), Bund der Industriellen (BDI), Hansa-Bund and Bund der Landwirte (BdL)**

	National Liberals					Left Liberals		Conservatives					Centre Party	
	1893	1898	1903	1907	1912	1907	1912	1893	1898	1903	1907	1912	1907	1912
CVDI	3	2	4	2	1	1	–	2	1	–	1	–	–	–
BDI	–	–	–	2*	1	–	–	–	–	–	–	–	–	–
Hansa				6	17	15	38					1	1	1
BdL	4**		3**	32	5	–	–	19**	15**	16**	78	54	–	7
Strength of parliamentary party	53	46	51	54	45	49	42	100	79	75	84	57	105	91

Note: where figures changed during a Reichstag period, the highest figure is given.

* Stresemann and Merkel for the *Verband Sächsischer Industrieller*.

** Senior positions in the BdL; how many deputies were committed to the BdL programme can only be established by parliamentary party for 1907 and 1912. Altogether, the numbers of deputies committed to the programme were: 1893 = *c*. 100 deputies; 1898 = 118; 1903 = 89; 1907 = 138; 1912 = 78; they belonged overwhelmingly to the *Deutschkonservative* and the Free Conservative *Reichspartei*.

Table 13 continued

(b) Members of the Prussian Chamber of Deputies in the CVDI and the BdL

	National Liberals					Left Libs.	Conservatives					Centre Party		
	1893	1898	1903	1907	1913	1908	1893	1898	1903	1908	1913	1903	1908	1913
CVDI	5	4	6	5	5	–	2	3	2	3	1	–	–	–
BdL a			9	7	3	–			144	158	146	1	1	1
b				28		3				202			7	
Strength of parliamentary party	90	72	77	65	73	36	209	204	203	212	202	97	104	103

Notes: a = members; b = committed to BdL programme; it is not possible to identify members of the BdL by parliamentary party before 1903; after 1893 the proportion of BdL members in the *Deutschkonservative* remained constant at approximately a third.

Table 13   continued.

(c)   **Members of the Hansa-Bund on the leading committees of liberal parties, 1912–13**

	National Liberals		Progressive Peoples' Party	
	Central Committee	Executive Committee	Central Committee	Executive Committee
Members	245	15	109	18
No. of whom in the Hansa-Bund	36	5	55	15
%	15	33	50	83

Source: H. Kaelble, *Interessenpolitik in der Wilhelminischen Gesellschaft: Centralverband Deutscher Industrieller, 1895–1914* (Berlin, 1967), p. 233f.: CVDI; Ullmann, *Bund der Industriellen*, pp. 150ff.; S. Mielke, 'Der *Hansa-Bund für Gewerbe, Handel und Industrie*', *1909–1914* (Göttingen, 1976) pp. 212, 215; H.-J. Puhle, *Agrarische Interessenpolitik und preußischer Konservatismus im Wilhelminischer Reich* (Hanover, 1967) pp. 167–71.

Some employers left the CVDI, which was oriented towards heavy industry, and in 1895 founded the *Bund der Industriellen* (BDI) (League of Industrialists) as an organization which exclusively represented the finished-product industries. It was strongly oriented towards exports, and represented above all smaller and medium-sized businesses. Although the BDI initially attempted to influence the state bureaucracy, after 1905 it increasingly focused on the Reichstag. It provided as many deputies as possible from all middle-class parties with information on issues which were important to the BDI. Under the leadership of Gustav Stresemann, the League of Industrialists changed its tactics in 1907–8. It now adopted the aim of creating a mass base for a German '*Weltpolitik*' which supported industry from 'national' workers, employees and peasants, whose political representatives were to be the National Liberals. This concept had failed at the latest by 1912, when not even Stresemann was re-elected, and the League of Industrialists was represented by a single deputy in the Reichstag and the National Liberal parliamentary party. Only in Saxony did it enjoy success. In 1907, twenty-five deputies of the Saxon legislature belonged to the Saxon League of Industrialists state association. Twenty-one of them operated in the National Liberal parliamentary party, which had thirty-one members, and which now became a branch of the *Verband Sächsischer Industrieller* (Association of Saxon Industrialists), gaining better access to the Saxon ministerial bureaucracy.[38] At Reich level the League of Industrialists was denied similar success. On the contrary, after 1912 the League underwent a swing to the right and became ever more distanced from the National Liberal Party.

The *Bund der Landwirte* or Agrarian League was one of the best-organized, politically influential large pressure groups in Wilhelmine Germany. A number of members or deputies in the National Liberal parliamentary parties had committed themselves to the programme of the League in return for electoral aid. But it was centred on the conservatives, above all on the German Conservatives, whose parliamentary parties in the Reichstag and in the Prussian House of Deputies fell into the hands of the League (Table 13). The Left Liberals received support from the Agrarian League only in rare and exceptional cases – as an emergency measure, when no other anti-Social-Democratic election alliance could be formed. Its relationship with the National Liberals was more complex and varied greatly from one federal state to another. Whilst the originally close links in the Province of Hanover had broken down by 1898, during this period they were only just beginning in Bavaria and in the Palatinate. After 1905, relations worsened everywhere. In the Reichstag elections of 1907, thirty-two of the fifty-four elected National Liberals had accepted the help of the Agrarian League, yet in 1912 this figure had fallen to five. Between these dates came the foundation of the *Deutscher Bauernbund* (German League of Farmers) in 1909, in which the National Liberals had participated. Although it was never able to compete with the Agrarian League in terms of political influence and membership – in 1914 it reached its peak with approximately 50 000 members, against the 330 000 members of the Agrarian League in 1913 – its foundation highlights the National Liberals' efforts to defend their rural base against the Agrarian League.[39]

Liberal attempts to create a dependable mass base in society included their close co-operation with the *Hansa-Bund* (Hanseatic League), created in 1909 (see Table 13).[40] With its 200 000–250 000 direct and 280 000 corporate members, it was one of the largest pressure groups in the immediate pre-war decades.

Table 14 Parties and denominations on district councils during the Kaiserreich

(a) Rhenish and Westphalian Towns with more than 10 000 inhabitants, 1911

	No. of towns in which the following parties had a majority							
	Liberals		Centre		SPD	No clear majority		Total
	No.	%	No.	%	No.	No.	%	No.
Rhenish	40	53	28	37	1	6	8	75
Westphalian	41	69	12	20	–	6	10	59
Total	**81**	**60**	**40**	**30**	**1**	**12**	**9**	**134***

* Of a total of 154 Districts with more than 10 000 inhabitants.

(b) Bavaria: Districts with more than 4000 inhabitants

	1908		1911	
	Votes	%	Votes	%
Liberals	945 711	38.7	1 170 403	35.3
Centre	475 530	19.4	621 065	18.7
Social Democrats	704 901	28.8	1 066 090	32.2
Others*	319 823	13.1	456 373	13.8
Total	**2 445 965**	**100**	**3 313 931**	**1002**

* Often Centre Party votes, since Centre Party supporters in safe constituencies often appeared in 'neutral' *Bürgervereine*.

(c) Silesia: proportion of religious denominations in the population and on town councils (I) and district councils (II), 1910 (in %)

		Catholics	Protestants	Jews
40 towns	Population	82.5	15	2.5
	I	67	20	13
	II	79	22	8
44 towns	Population	24	75	1
	I	15	81	4
	II	9	87	4

Source: Handwörterbuch der Kommunalwissenschaften, vol. III (Jena, 1924) p. 25 (taken from contemporary surveys which are far more detailed than the summary given here); cf. also H. Croon, *Die gesellschaftlichen Auswirkungen des Gemeindewahlrechts in den Gemeinden und Kreisen des Rheinlandes und Westfalens im 19. Jahrhundert* (Cologne, 1960) p. 59.

Table 14 continued

(d) **Frankfurt am Main: distribution of seats on the town council, 1899–1913**

	Democrats		Progress		Nat. Libs.		Soc. Dems.		Right		Independ.	
	No.	%	No.	%	No.	%	No.	%	No.	%	No.	%
1899	25	39.1	13	20.3	23	35.9	–	–	–	–	3	4.7
1901	23	35.9	11	17.2	20	31.2	1	1.6	9	14.1	–	–
1903	23	35.9	12	18.7	20	31.2	1	1.6	8	12.5	–	–
1905	23	35.9	11	17.2	12	18.7	3	4.7	15	23.4	–	–
1907	24	37.5	13	20.3	13	20.3	6	9.4	8	12.5	–	–
1909	17	26.6	12	18.7	10	15.6	15	23.4	8	12.5	2	3.1
1911	34			47.9	12	16.9	22	31.0	3	4.2	–	–
1913	32			45.1	12	16.9	23	32.4	4	5.6	–	–

Source: J. Rolling, *Das Problem der 'Politisierung' der kommunalen Selbstverwaltung in Frankfurt a. M., 1900–1918*, in *Archiv für Frankfurts Geschichte und Kunst* 57 (1980) p. 176.

Table 14   continued

(e)   **Munich: distribution of seats on the town council, 1869–1911**

	Liberals		Conservatives		Centre		Social Democracy	
	No.	%	No.	%	No.	%	No.	%
1869	37	61.7	23	38.3				
1896	33	55.0			26	43.3	1	1.7
1911*	30	50.0			14	23.3	14	23.3

* Remainder: others.

Source: L. Lenk, 'Katholizismus und Liberalismus', in *Der Mönch im Wappen* (Munich, 1960) pp. 384, 386.

Approximately two-thirds of its members were employees. More than 70 per cent of organized technical and merchant employees came into contact with the Hanseatic League as individual members, or via corporate links. Female membership was also allowed; this had been made possible by the Imperial Association Law of 1908.

The Hanseatic League's closest links were with the Left Liberals (see Table 13), whose success in the Reichstag elections of 1912 would probably not have been possible without its support. Approximately 90 per cent of Progressive People's Party deputies now belonged to the Hanseatic League; amongst the National Liberals the figure was approximately 38 per cent. The Hanseatic League campaigned for all liberal parties to form a united middle-class-liberal front against the agrarians, against the Agrarian League and against the black–blue bloc of the Centre Party and the conservatives. It argued openly for co-operation with Social Democracy. Discussions surrounding a political re-orientation of this kind were at the heart of the disputes conducted within the National Liberal Party between the 'Young Liberals' and the 'Old Liberals' in 1912. They were interwoven with the struggles between the Hanseatic League and the Central Association of German Industrialists, both of which attempted to win the party over to their political course. The influence of the Central Association waned – the National Liberals rejected the 'cartel of the productive Estates' in 1913, but a liberal party which was ready to co-operate with Social Democracy did not emerge. The Hanseatic League was not sufficiently strong and the interests which came together in the liberal parties proved to be too varied and contradictory for a social–liberal coalition.

Links between the large new pressure groups and the liberal parties varied. Their influence on the parties was considerable, but they did not 'dominate' them. Cooperation with the Hanseatic League offered the liberals the greatest opportunities in their search for new programmes, and for a broad social base in industrial society which could be built upon. For the liberals, whose dominant self-image was always one of a party of the *Mittelstand*, hoped to be able to use the Hanseatic League to win over large sections of the expanding 'new *Mittelstand*' politically. Workers, on the other hand, were lost to the liberals as a political clientele in the Kaiserreich. The large National Liberal–Social Democratic bloc, from 'Bassermann to Bebel', remained a short-lived experiment restricted to Baden (see Chapter 4, pp. 228–45). As parties, liberals were unable to compete for workers' votes with the Social Democrats and with the Centre Party, and all attempts to oppose the unions with their own workers' organizations ultimately failed. They were not entirely unsuccessful, however.[41]

The traditional Hirsch-Duncker trade unions, which were Left Liberal in orientation, organized around 100 000 workers after the turn of the century. The *Wirtschaftsfriedliche*, greatly promoted by employers, which in 1910 united in the *Hauptausschuß nationaler Arbeiter- und Berufsverbände* (Main Committee of National Workers' and Professional Associations) are thought to have had around 260 000 members by mid-1914. Like the Centre Party and the Social Democrats, the Left Liberals rejected the so-called 'Yellows' – the *wirtschaftsfriedlich* workers' organizations – while the National Liberals, as so often, responded in a number of different ways. Many of the 'Yellows' declared their support for the National Liberal Party, to which most of their association leaders also belonged. Only during the First World War, when the unions became indispensable to the war economy and to 'truce politics', did the National Liberals turn their backs on the *Wirtschaftsfriedliche*. Only in Bavaria did National Liberals succeed in founding their own workers' associations, in opposition to the existing Social Democratic, Christian and Hirsch-Duncker trade unions, and independently of the 'Yellows'. Thirty-four liberal workers' associations with a mere 6000 members existed in Bavaria in 1908, an unmistakable sign of failure.

This is true, too, of the Left Liberal attempt of 1912 to join all employees amongst their supporters in a *Reichsverein liberaler Arbeiter und Angestellter* (Imperial Association of Liberal Workers and Employees). A year later it had barely 3400 members. As these attempts make clear, the organization of workers was largely denied to the liberals. But this does not mean that liberals did not address the problems of proletarian life, or try to find ways of helping the proletariat. We will return to the issue of middle-class attempts at social reform, and the roles played by the liberals (Chapter 4, pp. 206–28). At this point it is sufficient to note that numerous social reforming organizations were founded, which also encompassed political liberalism and, more importantly, provided it with social and political impulses.[42] They include the *Verein für Sozialpolitik* (Association for Social Policy), the *Centralverein für das Wohl der arbeitenden Klassen* (Central Association for the Welfare of the Working Classes), the *Deutscher Verein für öffentliche Gesundheitspflege* (German Association for Public Healthcare), the *Evangelisch-Soziale Kongreß* (Protestant-Social Congress) and the *Gesellschaft für Soziale Reform* (Society for Social Reform), founded in 1901, whose committee always included National Liberals and Left Liberals in particular.[43]

These social reforming associations influenced the social 'climate' of the time, but they were not mass organizations with direct access to large sections of the population. Together with the fact that they transcended parties, a fact which they emphasized, that is why they could only help to a limited and indirect degree to form a 'liberal milieu' and to make themselves attractive to the lower social strata. This might have been more possible in their work in the field of adult education.[44]

A comprehensive network of adult educational facilities was built up during the Kaiserreich, especially towards the end of the century, which was also focused on the lower social strata. Taking education to the people was the name of the programme, which was aimed at all those who in their youth had been unable to acquire their *Abitur* qualification: the ticket into the 'educated class'. The deep fissures in German society are reflected in the fact that each of the great 'socio-moral milieux' developed its own adult education programme. Catholic associations included the *Volksverein für das katholische Deutschland* (People's Association for Catholic Germany) and the *Borromäusverein* (Borromeo Association), which provided parish libraries and parishioners with books suitable for Catholics. The socialist workers' movement also built up an extensive educational programme, which ranged from visits to the opera to Marxist instruction.

Working in adult education was a self-evident duty for liberals, since liberalism had always seen itself as a movement of the educated. 'Education' lay at the heart of liberal values. This remained the case during the Kaiserreich. Prussian National Liberals had often even demanded that 'better education' be rewarded with an 'improved right to vote'. The Saxon plural suffrage system of 1909 gave an additional vote to those who were entitled to a one-year period of voluntary military service, i.e. those who had attended at least six classes of a high or middle school. Under the Saxon law, even higher premiums (up to three additional votes) were awarded for income and property.[45] Although social and economic interests had also played a major role in the liberal parties' policies, liberalism as a philosophy and way of life was defined above all by means of education. Liberals necessarily therefore saw adult education as their own responsibility.

The liberal *Gesellschaft für Verbreitung von Volksbildung* (Society for the Dissemination of Adult Education) was founded in 1871 to bring together the many local educational associations. The political *Reichsgründung* was to be complemented by a cultural one. At the same time, the liberal founders hoped to be able to resolve the 'social question' by means of 'education for all'. 'The educated', they hoped, would bring 'the spirit into the organization, the property owners the capital, and the people the desire for education'.[46]

Yet the dreams of liberal adult educators remained unfulfilled. The Society never became a focus for the coordination of local educational efforts, though it supported many libraries – more than 11 000 in 1913 – organized lectures and included entertainment evenings and the theatre in its work, which spread to the countryside from the nineties onwards. Above all, it stimulated public discussion and encouraged the municipalities to recognize adult education as a municipal responsibility. In 1906 around 12 per cent (approximately 1.4 million readers) of the inhabitants of forty German cities, borrowed more than 5.4 million books, primarily from municipal public libraries.[47] Adult education, with which some universities also became involved after the turn of the century, did in fact widen, as the liberals had hoped. Liberals were leading participants in these successes, yet adult education did not create a self-contained liberal milieu comparable to the Catholic or the socialist proletarian milieux.

This is true, too, of the *Gebildeten-Reformbewegung* (educated reform movement), which reached wide circles of the population via societies such as the 'Dürer Association', the 'Goethe Association' or the 'Comenius Society'. The movement spread cultural values, which were shared by the liberals, and which they helped to shape, but again, it did not create a political liberal clientele.[48]

More significant for liberalism was the fact that similar developments were taking place in organized Protestantism. Here, too, liberals and liberal ideas were supported, but it did not constitute a self-contained milieu which would have been exclusively liberal in political terms. Prominent liberals including Ludwig Häusser, Rudolf von Bennigsen and Johann Caspar Bluntschli, were involved in the foundation of the *Deutscher Protestantenverein* (German Protestant Association) in 1863; Bluntschli was its first president (until 1881). However, the Association was politically open to conservatism, but not open to the left. This was even more true of the *Evangelischer Bund* (Protestant Assocation). Founded in 1887, by 1913 it had around 510 000 members. This organized *furor protestanticus* was aggressively anti-Ultramontane and anti-socialist. It was closely identified with the National Liberals: of the five deputies who belonged to its central committee between 1905 and 1914, four were National Liberals. But Free Conservatives also sat on the central committee. The Association, which described itself as a national Protestant watchdog, called for co-operation between National Liberals and conservatives, and maintained contacts with the *Alldeutscher Verband*, the *Ostmarkenverband* and the *Flottenverein* or Navy League.[49]

These national mass associations organized the same social groups that the liberal parties were trying to recruit – the repesentatives of 'education', 'the *Mittelstand*' and 'property' – and the National Liberal Party maintained close personal and programmatic links with the associations. With their large membership numbers – the Navy League organized more than 300 000 individual and almost 800 000 corporate members in 1913, while the approximately 32 000 veterans' associations had around three million members – they provided the National Liberals with a massive field which could be tilled politically. But again, it was a field which was cultivated not only by liberals, but to no small degree by conservatives too.

This openness is typical of the social spheres in which liberal ideas were rooted. As we have seen, political liberalism had a remarkably constant pool of voters, but unlike the massively expanding workers' movements, or stable political Catholicism, political liberalism was not bound into a 'milieu' which was fixed in ideological or organizational terms. Liberals could operate everywhere except amongst church-going Catholics and amongst Social Democratic workers. The life of Ludwig Friedrich Seyffardt is a good example of this liberal openness.[50] A textile manufacturer, Seyffardt was born in Aachen in 1827 and grew up in Krefeld, where he lived until his death in 1898. He joined the National Liberal Party when it was formed. From 1893 to 1898 he was a member of its central committee and for many years he represented it in the Prussian House of Deputies and in the Reichstag. He was also involved in countless municipal and other institutions and associations: in 1848 he joined the *Konstitutioneller Verein*; in 1852 he was elected president of a Lower Rhenish *Landwehr* support association; he was a member of the Krefeld gymnasts' association; at an early age he was elected to the merchant commercial court and in 1862 to the chamber of commerce, and attended many commercial conferences on its behalf. In 1863 he was elected to the poor relief board and the Krefeld town council. He was constantly expanding these fields of activity: he joined the *Volkswirtschaftlicher Kongreß*; the *Verein für Socialpolitik*; the *Gesellschaft für Verbreitung von Volksbildung*; the Krefeld Craftsman and Education Association; he had links with the *Lichtfreunde*, and, during the *Kulturkampf* (in which the Protestant Seyffardt participated), to the Old Catholics. He was a member of the *Verein der Realschulmänner für Rheinland und Westfalen* and other school associations; he sat on the central committee of the *Vaterländischer Frauenverein* and joined the *Deutscher Verein für Armenpflege und Wohltätigkeit*. He was on the committee of the *Verein für bürgerliche Interessen* – the list could go on. Seyffardt's career reflects the extent to which liberals and liberal ideas influenced the organized public.

It was here that liberalism's strength lay: its ideas permeated Kaiserreich society. But it is also here that we find the roots of the liberals' inability to develop a self-contained milieu. Subculturally fixed camps can only form groups that perceive themselves to be threatened or rejected by society. Only groups of this kind are able to form and sustain a 'closed' sphere of life, with clear boundaries between them and their 'hostile' surroundings. In the late Kaiserreich these boundaries began to dissolve in the socialist and Catholic milieux, but they nevertheless continued to exist. Boundaries of this kind had never even existed for the liberals. They regarded themselves as the political and cultural representatives of the German nation-state: they were part of the dominant culture. The segregation and organization of their political clientele in a sub-cultural grouping was therefore impossible. So as soon as the core of liberal thought in the Kaiserreich – the idea of the nation and the strong nation-state – was accepted by the public as no longer the preserve of the liberal parties, they became politically vulnerable. This is exactly what happened in the Wilhelmine era. Liberal ideas, above all as defined by the concept of the nation, had become common political property; it was one of the successes of liberalism which weakened it politically – to the advantage of its competitors who were firmly anchored in a specific milieu.

The 'Liberal Era' and the Shock of the 'Second *Reichsgründung*'

Contemporaries already regarded the internal political changes of 1878–9 as the end of an era, which, for all Bismarck's superior strength, had been profoundly influenced by liberals. Looking back on the 'heyday of the Reichstag' (M. Weber), almost without exception liberals proudly report on an era of reform which had furnished the nation's new state edifice with the liberal spirit. This had been possible because of the close co-operation between the Imperial Chancellor and the National Liberals. Yet the Progress Party, too, claimed a part in the reforms, which it regarded with pride. 'The great aims which the German Progress Party has pursued since it was founded have not yet been achieved by any means', said its election programme of 23 March 1873, 'however, some of them have been realized more quickly than even we had hoped, and if one compares the state of public affairs of 12 years ago with that of today, one has to admit that the changes which have taken place are more consistent with our programme than with those of our opponents'. In 1876 their election programme was no less self-confident, despite all the setbacks they had suffered; all laws, it said, even those which had been diluted by compromise, 'reveal traces of the work and the influence of our party'.[51]

The conviction that they were living in an era formed by liberals permeated the whole of liberalism, though it was at its strongest in the National Liberal Party. It was the National Liberal Party, its representatives pointed out again and again, which had helped to provide the content for the 'form' created with the North German Confederation and then with the German Reich; a form 'which was rather insubstantial for internal state life'.[52] Liberal achievements are impressive. In a long report, written after he left the National Liberal Party (15 March 1880), Eduard Lasker included the period between 1866 and the internal political *Wende* as one of the

> greatest phenomena in the history of reform in Prussia and Germany and indeed in any civilized nation. ... An understanding was reached in all areas of legislation, with the exception of taxation and finance, even on those government suggestions and on the demands for popular representation, for which agreement did not seem possible at all at the beginning, or at least not in the forseeable future. ... The greatest achievements of this kind are: the constitutions of the North German Confederation and of the Reich; the laws relating to the organization, equipping and maintenance of the army; to compulsory military service; the imperial trade and industry laws; the criminal code; the German justice laws; and laws relating to the districts, self-government and the administrative courts in Prussia. In all these cases enormous difficulties have been overcome in unbelievably short periods of time; countless other examples of smaller dimensions follow.[53]

They included currency reform and the foundation of the *Reichsbank*, the liberalization of stocks and shares law, the Imperial Press Law, the creation of imperial offices and the establishment of the imperial court in Leipzig. All this showed, Lasker believed, how much could be achieved 'with moderation on both sides, ... between a strongly monarchic, even authoritarian government and a moderate liberal party which is conscious of its responsibilities'.

The National Liberals consciously pursued a policy of being prepared to reach compromises, believing that this policy was vindicated by their electoral victories. They wanted to work together with the imperial leadership in order to prove their ability to rule, but they did not become a governing party. This was clear to them. They remained 'far away from the quietest beginnings of the so-called parliamentary system', as Julius Jolly, Minister in Baden until 1876, noted in his proud record of National Liberal achievements.[54] In doing so, he addressed the fundamental constitutional problem of the German Kaiserreich: did the constitutional organization of the Kaiserreich provide the opportunity for the long-term, gradual expansion of parliamentary authority, until the full parliamentary system was attained? Or would it ossify in an at best semi-constitutional compromise of power, incapable of reform, which would permanently be held against the liberal middle classes? Historians give differing, sometimes contradictory answers to this core problem.[55]

The liberals were optimistic. They knew that the amendments they had pushed through in the debates on the constitution did not venture anywhere near the centre of the ruling order: they failed to achieve imperial ministers accountable to parliament; the Reichstag did not co-operate in the appointment and dismissal of the Imperial Chancellor; the federal organ, the Bundesrat, also protected the imperial leadership from parliamentary intervention; and the army, too, remained largely beyond the Reichstag's control. Liberals had been forced to accept this distribution of power in 1867 and again in 1871, to allow the nation-state to be founded, and to enable them to co-operate in it at least to a limited degree. 'We cannot now go against Bismarck. He has made the Reich, we must tolerate his stamp.' Hermann Baumgarten's conviction was shared by the National Liberals and also by Max Weber, the sharp-tongued critic of the lack of desire for power amongst the Wilhelmine middle classes. In 1917 even Weber found sympathetic words for the middle classes' enforced position. A decisive 'battle for formal parliamentary rights with the creator of the Reich' would have paralyzed the institutional development of the new state, he said. The 'continued existence of the majority of the imperial institutions was owed' only to the National Liberals' readiness, which bordered on self-denial, to avoid the often-threatened break with Bismarck. The National Liberals wanted to secure these institutions for the post-Bismarck era. 'Their heartfelt desire, often expressed in the inner circle, was to steer those institutions through this magnificent person's period of rule in the Reich, for later, when they encountered politicians of more normal dimensions, the continuity of imperial politics would rest on the efficiency of these institutions alone.' Future developments proved them right – both in their permanent achievements and in what they had demanded, but had not been able to push through against Bismarck. Ultimately they were broken, Max Weber believed, 'not on practical grounds, but because Bismarck refused to tolerate independent power of any kind alongside himself, i.e. power which acted according to its own responsibilities'.[56]

Many liberals had similar thoughts when they experienced 'the great turn of events of 1878' (M. Weber) as the failure of their hopes. Julius Hölder was on the right-wing of the National Liberals. He went along with Bismarck's rejection of free trade, but spoke of the 'violent character' of the Imperial Chancellor, who allowed 'neither the Bundesrat nor the Reichstag, nor colleagues in the ministry, nor even the Kaiser to count for anything'. 'Ivan the Terrible! A nation must have great men at its helm! But – anything, even sacrifices like this, can become too much.' For 'his violence and ruthlessness are beyond measure; he is a modern major-domo'. Even Rudolf Haym, unshakeable in his admiration for Bismarck as the 'strong refuge of the Reich externally', complained that Bismarck had 'undermined every-thing' that would have made a constitutional system of govern-ment possible. But, he explained to a National Liberal meeting in 1881, if they wanted to get anywhere, liberals had no option 'but to come to terms with this man as he is'.[57] This they did. National Liberals worked closely with Bismarck in the Reichstag and the Prussian parliament. They made constant compromises, yet they did not become mere junior coalition partners for Bismarck's policies. Their main aim was to ensure that national unity was enshrined in the law, and that it was secured on a permanent basis. They subordinated many things to this aim, and were often forced to lower their sights.

This was true of the justice laws of 1876, which were hailed by Bennigsen and his colleagues as the culmination of all national legislative achievements. The Progress Party had supported some of the compromises, including compromises in the press law, but had then turned firmly against the compliance of the National Liberals.[58] This bitterly waged conflict between the two liberal parliamentary parties heralded the era of Eugen Richter, who

would later effectively shield the Progress Party from the temptation to capitulate simply in order to achieve partial successes.
In 'this internal disagreement in liberalism as a whole', it became
clear that more and more liberals were questioning the success of
the 'flexibility' of National Liberal policies.[59] They were extending the edifice which they had helped to build, but remained
subject to house rules which denied them the full right of abode.

   This was also true, and particularly so, of foreign policy, in
which the liberals had never questioned the government's
leading role. Indeed, after the *Reichsgründung* they would have
regarded any criticism of Bismarck's diplomacy as an offence
against Germany's national interests. The Reichstag had 'no say'
on foreign policy (J. Ziekursch). The liberals refused a say on
foreign policy as a matter of principle, for that was what the
nation had Bismarck for. He used international crises to put
pressure on both his rivals and his friends in domestic politics,
yet foreign policy remained indisputably his domain. Criticism of
Bismarck's policy of self-denial on national issues was heard, in
the run-up to the European Congress in Berlin (June–July
1878), for example, which took the Imperial Chancellor to the
peak of his international reputation; but this criticism was
expressed by liberals 'with one hand held over their mouths',
as it were (L. Gall). The parties' intensive engagement in foreign
policy did not begin until the eighties, when the German colonial
acquisitions began, and above all in the Wilhelmine era, when
Weltpolitik acquired a significance in domestic political discussions
which it had never had in the Bismarck period.

   However, international politics indirectly became a dangerous
problem, even in the 'liberal era' of the seventies and the following decade, when the Reichstag addressed the issue of the
military constitution. The army, the central pillar of monarchic
power in Germany, and above all in Prussia, had not been tamed
in constitutional terms, either by the constitution of the North
German Confederation, or by that of the German Reich, for
liberals had failed in their attempt to subject the military budget
to the annual budget authority of parliament. They had not,
however, entirely renounced this issue of power between the
crown and parliament, but had postponed it until 1874. It would
have been hard for the liberals who made this compromise
possible to achieve more in 1867 and 1871; their room for
political manoeuvre would have been too restricted by both

Reichsgründung wars. To begin an aggressive course on military policy just when the long-awaited nation-state had emerged as a military victory, lay outside the imagination of the liberals. Nor would they have encountered public support for such a course. The constitutional truce on the military issue came to an end in 1874, when it became necessary to establish the strength of the army in peace-time in legislation. Only now were the liberals able to become active again. The question was now whether to continue the constitutional conflict, which had ended in 1866 without a resolution, or whether parliament should retreat again from the centre of monarchic power. The government bill called for the permanent establishment of the army's strength in peacetime (*Äternat*). The Progress Party and the Centre Party, supported by the National Liberal left-wingers around Lasker, Stauffenberg and Forckenbeck, demanded an annual parliamentary decision. The issue was not about how many soldiers should be approved, but about who should decide the matter in the first place. All sides perceived this conflict as an important crossroads in domestic policy, as a choice between the constitutional state or military absolutism, as the Progress Party historian Ludolf Parisius put it. Many National Liberal deputies agreed with him whole-heartedly on this point. Lasker, for example, spoke of the 'abolition of constitutional rights'. Twesten believed that whoever accepted the bill was blurring the 'distinction between a political character and a mollusc'.[60] While Progress Party liberals remained with their decisive 'no' – for which they paid with the resignation of six deputies from the parliamentary party – the National Liberals agreed to the *Septennat* (the establishment of the strength of the army for seven years). Bennigsen and Miquel had negotiated this with Bismarck, who fell back on his 'favourite political measure – terror', as Oncken described his combination of threats and appeals to the public. The National Liberal decision meant the failure of the attempt to transform the military budget from its special status into a normal budget to be decided by parliament year on year, although in his speech to the Reichstag, Bennigsen tried to suggest that it was a compromise which had been determined by the situation, and which could be corrected at a later date.[61]

It was a speech which highlights the predicament the National Liberals thought they were in. They believed that the new nation-state was threatened by external and internal forces. With regard to the external threats, above all from France, he quoted General Chief-of-Staff Moltke – Bennigsen and his parliamentary party colleagues couldn't and wouldn't oppose Moltke's views with their own expertise – but it was the internal problems on which he focused. The great 'reorganization of Germany's circumstances', which had taken place according to 'principles … which in essence have been emerging from the liberal camp for thirty years', would remain under threat, as long as 'there are still large sections and classes of the population which say that the whole of German history since 1866 is an aberration'. At this point his remarks were aimed primarily at the Centre Party and the church-going Catholic population, yet in the future such sentiments would also be extended to new 'enemies of the Reich' at home and abroad.

In 1874 they succeeded in preventing what they were unable to hold back at the end of the decade: the collapse of National Liberal unity and the conservative *Wende* or change in course in imperial politics, when the liberals lost their role as a governing party without participation in government. This domestic political *Wende* took place during a period of economic crisis, which in 1873–4 brought about the spectacular end of the boom which had coincided with the *Reichsgründung*. Many recently founded joint-stock companies collapsed. Although in retrospect economic historians refer in a somewhat detached manner to the absorption of excess production capacity, contemporaries undeniably experienced the depression of 1873–9 as a deep and decisive break, which darkened their expectations of the future. This had profound political implications.[62]

Although the cheerful expectations associated with the nation-state initially served the liberal parties well, the tables turned when the economic boom ended in 1873–4. Lasker gave a graphic description of the 'change in climate in the state of political awareness and the ways in which people reacted' (H. Rosenberg). With the economic collapse, he said,

Dissatisfaction spread to all regions of the Reich, to all classes of the population, creating an atmosphere in which everyone inhaled ill-feeling as they breathed. It was not hard to exploit this mood in an agitatory fashion, it was not hard to blame it on the ruling direction. This was done by all the parties who had not been major participants in the ruling direction, with varying degrees of skill and effort. ... But this manner of agitation was only elevated to the level of a political historical motive when the organs of government joined in.[63]

Here Lasker was summarizing in retrospect (1883) a course of development which took place over many stages, and which saw the collapse of the former National Liberal–Free Conservative 'governing coalition' by 1879. It was not an inevitable process steered by Bismarck in a planned fashion, and no new workable alliance emerged against the background of a protectionist *Sammlungspolitik* of solidarity between 'blast furnace and harrow' – between heavy industrialists and large-scale agrarians.[64]

We will examine below the new things that did emerge. But first we should describe what was destroyed. At the end of the 'liberal era' the National Liberals had lost their virtual monopoly in imperial politics. There were several reasons for this. After 1874 the Conservatives, who had now become reconciled to the foundation of the nation-state, were able to more than double the number of seats they held, and as a result their political significance for Bismarck was considerably increased. In particular, he began to phase out the *Kulturkampf* (cf. Chapter 4, pp. 199–206) from 1878 onwards. He did so with the intention of making the Catholic deputies, hitherto demonized as 'enemies of the Reich', into coalition partners. But it also meant that the way was now clear for what the National Liberals had always feared: they could be outplayed in parliament, whilst Bismarck came together with the Centre Party on individual issues.

The public change of mood which took place under the impact of the economic crisis made it possible for the Imperial Chancellor to exploit this new scope for political action against the liberals. The liberals found themselves blamed by growing sections of the public for *Gründerkrach* and 'stock market swindles': the contemporary slogans which sought to describe the grounds for the unexpected end of the economic boom. The *laissez-faire* principle had never been part of core liberal ideas, yet in the sixties, when Prussia introduced free trade as a national political weapon against the economically weaker Austria, in economic political terms liberalism became increasingly equated with free trade and the unrestrained economic society. The liberal parties were therefore profoundly affected by the recession of 1873. Political liberalism was discredited along with economic liberalism. More than any other party, the liberals found their ability to assert themselves on a political level weakened by economic conflicts of interest, which were now carried out more aggressively and in an increasingly organized fashion. For both large liberal parties drew their unifying force from political aims and only as primarily political parties could they hope to remain parties of national integration. The growth of the protective tariff movement, which was encouraged, though not created by Bismarck, and above all its expansion to include agrarians who had formerly supported free trade, began fundamentally to alter the political situation. Lasker's astute analysis of this development was written in 1883. Subsequent research has not been able to add anything fundamentally new to it:

> The political significance of this volte-face in economic perspectives is immediately obvious. On the one hand, the mass transfer of members of the Old Prussian Conservatives to the protective tariff system vastly improved the ability of the supporters of protective tariffs to agitate and to be effective, and on the other hand Old Prussian Conservatism emerged from its politically isolated position and recruited new allies in regions of Germany and in professional circles which it had never before been able to penetrate. The government, or should we simply say Prince Bismarck, who liked to hold all the cards and to be able to determine the outcome of the game as far and as long as possible, must have welcomed a movement which provided the opportunity for many permutations, which allowed any number of party reorganizations, and which for the time being created a powerful and active coalition, whose purpose was to appeal to the government for support and help, so that it could seize the initiative in the reorganization of the trade system and of customs tariffs.[65]

This was directed, as Lasker stressed, 'against the liberal spirit', but it did not make Bismarck's break with the National Liberals inevitable by any means. At the end of 1877 Bismarck began negotiations with the National Liberal Party leader, Bennigsen, whom he offered a Prussian ministry and the post of Imperial Vice Chancellor. Negotiations broke down, probably because Bennigsen demanded that two other prominent National Liberals, Forckenbeck and Stauffenberg, both of whom were on the left wing of the party, should also join the government. Whether this was the main reason for the failure, even contemporaries couldn't say, and it remains unclear today. 'The internal situation changes as quickly as a kaleidoscope', a well-informed observer noted at the time.[66] It is also uncertain whether the Kaiser had agreed; the Imperial Chancellor remained dependent on him. This was true even of Bismarck, who had risen to become 'the hero of the *Reichsgründung*'. His methods may have been 'bonapartist', but he was certainly no 'Bonaparte'.

With three National Liberals as Prussian ministers and in imperial offices, the chances of implementing a parliamentary system in the Reich and in the most important German federal state would certainly have increased, and it may have marked the beginning of the transition to the parliamentary system of government which had failed in 1867 and 1871. Whether that would have been made possible if Bennigsen alone had assumed ministerial office is doubtful. There had often been individual liberal ministers during the Kaiserreich, but they were isolated from their parliamentary parties, just as Bismarck had envisaged would be the case with Bennigsen in 1877–8. In the absence of the party or parliamentary grouping, the parliamentary practice of government could not evolve from the entry of one liberal into the government; in other words, there was no firm co-operation between government and majority parliamentary parties, and the government was not formed from these groups. This is true of Miquel, who was appointed Prussian Finance Minister in 1890, and of Hölder, who took over the Württemberg Ministry of the Interior in 1881. Both were appointed, not as trusted men of their parliamentary parties, but as experts who, during their long political careers, had won the trust of the monarch and the government leader. Miquel set great store by the assertion that he did not pursue 'National Liberal Party policies'.[67] As a single liberal in the Prussian cabinet, Bennigsen, too, would probably have been neutralized in party-political terms.

Only after the National Liberals failed to seize government power did developments lead in rapid stages, from the end of February onwards, to the *Wende*, which is usually called the 'second' or 'internal' *Reichsgründung*: the 'greatest, most radical internal change in the history of the modern German Reich', as later, in 1910, Oncken described the feelings of those who experienced it.[68] Developments did not run as Bismarck had calculated, even after negotiations had broken down. The National Liberals remained prepared to make compromises. They were not committed to the principle of free trade, but as a majority under Bennigsen's leadership, they would have helped carry through the transition to protective tariff policies that Bismarck desired. They would also have agreed to a financial reform, though not solely under Bismarck's conditions.[69] Customs and financial reforms formed a unit in his plans. His aim was to set the Reich on its own feet financially, to make it independent of the Bundesrat and above all of the Reichstag. For these institutions annually fixed the division of the funds paid by the individual states to the Reich, which was unable to make ends meet on its own low income. The National Liberals would not have resisted a financial strengthening of the Reich, but they demanded 'constitutional guarantees' in return. They did not want to see parliamentary budget rights devalued by permanently agreed customs duties, indirect taxes and income from state monopolies. Yet a rational course of the kind which Bennigsen suggested in his great Reichstag speech of 5 May 1879 could no longer be implemented. Bismarck refused to agree to it. Instead, he accepted the Centre Party's offer of a financial reform which failed to realize his aims. For the so-called Franckenstein clause, which was decided by the Centre Party and the conservatives against the liberals and Social Democrats, prescribed that the Reich should pay to the federal states all income from the new tobacco tax and from customs duties which exceeded 130 million marks. This was not an effective imperial financial reform. That remained a task for the future.

Why did Bismarck agree to a financial reform which amounted to a defeat for him, when he would also have been able to push through a change in economic policy with the National Liberals? His Reichstag speech of 9 July 1879,[70] in which he settled the score with the liberals and the 'liberal era', provides the answer: he feared a fundamental shift in the political ruling order in favour of the parliamentary system and of the liberal middle classes. The government, he declared, needed the 'support of the parliamentary parties', but it must not submit to the 'rule of one parliamentary party'. It is true that in his apologia he ascribed to his policies of the crisis years of 1878–9 a principled direction which they had not in fact yet had. But his sharp contrasting of the constitutionalist state with the middle-class liberal state ruled by parliament, described the two competing principles between which many people believed they had to choose after the Imperial Constitution had left the matter open. This went against liberalism as a whole in 1879, for the 'bankruptcy of liberalism', of which Windthorst, the leader of the Centre Party, spoke in the Reichstag, did not affect the National Liberals alone by any means. It also represented a failure for the Left Liberals. They were proud of being not a 'government party', their election announcement of 1873 proclaimed, but a 'party of independent men, who have no obligations towards the government or towards individual members of the same'.[71]

The Left Liberals' decisive opposition underlined how far even the 'liberal era' remained behind liberal principles. Yet their policy of remaining true to their principles meant that their opportunities to participate in the formation of policy were extremely limited. They attempted to prevent the undesirable, but left everything else for the future, for the post-Bismarck era, to decide, whilst the National Liberals did their utmost to help determine the development of the nation-state from the beginning.

The German liberals' lack of desire for power, and their reluctance to fight resolutely for the introduction of the parliamentary system in the Reich, have often been criticized. But such criticism ignores the constant attempts made by liberals and National Liberals in particular during the seventies to shift the political balance in favour of parliament. The readiness of the National Liberals as an overall parliamentary party to take over government responsibility, but not merely via an individual member 'isolated' from the party, was to be the culmination of the 'liberal era', and was envisaged as a firm step on the road to the parliamentary system of government. When that failed, it seemed as though the National Liberals had been duped. All the concessions they had made now seemed to be worthless, or else they hampered subsequent developments.

This is true above all of their agreement to the Anti-Socialist Law. In order to avoid a break with Bismarck and to safeguard liberal opportunities to play a part in the shaping of imperial policy, they had accepted an illiberal exceptional law, though their reservations had been great, and the law had been toned down in relation to the original draft. 'This change in principle and in political behaviour, as far as it was determined by momentous events, played a key role in damaging the National

Liberals' reputation externally, but also in shattering the internal structure of the organization.' Lasker's retrospective verdict can also be applied to other concessions which the National Liberals found it hard to make, including those made in the justice laws. Yet if their politics before 1878–9 is judged simply in terms of a rapid succession of compromises on a steep path towards the rather feeble renunciation of participation in power, we overlook what lay before the failure: the 'heyday of the Reichstag' (Weber) was shaped by the National Liberals. They could not have foreseen the fact that the parliamentary system of government they hoped to reap would be denied them. And they could not enforce this harvest. 'A frost has fallen on the blossom of our national seed, and we cannot now say how much of it remains healthy, how many of our achievements ... remain in existence'.[72]

Their failure was not only attributable to Bismarck, although his ruthless readiness to weaken political opponents was partly responsible for 'thoroughly shaking up' (Lucius von Ballhausen) the parties and their policies in 1879.[73] There were other reasons too. They include the death of Pope Pius IX on 7 February 1878, which made it easier to phase out the *Kulturkampf*, and which paved the way for Bismarck to find parliamentary majorities which did not include the National Liberals. The ending of the *Kulturkampf* is one of the normalizations of political life in the Kaiserreich. It was vital for democratization, but for the liberals it came at the worst possible moment. Bismarck the power politican seized the moment – and the National Liberals were unable to defend themselves.

However, it was above all the 'economization' of politics, which began in 1873 with the economic crisis, which hit liberalism as a whole at its most vulnerable point: a wound which Bismarck ruthlessly tore open. It should be stressed once again that liberalism's unifying force lay in its political model; the nation-state as a liberal constitutional state. As soon as public interest focused on the economy and the social sphere, this national and constitutional unifying force was bound to be weakened. They did not have, nor could they have, a new socio-economic unifying idea with which the one which was on the wane could be replaced. In the wake of heavy industrialization, the middle classes were becoming ever more diverse, and their social interests varied too greatly for that to be possible. The 'economization' of politics therefore threw political liberalism into a deep

existential crisis, which saw the decline of the old form of
liberalism, with its educated middle-class values. The pre-
eminence of economic interests had never been part of these
values. Economic interests, they believed, would be resolved in
the political ideal of the liberal nation-state: political progress
would be the prerequisite for economic progress. It now seemed
as though this bond had been broken, and the prioritization of
political progress was called into question.

State protectionism, as Richter of the Progress Party described
Bismarck's new course, brought 'class interests' into Reich politics
'from above': 'This is far more dangerous than the socialist agitation coming from the other side.' The National Liberal Rickert
spoke of the 'bedlam of the hunt for interests', which united
everyone in an 'all-encompassing confusion': 'Agrarians, supporters of protective tariffs, supporters of guilds, tax reformers
of opposing directions, Ultramontanes, Bismarckians, socialists,
union men, sanctimonious hypocrites, free traders who want no
customs duties at all but who do not like paying direct taxes
either, crass militarians and the opposite.' Liberalism was permeated by the feeling that liberal central values would be destroyed
if policies were determined by the incipient economic–social
conflicts of interests.

> What we call the liberal party leads only a galvanic pseudo-
> life and *only* an appeal to personal interest is capable of
> achieving anything with people. Our role seems to be finished,
> and every day I find it harder to ward off the feeling that I have
> worked for half my life pro nihilo. . . . Even the thought of party
> politics is unspeakably disgusting. . . . Surely one shares in
> the guilt of this great lie of parliamentarianism if one continues
> to participate; surely a united, reasoned resignation from
> parliamentary life is the right thing to do. (Franz von
> Stauffenberg)[74]

The National Liberals did not resign, but they did split. On 12
July 1879 a first group of fifteen right-wing deputies left the
parliamentary party. They had voted for the customs tariff law
for different reasons. Some were staunch supporters of protective tariffs, others hoped that the financial reform would
strengthen federalism. The real break, however, did not take
place until 28 August 1880, which saw the so-called 'Secession' of

the National Liberal left-wingers around Ludwig Bamberger, Franz von Stauffenberg and Max Forckenbeck. Lasker had already decided to take this step on 15 March 1880. The 'Secession' was prompted by the military law of 1880, which once again fixed the army budget for seven years, and above all by the laws which heralded the end of the *Kulturkampf*. The National Liberals failed to reach a consensus on a parliamentary party vote in these ballots. Yet the deeper reason for the split in the National Liberal party lay in their different perspectives of the future.

Bennigsen articulated the hopes of those who remained together under the old party name: they wanted to form a centre party, which was open to the right, but not merged with the conservatives; a 'practical party'; one which was prepared to continue to 'pursue practical politics' with the Imperial Chancellor. 'As long as a man of such historical standing and authority is in office', they had no option but to 'seek an understanding with him.' But hopes that this policy would allow a parliamentary system to evolve under Bismarck had vanished. Only now, after the great *Wende* in imperial politics, did the National Liberal desire for a parliamentary system fade away into a distant, indeterminate future.

> If later, after a long period of training in political and parliamentary activity, a situation should arise in Germany where the parties which form the majority in the parliaments also assume responsibility for the affairs of government, a different structure of political party relations may also gradually emerge. For the time being, however, this situation does not yet exist.[75]

Jolly went even further than Bennigsen in his analysis of 1880. He believed that the parliamentary system of government could never be realized in Germany. The 'power' of the Prussian crown had never been sufficiently reduced for that. Its main crutches – the army and the bureaucracy – were too strong, and the parties were incapable of ruling. Either they rejected the parliamentary system or, he said, like all the liberal parties, they were too fixated on their 'ideals'. Jolly regarded 'constitutionalism' as the 'necessary product' of German history. It was unfinished, it had to be expanded, but it should not be misunderstood as 'the parliamentary system in evolution'.[76]

The Secessionist left-wingers used the decisive rejection of Bismarck to counter these perspectives of the future, which sought to continue the National Liberal course of compromise, but were now associated with the open or thinly veiled renunciation of the adoption of the parliamentary system. In his *Die Sezession* ('The Secession'), four editions of which were published in 1881, Bamberger gave an astute analysis of the break with the National Liberal policy of taking one small step at a time. It was a break, as is also highlighted in the work, which was by no means carried out in the confidence of victory. Even the liberal left thought in long periods of time, placed their hopes in the post-Bismarck era, and feared the secret alliance of extremes between which liberalism could be crushed. The policy of the 'preferential treatment of everyone against everyone else' would be 'economically reactionary', and at the same time follow 'the most modern impulse of the time, the socialist impulse'. 'Reaction with socialism!' Bamberger regarded it as an open question 'whether the middle classes are a match for their calling' of safeguarding 'the peaceful development of humanitarian culture', which he believed was threatened by 'state socialism', cloaked in 'conservative robes', which stood there with 'the respectable face of maintaining the state' and yet 'was aimed at completely new and completely outmoded conditions'.[77]

Liberals were clearly convinced that the foundations of the state and of society were shifting, and that the style of political practice was changing. They feared these changes, for they thought that they would bring about the downfall of everything on which middle-class liberal policies were based. Baumgarten is a good example of this change in the liberal view of the future from optimistic visions of progress to premonitions of doom. In his 'Selbstkritik' (Self-criticism) of 1866 he had called upon the liberals to become capable of governing at Bismarck's side. By the eighties, however, though he continued to regard Bismarck's foreign policy as 'wonderful and admirable', he had come to regard Bismarck's domestic policies as the reflection of the 'autocratic demagogue' who whipped up 'the fanaticism of the masses', who made politics 'violent, yes, raw and brutal', and who prepared the ground for 'radicalism'.

If the liberal middle classes have been destroyed as a political factor by Bismarck's enmity and their own political weakness of thought, and now only large property owners and the greedy masses stand opposed to each other, then given such political and intellectual impotence and the uneconomic tendencies of our aristocracy, it would be very strange indeed if demagogy did not become master, at least temporarily, using the tools prepared by Bismarck.[78]

Liberals changed during the *Wende* of 1879. Organizationally, two transformed liberal parties emerged from the 1884 split: the National Liberal Party created a new programme in the form of the Heidelberg Declaration; and the liberal left joined to form the *Deutsch-Freisinnige Partei* (German Radical Party). Before we examine the final stage of liberalism in the Kaiserreich which now began, we will briefly outline the liberal position on three central areas of domestic politics: the state and the church, anti-socialism and social reform, and municipal politics.

The State, the Church and the *Kulturkampf*

A secular state was at the heart of liberal beliefs. German liberals were not opposed to the church. They wanted a confessionally neutral state, which enjoyed administrative sovereignty, enshrined in constitutional law and not shared with other institutions. The state would assume administrative tasks which were now the preserve of the churches, including the supervision of schools or the maintenance of the births, deaths and marriages register. The churches as voluntary religious organizations, from whom all state administrative responsibilities had been removed; the 'de-churched' state as a guarantee of the freedom of the individual to live a rational life: this liberal ideal raised learning to a central cultural value, which shaped private and public life, and which it had to try to live up to. In the model of the 'educated' – in the nineteenth century this increasingly meant the model of the academically educated – the educated middle class turned its own ideal into the measure of cultural progress.[79] Liberalism, which was shaped by the educated middle class, also submitted church doctrines to this authority. When the church hierarchy, and at the same time a broad 'pious' movement, rooted in the church-going public, turned against the comprehensive judicial office which the liberals attributed to learning, a struggle began for the ideological monopoly which both liberalism and the churches claimed for themselves. This inevitably led to a clash between the two. There are a number of reasons for the fact that these pan-European conflicts were vented above all between Catholicism and liberalism, and between the Catholic Church and the states.[80]

After the revolutions of 1848, a development was reinforced and continued under Pope Pius IX, in which papal authority was extended in matters of belief, and in which the national churches' relationship with Rome as the centre of Catholic Christianity was consolidated. This process (contemporaries referred to it as Ultramontanism) was accompanied by remarkable decisions in Catholic doctrine, which the educated Protestant liberal experienced as anti-learning, anti-culture, and as a battle against the 'spirit of the time'. This is true in particular of the doctrine of the Immaculate Conception, which was pronounced in 1854. For Droysen, for example, it was nothing short of 'idolatry', aimed at the 'rabble'. The same was true of the *Syllabus Errorum* of 1864, which described the demand that the Pope should 'reconcile himself to liberalism and modern civilization' (Thesis 80) as one of the 'major errors' of the century. It is also true of the proclamation of papal infallibility on issues of dogma (July 1870). 'What our fathers said is still true', shuddered the liberal cultural Protestant Treitschke, 'the Pope is the anti-Christ'. He regarded the Catholic movement against the Badenese school law of 1864, which ended the clergy's supervision of schools, as 'pranks' and 'rabble rousing', staged as a result of 'the clergy's thirst for power'. Only now, he said, did he recognize 'what great fortune it is to be Protestant. Protestantism is capable of endless further development. The Roman Church always remains what it was'.

The liberal Protestant educated middle classes' conviction that they had to defend the 'independence of modern society and its culture'[81] from the Catholic Church acquired a particular political dynamic in Germany, because in the decade of the *Reichsgründung*, the national political and religious camps extensively overlapped. The liberal interpretation of the *Reichsgründung* as the political culmination of the Reformation, pushed Catholicism to the periphery of the Protestant nation from the start. This was also true of liberals such as Miquel, who stressed that, 'We are fighting the battle, not from the position of the Reformers, of Luther and Melanchthon.' But, he went on, 'we are fighting the battle from the position of Ulrich von Hutten, who even then wanted every German to be granted full freedom of conscience and the right to practise religion, and whose sole aim was the national liberation of Germany from the political rule of Rome and from the external bonds of the hierarchy'. When a Catholic parliamentary party subsequently formed in the first Reichstag, the liberals no longer had any doubts at all that there was an Ultramontane 'war party' which was acting against the German nation, against the modern state, and for the 'rule of the Pope over the secular sphere' (Lasker). They believed that the 'Middle Ages, where the battle [had been] waged once before' had risen again in the guise of Ultramontanism: the Kaiser and the Reich versus the Roman Pope; secular versus Church rule; nationality versus internationalism; 'true learning' versus 'divine mission' (Bennigsen).[82] In short, they believed that the Ultramontane church was threatening political and cultural 'modernity', just as this 'modernity' had acquired its state edifice in Germany, which liberal ideas had helped to shape, and now wanted to furnish.

Several currents joined together in the *Kulturkampf* or cultural struggle – contemporaries already referred to these conflicts in this way, adopting a word coined by Rudolf Virchow in a Progress Party election announcement:[83]

- The development of modern state rule subjected the churches as public institutions more strongly than ever before to state regulation, and removed from them spheres of authority which now became the province of the state administration.
- A philosophical belief in progress, coloured by cultural Protestantism and oriented to 'learning' as the lodestar of 'modernity', closed itself to religious doctrines of salvation. The Catholic Church responded with a renewed offensive demanding authority in opposition to the state and society.
- During the formation of the Protestant–*kleindeutsch* nation-state in 1866–71, which was completed with military force against the 'Catholic' major powers of Austria and France, any group which did not, or did not primarily, base its aims on the nation-state from the beginning was suspected of being nationally unreliable.

Broadly speaking, educated Protestant liberals regarded the 'Ultramontanes' as anti-culture, anti-progress, as internationalists and enemies of the state. But there were other factors, too, which strengthened liberal resolve in the *Kulturkampf*.

The conflicts between the state and the Catholic Church began in 1871 in Prussia and in the Reich, and peaked in 1875. Before that time, however, liberals in Bavaria, and above all in Baden, had already seen that a policy of social and economic liberalization could lead to a broad anti-liberal movement. For a massive counter-movement had been unleashed amongst the rural population and Badenese small traders by freedom of enterprise and movement, by central reforms on the part of the liberal Badenese government (1863), and by the attempt of the liberal middle classes in 1870 to use the Foundation Law to make 'productive' use of the assets of the foundations – i.e. to withdraw them from poor relief.[84] The fact that this anti-liberal popular movement was also a Catholic movement, increased the liberal readiness to pursue the *Kulturkampf* as a domestic preventative war against 'Ultramontane anti-modernity', in which, liberals believed, the Church hierarchy and 'unenlightened' popular belief had entered an unholy alliance.[85] In the seventies, liberals were then forced to accept that economic and social conflicts of interest, even without Ultramontane aid, had stripped them of their claim to represent the nation.

Liberals also regarded the *Kulturkampf* as one of the most important ways in which the 'liberal era' could be prevented from moving to the right and in which Bismarck could be bound to them. The oppositional Progress Party also saw matters in this light.

> Only in the so-called 'Kulturkampf' [wrote the left liberal Parisius in 1878] was Bismarck forced to break with truly conservative traditions and distance himself from the High Church hordes. ... Without the doctrine of papal infallibility, liberal achievements such as the introduction of civil marriage and the births, deaths and marriages register and the severing of links between schools and the church through the school supervision law would have remained pious hopes for a long time.[86]

Liberal reforms in the young, still incomplete nation-state, the repulsing of conservative counter-forces and the *Kulturkampf* were combined in liberal thinking, and it was this alone which allowed the 'liberal era' to take place. Even Bismarck, they believed, needed the isolation of the Centre Party for his attempts to form a Reichstag majority, pushed to the right and comprised of conservative moderates and National Liberals. For this reason, Lasker later wrote, like the liberals, though with different aims, Bismarck had shown himself to be ready to brand the Centre Party with 'the moral outlawry of enemy of the Reich ... which, like the declaration of outlawry of the Holy Roman Empire, was designed to prevent the other opposition groups from even only rarely coming into contact with the Centre Party, since all voluntary, even occasional, contact with an enemy of the Reich brought with it an irredeemable stigma'.[87]

Liberals like Ludwig Bamberger later described the *Kultur-kampf* as a mistake, and accused Bismarck of having initiated it as a 'necessary evil in the safeguarding of the state'. Yet Bamberger had previously agreed with most of the *Kulturkampf* laws, even special laws such as the Expatriation Law, which allowed for priests to be stripped of German nationality and deported from the Reich if they continued to practise when dismissed from office by order of a court. Even some Left Liberals approved the special laws or 'measures', as they were called in legalese; they voted unanimously in favour of the laws separating Church and state, for example.[88]

The German liberals pushed on the development of modern government by the state during the *Kulturkampf* – a development which also took place in other countries – yet they did so in a manner which actually undermined the constitutional state as they were building it up. Where liberals went beyond the separation of state and church in *Kulturkampf* legislation, they sought to safeguard their ability to rule by attempting to isolate Bismarck from the Centre Party and rendering it politically untouchable as an enemy of the nation. This policy unwittingly exposed the weakness of German liberalism, even in the 'liberal era', when liberalism had become a decisive force in the parliaments. Liberals believed they needed a clear concept of the enemy in order to be able to push through liberal policies without participating in government, and as a means of uniting the nation internally after the 'external' *Reichsgründung*. The political function of the national idea now changed. At one time the strong adhesive force around the broad spectrum of the liberal and democratic emancipation movements, it now became an instrument which united by excluding parts of the nation as enemies of the Reich. The change in direction from 'left-wing to right-wing nationalism' (H. A. Winkler) was fully exposed for the first time during the *Kulturkampf*. The liberals had helped prepare it with their agreement to illiberal special laws, because they wanted to prevent a 'clerical–conservative era' (E. Lasker).[89]

In the legislative phasing out of the *Kulturkampf* after 1880, National and Left Liberals cast their votes in different ways, since their views differed on what should be regarded as an exceptional law, enacted for a specific period only, and what was indispensable for the separation of the state and the church. The end of the state *Kulturkampf* did not signify a rapprochement between liberalism and Catholicism. There might have been significant numbers of Catholic deputies in the liberal parliamentary parties of the parliaments and chambers,[90] but the liberal parties remained Protestant parties. The 1907 edition of the *Political Handbook of the National Liberal Party* still defined 'liberal' above all by distinguishing it from political Catholicism, which, in contrast to liberalism, rejected the 'free individual' (p. 705). And under the heading 'Catholic Church', the *Kulturkampf* continued to be defended as necessary: 'Liberalism fights for the independence of modern society and its culture and for that of the Catholic layman against the one-sided clerical desire to rule the world through the Church, and against the indirect dependence of the state on the Church' (p. 561).

When the state *Kulturkampf* ended, the social *Kulturkampf* continued. The Protestant spearheads were now no longer the liberal parties, however, but the extra-parliamentary organizations. The *Evangelischer Bund* (Protestant Association), founded in 1886 and linked to the National Liberals, was a prominent Protestant campaigning association with many members, which continued to work against the 'enemies of the Reich'. Alongside the 'Roman arch-enemies', it also described Social Democrats as 'infidels and unpatriotic'.[91]

The separation of state and church did not affect Catholicism alone. In the Protestant established churches of the states, the *Landeskirchen*, the liberals' ambition was to weaken the sovereign's regime by strengthening and liberalizing the church councils. The synodal constitution would thereby form the ecclesiastical counterpart to constitutionalism at Reich and individual state levels. But liberal attempts to push through their aims were even less successful in the Protestant churches than they were at state level: 'The parishes developed less of an independent life than the municipal organs of self-government, and the synods less than the parliaments of the Bismarck era. German Protestantism's separation of the established state churches certainly took second place to the growing national unity of the Reich. In this respect, the development of the church constitution remained far more conservative'[92] than that of the state constitution. Only the south west German state churches, where liberal ideas had taken a firmer hold, represented an exception to this rule.

The attempt to establish a national church, in which at least some liberals had placed their faith, was also unsuccessful, both in Protestantism and Catholicism, where the *Altkatholiken* or Old Catholics were little more than a small 'middle-class sect'.[93] The Old Catholics supported the liberal *Kulturkämpfer*, yet this 'Rome-free' Catholic liberal outpost can only have weakened their chances of recruiting Catholics.

Despite all the obstacles between them, it would be wrong to assume that the gulf between Catholicism and liberalism during the Kaiserreich was unbridgeable. The 'second *Reichsgründung*' signalled the beginning of a long road to mutual openness in the political relations between the Centre Party and the liberals. This became possible only when the National Liberals lost their role as 'government parliamentary party' and the Centre was able to move away from its position of moral ostracism as an 'enemy of the Reich'. Contemporaries were unable to predict this effect, and it is usually overlooked in retrospect too. The reconciliation of the Centre Party and the liberals peaked in the 'Weimar Coalition'; it had been heralded in the co-operation between the two which was sometimes possible in the elections and the parliaments already during the late Kaiserreich.

Intellectual barriers held longer and remained more entrenched than political ones. This is true of both sides. It was not only liberals who perpetuated the social *Kulturkampf* after the state *Kulturkampf* had ended. A Catholic Church lexicon of 1891, for example, introduced liberalism to its readers as the philosophy which from time immemorial to the present day had paved the way for all the evils of the world; 'the serpent in Paradise already uttered the temptations and false promises of liberalism'. The 'decisive, basic liberal principle emerged with the Reformation' and 'the most advanced socialism' represented its latest sad fruit.[94] This article, which otherwise offers a perceptive analysis of liberalism, was by no means an isolated example. The gulfs between liberalism and the Catholic Church could extend even to the grave. When Forckenbeck died in 1892, the public and the highest dignitaries of the state expressed their sympathy, yet this prominent liberal, who had remained a Catholic all his life, was denied a church burial by the Catholic hierarchy.[95]

Anti-Socialism, Social Policies and Liberal Social Models

The relationship between liberalism and the socialist workers' movement changed with the foundation of the German nation-state.[96] Until that point, both workers' parties had belonged to the German national movement (cf. Chapter 3, pp. 102–20). The visions of the future which they associated with the nation-state differed from those of liberals and middle-class democrats, yet all shared the one great hope that national unity would be a starting point for a better future. The fact that they would not be able to share a path to this future was made symbolically clear at the birth of the new Kaiserreich. While the liberal middle classes experienced national unity as the high point of their lives, the founders of the Social Democratic Workers' Party experienced it in prison. The war against France, annually commemorated as the basis of the new Reich by the national middle classes on 'Sedan Day', had been regarded by the Social Democratic Workers' Party as a war of aggression and conquest, and this had led them to be charged with high treason. The 'national' public's verdict was clear: they were 'enemies of the Reich', 'vagabonds without a fatherland', destroyers of society and enemies of morals and order; the Paris Commune uprising had provided a foretaste of the threats they posed.

Treitschke, who was still a member of the National Liberal Party at the time, summarized these fears for a wider public in his 1874 polemic *Der Sozialismus und seine Gönner* (Socialism and its Patrons).[97] Social Democracy, he said, was a 'party of moral decadence, of political indiscipline and social unrest' (p. 141). Treitschke did not stop at accusations of this kind, however. Against this socialist negative, he developed a picture of 'civil society' which demanded both the resolute defence of the existing order, and at the same time its reform. It was an educated middle-class social model, which barely addressed the issue of the socialist workers' movement, but which had a great deal to say about the hopes and fears of large sections of the educated liberal middle class, and on the limits it wished to place on all social reform. Treitschke described as sacrosanct the bases of 'civil society': 'Marriage, property and the structuring of society'. Tampering with these things, he said, would destroy everything. The ideal of equality was the focus of his tirades against the 'madness of Communist teachings' (p. 103), and against the criticism of the present-day 'social order', with which middle-class scholars were unwittingly providing socialists with an 'easy flank defence' (p. 94). In the name of equality, Treitschke tried to frighten his readers, the socialists wanted 'free love', the 'goddess of the bordello born in the mire', to replace the 'monogamy of modern Christian peoples', which included the 'absolute form of marriage, ... immutable until the end of time'; 'the full and indissoluble relationship for life', in which 'the woman is equal to the man morally', but 'subordinate under the law' (p. 102).

For the middle classes who placed their faith in history, Treitschke's historical philosophical speculations confirmed their position as the culmination of creation, the result of a long historical process which could only be improved upon to a moderate degree. For Treitschke defined 'civil society' as a cultural society, which was based on inequality. 'Millions have to plough the fields, forge and plane, so that thousands can research, paint and rule. In vain does socialism try to use empty outcries of rage to eliminate this bitter knowledge from the world' (p. 105). Treitschke's educated middle-class view of the world polemicized against socialism as a 'community of class hatred' (p. 137) and against the 'rule of the purse', of which, however, there was 'no immediate prospect' in Germany (p. 147). Only education could lead to an aristocracy of educated people, and only they could participate 'in the greatest blessings of culture' (p. 113).

Within the cast-iron edifice of cultural inequality which he called 'civil society', Treitschke approved of state-aided social reforms, such as the extension of factory legislation, improvements in elementary education, and measures to combat the 'terrible misery of workers' housing' (p. 165). But reforms of this kind, he said, should not rebuild the edifice itself, whose first floor was reserved for those few who had been chosen by education. Treitschke used speculative historical and Social Darwinist terminology to underpin his belief that social promotion could only ever be possible at individual level and not collectively. It was a view which permeated all liberal activity in the sphere of education, and sharply distinguished it from its socialist counterpart, despite the common ground that the two shared.[98]

As we shall see, liberals reacted to the 'workers' question' and to the development of the socialist workers' movement in too many different ways for Treitschke's stance towards Social Democracy and social reform to be regarded as typical of German liberalism as a whole. Yet his plea to stigmatize socialists as enemies of the Reich and of society, and at the same time to carry out limited social reforms in favour of the workers, was more typical of state policy and the policies of the liberal parties in the Bismarck era than the recommendations for social reforms suggested by the middle-class *Kathedersozialisten* (socialists of the Chair), against whom Treitschke polemicized. Before we address the issue of these *Kathedersozialisten*, we will turn our attention to liberal attitudes to anti-Socialist measures.

Bismarck's contemporaries correctly assumed, as historians have in retrospect, that he intended the Anti-Socialist Laws of 1878 to deal a blow against both the socialist workers' movement and the National Liberals, who would then be forced to decide for or against Bismarck's new political course (see Chapter 4, pp. 183–99).[99] With its approximately 500 000 Reichstag voters and 50 000 unionists, the workers' movement was too weak alone to represent an enemy, on which the forces which sought to 'maintain society' could focus and forget their conflicts. Bismarck therefore set about ruthlessly exploiting the two attempts to assassinate the Kaiser of 11 May and 2 June 1878 to dramatize the political situation. The attacks on the 'beloved first Kaiser of our reunited Fatherland' (Philippson) were publicly blamed on the Social Democrats, despite evidence to the contrary. The assassination attempts could not have come at a better time for Bismarck, for he had got himself into a rather difficult situation; he was on the verge of losing the support of the National Liberals, but there were no prospects as yet of a new 'coalition'. No one wanted to 'climb aboard ... when the helmsman had lost his way', as in April 1878 the Badenese Grand Duke described the domestic political impasse which Bismarck's new political course had brought about. A law to combat Social Democracy was designed to force the National Liberals, if possible without their left wing around Lasker, back to the Imperial Chancellor's side. Yet this was not initially successful. With the exception of Treitschke and Rudolf Gneist, all the National Liberals belonged to the large majority of 251 deputies (of a total of 309) who brought down the first bill. Yet the splits in the National Liberal parliamentary party were already evident in the explanations given by Bennigsen and Lasker for their rejection of the bill. Whilst Lasker, like Richter from the Progress Party, extended his sharp criticism to a general condemnation of Bismarck's domestic policy, Bennigsen described the bill in its concrete form as a violation of the principles of the rule of law and as politically premature. 'Existing laws', he said, should first 'be applied to the limits of what is permissible', before a 'return to the question of exceptional measures' could be contemplated.[100]

Bismarck refused to accept the parliamentary defeat. He decided to appeal to the public, and called new Reichstag elections. No one could have predicted that the conservative parties would be amongst the great winners and the liberals amongst the losers of these elections (see Table 4). The political climate amongst the German middle classes had changed; from the 'German bedlam' of the elections (Hölder) a Reichstag emerged which had moved to the right. The National Liberals had also been pushed to the right. They were still able to modify the second bill, but it remained an illiberal exceptional law, and they voted for it unanimously. Whilst this was a difficult decision of conscience for Lasker, which he corrected two years later when the Anti-Socialist Law was extended, Bennigsen justified the law in his Reichstag speech as a necessary combative measure on the part of the state to prevent the 'catastrophe' of the decline of law, morals and 'traditional culture', which separated 'the seducer and the seduced' just in time.[101]

Over the next few years, the National Liberals resisted several attempts on Bismarck's part to tighten further the Anti-Socialist Law, yet they played a part in extending the law on four occasions (1880, 1884, 1886, 1888). And even when a renewed attempt to extend the Anti-Socialist Law failed in 1890, National Liberal newspapers demanded a replacement for it.

Left Liberals were more decisive than National Liberals in condemning the way in which exceptional laws undermined legal principles. Yet even they did not remain steadfast in their rejection of them. When the government threatened to dissolve the Reichstag in 1884, they lifted the party whip so as to be able to reject the law by means of a split vote, and yet still allow it to be extended. Twenty-six Left Liberal deputies voted in favour, thirteen did not attend the vote, and the remaining twenty-eight voted against it. Although in 1878 Richter had referred to the Anti-Socialist Law as 'middle-class society's declaration of bankruptcy', in 1884 the unity of the *Deutsch-Freisinnige Partei* (German Radical Party), recently formed from the Progress Party and the Secessionists, was more important to him than the principle of the state founded on the rule of law, of which he was usually the most ardent defender.[102]

Even after the Anti-Socialist Law had lapsed, governments in the Reich and in Prussia made frequent attempts to push through new anti-socialist legislation – both as a replacement for the Anti-Socialist Law and to avoid a military *coup d'état*, of which the Kaiser was terrified, despite his verbal shows of strength against those 'vagabonds without a fatherland'. Important examples of such anti-socialist legislation include the *Umsturz-vorlage* of 1894, the so-called 'small Anti-Socialist Law' in Prussia (1897) and above all the *Zuchthausvorlage* of 1899, which was to create a special penal law for workers, and which was intended to weaken the negotiating power of the unions, and therefore Social Democracy. The liberal parties played a key role in the failure of all these bills.[103] During the final decade of the nineteenth century, they began their search for a policy which would re-establish a broader base in the population for liberalism. Openness to the right and increased attempts to recruit the *Mittelstand* and the peasants were part of this search, as were plans to win the workers back to liberalism, to bring together liberal and Social Democratic 'revisionists', or even to create a political reform bloc from 'Bassermann to Bebel' – from the National Liberals to the Social Democrats. We will return to these Wilhelmine-era efforts to renew liberalism on a political and social level (in Chapter 4, pp. 228–45). First, however, we will turn our attention to the socio-political stance of the liberals, and discuss the ways in which their anti-socialism and their social policies complemented each other.

Despite the increase in industrialization after the middle of the century, the early liberal ideal of a classless society of citizens only gradually began to wane (cf. Chapter 3, pp. 102–20). In the era of the *Reichsgründung* even free traders frequently set their sights on the 'pre-capitalist motive of the satisfaction of one's needs', rather than the fundamental bourgeois 'enrichissez-vous' principle.[104] The appeal of the co-operative idea, which extended into the working class and the workers' movement, also testifies to the durability of the model of the economically independent citizen, and the wide social circles into which it extended. In the seventies, however, it was no longer possible to overlook the fact that the early liberal Utopia of a 'classless society of citizens' (L. Gall) had been overtaken by the reality of the industrial class society. Those who continued to promote the early liberal Utopia seemed now to be mere ideologues with nothing but false promises to offer. The economic recession and the increased calls for state intervention in the battle for economic distribution which went with it, accelerated the liberals' abandonment of their old social model. But even now they did not surrender it entirely: 'middle class society' remained the ideal of the liberal parties, but it was now revised so that it could be brought into line with industrial capitalist reality. Treitschke's social model was an educated middle-class attempt to adapt to the new social conditions. He came to terms with the class-based society, but redefined it in educated middle-class terms, transforming it into something that was indispensable for cultural progress of any kind: 'There can be no culture without servants; that is an inevitable consequence of the law of the division of labour'. Hopes that co-operatives could be used to turn workers into small property owners, Treitschke said soberly, had already failed. They had 'been turned into co-operative banks for the lower middle classes, almost inaccessible to the worker'.[105]

What could 'civil society' do for the worker? We have already heard Treitschke's answer: aid from the state and from the middle classes could be combined with the workers' own efforts to help themselves, to bring the workers' social position closer to middle-class standards, though without blurring the distinctions between the classes. 'Let us genuinely provide for the education and welfare of the small man; but let us beware of supporting the gospel of envy by conjuring up vague dreams of the future and by making emotional complaints about things that cannot be changed' (p. 169). Treitschke's plea to combine anti-socialism with social reforms to help the 'little people', but without blurring the class distinctions of 'civil society', is only one of the socio-political positions adopted by liberals in the Kaiserreich. Another

stance, which had a major impact on the policies of the liberal
parties, is known as *Kathedersozialismus*, although the differences
between the two were not as great as were suggested by
Treitschke's polemics against the 'economic doctrine of original
sin' (p. 94), which he attributed to the 'socialists of the Chair'.

Kathedersozialismus, a derisive term which became a badge of
honour, referred to intensive discussions during the Kaiserreich
on the part of middle-class social reformers who were looking for
a 'third way' between 'communism' and 'capitalism'.[106] The
Verein für Sozialpolitik (Association for Social Policy) founded in
1872, was an effective forum for discussion for this middle-class
desire for social reform. The Association had no ambitions to
become a political party. Scholars, and above all 'anti-Manchester
economists', such as Gustav Schmoller and Lujo Brentano,
formed its core, which was to be supplemented by 'members of
all parties who are not absolute opponents of factory legislation
and of unions', as Schmoller wrote to Lasker when he invited
him to the founding meeting.[107]

The attempt to expand the core of the Association in this way
was not successful. The liberal left wing in particular, including
the National Liberal left-wingers around Lasker and Bamberger,
refused to co-operate with the Association for reasons which will
be examined below. None the less, various channels of influence
brought the debates of the *Kathedersozialisten* on reform into
liberalism as a whole. Their impact on the liberals and the other
parties, the state bureaucracy and the public was considerable,
though hard to quantify. The scholarly debates lent the demands
for social reform a scientific weight which ensured the attention
of the public and seemed to transcend party conflicts. They
thereby came close to the bureaucratic ideal of neutrality and
fostered a climate of readiness for social legislation and welfare
administration.

The political stance of the middle-class social reformers ranged
from moderate liberalism to staunch conservatism. Socio-politically, too, their views varied widely, ranging from state socialism
to the liberal ideas of Brentano, who described freedom of
coalition and the recognition of unions as indispensable for the
controlled reconciliation of the interests of the employment
market parties. In the Wilhelmine era the Association for Social
Policy lost its leading role in the socio-political debate, but it
continued to influence many of the numerous organizations

which were now being founded, and which created the basis
for the 'socialism of the educated' to which various contemporaries referred.

The *Gesellschaft für Soziale Reform* (Society for Social Reform),
founded in 1901, was a new kind of umbrella organization for
social reform, whose leadership included National and Left
Liberals. The Society argued for a social policy which would
defuse domestic political conflicts. This stance provided a
starting-point for co-operation with Social Democracy and the
unions, although this was effectively restricted by the combination of social policy and *Weltpolitik* demanded by the Society,
which was sharply criticized by the Social Democrats. In 1903, the
Chairman Freiherr Hans Hermann von Berlepsch[108] described
the Society's hope that socialism could be removed from Social
Democracy and that it could be transformed into a workers'
party, 'which attempts without class hatred, and without a war
of extermination against the existing order, to fight on the path
of reform and development for a place in the sun for workers, to
which they, like every other citizen of the state, are entitled'. This
was a programme which was approved of by some liberals, but by
no means by all of them, and not even by the majority.

Liberal positions during the almost five decades of the monarchic nation-state changed too greatly to allow political liberalism's attitude to Social Democracy and social policy to be
reduced to a clear and simple formula. Most importantly, political and socio-political 'progressiveness' did not necessarily over-
lap. 'Manchester liberal' blindness to social problems went hand
in hand with decisive political liberalism, and a 'social liberal'
understanding of the hardships of unrestrained industrial capitalism was linked to a political stance which sometimes extended to
illiberality. The attitude of the liberal parties to the anti-socialist
laws and the social legislation of the 1880s highlights the mean-
inglessness of labels such as 'left' or 'right' when it comes to
characterizing the socio-political attitudes of Left Liberalism and
National Liberalism as a whole. Richter regarded the anti-socialist
laws as combative measures against the 'majority of the Reichstag', and as 'middle-class society's declaration of bankruptcy'.[109]
Yet under his leadership, Left Liberalism also rejected social laws,
such as sickness insurance (1883), accident insurance (1884) and
old age and invalidity insurance (1889), with which the German
Reich had embarked upon a path to modern state social

provision; a course which the other European states soon adopted too. The National Liberals, on the other hand, were amongst the parties which allowed this first step in the direction of socio-political modernity to be taken. Yet at the same time, they helped push the illiberal anti-socialist exceptional laws through parliament. The two major liberal camps were therefore not separated by a clear line of 'progressiveness', which encompassed both political and social progressiveness.

The small German People's Party, on the extreme left wing of liberalism, also had difficulty in reconciling its desire for socio-political reform with its uncompromising political liberal stance, which was expressed in the rejection of all exceptional laws. In the Reichstag it voted in favour of the sickness insurance law, but against accident, old age and invalidity insurance legislation. However, the group around the *Frankfurter Zeitung*, which was more open to reform, was then able to assert itself against the Württemberg democrats' position of rejection. The new party programme of 21 September 1895 accepted the idea of state social insurance, and also called for an extension of measures to protect workers, and for the creation of municipal unemployment insurance. In 1910, the south German democrats also brought this list of socio-political reforms, which was wider-ranging than those of the other liberal parties, into the programme of the Left Liberal merger, the *Fortschrittliche Volkspartei* or Progressive People's Party.[110]

The Left Liberals' rejection of the progressive social insurance laws of the eighties reflects the liberal belief in society's power to heal itself, which sometimes verged on 'Manchester liberal' blindness and 'economic Darwinism'.[111] This belief was combined with the fear of the authoritarian state, which they believed would be impossible to liberalize if it also had a 'socio-autocratic' (E. Richter) hold on society. Left Liberals regarded the state social insurance laws as the strongest grip on 'civil society' since the 'second' *Reichsgründung*. The introduction of protective tariffs; economic aid and economic activity on the part of the state; government co-operation with conservatives and the Centre Party; the growing power of pressure groups and associations; and public criticism of capitalism from the left and the right were all leading, Left Liberals believed, to a 'clerical–aristocratic–socialist alliance' (Bamberger), of which state social insurance represented a further important element.[112]

A comparison of Bamberger and Miquel shows that the desire for political and social reform was shared by liberals on the 'left' and the 'right', and that there was no comprehensive socio-political reform bloc in German liberalism. As we have seen, Bamberger was a sharp critic of the *'Wende* of around 1880'. The political compliance of his National Liberal Party eventually moved him to join first the Secessionists (1880) and then the Left Liberal German Radical Party, which was founded in 1884. The German middle classes would now have to prove that they 'were a match for their mission' of protecting 'the peaceful development of humanitarian culture', which he claimed would be threatened if the 'finances of a military state, which was always armed to the teeth, also had to assume responsibility for a colossal state industry and finally for the redemption of the most wide-ranging social promises'. Bamberger felt that his time had been spent in a dispute about principles, a fight for 'life and death on the battlefield of free, peaceful modern development'. He believed that one of the great threats to a humanitarian society of citizens was the 'plan for a social tower of Babel, in which the plans for a general life pensions institution for its inhabitants are already clearly visible'.[113]

Bamberger therefore regarded the rejection of the state social insurance laws of the 1880s as a civic duty for liberals. It was this very respectable political stance on the front against the alleged threats of authoritarian 'state socialism' which seduced Left Liberals like Bamberger into singing the praises of the 'free middle-class individual', whilst ignoring the social reality of the non-middle-class strata. Bamberger's inability to incorporate the lives of workers into his image of middle-class individuality and political liberalism meant that he could only see the proposed accident insurance, for example, as a further element in the 'restructuring of the whole world of work in the Gothic style' – like the attempts to eliminate freedom of enterprise by reviving 'compulsory guild membership' or by means of apprentice regulations. In his prophecies of doom against the social-reforming 'crusades against capital', in which government and agrarians, 'the pulpit and the lectern', would come together to make the socialist criticism of capitalism socially acceptable, Bamberger employed a language which already came close to Social Darwinism: the socialism of the left and the right would foster an omnipotent interventionist state, which would finally realize the 'famous new ideal', 'which reads: the weak must be protected, the strong must be broken – that is to say, the economically diligent must be suppressed, and the idle pampered'.[114]

Other Left Liberals were haunted by similar nightmare visions of the consequences of the plans for state social insurance in the eighties. Barth, for example, referred to 'this kind of humanitarianism' which uses the methods of the state to undermine the individual's 'feeling that he should take responsibility for himself'. It was misguided, he said, because it would discourage many waged workers from 'saving up a small amount of capital, which they can use to advance to a higher economic level'.[115] His advocacy of the principle of self-help, which he wanted to see safeguarded in social insurance too, transferred the idea of co-operatives to social provision, whilst apparently forgetting that the liberal hope in the production co-operative as a method of turning workers into businessmen had already been disappointed.

National Liberals also rejected the idea that the state should assume full responsibility for social provision. The state may only 'point the way', thought Bennigsen, but the 'decisive factor' must 'always remain the individual, the corporations and the local authorities'. Otherwise a 'social bureaucracy' would emerge, which was as alien to the 'innermost essence of the German character' as Social Democracy was.[116] In contrast to the Left Liberals, the National Liberal Party did not stop at bringing down Bismarck's plan of turning workers into state pensioners. They also played a major role in the fact that the social insurance laws turned the workers into insured individuals, who paid their own contributions. Only in old age and invalidity insurance did Bismarck manage to find support for a state contribution; accident insurance was financed by employers alone, and one-third of sickness insurance by the employer and two-thirds by the insured individual. Since administrative bodies (local sickness insurance companies, professional co-operatives and state insurance companies) were also established for all types of insurance, the National Liberals believed they had achieved their objective: the state established the framework, and those affected – workers and employers – paid the insurance contributions, which were jointly administered.

Miquel also argued for this procedure, although he had nothing against the state making a contribution to insurance provision, for, as he reproached the Left Liberals in 1889, 'the

German state [has] never been as individualistic ... as a certain economic theory likes to believe'. He welcomed the overall state social insurance framework of the 1880s as an important first step, which would soon be followed by others. For it established new standards which would soon be extended to other areas. He was not even against a single organization for all types of insurance or the extension of social insurance provision to all workers, including rural workers.[117] Miquel regarded these new social benefits as a 'progressive cultural responsibility on the part of the state', like the imperial housing law which he demanded in 1888, in order to gradually eliminate the 'colossal physical and moral devastation wrought by people living on top of one another'. His programmatic speech at a National Liberal Party meeting of 1886 reflects his conviction that 'all other issues vanish' before 'the great social question'. 'Social reforms will be addressed, above all the equitable distribution of property and an increase in medium- and small-scale property-ownership. The just satisfaction of a class which is rightly striving for emancipation; that is the great duty of the middle classes!'[118] Miquel argued for a policy which brought together state, municipal and corporate aid and – he referred here to England – which would recognize even unions as useful elements in bringing about the 'social peace' he hoped for. 'In many issues I am far more progressive than the Progress Party ever was,' he rightly believed, 'but in others I am more conservative than the parties which may stand behind me.'[119]

Miquel's self-portrait fittingly described the lines of 'progressiveness' which were so intertwined in Germany. Those like the Left Liberals (and the Social Democrats) who demanded far-reaching political reforms, firmly rejected the German Reich's first attempts to create social insurance. Those who were closer to this state and to its conservative ruling élites, like the National Liberal Miquel, whom the Left Liberal Parisius rightly called a 'professional maker of compromises',[120] were clearly more open to the introduction of state social insurance policy. This sociopolitical front, which ran right through German liberalism, counter to the division between right and left, weakened in the Wilhelmine era, when all parties, including the liberals, were searching for new political directions in a changed society (see Chapter 4, see pp. 228–45). The German liberals' experiences of municipal politics played a major role in this development. For in

the Kaiserreich the municipalities became a field of experimentation for the emerging interventionist state, actively fostered by
liberals in the sphere of municipal politics, which was regarded as
being 'close to the citizen'. This is also true of the Left Liberals.
What they rejected at national level, describing it in terms of the
state's overwhelming of society, they promoted or at least toler-
ated at municipal level. Without this social reforming municipal liberalism, the German variant of 'social liberalism' in the
Kaiserreich, it would not be possible to understand the desire for
social reform on the part of liberals of all camps and their ability
to implement those reforms.

Liberalism and Municipal Politics

No political alignment of the nineteenth century had been able to
entirely distance itself from the aim of the state as a union of equal
citizens – this had been a core element of all hopes for the future.
Yet reconciling the ideal of the citizen of the state with that of
the 'citizen of the municipality' posed considerable problems.
It was the liberals in particular, who had always been staunch
supporters of municipal self-government, who were forced to
confront this issue. Though they regarded the municipality as a
'living, integrated personality' (Rotteck), the basis of civil society
and the free state, there were different levels of municipal rights.
This historically evolved order, which distributed participatory
rights and protection in an unequal fashion, corresponded to the
early liberal social model. Even the Imperial Constitution of
1849 had not attempted to use the constitutional norm of the
equality of citizens of the state to deny the municipality the freedom to remain a union of unequals. Although the Constitution
aimed to bring the 'municipal citizen' closer into line with the
'state citizen', its implementation was postponed to the future
(paragraph 133), and the municipalities were left to decide their
constitutions as they saw fit (paragraph 184).

   The process of assimilation between citizens of the state and
municipalities advanced over the course of the nineteenth
century, but remained incomplete at the end of the Kaiserreich.
With freedom of enterprise and the lifting of the remaining
marriage restrictions, the nation-state immediately destroyed
major bulwarks which had reinforced the hierarchical and

exclusive municipal freedoms which existed in many Germany states. Yet the principle of equal rights for all continued to be realized to a far lesser degree at municipal than at Reich or state level. Broadly speaking, the municipalities remained places where the democratization of political institutions was blocked, and yet at the same time they were sites of the most profound social change. It was in the municipalities that Germany's transition to an industrial society, which was centred on the towns, took place.[121] In 1910, 56 per cent of the population of the Reich lived in towns with more than 20 000 inhabitants, compared to a mere 17 per cent in 1871. In these towns the image of society was transformed, with new ways of life and new social and cultural demands and obligations, which gave rise to administrations which made major achievements in municipal social provision.

All this was carried out under extensive municipal self-government. It was dominated by the middle classes, at a remove from the lower social strata, and on a political level it was largely determined by liberals. This political colouring was by no means self-evident. Indeed, it is one of the most striking aspects of the history of the German Kaiserreich, that of all places it was in the centres of the emerging urban industrial society – which became strongholds of Social Democracy in the Reichstag elections – that the liberals were able to assert their supremacy in municipal politics for so long. The liberals, who had begun as representatives of the nation-state movement and as the real parties of the *Reichsgründung*, had long since been forced to sacrifice their dominant position at Reich level, where they had lost urban voters above all to the Social Democrats. Yet they continued to set the tone on the urban governing bodies, where they approved of policies which do not conform to the usual image of bourgeois liberalism, frozen in the representation of its material interests, incapable of reforms based on a sense of social responsibility. Research into municipal liberalism has so far been neglected, and it is only rarely mentioned in studies of liberal-ism.[122] Here, too, we can do little more than provide a broad outline. Without it, however, we would be left with an image of liberalism which was unbalanced and alien to reality.

What did municipal social provision mean in the Kaiserreich? The answer to this question should be prefaced by a brief description of municipal political liberalism.

The vast population increases of the second half of the nineteenth century made it necessary for the towns to take on a number of new responsibilities,[123] one of the most important of which was sanitation. As late as 1892, more than 8000 people died in a cholera epidemic in Hamburg. It was the last in Germany, for new water works, and above all improvements in the sewerage system, brought about a 'cultural revolution on the greatest scale', after which the great plagues caused by inadequate hygiene became a thing of the past. Abattoirs overseen by veterinarians were also a major element in municipal social provision. From the last third of the nineteenth century onwards, they rapidly replaced private slaughterhouses. Gas and electricity works were also important, as were trams, which became indispensable in the growing towns. But citizens demanded other facilities too, including better schools, public baths and parks, theatres and museums. Most of these facilities were erected and run by the municipalities from the beginning, or increasingly came under municipal control.

The towns, above all the larger ones with 20 000 inhabitants or more, developed a range of provision which had a profound effect on people's lives. Not everyone could make use of all that was on offer. Some, like theatres and museums, met specifically middle-class needs and opportunities, but others were for everyone's benefit. The municipal interventionist state, which emerged in the Kaiserreich under middle-class leadership, did not serve purely middle-class interests, by any means.

Liberals were instrumental in building up and expanding this wide-ranging municipal social provision. They helped to establish municipal works and to run them, or at least came to terms with the fact that such things were necessary. Contemporaries spoke of municipalization and bringing certain spheres under local authority control, but they also referred to 'municipal socialism' – a term which in Germany, in contrast to England, did not mean socialist programmes of reform, but municipal 'public welfare' schemes, which were based on social reform, and which rejected notions of private economic profit. That liberals helped to support such policies is not self-evident. It shows that the economic liberal *laissez-faire* principle had never managed entirely to suppress the old tradition of the municipality as a middle-class protective association, entitled to limit the individual's scope for economic development for the common good.

Liberals seem to have been well aware of the conflict between their efforts to free the economy from state regulation and their readiness to bring the growing areas of social provision under municipal control, and to remove them from the 'free market'. This was highlighted by their extreme reluctance to address municipal political issues in their party programmes. At best they are touched upon on the periphery. They were issues which were best left to municipal liberalism, which could then adapt to each local situation, without being bound to programmatic suggestions on the part of the national parties. This avoided a conflict between national and municipal liberalism's different perspectives on the interventionist state.

For this reason, it is not possible to extrapolate the municipal policies of the liberal parties from party programmes. One can only look at the behaviour of liberals in the municipalities and their institutions. Apart from the small *Nationalsozialer Verein* (National Social Association), the Left Liberal Berlin *Sozialfortschrittlicher Kommunalverein* (Social Progressive Municipal Association), of which Barth and Hugo Preuß were active members, and the Alsace Progress Party (1913), only Social Democracy developed a municipal political programme. While it declared its firm support for municipal socialism, the National Social Association called for municipal works only in those areas which were 'far removed from healthy competition' and which 'serve the lasting needs of the municipalities'.[124] Yet the circle it drew was a wide one; in addition to transport services, gas, electricity and water works, etc., it encompassed abattoirs, pharmacies and savings banks. Left Liberals seem generally to have been more reticent towards municipalization than National Liberals, but at the end of the day they all came to terms with it and supported the irreversible trend towards public works. This is also true of the conservatives and the Centre Party. The expansion of social provision through the establishment of public works was not, therefore, a specifically liberal achievement. It was widely supported by all middle-class parties, including the liberals, but it was not a foregone conclusion for these representatives of middle-class independence who sought to avoid state monopolies at Reich and state level.

During the Kaiserreich, liberals encouraged the growth of the municipal interventionist state as representatives on the elected town councils, and also led the municipal administrations in many towns. This was above all true of the National Liberals, while Progress liberals such as Hermann Becker succeeded only rarely in becoming mayor. Becker, known as 'red Becker' after he was imprisoned for his democratic activities during the 1848 revolution, became mayor of Dortmund (1871–5) and then of Cologne in 1885. Yet the National Liberals were the 'preferred party of mayors'.[125] Their most important representatives included Miquel in Osnabrück (1867–9, 1876–9) and Frankfurt (1880–90), Leopold Winter in Danzig (1863–91), Otto R. Georgi in Leipzig (1876–99) and the mayor of Berlin, Arthur Hobrecht (1872–8), whom Forckenbeck succeeded, having served as mayor of Breslau from 1872 onwards.

Forckenbeck (1821–92), one of the leading National Liberals, joined the Secessionists in 1880 and with them founded the Left Liberal merger, the German Radical Party, in 1884.[126] As an esteemed parliamentarian, he rose to the highest offices open to a deputy: he was President of the Prussian House of Deputies from 1866 to 1873, and Reichstag President from 1874 to 1879. He could have become President of the Court of Appeal in 1872, but opted instead to accept the post of mayor of Breslau. Race courses, the town gas works and a museum were built in Breslau under his leadership. A town statistical office was also established, and the theatre was brought under local authority control. He also established a town trade school and a new *Gymnasium*. For the first time, the *Volksschulen* or elementary schools were overseen by two secular inspectors. During his period of office, Breslau also acquired new water works and a modern sewerage system. He continued this work in Berlin until his death in 1892. Under his leadership, town expenditure on *Volksschulen* rose considerably, when school fees were waived for around 82 per cent of *Volksschule* pupils. After 1884 the town established higher *Bürgerschulen* and new *Gymnasien* and *Realgymnasien*. The girls' schools, however, remained overwhelmingly private. Regular street cleaning was also introduced in Berlin, streets were lined with trees, the Victoria Park and other parks were established, and Forckenbeck and his public servants asserted themselves against the small businessmen who tried to block the building of town abattoirs and market halls. The Berlin municipal authorities also used petitions to introduce a regulation which took effect in 1881, which prevented municipal abattoirs in Prussian towns from selling meat which had not been slaughtered on the premises.

These facilities were owned and maintained by the towns, as were the water works which were now built or improved. The financial risks associated with electrification in Berlin, however, seemed too great to Forckenbeck and the town councillors, and the concession was awarded to a private company. Liberal mayors and *Bürgerkollegien* also set about reforming the poor relief system. This was carried out under Forckenbeck in Breslau and Berlin and Miquel in Frankfurt, where in 1883, on the model of the Elberfeld system, the town took over poor relief which had previously been in the hands of charitable foundations.[127] Miquel was no supporter of unrestrained municipalization. The town council, on which the Left Liberals had the majority (see Table 14), was pressing for a greater expansion of municipal works than Miquel wished to allow on money-saving grounds. He therefore prevented the town from taking over the administration of the gas works and trams during his period of office, although he was willing to go further than the town councillors on the matter of building regulations and the construction of small municipal flats. He was not able to push through the construction of housing for public sector employees until 1887 and 1889. He left Frankfurt in 1890 to take up the post of Finance Minister in the Prussian government. In his farewell speech he named three things which he hoped to 'entrust' to the town councillors. One of them was the readiness of the municipality to participate more fully in 'great works of social improvement'. 'Limits which have hitherto been placed on municipal power' would have to be moved, he said; carefully, testing every step, but moved nevertheless. Some things had been done: school fees had been waived for those 'classes without means', as had water rates and to a large degree rents too. But this, he said, was not enough: the municipality had to do more.[128]

Similar demands were made in the programme of the Left Liberal Social Progressive Municipal Association, referred to above. Its demands included improved social services for town workers, public labour exchanges with equal representation on the part of employers and employees, free municipal nursery provision for those in need, subsidies for public housing associations, capital gains tax on municipal works 'in a fair fashion' and tax exemption for lower income groups. In 1913 the municipal programme of the Alsace Progress Party included similar social reforms, but it focused more closely on the small businessman. All 'businesses which were virtual monopolies (for example, abattoirs, water works, gas works, electricity works, trams and small railways)' were ideally to be operated by municipalities or associations, but at the very least they should be run by 'mixed concerns', with a strong municipal influence and a sharing of profits.[129] Although not all liberals went as far as this, it is generally true to say that liberal municipal politics was not the bourgeois politics of pressure groups. Nor was it Manchester liberalism, which would leave the individual at the mercy of self-help, even at the risk of poverty.

Municipal liberalism did not embrace the 'free market' or the cult of economic strength. It helped implement municipal policies of social reform and social provision, but rejected political reforms and the democratization of the town administration. Municipal social policy was implemented behind the walls of political illiberality, without which municipal liberalism would have been forced to sacrifice its strong position in the municipalities, as it had at state and above all at Reich level.[130] Suffrage was its strongest crutch. Equal and universal suffrage had never been part of the liberal programme, but in comparison to suffrage at national and individual state level, municipal suffrage was particularly backward during the Kaiserreich. Regulations varied greatly from one federal state to another and even within states themselves. But it is generally true to say that municipal suffrage promoted middle-class supremacy on the town councils by means of 'many variable restrictions and preferential treatments, such as property suffrage restrictions, the poor law clause, the suffrage of public limited companies, the division by a third or a twelfth of taxable income, the home ownership clause and open casting of votes'.[131] Municipal suffrage was also bound to numerous taxes on the acquisition of citizens' rights. As late as the turn of the century in the area covered by the Prussian three-class suffrage system, only 50–60 per cent of Reichstag voters in large towns were also entitled to vote in municipal elections. In Badenese and Hessian towns this figure was 60–70 per cent, in Frankfurt am Main and Kiel only half, in Hamburg around 23 per cent and in Rostock a mere 8 per cent. Not only workers, but even local notables could be disadvantaged by the extreme suffrage restrictions, which favoured the property-owning middle classes. In Cologne in 1898, for example, the Government President and the President of the Provincial High Court voted in the third class.[132] After 1900, suffrage was liberalized in some German states (though regulations were tightened in Hamburg and Saxony, for example), yet until the end of the Kaiserreich municipal suffrage remained the most important means by which middle-class rule was defended against emerging Social Democracy in the towns (see Table 14).

Social Democracy was the only party to demand democratic suffrage – to be extended to women – for the municipalities. The National Liberals lamented the fact that educated people who did not own property were disadvantaged, yet the fear of further strengthening Social Democracy and the Centre Party led them to reject reforms which would liberalize municipal suffrage. The Left Liberals were against class suffrage and against open, non-secret ballots, but only small groups – the German People's Party, the National Social Association and the Social Progressive Municipal Association – demanded equal, secret elections for all men. The Alsace Progress Party made similar demands in 1913, but like the National Social Association, it believed that only those who had lived in the constituency for at least a year should be allowed to vote. In the Left Liberal merger, the Progressive People's Party, the rejection of a liberalization of municipal suffrage which had always dominated progressive liberalism, won the day. At its party conference in 1894 the Radical People's Party adopted Richter's position.

The political communities represented by the municipalities are not the same as the community represented by the state. A boarder who has moved into a municipality on the day that the electoral roll is compiled is entitled to vote in a Reichstag election, but he does not yet have any interest in or understanding for the finer issues of municipal affairs. A fluctuating population is not a suitable representative for municipal suffrage. Municipal rights must be dependent on duty and on the payment of taxes.

Liberals had always represented the view that the fully political municipality should consist of tax payers. The Left Liberals continued to pursue this argument in the Prussian Parliament in 1914, when they called for the active right to vote in municipal elections to be awarded to economically independent women – and only those who were economically independent.[133] The line of argument remained the same, yet their objective had changed: views of suffrage which in the first half of the nineteenth century had corresponded to aggressive middle-class liberalism were now, towards the end of the century, simply attempts to defend a bastion of middle-class control which was perceived to be under threat.

Strictly limiting the circle of citizens who were entitled to vote was not unlike liberal *Honoratiorenpolitik*. It had the effect of slowing down the penetration of political parties into the municipal governing bodies. District associations chose the candidates for the municipal elections and they discussed the subjects which the town councillors and the municipal authorities were to address. In Münster, for example, around 30 per cent of all district councillors between 1835 and 1870 belonged to the 'Civilclub'; between 1870 and 1914 the figure was around 21 per cent. A further 13 per cent met in the 'Two Lions Club', the town's other important association in terms of municipal politics.

The old families lost their influence in the expanding towns in the second half of the nineteenth century. The new industrial social groups advanced and the economic pressure groups increased their importance on the municipal representative bodies. Yet the local associations retained their importance for the new leading local groups as focal points of influence for municipal politics. In Dortmund, for example, from the seventies onwards, the new municipal leading stratum was comprised of the directors of the mines and the iron and steel works, the middle-class owners of firms which had sprung up in the wake of industrialization, and merchants and lawyers. Their representatives sat on the town council and they met in the 'Casino' Association. For the Dortmund upper- and upper-middle classes – craftsmen did not belong to the association – this was the place where town issues could be settled in advance. In 1912, twenty-six of the fifty-five town councillors and ten of the twelve unpaid members of the municipal authority were members of the 'Casino'.[134]

Municipal local government was played out in these small, clearly defined circles, where everyone knew everyone else. They were ideal places for *Honoratiorenpolitiker* to operate. As Miquel said to the Frankfurt town councillors when he took office in 1880,

They have elected me as their mayor, not as a political man, but as a man of the administration, a servant of the municipality. . . . I interpret this as a nice way of saying that the municipal administration has nothing to do with political, social and confessional conflicts, and that it should remain a neutral area in which everyone can work together for the good of the whole, unhindered by differences of opinion.[135]

The liberal ideology of a society of citizens in which all interests coalesced can be clearly heard here, and Miquel was not entirely wrong. Certainly, in many areas municipal social provision was geared to the 'good of the whole'. What was meant by that was increasingly determined by the political parties, who were now beginning to play a greater role in municipal politics. Two things above all fostered this process: the *Kulturkampf* and the growing success of Social Democracy in the municipal elections.[136]

In the areas with a large proportion of Catholic inhabitants, the Centre Party remained the liberals' most important rivals. The liberals therefore rigorously exploited the opportunities offered by the Prussian municipal election law of 1900: they used a local statute to impose a regulation which would undermine the law's aim of including more voters in the second class. The liberals' intention was clear. The issue, as the Rhenish National Liberal central committee declared in 1899, was to prevent 'the surrender of a whole series of flourishing liberal town councils in the Rhineland to the Ultramontane Party'.[137] The Centre Party was wrestling with the liberals for supremacy in the municipalities, yet both agreed on limiting the democratization of suffrage to prevent Social Democracy from becoming too strong. Alliances were even forged between National and Left Liberals and the Centre Party, in order to halt the advance of Social Democracy in municipal politics.[138] At the end of the day, however, it could not be prevented, and the face of municipal election campaigns and debates in the town councils was changed.[139] Nevertheless, liberals were remarkably successful in defending their municipal bastion until the end of the Kaiserreich (see Table 14).

The towns, the centres of industrial society, had remained liberal strongholds where liberals pursued policies which sometimes appear confusing and contradictory. They defended *bürgerlich* self-government from state intervention, yet *bürgerlich* referred not to the 'citoyen', but to the 'bourgeois'. With the aid of the Centre Party and the conservatives, liberals attempted to apply suffrage restrictions in order to stabilize the supremacy of the property-owning middle classes. In this bourgeois citadel, however, they pursued policies which advanced the municipal interventionist state and implemented social reforms and social provision for non-middle-class strata too. In short, political illiberality and readiness for social reform combined to form a curious mix in municipal liberalism.

This municipal liberalism, clearly distinguished from national liberalism, also provides a clue as to why, in contrast to England, a viable social liberalism did not emerge at national level. Liberals seem to have been capable of policies of social reform only where their political position was not threatened by an independent socialist workers' party. In this respect, the political illiberality which liberals employed to prevent Social Democracy from gaining access to the municipal parliaments was probably a prerequisite for urban social liberalism in the Kaiserreich. Yet this suggestion is certainly inadequate as a sole explanation. We should also consider the fact that social liberal currents were slowed down at national level by factors such as the socio-political involvement of the state. As we have seen, many liberals feared that state social policies would lead to a powerful illiberal alliance between the bureaucratic authoritarian state and the socialist desires of the working class: 'Reaction with socialism', was Bamberger's description of this fear of an alliance of extremes. This threat existed to a lesser degree in the towns. This was at least true of the towns with a historically evolved middle class. Conditions were different in the 'industrial villages' of the Ruhr which had grown into cities,[140] where it was not possible for middle-class, liberal-determined social provision to develop as it had in the towns with a middle-class tradition and a middle-class identity. To clarify the point once more; in the *Bürgerstädte* too, interventionist social provision fulfilled middle-class interests, but not only those. Middle-class pressure group politics and the social liberal desire for reform were not mutually exclusive in liberal-led towns.

'Weltpolitik' and Internal Reform: The Wilhelmine Era

From the last two decades of the nineteenth century onwards, the conditions under which German politics was pursued changed profoundly, and the fundamental politicization of society reached a new level. The *Kulturkampf* and the persecution of the socialist workers' movement were instrumental in these processes, as were state and municipal social provision and the internal political tensions which were played out against the backdrop of German 'Weltpolitik'. The large numbers of mass organizations, which were established above all from the nineties onwards, reflect this qualitative change in politics, and played an important role in advancing the process of change. Political decisions affected the lives of all people to an increasing degree, and more and more people attempted to take part in political decision-making processes. Their chances of doing so were vastly increased by the many new organizations and institutions, which ranged from political associations and workers' unions, to social or religious associations and the elected administrative bodies for social security. Women also entered politics via their organizations, although they did not gain full political rights until the Weimar Republic. Almost all social spheres were politicized, even areas such as sport or adult education, which seem far removed from politics. The existence of Social Democratic shorthand courses, chess clubs or libraries, and political Catholic drama groups gives some indication of the areas of society which now became politicized.

These developments presented the parties with a great challenge. If they were to be a match for their primary task of reconciling competing interests and pushing them through on a political level, their programmes and organizations would have to seek to address the enormously expanded areas of political life. The social integration now demanded of the parties increased rapidly and none of the large parties was more profoundly affected by this than the liberals. They had always seen themselves as the representatives of the entire nation, and they regarded their dominant position in the German national movement of the era of the *Reichsgründung* as a kind of historical attestation of this claim. The '*Wende* of around 1880' had shaken this liberal self-image for the first time, and the Reich and state election results, together with the growing numbers of non-liberal pressure groups and organizations, left them in no doubt that the political unifying force of the liberal parties was beginning to dissolve. We have already discussed (Chapter 4, pp. 128–83) the way in which they reacted to this in organizational terms, so as to avoid being crushed between the Catholic, Social-Democratic and conservative milieux. We will now turn to the manner in which the liberals responded to the qualitative political changes in their programmes.

The loss of their leading position in the Reichstag had forced the liberal parties to enter into parliamentary coalitions to enable them to continue to influence Reich politics. Yet the number of coalition partners open to them was small. The liberals' national and Protestant perception of their party and their clientele did not permit an alliance with the Centre Party. This was as true of the Left Liberals as it was of the National Liberals. Anti-Catholic sentiments were the strongest 'mortar' in the fragile common ground in and between the liberal parties. It did not exclude the possibility of selective co-operation with the Centre Party, which increased in the last few pre-war decades. Yet it was only during the First World War that the gulfs which the *Kulturkampf* had opened up were bridged again, before in 1917 a strong parliamentary coalition between Left Liberals (and temporarily the National Liberals) and the Centre Party and the Social Democrats became possible in the *Interfraktioneller Ausschuß*. Before the First World War, in contrast, one of the main aims of liberal politics had always been to force the Centre Party out of the key political position it had acquired between 1894 and 1906 in particular, as 'not the government party, but the governing party', as the Centre Party leader Ernst Lieber put it.[141]

In order to be able to assume this position of 'governing party' once more – to be the main parliamentary party with which the Reich leadership co-operated in the Reichstag – the National Liberals would only consider a coalition with the conservatives before the turn of the century. The Left Liberals' room for manoeuvre was even more restricted. Barriers had been created to the right, to the National Liberals and the conservatives, by the conflicts surrounding the 'second' *Reichsgründung*; barriers which would take a long time to dismantle. The only significant political force to their left was Social Democracy, which Left Liberals like Richter regarded as an 'artificial product' of the reactionary state, which itself was pursuing a 'vulgar state socialism'.[142] Left Liberals therefore had no option but to retreat into opposition and to put their faith in the post-Bismarck era. However, the early death in 1888 of Frederick III, who was granted only ninety-nine days as German Kaiser, destroyed all the plans made by the 'Crown Prince Party', as the Left Liberals were called, and the attempt under Bismarck's successor, Leo Graf von Caprivi, to win the liberals and the Centre Party over to government policies in the Reich and in Prussia had failed by the end of 1891.

Only after the turn of the century did the political fronts shift to allow the liberals' scope for political action to grow. A major role was played here by developments in Left Liberalism, which was attempting to expand liberalism's social base and to open it to the left to Social Democracy. Liberalism as a whole also became more prepared to co-operate with the conservatives.

Between the 'second' *Reichsgründung* and the beginning of the First World War, liberals had only two parliamentary alternatives: coalition with the conservatives, or – from around the turn of the century onwards – cooperation with Social Democracy. The opportunities and problems associated with these opportunities for alliances will be examined here in the context of three points of intersection: the National Liberal–Conservative Cartel of 1887; the liberal–conservative Bülow Bloc (1907–9); and the Badenese Grand Bloc experiment, which brought together liberals and Social Democrats between 1909 and 1913.

After the '*Wende*' of around 1880' a period of political reorientation began in which a regrouping of the conservative and liberal parties to form a middle-class Protestant two-party bloc appeared to be possible. Left Liberals joined together to form the German Radical Party, whose programme of 5 March 1884 emphasized the core elements of oppositional liberalism: the safeguarding of the rule of law; the strengthening of parliament, though without a demand for the parliamentary system of government; the rejection of interventionist economic and social policy on the part of the state ('state socialism'); and support for the regular establishment of the strength of the army in every legislative period.

Later that month (23 March 1884), south German National Liberals opposed this programme with their Heidelberg Declaration, which proposed co-operation with the Imperial Chancellor and the conservative parties. Their programme included calls for an extension of the anti-socialist laws, assent to the state policies on workers, measures which favoured agriculture and the readiness for 'any sacrifice necessary' to safeguard German military might.[143] This programme, which the north German National Liberals adopted under Bennigsen's leadership, created the basis for the Cartel of 1887. The alliance of the 'middle-class centre parties' desired by the National Liberals was triggered by the conflict surrounding the army bill of November 1886. When the Reichstag majority, including the Left Liberals and the Centre Party, agreed only a three-year army budget, instead of the seven-year budget applied for, the Reichstag was dissolved and in 1887 the National Liberals and both Conservative parties united to form a cartel for mutual electoral support.

Bismarck had wanted this conflict. He set about engineering a war hysteria intended to persuade people that 'without a seven year budget, the French would arrive tomorrow' (Bamberger), and reduced the elections to a battle on the 'issue of principle of whether the German Reich should be protected by an imperial army or a parliamentary army' (Bismarck).[144] The National Liberals gratefully accepted Bismarck's interpretation of the crisis, for they regarded the 'national interest' as the only adhesive force that could bring the disparate middle-class interests together politically, and create a practicable link to the leadership of the Reich.

In a speech to a National Liberal state conference in Hanover on 23 January 1887, Bennigsen spoke of the danger of a new constitutional conflict and pleaded that the army, 'the secure basis of our existence', should not be exposed to the 'passions of party debates and party struggles' every three years. The guarantor of national security must not be subjected to a Reichstag which was 'torn apart by the parties' – this was Bennigsen's message, though it was toned down by a proud record of liberal achievement which not only celebrated the 'liberal era' between 1867 and 1878, but also looked back to the era of reform. Since that time, he said, 'in the civil service, in learning, in middle-class activity, in art, industry and technology' in Germany 'a great chapter of liberal views and principles [had been] built up and developed to form the secure basis of a free constitutional life'. For this reason, a period of reaction was not to be feared.

Whilst Bennigsen emphasized the peace-keeping role of a strong army, at a remove from 'the seamy side of party life', Miquel, the architect of the Cartel on the National Liberal side, was rather more explicit. In his acclaimed speech at the south west German party conference in Neustadt on 30 January 1887, he spoke of the 'new showdown' with France, which could come at any time: 'Stay on the side of the Kaiser in the argument, and on that of his great advisors in war and in peace! We want to help them to maintain what we have achieved on the bloody battle-field through them and with them. That is what we pledge today – yes, we pledge it!' He found more moderate words for the peace-keeping mission of the army.

It was above all the centre parties which reaped the benefits of the 'appeal' to the nation, to the 'simple people who think impar-tially', as Miquel described them.[145] Whilst the German Con-servatives gained only a further two seats, the number of Free Conservative deputies (*Reichspartei*) rose from twenty-eight to forty-one, and the National Liberals were able to almost double their seats (from fifty-one to ninety-nine). The Left Liberals were the great losers. Bamberger spoke of the 'crushing' of his party, as its share of the seats decreased from 18.7 per cent to 8.1 per cent (see Table 4).

The National Liberal–Conservative Cartel had the absolute majority in the Reichstag elected in 1887, but its political com-mon ground was soon exhausted. The acceptance of the seven-year budget, the extension of the Anti-Socialist Law, the new sugar and spirits tax law and old age and invalidity insurance are all included in the Cartel's record of achievements. However, rifts were soon exposed in the increase on customs duty on grain and the phasing out of the *Kulturkampf*. Neither in the Reichstag, nor in the Prussian House of Deputies did the Cartel parties form a closed coalition. National Liberal deputies broke ranks and moved to the left, and German Conservatives sought and found the support of the Centre Party.

Miquel's hopes for a liberal–conservative reforming alliance were utterly dashed. His programme of reform, described to an audience of around 4000 on 2 February 1890 at a National Liberal Party conference in Kaiserslautern, included improved association and coalition rights; further 'profound social reforms'; increased taxation of 'immense wealth' and 'tax relief for those with less property and for medium-scale property owners in the town and the country'; and the reform of imperial finances. But this programme could not be pushed through with the conservatives, and was even a controversial subject amongst National Liberals. There was no option but an appeal to con-tinue the Cartel as an 'alliance to repel opponents, who are

waging a life or death war with us'.[146] But repelling opponents
was not enough, not for the voters; in 1890 the National Liberals
and the Free Conservative *Reichspartei* (Reich Party) lost more
than half of their seats. Nor was it enough for the young Kaiser
William II, whose political course was 'onward', not the defence
of what had already been achieved.

1890 saw 'the lacklustre collapse' (Herzfeld) of the Cartel,
and the beginning of the 'latent crisis of the Wilhelmine Reich'
(W. J. Mommsen).[147] For the National Liberals this initially meant
the bitter experience of losing the key parliamentary role to their
main rival, the Centre Party. On both wings of liberalism,
however, a rejuvenation of personnel and programme began,
which culminated in the two bloc experiments of the pre-war
decade: the liberal–conservative Bülow Bloc at Reich level and
the liberal–Social Democratic Grand Bloc in Baden.

During the nineties, and increasingly after the turn of the
century, a broad discussion began on the liberal ideas of the
future and on the ways in which these aims might be implemented. This has been largely neglected by research. The discussion, which was conducted in many political and cultural
spheres, centred on the German liberals' attempts to adapt their
social models to a dynamic industrial society. This was an extraordinarily difficult task, for as we have seen, German liberalism
had arisen as a pre-industrial movement, with pre-industrial
views of the world, which had survived even the period of
industrialization from the middle of the nineteenth century
onwards.

There are a number of reasons for the fact that even liberalism, the herald of the modern 'middle-class' world, retained this
colouring for such a long time. One in particular should be
referred to here. The late stage at which the nation-state was
founded, which failed on several occasions and which was threatened with failure to the very end, had allowed German liberalism,
in contrast to Western European liberalism, to become the
organizational and intellectual shell of a national movement,
which subordinated all political and social interests to a single
great aim: that of the nation-state. This focus on the idea of the
nation, in which the liberals were able to forget their internal
conflicts, was possible because of the favourable economic situation of the era of the *Reichsgründung*, which largely postponed
the middle classes' internal conflicts of interest. Liberals of all

alignments attempted to continue this course after the *Reichsgründung*: they used the appeal to the nation as a clearing house for interest politics, but above all as a source of legitimacy. Only interests which were recognizably national were regarded as valid. Anyone who did not obey these was stigmatized as an enemy of the Reich and excluded from the 'nation'.

This fundamental position, which aimed to determine policies based not on specific social interests, but on the overridingly important nation, particularly appealed to liberals. It formed the basis of their existence, for German liberals of all camps did not see themselves as representatives of middle-class interests. They continued to regard 'civil society' as an 'open society': anyone could rise into it; social harmony was its aim. During the period of high industrialization in the Wilhelmine era, this claim completely conflicted with reality, which was not the 'classless society of citizens', the old dream of German liberalism, but the industrial class society, which had organized itself in a multitude of pressure groups. Between the 'second' *Reichsgründung* and the eve of the First World War this new society deprived liberalism as a whole of almost half its Reichstag seats (1881: 40.8 per cent; 1912: 21.9 per cent). The liberals of Wilhelmine Germany did not react to this development by openly and aggressively emphasizing the class character of their liberalism. They did attempt to build up economic pressure groups and organizations, or to attract existing ones to their side (see Chapter 4, pp. 128–83). They also pursued policies which aimed to push through the interests of their middle-class clientele. Yet they did not follow Max Weber's demand to gather the *Bürgertum* as a class into a class-conscious liberal party, and to lead it against the 'class of conservative large landowners'.[148]

The national self-image with which German liberalism had developed and with which it continued to identify, ruled out a declaration of this kind. But liberalism's insights into the difficulty, if not impossibility, of defining middle-class interests 'in total middle-class terms' also closed them to a middle-class liberal class programme. When they attempted from the nineties onwards to assimilate liberal values and liberal politics to the changed conditions of industrial society, liberals were forced to confront this core problem: they were living at a time of increasing class tensions, and did not represent any class whose interests were uniform enough. 'In some respects the National

Liberal Party is in a less favourable position than others',
Hobrecht, the National Liberal deputy and former Prussian
minister, declared in 1897, for example.

> Alongside their political programme, and outside the sphere of
> actual politics, almost all other political parties retain a
> particular point of origin and unity ... which holds them fast,
> perhaps in the sphere of the Church, or in the representation
> of a particular class or *Stand*, or in the representation of specific
> material economic interests. The National Liberal Party lacks
> all these things; the representation of economic interests is
> more of a threat to us than a unifying element. We must seek
> our reputation in the attempt to reconcile conflicting economic
> efforts wherever possible, and to bring them into harmony. We
> are not representatives of a class or a *Stand*; people often say
> that we are the true representatives of the educated *Mittel-
> stand* – but that is only a rhetorical expression – this term has
> never really meant anything concrete to me. The so-called
> middle classes are a substance which is too vague, too diverse
> and loose for one to be able to make a strong bond of them, and
> the German middle class is too German to be able to work in a
> particularly unifying and binding manner. All the more
> valuable for us is the mortar of history, which is inevitably
> created by a long period of common work on great tasks, and of
> shared battles on great issues.[149]

Hobrecht's hope that the liberal future might be found in the
national past reflects a stance in which the older generations in
particular sought refuge. Yet even forward-thinking liberals,
who wanted to make liberalism viable in the future, referred to
the 'nation'. 'Every standstill', said Miquel, was 'a grave national
loss' and for a young empire such as the German Reich, a
'standstill [was a] reversal'. Miquel's conviction led him in 1890 to
demand a careful but determined colonial policy, which did not
recoil from financial sacrifice. All great peoples, he said, had
acquired colonies; it was by their colonies that a nation's desire
for power and formation could recognized. Five years later Max
Weber famously expressed his belief in the power of a dynamic
liberalism to rejuvenate domestic politics: 'We must grasp the
fact that the unification of Germany was a youthful escapade,
which the nation committed in its old age, and which would have

better been omitted on the grounds of cost, if it was going to be the conclusion and not the beginning of German world power politics.'[150]

Wilhelmine liberalism was particularly receptive to the idea of an imperialistic German *Weltpolitik*, since its belief in the nation as the highest measure of state existence and political action had prepared it for the idea of a German world mission.[151] *Weltpolitik* seemed to provide a new task which would safeguard the future, a suitable means of uniting the nation across its social divisions. This is particularly true of the National Liberals. They became the 'colonial party *par excellence*' (H. Gründer), constantly under threat from social and economic conflicts, which they sought to counter with the 'battle for national needs', the 'battle for ideal goods' as a source of national harmony and liberal strength: 'The era of political confusion and decay, the years of the reckless pre-eminence of the economic interests of individual *Stände* were also the years of the low point of the National Liberal Party. Each high tide of national sentiment, each period of political and economic resurgence brought it up again.'[152]

Most National Liberals advocated not an aggressive imperialism, but 'an imperialism based on *realpolitik*' (W. J. Mommsen), which was used as a defence against Social Democracy on a social level, and which argued fiercely for increased middle-class participation in political rule. The National Liberal plea for a German colonial policy combined the arguments of power politics and economic politics with the idea of a cultural mission which seemed ideally suited as a means of stylizing the 'seizure' of 'apparently rulerless countries' as a common national task, in the face of which all domestic conflicts would be silent. The German nation would provide 'cultural benefits' and would receive settlement areas and raw materials 'in return'; it would pay less money to foreign countries for imports, but would, as it were, 'take money from one trouser pocket and put it in another'. But it would not just go into capitalist pockets; it would also go into the pockets of the 'little people', and even into Social Democratic pockets.[153] The social imperialistic vision that the National Liberal Party brought before the public was German *Weltpolitik* in the service of national power externally, and social harmony internally, made possible by increased wealth for all.

Left Liberals initially opposed a colonial state policy, but slowly abandoned this position by 1906.[154] The *Freisinnige Vereinigung*

(Radical Union) was the first to turn. Its agreement to the German military, fleet and colonial policy combined economic interests with the hope of restraining the large-scale agrarian–conservative circles on a domestic political level, and the hope that progress could be made on the introduction of the parliamentary system in the Reich. Georg von Siemens was one of the representatives of a policy of this kind, which was to be self-consciously middle class, though without being frozen in opposition like Richter's Radical People's Party. Siemens was not afraid of an aggressive defence of capitalism as the most important fruit of the 'most revolutionary century of the last two thousand years'. He described it as the new basis 'of the state and culture' which made 'the party of landowners and the army largely superfluous'. He regarded politics and the economy as inseparable. The economic battle of the 'European nations to secure their food' had now joined the 'soldiers' war'. Colonial politics was for Siemens a necessary part of this economic battle, which should only be supported by the state, but led by 'capital' and steered by the stock exchange as the economic 'general staff' of the nation.[155]

Richter's Radical People's Party, which had forced the split of the German Radical Party in 1893, following its rejection of the military bill, did not pursue a fundamentally anti-imperialistic policy either. It certainly supported an 'informal imperialism': economic expansion overseas, but privately financed, not subsidized by taxation, as the 'business patriots' (Richter) desired. One of the main criteria by which Richter and his Left Liberal supporters measured German colonial and fleet policy was the profitability which they did not necessarily regard as inevitable in state colonial ownership. Franz Mehring's phrase (1898), 'calculated opposition',[156] is a fitting description of Richter's stance.

Between the turn of the century and 1906, amidst vehement internal parliamentary party disputes, the Radical People's Party abandoned its rejection of an active state colonial policy. This created the conditions for the Bülow Bloc. The death of Richter (10 March 1906) facilitated the Left Liberal reorientation, which was avoided only by the *Demokratische Vereinigung* (Democratic Alliance), founded in 1908. The deeper reason for the reorientation, however, is to be found in the mass suggestion which began when the nation's dreams of power began to stray into the realms of *Weltpolitik*. Had the liberal parties tried to distance themselves from this, they would have lost their middle-class clientele, which needed no manipulation from above to desire the nation's launch 'into the world'. The combination of *Weltpolitik*, a powerful national state and industrial social modernity exercised a fascination against which the liberal middle classes had no resilient defences, given their political and social philosophies.

The strongest impulse for liberal change came from the 'progressive imperialists', whose spiritual leader was Max Weber and whose most effective propagandist was Friedrich Naumann.[157] For both men the nation and the national powerful state were synonymous; and the 'national' the highest value of all. For Weber it became a kind of secularized belief, the 'belief in Germany' (W. J. Mommsen). But it was a belief in a renewed Germany; a Germany which was externally strong and internally open to political and social reform; an, 'as it were, progressively changed social imperialism' (P. Theiner). Naumann failed in his attempt to create a 'liberal revisionism' (T. Barth) which was capable of forming an alliance with Social Democratic revisionists. But he anticipated ideas which would only be translated into action after the Second World War. He had a profound effect on liberalism as a whole, and helped to draw it out of the political ossification in which it had been stuck since the eighties.[158]

The Bülow Bloc was the first attempt to make this changing liberalism politically viable.[159] When the Centre Party and Social Democracy rejected a colonial supplementary budget, Imperial Chancellor Bernhard von Bülow dissolved the Reichstag in December 1907. The 'coupling of the conservative spirit with the liberal spirit', as Bülow described his aim, was incomplete from the beginning. The merger of the National Liberal Party with the conservative parties or with the Left Liberals to form one large centre party was considered. Yet these were not so much realizable plans as a reflection of the hopes of contemporaries that it would finally be possible to bring an end to the fragmentation of the parties.[160] All the same, Left Liberals succeeded in 1907 in founding a joint parliamentary party.

What did the liberals achieve with their co-operation in the Bülow Bloc? Why did it fail? Its achievements include a number of economic laws, a restriction of the criminal offence of *lèse majesté*, and above all the Imperial Association Law of 1908. Although this law did not entirely satisfy the Left Liberals, since only restricted permission was given for non-German languages

to be used at public meetings, it did represent an important
advance. Women were also permitted to join political associations and to attend political meetings. The Reichstag's influence
on Reich politics increased, yet a decisive step in the direction of
the parliamentary system failed, as did attempts to reform the
Prussian three-class suffrage system, and to expand the liberal–
conservative bloc to the Prussian House of Deputies. This was
not only due to the conflicts between liberals and conservatives.
Even amongst liberals there was no clear consensus on objectives. Whilst some of the Left Liberals saw the liberal–conservative
bloc, as Naumann did, as a means of achieving a Left Liberal
merger and as a preparation for a liberal–Social Democratic
alliance, others regarded it primarily as a means of warding off a
renewed conservative–Catholic supremacy.

The fact that there was no overall liberal desire to seize
government power was made clear by the *Daily Telegraph* affair of
1908. All parties distanced themselves from the Kaiser's inter-
view, which had triggered an international sensation and out-
rage. However, the Reichstag was clearly unable and unwilling to
exploit the damaged position of the Kaiser and the Imperial
Chancellor for political purposes. The National Liberals did not
go beyond the demand for a return to the rules of constitutionalism. They wanted to strengthen the position of the Chancellor and prevent the Kaiser's 'personal regime'. The parliamentary system of government was no longer included in their
demands. In the decade of the *Reichsgründung* until the '*Wende* of
around 1880' things had been quite different. By the pre-war
period, however, only a minority of National Liberals still
regarded the parliamentary method of government as desirable.
The motives for this change in attitude were complex. They
regarded parliamentarianism as irreconcilable with a strong
monarchy, which, in turn, they held to be indispensable on
military grounds. They also believed that the party system would
weaken federalism and, in combination with democratic suffrage,
would encourage the 'rule of the masses'. Given the development
of the elections, they also feared that they would be permanently
excluded from influence on government policy.[161]

Nor was there a clear consensus on the parliamentary system
of government in the Left Liberal parliamentary group during
the Bülow Bloc. Only a tiny section openly demanded that the
parliamentary majority should form the government. In his

1907 article on 'Parliamentarianism', Conrad Haußmann of the German People's Party, said, in rather veiled terms, that the 'administrative leaders must be the trusted men of the [parliamentary] body or its majority'.[162] But the liberal left had its sights on a clear strengthening of parliamentary power, even though it failed to devise a constitutional model which could have been assimilated to the German situation, above all to the federal structure of the state, the strong position of the monarchies and the fragmentation of the parties.

The Bloc finally collapsed in 1909, when the conservatives 'terminated' it (Eschenburg) because they were unable to accept an imperial finance reform which ran counter to their agrarian interests. The conservatives succeeded in preventing the reform when they were joined by the Centre Party in rejecting the planned inheritance tax and instead taxing movable capital at a higher rate, whilst defending the tax privileges of the agricultural spirit distilleries. As Naumann said in triumph, 'the rift in the bloc occurred at the right point and at the right time': 'to the right of the National Liberals' and at a time when the 'source of friction' between liberals and Social Democrats had decreased.[163] Now, he hoped, the failed liberal–conservative reform coalition would be replaced by the liberal–Social Democratic Grand Bloc 'from Bassermann to Bebel'.

The Grand Bloc was only realized in Baden, however. It had been initiated after 1905 in the election agreements between National Liberals and Social Democrats and in their limited parliamentary co-operation, above all in the spheres of cultural politics. Only in 1909 did a parliamentary coalition emerge from it, which was capable of 'logical, systematic bloc politics' before 1913.[164] Progress of this kind could be made because liberals and Social Democrats had already begun to come closer before 1909. Their rapprochement was aided by the revised constitution of 1904, which had brought the suffrage of the Badenese legislative chamber into line with Reichstag suffrage. The Social Democratic election victories of 1905 and 1909 – the number of seats rose from six in 1903, to twelve, and then to twenty – strengthened the reformist course of Badenese Social Democracy. The increase in Centre Party seats and their own losses initially forced National Liberals and Left Liberals or democrats to form a small overall liberal bloc (1905) which was expanded to form a Grand Bloc in 1909. Rejection of the Centre Party was their most important common goal, but it was not the only one. In 1910 the coalition pushed through a reform of the *Volksschule* curriculum against the Centre Party, and brought about a revision of municipal suffrage which was now linked only to a direct state tax of 20 Marks. It was even possible to address a subject in which a break between National Liberals and Social Democrats seemed assured: in 1910 a tax reform was implemented with which no one was satisfied, but which was pushed through by the bloc parties against the Centre Party.

These reforms, however, exhausted the common ground between them. In the *Landtag* elections of 1913, many National Liberal associations openly resisted the election agreement their party leadership had struck with the Left Liberals and Social Democrats. The leading committees had ventured further than the National Liberal party base was prepared to accept. This was the main reason for the failure of the Grand Bloc inside Baden, which dissolved in 1913–14, despite the fact that it had not been formally revoked. There were other reasons too, based on Reich politics.

The collapse of the Bülow Bloc had strengthened the conflicts surrounding the liberals' future political course, but it had also increased efforts to unite the liberal parties. In 1910, the Left Liberals merged to form the Progressive People's Party, whose programme was in many respects only a vague compromise, but which also highlighted the renewed reforming zeal of Left Liberalism. The programme called for the equality of citizens of the state, to be achieved by means of democratic suffrage in the states and (it was not quite so decisive on this point) in the municipalities. However, the programme postponed the inclusion of women in the society of citizens of the state to the future, to be preceded by intermediate steps, such as equality in the elections to merchant and trade courts and to the legal imperial insurance bodies. Naumann had demanded equal suffrage for women as a programmatic point, yet before the First World War this demand could not even be pushed through amongst Left Liberals – of all the middle-class parties, the one which was least opposed to the political women's movement. During the war, too, the Progressive People's Party continued to refuse to extend their demand for the democratization of Prussian suffrage to women. National Liberals regarded female suffrage as a 'Utopian' demand anyway, which took 'no account of the differences between the sexes desired by nature, or between the male and the female psyche'. For the same reason, they rejected any criticism of the marriage law clauses of the *Bürgerliches Gesetzbuch* or Civil Code, which had come into force in 1900. The decision-making rights of the husband 'in all affairs affecting shared married life' (paragraph 1337) corresponded to the 'essence' of the family, which was 'leadership on the part of the man'.[165]

The extent to which liberalism had changed was revealed most clearly in the programme's sections on social policy. 'Self-help' was no longer a fixed doctrine, state regulation was now regarded as permissible and was also demanded for employees. The Left Liberal programme also provided for help in cases of 'blameless unemployment'. This corresponded to a demand from the German People's Party, which had been the first of the middle-class parties to raise this point, as early as 1899. On this matter, however, National Liberals were more inclined to put their faith in the self-healing powers of the economy.[166]

The opening up of Left Liberalism on a social level was unmistakable. Even in German early liberalism, the core aim of liberating the individual from compulsion had always also meant the protection of the individual's social rights. Only after the turn of the century did Left Liberals succeed in adapting their ideal of the independent individual to the conditions of industrial society. The *Nationalverein für das liberale Deutschland* (National Association for Liberal Germany) went particularly far in this respect. The foundation statement of 15 March 1907 stated that,

Being liberal means recognizing the right to economic organization, the full freedom of coalition for members of both sexes, and the equality of employees and employers. We do not regard the economic struggle as an end in itself, but as a means of achieving social peace. The extension of social legislation and its expansion to include further circles of the population will also serve this purpose.

The National Association's programmatic work of 1910, *What is Liberal?*, described the distribution of income in Germany as illiberal, since 'approximately 2/3 to 3/4 of the total German population does not have the income needed to satisfy its absolutely basic needs. This means that it lacks that fundamental condition which is vital for the free development of talents and higher moral development'. The cultural ideal of the free individual meant that liberalism's 'most important task' was to provide 'as large a part as possible, and an ever larger proportion of our people, with the means to acquire the minimum amount of external possessions which will keep them free from poverty' and allow 'them to lead a moral way of life'.[167]

Whether this ideal required co-operation with the Social Democrats – the central question for all who sought an alternative to an alliance with the conservatives – was a controversial issue, even amongst Left Liberals. Although one of the large pressure group organizations, the Hanseatic League, was urging the liberals to work together with the Social Democrats to create a reform bloc against conservative agrarian forces, Naumann could not even find a majority in his own party for his slogan 'from Bassermann to Bebel'.[168] The chairman, Otto Fischbeck, referred to the 'Grand Bloc Utopia' and both the Social Democratic Chairman August Bebel and the National Liberal Chairman Ernst Bassermann rejected the idea of the Grand Bloc. However, party fronts were not fixed. Numerous attempts were made to form party coalitions, and contemporaries referred to the 'black–blue bloc', comprised of the Centre Party and the conservatives, and to the 'Grand Bloc', and to the conservative 'cartel of the productive estates'. These efforts, and the internal party forces which opposed these coalitions, highlight the extent to which the political fronts had begun to change after the end of the Bülow Bloc. The agreements reached in the Reichstag elections of 1912 had brought Left Liberals and Social Democrats closer together, sometimes including the National Liberals, who in 1912 also contributed to Bebel almost being elected to Reichstag President, and his fellow party member Scheidemann becoming the first Vice President. Finally, in 1913, together with the Centre Party and Social Democracy, the liberal parties managed to push through against the Conservatives a tax on capital, which had become necessary to finance the huge increase in the size of the army. This reform alliance from the liberals via the Centre Party to Social Democracy, had already made possible the Alsace-Lorraine constitutional reform of 1911. The 'Weimar Coalition' was therefore already being formed in the last few pre-war years, but only as an uncertain possibility, constantly under threat, which also encountered a great deal of resistance from liberals.

It was certainly not a point of development which could already be envisaged as realizable.

War Aims and Aims for Reform: Liberals during the First World War

'We are fighting for the fruits of our peaceful work, for the legacy of a great past and for our future.' Imperial Chancellor Theobald von Bethmann Hollweg's belief, voiced on 4 August 1914 in the Reichstag, was probably shared by almost the entire German population. Hardly anyone doubted the fact that Germany was entering a defensive war. But which 'great past' were they defending? For which 'future' were they to fight and die? Later, in 1918, Friedrich Meinecke described the hope for a great national reconciliation of all internal conflicts as a 'honeymoon mood'; but it was a mood which rapidly evaporated.[169] The internal political 'truce' announced by the Kaiser, which all parties had enthusiastically welcomed, held longer. It will come as no surprise to learn that German liberalism as a whole shared a pathos-filled longing for national unification, which no longer recognized parties, only defenders of the Fatherland. Those who had always defended the idea of the nation as the highest guiding principle of political action, could not distance themselves from the longing for unity which broke out with the war. That is why even the decided Left Liberal critics of Wilhelmine Germany initially went along with the suggestion of the imperial leadership that internal reforms should be postponed until the war was over. National unity, the 'duty to seek internal peace' (E. Müller-Meiningen) in the war 'which has been forced upon us' was the motto. The confidence of victory and the belief that the war would be a short one, also played a part in the fact that hopes for reform were completely eclipsed by war policies.

This was also true in 1915, when a broad discussion of war aims began amongst the German public, in which of all the liberal parties, the National Liberals played the largest part.[170] They formed the party political core of the war aims movement, which placed the Imperial Chancellor under enormous pressure to publicly commit himself to a 'greater Germany' in the face of the alleged threat of an 'insipid peace'. Prussian National

Liberals were the first parliamentary party to voice demands, which already in the spring of 1915 comprised a broad programme of war aims. These extensively overlapped with those of the *Alldeutscher Verband* or Pan-German League, with whom the National Liberals enjoyed close personal links (cf. Chapter 4, pp. 128–83). Their demands included settlement land in the east – and the west, too, if possible. For the annexation of Belgium, which was accepted without question, was also envisaged by some as an annexation without the Belgians, who were to be expelled to France. Although from the beginning there was an internal party opposition to such dreams of power, the National Liberals remained the party of 'the expansion of the Reich, of the increase of the Reich and the powerful position of the Reich in the world', as the Westphalian legislature deputy Carl Cremer put it.[171]

National Liberal jingoism initially concealed internal party conflicts. This changed after 1916, however, when a fierce conflict on the extent of the internal reforms to be striven for was added to the differences of opinion on the aims of the war. One of the apparently paradoxical aspects of German politics in the war years before 1917 is the fact that, of all the parties, it was the National Liberals who most resolutely advocated an increase in Reichstag power, while the Left Liberals sought to strengthen the position of the government. The pre-war situation had therefore been reversed. This reversal of Left Liberal and National Liberal roles came as a result of the policy of Imperial Chancellor Bethmann Hollweg. Those who condemned his war aims as 'weak' and who called for a concerted course of annexation, demanded internal reforms, such as the lifting of press censorship, so that the government could hear the 'voice of the people'. Above all, they demanded a strengthening of Reichstag authority, in order to end what was described as the 'politics of rapprochement and concessions' to the opponents of the war (Stresemann). Those like Naumann, on the other hand, who regarded the 'grasping around in unconquered countries' and the 'minister-overthrowing' of the extreme annexationists as irresponsible, attempted to support the Bethmann Hollweg government against the 'democratization from the right' by adopting a reticent stance on internal matters.[172]

The Left Liberal Progressive People's Party did not voice its opposition to German war acquisitions by any means.[173] Three groups can be roughly distinguished from the beginning of the discussions on war aims. The first comprised the defenders of a 'victorious peace', who strove for German hegemony on the European continent, which was to be safeguarded by a combination of annexations, dependent buffer states and economic spheres of influence. The second was a more moderate group of those who desired a 'protective peace'. The third group argued for a 'peace of understanding'. The aims of these groups and their influence on the party course in the Reich and the states changed as the war progressed. Generally speaking, however, the Progressive People's Party adopted a moderate position in the discussions on war aims, and sought to use internal political reticence to support Bethmann Hollweg against the faction of extreme annexationist reformers.

The conflicts surrounding the aims of the war and internal politics intensified in 1916, and reached a first climax with the July crisis of 1917, which led to the fall of Bethmann Hollweg. A series of developments combined in this crisis, which had emerged from the shifting of power between the government, the Third Supreme Command and the Reichstag, and from the political rethinking process being undertaken in the parties. Under the leadership of Matthias Erzberger, Centre Party foreign policy aims had begun to come closer to those of the Progressive People's Party and the Social Democrats. This had created the basis for a parliamentary majority coalition, which National Liberals also joined for a time. This rapprochement was reinforced in July 1917 in the form of the *Interfraktioneller Ausschuß*, with which the majority parliamentary parties created a politically important informal committee. It made possible the Peace resolution of 19 July 1917, with which the three parliamentary parties of the Centre Party, the Social Democrats and the Progressive People's Party demanded a peace without annexations and without 'economic barriers and the estrangement of the peoples'.[174]

A fundamentally changed constellation of parties emerged from the July crisis of 1917, in which the 'Weimar Coalition' of Social Democracy, liberalism and the Centre Party assumed a concrete form. Initially, however, a kind of negative coalition of Reichstag parliamentary parties asserted itself, which ranged from the parties of the right, to the Centre Party and the Supreme Command. Bethmann Hollweg was forced to resign, though the introduction of the parliamentary system was not associated with this. It now became clear that internal and inter-party views on the meaning of 'parliamentarianism' diverged widely, and that mutual distrust prevented the Reichstag from reaching for government power.

Amidst vehement internal conflicts, which climaxed in the disputes surrounding the reform of the Prussian three-class suffrage system, the National Liberals turned away from the constitutional monarchy – a milestone in the history of German liberalism – yet only a small wing declared its support for the parliamentary system of government. The majority sought a 'German form of parliamentarianism', which would be satisfied with a 'closer feeling' between parliament and government, and which would prevent imperial politics from being exposed to changing parliamentary majorities, The particular foreign political danger to Germany was the core argument of the National Liberals, many of whom were linked with the *Deutsche Vaterlandspartei* or German Fatherland Party, which was founded in 1917 as a melting pot of extreme annexationists.

The Left Liberals, whose programmes had always shown them to be the most resolute champions of the parliamentary system amongst the middle-class parties, also avoided this aim in their political practice. Even when the Württemberg Left Liberal Friedrich Payer joined the Hertling government as Vice Chancellor (1 November 1917 to 3 October 1918) this did not mean a parliamentary system, and nor did it testify to a desire for it. This was clearly revealed when the government of Prince Max of Baden was formed on 4 October 1918, after Payer had refused the chancellorship. The 'quiet introduction of the parliamentary system' (C. Haußmann) advanced under this government, in which members of all the majority parliamentary parties participated, but it never became anything more than an 'incomplete parliamentary system' (K. von Beyme).[175]

Despite all the historical legacies which stood in the way of a parliamentary system of government in Germany, and despite the war – which helped effect a quiet change in the constitution, but also restricted it – the political system underwent a fundamental transformation during the First World War. The October reform of 1918 finally completed the introduction of the parliamentary system in the German Reich. Yet this step came too late to be accepted by the war-weary population as an alternative to the revolutionary downfall of the Kaiserreich. The Supreme Command had demanded that its power be trans-ferred to the Reichstag, so that it could flee into an uncertain peace from its responsibility for the military defeat, which could no longer be hidden, the consequences of which it tried to blame on parliament and its majority parties. But this change in the system was not simply ordered 'from above'. It was prepared and finally also demanded by the majority parliamentary parties. When the main support of the old powerful élite, the Prussian officer corps, capitulated, political leadership fell to the Left Liberal opponents of the Prussian monarchic powerful state and the 'enemies of the Reich' of yesteryear. The fact that it was able to veil this capitulation – the military collapse was totally unexpected by the public – while the parliamentary system was introduced in the Kaiserreich, would prove to be a heavy burden for the new parliamentary republic.

5 The Deliberalization of the 'Middle-Class Centre': The Decline of Political Liberalism in the Weimar Republic

The Overburdened Republic

Emphasis on a new departure and visions of decline mark the beginning of the young Republic, which achieved significant things, but which was burdened with great problems which never allowed it to achieve a sense of normality. Whether these problems were insurmountable is one of the unresolved, and probably insoluble, controversies of historical research; we have no intention of rehearsing the arguments again here.[1] We will content ourselves with a brief outline of the crises and developments which took place between the end of the Kaiserreich and the National Socialist dictatorship, in order to assess the scope for liberal politics and the liberal parties.

The Republic began as a promise and a threat at the same time. The dreadful war was over, but just when hopes had risen that the hardship created by the war might be eliminated, and the way to a democratic future seemed assured, the German Kaiserreich collapsed in 1918. Yet the bankruptcy of imperial Germany did not only liberate; it also placed great burdens on its republican heir. Given that Germany had lost a war which left behind it around ten million dead, huge material losses and which had whipped up national passions in the affected states, this was unavoidable. But it was not the burdens themselves, but what was made of them in Germany that so poisoned the political climate of the young Republic. Since the military defeat had been largely hidden from the German population – the troops were still on foreign territory at the time of the armistice – the *Dolchstoßlegende* which was now launched, the myth that Germany had been stabbed in the back by its own politicians, fell on fertile soil.

'Undefeated on the battlefield', the army was said to have been forced to capitulate by the revolution at home. This lie on the part of the old Germany seriously hampered the new Germany's chances of accepting the military defeat and its consequences. The Treaty of Versailles, experienced as a national disgrace and humiliation, was blamed on the Weimar democracy and its political foundations, and not on the élites of the defunct Kaiserreich. The anti-Versailles mood to which the German population now succumbed, was not simply blindly consolidated to form a powerful enemy image, in which the actual and imagined suffering, the grief for what had been lost and the hatred of the new was subsumed and directed against the 'Weimar system'. In fact, the authorities, associations and parties worked on the public in a sustained fashion in order to create a revision movement which, it was hoped, could be employed on a foreign political level against the Treaty of Versailles, and which could be used on a domestic level to bridge social and political divisions.[2] Yet with the active help of the liberal parties, a weapon was forged which could be used only by the enemies of the Republic. This wide-ranging agitation, which was pursued or at least approved of, by all the large parties, persuaded the German population that the nation had been morally humiliated by the Peace Treaty. Without such agitation, the struggle against Versailles could never have been transformed so easily into a fight against Weimar. The liberals shared some responsibility for the fact that this occurred, even if, as we shall see below, they themselves advocated a more rational and restrained nationalism.

Refusal to recognize the defeat and its consequences, which included the democratic Republic, had a profound impact on developments in the crisis-wracked early phase of the Republic before 1923. A few of the most important events will suffice here. A series of political murders revealed the demoralization to which the judicial system also contributed, with its verdicts which listed to the right. The anti-republican Kapp–Lüttwitz Putsch of

1920 may have failed, but it highlighted the distance between the national army and the Republic, and made it possible for Bavaria to become a stronghold of militant right-wing forces. The period of crisis culminated in the events of 1923: the occupation of the Ruhr and passive resistance; renewed putsch attempts from both right and left; and above all the shattering of the German currency by hyperinflation, which alienated large sections of the middle classes in particular from the Republic, and firmly restricted the opportunities for action of the middle-class parties who were loyal to the Republic.

Yet it would be wrong to judge the Weimar Republic's chances of survival only by its birth defects or by its death. The young democracy managed to withstand the permanent crisis of its beginnings and was consolidated in the period of stabilization from 1924 to 1928. In the elections of December 1924, the parties of the 'Weimar Coalition' were able to halt their loss of voters for the first time (see Table 16), the right-wing liberal *Deutsche Volkspartei* (DVP), or German People's Party, had reformed under the leadership of Stresemann, and had become a party capable of sustaining the Republic. Even the conservative *Deutschnationale Volkspartei* (DNVP), the German National People's Party, was coming to terms with the republican order. In 1925 it was represented in a government for the first time. And the 'historical compromise' between capital and labour, with which the Republic had begun, seemed to be proving its viability with the labour exchange and unemployment insurance law, which was enacted in 1927 against the votes of the KPD, the NSDAP and parts of the DNVP. However, criticism on the part of employers of the 'welfare state', which had made possible the creation and survival of the democratic parliamentary Republic in the first place, was now on the increase. Just as the 'middle-class' government began to expand the 'welfare state' by introducing unemployment insurance, heavy industry prepared to bring about the failure of the policy of reconciling social differences.[3] Given their close links with economic pressure groups, the liberal parties were inevitably profoundly shaken by these conflicts. In the global economic depression the liberals ceased to be a serious political force. They became splinter parties with little influence, as the 'panic in the *Mittelstand*' (T. Geiger) drove traditional bands of voters to the right, where they hoped to find economic salvation and political stability.

Even before the liberal parties 'disappeared almost unnoticed' (K. D. Bracher) in 1933, the decline of liberalism reflects the way in which large parts of the population and the old élites turned away from the welfare state parliamentary democracy. It signalled the breaking of the 'historical compromise' between the Social Democratic workers' movement and the democratic liberal middle classes, which had made the Weimar Republic so astoundingly viable, despite all its existential crises. The 'Ruhr iron conflict' of 1928 testifies to heavy industry's desire to destroy the social 'founders' compromise'. The 'middle-class centre's' abandonment of its traditional liberal and conservative parties (DDP, DVP and DNVP) as it moved to the splinter parties of the right – and then to the NSDAP in the elections of 1928 and after 1930 – bore witness to the fact that the Republic had also lost those middle-class circles which had wanted it or which had been forced to come to terms with it. 'After the Reichstag elections of 1928', noted Arthur Dix in 1930, 'talk of the *crises of parliamentarianism* and "*partyism*" could no longer be silenced'.[4]

This 'talk' was carefully prepared and translated into action in 1930, when President Hindenburg asked Brüning to form the first presidential cabinet. The 'dualistic birth defect of the Weimar Republic, its ambivalent structure of power between the parliamentary and the presidential system' (Bracher) was now exploited to enable the dictatorial power of the *Reichspräsident* or National President to be used to break through the constitutional restrictions on that power. Parliament was forced out of the centre of politics; its place was taken by the executive and the informal circles which enjoyed the trust of the President. The Brüning cabinet had tested out the presidential emergency constitution; an 'ever-present temptation to dictatorship'.[5] The two subsequent presidential cabinets then extended it so far that many contemporaries perceived the beginning of National Socialist rule simply as a further stage in the gradual transition of the Weimar parliamentary system to something new. Quite what this new system would look like, none of those who had turned away in disappointment from the Weimar Republic could guess.

'What followed the Republic became a judgement on it. It did not go down fighting; the bankrupt business simply went into liquidation.'[6] This inglorious end was not inevitable, however, and it should not prevent us from assessing the achievements of which the Republic was clearly capable, despite its extraordinarily heavy burdens.

Why did the first German democracy fail? We will ask this question again at the end of our analysis of the developmental problems after 1918, with an examination of the conditions to which liberalism had to adapt. The scholarly literature offers three major reasons: the serious birth defects, which made a premature death at least likely; the capitulation of a 'republic without republicans'; and its deliberate destruction by forces hostile to democracy. These three theories of decline focus on different burdens and regard different periods of time as decisive. The period of stabilization, from time to time retrospectively transfigured into the 'golden twenties', is of little importance in comparison to the extreme situations of the rise and dissolution of the Republic. However, any attempt to correctly assess and establish the political parties' room for manoeuvre must include an attempt to evaluate the entire life of the Weimar Republic and to define its position in the process of social development.

Significant processes of social change culminated in the postwar era. Some of them had started before the war, and now came together in mutual reinforcement. Many contemporaries felt that they were living in a period of radical change, in which everything seemed to have been transformed. Their expectations of the political system were correspondingly great, and a heightened degree of adaptation and control was demanded of it.

The changes which profoundly affected people's lives included the change in reproductive behaviour. From around the turn of the century onwards, population growth slowed, and the Weimar Republic saw the beginnings of the 'industrial method of population', with its low birth and death rates. Married fertility rates halved between 1900 and 1925. At a time when people were grieving for the lost greatness of the nation, it was easy to blame the young Republic for the restricted population growth, which was experienced as a national loss. Complaints about the 'nation without young people' (F. Burgdörfer, 1932) or about 'immoral' methods of contraception were directed at a state which was criticized for failing to fulfil its 'völkisch task' of the 'biological self-assertion' of the nation.

Those who held such erroneous views will have seen their fears confirmed by a series of developments – the proportion of women in work rose; demands for the liberalization of sex education and abortion, for marriages of partnership and for sexual freedoms became more urgent; women's fashions changed to the point where the bob became an emancipatory hairstyle – all this could be condensed into an image of moral decline, which represented a particular threat to those middle-class parties which were loyal to the Republic. For their voters felt extremely insecure.[7] This insecurity probably contributed to the flight of the 'middle-class centre' from the liberal parties to the opponents of the Republic, who made political capital out of the widespread delusion of a biologically and morally decaying nation.

The plateauing population growth indicates a general restriction in social growth after the First World War. The rapid urbanization which had characterized the industrialization period before 1914 began to slow down and the enormous internal migrations associated with it were dramatically and permanently reduced. The population of the Weimar Republic had become 'older' and 'quieter' in comparison to that of the Kaiserreich. Yet this 'calming down' in population growth did not stabilize the Weimar Republic. For it coincided with the end of the period of high industrialization, during which the German Kaiserreich had developed into one of the leading industrial states of the world. In all sectors of the population, a belief in progress had emerged, which meant that the end of the frenzied period of growth was experienced as a collapse. Inflation, consistently high unemployment rates and finally a recession which ran deeper than anything ever seen before, presented them with entirely new experiences: experiences of decline which were blamed on the Republic.

The tendency to make the state responsible for social crisis had been laid down in the German tradition of the 'strong state'. The rise of the modern social welfare state during the last three decades of the nineteenth century, and state–corporate dirigisme in the First World War had only served to reinforce this tradition. Weimar social interventionism – public housing projects, health care, unemployment insurance, and compulsory arbitration in workers' conflicts, to name but a few – continued this line of development with remarkable success. Yet the Republic had no time to consolidate its achievements. That would have required a basic social consensus, which expanded naturally to form a social state. But this was something which could only have emerged gradually. The chances of it happening certainly existed. But they were destroyed by the global depression. The depression was too much for the welfare state, and the great hopes it had raised were now dashed. The economic crisis became a state crisis which benefited most those political forces who rejected the state and its foundations most radically.

The state crisis necessarily affected the liberal parties more profoundly than any other political alignment. Of all the parties, it was they who had attempted the political integration of competing interests by the adoption of a pluralistic social concept using the guiding values of the 'state' and the 'nation'. The decline of liberalism was therefore a symptom of the declining attraction of the pluralistic model of a democratic republic.

Cultural developments also played a part here. Like Weimar society and its politics, 'Weimar culture' was split, as avant-garde culture and 'mass culture' diverged more strongly than ever before. Here, too, liberalism suffered to a particular degree. For the German educated middle class, which had always been the backbone of liberal organizations and had been the herald of liberal views of the world, believed that it had been exposed to a pressure which threatened to destroy its social position. When the avant-garde shattered the educated middle-class under-standing of culture and when a commercialized 'mass culture' arose which also distanced itself from educated middle-class norms, the educated middle class lost the general cultural authority which it had always used to legitimize its socio-political demands. This development had begun before the First World War, but only really asserted itself in the twenties. It expanded opportunities for cultural participation, and to that extent is part of the democratization phase of the Weimar Republic. But it did not strengthen the Republic. On the contrary, the 'élite culture' 'ignored reality' and in so far as it was republican, it had its sights on the 'futuristic republic of poets ... not the Weimar Republic' (H. Kuhn).[8]

The new cultural industries, such as film and radio, or the wider range of 'adult education' on offer, also accelerated the process of dissolution in which the 'social moral milieu' (Lepsius), which had been formed and consolidated in the Kaiserreich, now found itself. This dissolution of the socio-political camp cer-tainly contributed to democratic pluralism. But it also heigh-tened society's susceptibility to the new radicalism which the old milieux fought most decisively, but which at the same time offered new bonds of tempting simplicity. Here the 'fear of modernity' (P. Gay) fused with an irrational faith in a planned future to form a 'reactionary modernism',[9] which did not adhere to the past and seemed unburdened by the present.

This form of radical flight into the future undermined the foundations of the Weimar Republic, which were not terribly sound to begin with. For large parts of the Protestant middle classes, in particular, it always remained tainted with the stigma of illegitimate birth, and yet at the same time it was fettered to the old Germany, whose legacy it had to bear. One of the lasting achievements of the Weimar Republic is that it formed a state despite all the old problems and new burdens, and achieved more democracy than had ever been achieved before in Germany history. The middle-class liberal centre and its parties played a major role in this achievement. But they must also share responsibilty for the fact that the parliamentary system could be destroyed from within in 1930, which allowed the enemies of the Republic to move into the centres of state power.

Party Organization, Voters and Pressure Groups: The Dissolution of the Liberal 'Milieu'

The lines of continuity linking the Kaiserreich with the Republic include the parties.[10] The 'fundamental character of the pre-war parties' (S. Neumann) did not change, and the distribution of political power also remained almost unchanged until, from 1928 onwards, with the emaciation of the middle-class parties, the party system, which had been astoundingly stable for more than half a century, began to collapse. The lines of continuity should not be exaggerated, however. The radical political and constitutional changes transformed the parameters of action to which the parties sought to adapt themselves in their pro-grammes and organizations. The Centre Party found the transition easier than most; its voters were defined by religion and were least affected by the change in the form of the state.

The Social Democratic workers' movement, on the other hand, split into two main parties. The SPD became the party which supported the state; it accepted the Weimar Republic as its state, as a state in need of reform, but worth defending. Those parts of the socialist proletarian milieu which rejected the

Republic outright as being incapable of reform aligned themselves with the KPD. The conservatives, in contrast, initially
succeeded in uniting their organizations; in November 1918
the old conservative parties and a smaller number of National
Liberals joined together in the *Deutschnationale Volkspartei*
(the German National People's Party). Politically and socially
it encompassed a broader spectrum than pre-war conservatism.

Liberal attempts to join together to form a single party failed
from the beginning. A Berlin announcement of 16 November
1918, signed by Left and National Liberals, called for the creation
of a 'large democratic party for the united Reich'. It was enthusiastically welcomed by the public, and in many places mergers
were agreed. Yet it rapidly became clear that 'the old party
structures [had by no means been] broken'[11] on 9 November
along with the monarchy. German liberalism's perspectives of the
future were too divergent (Chapter 5, pp. 271–99) to be accommodated under the umbrella of a single party. When Stresemann successfully torpedoed the unification negotiations, he was
simply executing existing conflicts, which had only seemed
surmountable for the short period in which the liberals were
affected by the shock of the collapse.

The author of the Berlin foundation announcement believed
that people like Stresemann should later acquire a modest place
at the very most in the new democratic party, since they were too
greatly 'burdened by annexationist declarations or other war aim
declarations' (G. Gothein). Of all things, it was this which made
Stresemann the ideal focal point for that section of the liberals
which wanted to salvage as much as possible from the past in
the Republic. With the DVP, which was formally founded on
15 December 1918, they brought about 'the somewhat mutilated
rebirth of the old National Liberal organization',[12] while the
DDP, which was constituted as early as 20 November, became the
successor to the Progressive People's Party and the small Democratic Alliance. It also absorbed a section of the National Liberals.

Neither the DDP nor the DVP succeeded in continuing the
development of pre-war liberalism to form more tautly organized membership parties, though the DDP made great efforts
to do so. In January 1919, it launched an election campaign
which was unprecedented in the history of German liberalism.
An election film was made, for example, which was to be shown
in cinemas, and 15.5 million leaflets were distributed, some of

which were dropped from planes. But by 1920 at the latest, the attempt to build up a modern membership party had failed. The DDP and the DVP remained voters' parties. The Democrats recorded almost 788 000 members in July 1919 – about 14 per cent of the DDP voters of 1919! – but over the ensuing years they suffered heavy defeats. Between 1922 and 1929, DDP membership fell from approximately 210 000 to around 113 000. No reliable figures are available for the DVP. In 1920, when it achieved its best election result, it is said to have had approximately 500 000 members, in 1930 the figure was still around 250 000. The DVP did not need to know the number of its members, for they played no role on an internal party level. Representation of the constituency associations at party conferences and in the central committee was dependent on Reichstag election results.

In both parties, from 1920 onwards the political weight increasingly shifted to the parliamentary parties, whose course was not laid down by the party committees but approved retrospectively. Stresemann became almost an independent institution in the DVP. Without him the reconciliation of the widely diverging interests in the party would never have been possible. His charisma fed not only on the successes of his foreign policy, to which no one could offer a realistic alternative, but also on the fact that he was a brilliant speaker and journalist, he was the founder of the party, he built up the party apparatus and held the highest posts, he influenced the image of the DVP as its 'chief ideologue' (W. Hartenstein), and at the same time he was a skilful tactician. The DDP did not have a comparable 'figure who carried the party' (Bracher). Naumann, who seemed to be growing into this role, died in 1919 and subsequently, as Payer said in 1920, the DDP only offered 'good average wares'.[13] He emphasized the word 'good', but it wasn't enough to fulfil the democrats' longing for a charismatic 'leader', which grew with the crises in the Weimar Republic.

One of the liberal parties' main problems had always been holding together the wide range of middle-class interests politically, so that they could organize. Even during the Kaiserreich they had been less and less successful in doing this. Their election defeats reflected this, as did the growing numbers of middle-class pressure groups and organizations which influenced the liberal parties, but which distanced themselves from their political claim to leadership. This line of development continued in the Weimar Republic, but it now grew to the point where the parties were overwhelmed by pressure groups and became utterly emaciated in the elections. The liberal milieu, which had never been as clearly defined as its rivals, now completely dissolved. We will turn our attention first to the elections.

The DDP achieved its best election result (18.6 per cent) in the National Assembly elections of 1919. The DVP, on the other hand, which did not stand in eleven of the thirty-six constituencies in 1919, and which still had no organization to speak of, reached its peak in the Reichstag elections of 1920 (13.9 per cent). With the exception of a slight recovery in the December elections of 1924, both parties then continued to lose seats, with a dramatic acceleration in 1930, when the DDP and the DVP dwindled to splinter parties in the Reichstag, and in 1932, when they finally became insignificant (Table 15). Liberals suffered a similar decline in the states (Table 16). During the Kaiserreich, the liberals had been unable to keep pace with the huge rise in the population and above all in participation in elections. For this reason, their share of the votes decreased, although the number of votes they won rose. In the Weimar Republic, on the other hand, the DDP and DVP collapsed completely. Absolute as well as relative figures fell.

The question remains as to why voters allowed parties to go under within a few short years, whose predecessors had been instrumental in the formation of the nation-state from its beginning. First we will ask who these voters were, and to which parties they transferred their allegiance.

There has been a broad consensus amongst contemporaries and historians alike in the answers given to these questions. The DDP and the DVP were above all elected by urban Protestants, by 'the industrial, commercial and financial middle classes, independent craftsmen, civil servants, employees and intellectuals'.[14] The number of peasant voters rapidly declined. Worker voters did not play a significant role for the DDP; the 'German Unions' which sympathized with it had few members (c. 226 000 in 1920; c. 150 000 in 1931). The DVP was the 'non-proletarian party *par excellence*' (Hartenstein). Under certain conditions it could certainly receive workers' votes; workers amongst the 'Kruppianer' of the 'Krupp town' Essen-West, for example, must have voted DVP and DNVP.[15]

Table 15 Reichstag elections during the Weimar Republic (proportion of votes in %)

	1919	1920	1924 May	1924 Dec.	1928	1930	1932 July	1932 Nov.	1933
1. DDP	18.6	8.3	5.7	6.3	4.9	3.8	1.0	1.0	0.9
2. SPD	37.9	21.7	20.5	26.0	29.8	24.5	21.6	20.4	18.3
3. Z/BVP	19.7	17.8	16.6	17.4	15.2	14.8	16.2	15.3	13.9
4. DVP	4.4	13.9	9.2	10.1	8.7	4.7	1.2	1.9	1.1
5. DNVP	10.3	15.1	19.5	20.5	14.2	7.0	6.2	8.9	8.0
6. KPD/USPD	7.6	20.0	13.4	9.3	10.7	13.1	14.5	16.9	12.3
7. NSDAP	–	–	6.5	3.0	2.6	18.3	37.4	33.1	43.9
8. Others	1.6	3.3	8.6	7.5	13.9	13.8	2.0	2.6	1.6
1–3: Weimar coalition	76.2	47.8	42.8	49.7	49.9	43.1	38.8	36.7	33.1
1–4: Grand coalition	80.6	61.7	52.0	59.8	58.6	47.8	40.0	38.6	34.2
1, 3–4: Bürgerliche coal.	42.7	40.0	31.5	33.8	28.8	23.3	18.4	18.2	15.9
5–7: Anti-Weimar parties	17.9	35.1	39.4	32.8	27.5	38.4	58.1	58.9	64.2
No. of deputies	421	459	472	493	491	577	608	584	647
Election turnout	83.0	79.2	77.4	78.8	75.6	82.0	84.1	80.6	88.8

Source: J. Falter *et al.*, *Wahlen und Abstimmungen in der Weimarer Republik* (Munich, 1986) p. 44.

Table 16 *Landtag* elections during the Weimar Republic

Proportion of votes in %

election years

Lander		1918	1919	1920	1921	1922	1923	1924	1925	1926	1927	1928	1929	1930	1931	1932	1933
Anhalt	DDP	34.0		15.7				3.5/7.3				4.2				1.5	
	DVP			13.4								15.5				3.7	
Baden	DDP		22.8		8.5			16*	8.7				6.7				
	DVP				6.0				9.5				8.0				
Bavaria	DDP		14.0	8.3				3.2				3.3				–	
	DVP		–	–				1.0				3.3				1.7	
Brunswick	DDP	21.8		9.5		10.7		5.3			4.6			3.0			
	DVP	–		–		–		17.2			14.3			–			
Bremen	DDP		19.9	13.9	16.1		12.7	11.8			10.1			4.1			
	DVP		(13.4)	20.1	23.2		20.2	(29.1)			–			12.5			
Hamburg	DDP		20.5		14.1			13.2			10.1	12.8			8.7	11.2	
	DVP		8.6		13.9			14.0			11.2	12.5			4.8	3.2	
Hesse	DDP		18.9		7.3			8.5			7.8				1.4		
	DVP		10.1		14.6			11.8			10.7				2.3		
Lippe	DDP		19.8		11.5				8.1				5.6				0.8
	DVP		–		19.6				(15.7)				12.4				4.4
Lübeck	DDP		36.3		–				8.9	2.3			3.3			1.6	

Mecklenburg-Strelitz	DDP	27.3	6.9	4.3			3.6		3.0	2.9	2.8			–
	DVP	4.3	15.4	17.5			7.3		8.4	7.9	–			–
M-Schwerin	DDP	39.9	21.0	14.7	14.5		14.9	13.7		6.7	4.6			5.1
	DVP	–		–	5.5					4.4	3.6			–
Oldenburg	DDP	31.1	14.6		18.6		14.9	13.7			10.7		3.3	2.2
	DVP	11.4	19.6		22.6		(34)	(34.6)			(17.7)		4.1	0.8
Prussia	DDP	16.2		6.1			5.9				4.5			1.5	0.7
	DVP	5.7		14.0			9.8				8.5			1.5	1.0
Saxony	DDP	22.9	7.7		8.4				4.7			4.3	3.2
	DVP	3.9	18.6		18.7				12.4			13.4	8.7
Schaumburg-Lippe	DDP	15.8		4.9				7.2		7.9		5.1
	DVP	5.9		14.6				–		8.6		5.5
Thuringia	DDP	7.3	5.6				–			3.3	2.9	(1.9)
	DVP	15.8	16.2				–			–	8.8	1.8
Württemberg	DDP	25.0	14.7		10.6					10.1		4.8
	DVP		3.4		4.6					5.2		1.5

Note: Where two figures are given, two elections took place that year.
* Merged with other parties. ( ) = with the DVP: Bremen, Oldenburg; with the Z: Lippe, Schaumburg-Lippe. – = did not stand.

Source: Falter *et al.*, *Wahlen und Abstimmungen*, pp. 89–113.

The 'old' and the 'new' *Mittelstand* represented the majority of the urban Protestant voters of the liberal parties; that is to say, independent businessmen as well as employees and civil servants. But these social groups were courted not only by the DDP and the DVP, but also by their main rivals and by the numerous small pressure group parties whose rise and success was an indication of the waning political unifying force of the old party system.

Already after the next election, the 'middle-class centre' which in 1919 had made the DDP the strongest non-socialist Protestant party, 'turned away from the Republic in a wave-like motion, ... always choosing the next alternative to the right'.[16] In 1920 voters turned to the DVP and the DNVP, between 1924 and 1928 to the DNVP in particular, but also to the new splinter parties, until in 1930 and above all in 1932, the 'panic in the *Mittelstand*' led to the NSDAP becoming the supposed refuge for the 'middle-class centre' – and others (see Table 16).

The advantage of this interpretation is that it brings the experiences, observations and opinions of contemporaries into line with the wave-like swerve to the right of the election results. However, this kind of interpretation is described in the present-day historical sociology of elections as 'electoral history folklore' (J. Falter). This is by no means an inappropriate description; the electoral successes of one party cannot simply be 'offset' against the failures of others. If the DDP lost around ten percentage points between 1919 and 1920 and the DVP won 9.5 per cent, it does not necessarily follow that DVP gains had come from DDP losses. Those who unquestioningly accept a voter migration of this kind do indeed perpetuate 'election folklore'. But folklore does not have to be untrue, and in this case it is not. Many studies demonstrate the likelihood of the exchange of voters at constituency level assumed by historians and contemporaries alike. The statistics which anti-folklorists such as Jürgen Falter published in around 1986 either fail to contradict the old assumptions, or partially confirm them.[17] They cannot identify voter migrations, they can only identify changes between the parties at constituency level. For there are no contemporary surveys on voter migrations between the parties. Even modern statistical methods cannot make good this lack. They can only ascertain whether, for example, in areas with above-average DDP losses, the SPD or the NSDAP gained above-average numbers of votes.

But whether those voters who turned away from the DDP did actually move to the SPD or to the NSDAP cannot be extrapolated from the data.[18] We remain dependent on evaluating the reports of informed contemporaries on the shifts between the parties. And everything seems to point to the fact that shrewd observers have handed shrewd observations down to us. For small parties like the DVP and the DPP, there is the additional problem that the correlation values calculated from the election statistics are generally too small to allow any meaningful statements to be made.

There is some value in the attempts to calculate 'voter migrations' to the NSDAP over the course of several elections, in order to ascertain whether particular parties lost voters to the National Socialists in stages, via 'intermediate hosts'. As one might expect, the clearest findings show positive correlations between NSDAP shares of the vote after 1930 and the areas in which the DNVP enjoyed their greatest electoral successes before 1928. For the DVP, statistical correlations with NSDAP victories after 1930 are markedly less clear, but they are clearer than those for the DDP. It seems that the democrats forfeited voter circles who came to them before 1920 most strongly via 'intermediate host' votes to the NSDAP, while voters who had remained loyal to the DDP even after the party began to decline, probably did not vote for the NSDAP in large numbers in the final phase of the Republic. It is also likely that the DVP was forced to yield to the NSDAP most of the voters who had flocked to it during its 'boom phase' (1920–1928). Those who remained with this party after the collapse of the DVP in the elections of 1930, then proved to be more resistant to the NSDAP.[19]

These interpretations, which can be gleaned from the most recent sociological electoral data for the DDP and the DVP, confirm the image drawn above, which has always been offered by 'electoral historical folklore' and the reports of intelligent contemporaries of the Republic.

The number of those entitled to vote had more than doubled in 1919, since the voting age had been reduced to twenty, and women had been awarded the right to vote. The Centre Party in particular profited from women's suffrage, which only the socialist workers' movement had decisively demanded during the Kaiserreich. Then came the DNVP and the DVP, whilst towards the end of the Republic the SPD and the DDP were voted by almost equal numbers of women and men, though both parties had initially fared worse amongst female voters. But there were strong regional deviations from the Reich average.[20] For the liberals as a whole, female suffrage was not disadvantageous (DDP) and was sometimes even advantageous (DVP). However, the liberals reaped below-average numbers of votes from those who were allowed to vote for the first time in the Weimar Republic – people born between 1899 and 1913. The liberals often complained about this. Those who 'could find suitable words and formulas for the war generation', wrote Arthur Dix with reference to the 1930 elections, would be able to recruit a 'million-strong reserve for a new political movement'.[21] The liberals failed to find such 'words and formulas' for any population group, least of all for the increased numbers of young voters.

The DDP and the DVP courted all social groups, but only those groups who had pressure groups at their disposal were able to influence party politics. And even these opportunities were rather unevenly distributed. Both parties established a series of national committees in the party executive to represent special interests: there were committees for employers from trade and industry, for the independent *Mittelstand*, for freelance professions, peasants, workers and employees (DDP), civil servants, employees (DVP), youth, students, women, and for culture and municipal politics. Little is known of the activities of most of these national committees. Committees which were not backed by a powerful interest group were probably little more than popular party window-dressing. This was true, for example, of the National Youth Committee of the DDP, based in the *Reichsbund Deutscher Demokratischer Jugend* (National Association of German Democratic Youth), which had only around 25 000 members in 1925. The DVP's Hindenburg Association was equally weak.[22]

The demand from women's associations to promote female candidates was of greater domestic political significance, since it promised to tap a major pool of voters. In 1919 the Württemberg DDP awarded every sixth place on its list of candidates for the state assembly elections to a woman. The proportion of women in the DDP Reichstag party was only around 8 per cent; this figure was exceeded by the SPD, and temporarily by the USDP (1919–20) and the KPD too (1930). At 4.5 per cent (1919) to 3.5 per cent (1930), DVP figures were even lower. These politically active women came almost exclusively from the women's movement.[23]

The growing numbers of employees were courted by both parties and they enjoyed close personal links with the employee associations, although these varied according to the differing political stance of each party. In their leading committees – there is no information on membership – as well as in the municipal councils, the DDP enjoyed close personal links with the *Gewerkschaftsbund der Angestellten*, the Union of Employees. The DVP, on the other hand, had its base in the right-wing anti-Semitic *Deutschnationaler Handlungsgehilfen-Verband*, the German National Association of Commercial Employees, which also made use of other parties, above all the DNVP, and which entered the slipstream of the NSDAP in the concluding phase of the Republic.[24] This openness to the right, which sometimes went as far as illiberal anti-Semitism, linked the DVP with its predecessor, the National Liberal Party.

As with the employees, the DVP and DDP competed with each other to recruit civil servants. The extent to which the party organs functioned at all was owed to the civil servant groups. Not only from the point of view of their political interests, but also in terms of the professional profile of the parliamentary parties, the left-wing and right-wing liberals could be regarded as civil servant parties. In the Prussian parliament civil servants always represented between more than a third and almost a half of all deputies in the DDP parliamentary parties. In the DVP this figure was even higher. No other party achieved higher figures; only the Centre Party came anywhere close to them.[25]

By 1928, there was a higher percentage of civil servants in the DVP parties of the Prussian parliaments than in the Prussian government parties, the SPD, the Centre Party and the DDP. This would suggest that many civil servants were becoming distanced from the republican state which they were supposed to be serving. In absolute numbers, however, there were more civil servant deputies in the republican government parties. Until the late twenties, the three parties managed to hold back conservative political civil servants – provincial governors and government presidents and their representatives, chiefs of police and district administrators – in favour of members of their own parties. The right-wing liberal DVP also benefited from this republicanization of senior civil servant posts.[26]

None of the professional groups and pressure groups referred to above acquired the political influence which the major industrial circles and representatives of large-scale trade and the banks exercised in the DDP and the DVP. As even the party leadership was forced to concede, 'in the eyes of the ordinary man' the DDP was 'the party of big capitalism'. As for the DVP, when Stresemann's party was forced to the right under the pressure of representatives of industrial interests in 1929, he complained that the party was becoming 'increasingly and purely a party of industry'.[27]

Because of their small and ever-decreasing membership numbers, both parties were largely dependent on financial donations from commercial circles. As this dependence grew, it was exploited by donors to push through political desires and, to an even greater degree, to block what they regarded as undesirable. Anton Erkelenz, representative of the left-wing employee wing in the DDP, lamented this situation, which made it hard 'to represent an independent opinion'. His party chairman Erich Koch-Weser noted in 1926 that, 'it is unpleasant to have to pursue politics when one feels that one is lost without donations from powerful financial circles'.[28]

In the expensive election years, donations from commercial circles covered more than 90 per cent of the DDP budget. Its treasurer Hermann Fischer embodied the party's links with pressure groups and associations and the dependence of the DDP on those associations. He sat on the supervisory board of fifty-one firms and maintained links with countless commercial associations, including the industry committee, which arranged donations to parties. He was chairman of the *Hansa-Bund für Gewerbe, Handel und Industrie* (Hanseatic League for Trade, Commerce and Industry) between 1922 and 1933.[29]

The DVP probably had an even higher number of representatives from commercial associations. Forty per cent of the 'party core' established by Lothar Döhn – comprised of almost 3300 people whose internal party position extended beyond 'mere membership' – was made up of men from large- and medium-scale industry (25.7 per cent), large-scale trade (9.3 per cent) and the banks (4.8 per cent). DVP members sat on the leading bodies of most commercial associations and were strongly represented in the spheres of heavy industry (35 per cent) large commercial concerns (*c.* 33 per cent) and the processing industries (*c.* 31 per cent). All middle-class parties, including the Centre Party, were represented in the powerful *Reichsverband der Deutschen Industrie* (National Association of German Industry). In 1925 between a fifth and a third of all members of the leading committee and the executive, and of the main and specialist committees, were also members of the DVP. Representatives of heavy industry dominated amongst the politically active party members from commercial circles. In the committees and supervisory bodies of industry and the major banks, the DVP acquired membership shares of up to 25 per cent in 1927.[30]

The close links between the DDP and the DVP and commercial and professional associations continued traditions from the Kaiserreich. But a new situation was brought about for both parties, which was associated with the trend towards the 'economization of politics' (S. Neumann), which had accelerated since the war, and with the trend towards corporative political models, combined with the increasing organization of special interests.[31] The liberal parties, who had never been anchored in a clearly defined milieu, had to defend their claim to being a popular party if they were not going to go under in the elections. Becoming a party of special interests was therefore ruled out for them. Nevertheless, they adopted this course as a makeshift solution, under the pressure of their financial dependencies and their personal links with commercial associations. Yet no concerted interest policy emerged in either liberal party from this 'economization' of liberal politics, the extent of which had not been seen in the nineteenth century (Chapter 5, pp. 271–99). Indeed, such a policy would have been impossible, given the contradictory nature of the interests of the different associations. This became abundantly clear when in 1929 the DDP failed to agree on an economic programme. The liberals responded in time-honoured fashion to the dilemma of no longer being able to bind together the diverging interests of their clientele in a practical fashion. With mottoes such as the 'state', 'the people' and 'the nation', they offered unifying bonds which, however, were proving to be less and less effective. Before we turn to this decline in the liberals' viability as a political force, we will briefly examine the rapid organizational end of German party liberalism.

Voters had abandoned the liberal parties by 1930 at the latest. But not just the voters; even the liberal newspapers distanced themselves from them. In the 1930 elections they already revealed an 'unprecedented abstinence', as an observer for the *Berliner Presse*, which was close to the DDP, noted.[32]

In order to try to halt the decline of liberalism, from 1928 onwards a series of renewed attempts were made by both liberal parties to create allies outside the parties, or to unite the DDP and the DVP. The efforts to find external aid included the DDP's co-operation with the 'Reich Banner Black Red and Gold' (*Reichsbanner Schwarz-Rot-Gold*) and the DVP's co-operation with the 'Stahlhelm' movement. But alliances of this kind clearly did not conform to the political style of middle-class liberal politics. Other attempts, such as the 'Republikanische Union', which attempted to form links between the DDP, the Centre Party and the SPD, or the 'Arbeitsgemeinschaft für jungdeutsche Politik' were equally unsuccessful.[33]

The DDP's attempts to revive their organization and their programme led to the foundation of the *Deutsche Staatspartei* or German State Party, on 27 July 1930, which was made up of the DDP, the *Volksnationale Reichsvereinigung* (People's National Alliance) and individual members of the DVP and the Christian unions. The foundation of this party represented a surprise coup from the ranks of the leading groups, because talks had been going on for some time to assess the chances of a merger between the DDP and the DVP. The chances were probably small anyway, but they were destroyed by the foundation of the State Party. Only in Württemberg were successful attempts made to create a liberal unity list in the 1930 Reichstag elections, though this did not halt the decline of the liberals.

The new party ended in the year in which it was founded with a 'wretched fiasco'.[34] As early as 7 October 1930, the *Volksnationale Reichsvereinigung* left the State Party in which from now on only the former DDP continued to exist – but as a rump party. Koch-Weser, one of the founders of the party, resigned the party leadership and his Reichstag seat. The decisive opponents of the merger with the *Volksnationale Reichsvereinigung* had already left the party. Some pacifists around Ludwig Quidde founded the *Vereinigung Unabhängiger Demokraten* (Alliance of Independent Democrats), which remained an extra-parliamentary splinter group, even after its transformation into the *Radikal-Demokratische Partei* (Radical Democratic Party) in November 1930. Other democrats, including Erkelenz and Ludwig Bergsträsser, joined the SPD.

With the foundation of the new party and the subsequent splits, Left Liberalism declined from 1930 onwards, and not only on an organizational level. The merger with the *Volksnationale* ('Jungdeutscher Orden' or Young German Order) would, members of the DDP had hoped, bring ageing Left Liberalism up to the 'bündische Jugend' youth movement, where it would regain its youth. The youth movement sought not the management of old ideals, but a departure into the future. But the *völkisch* ideas of the Young Germans could not be fulfilled by liberalism. The 'Ariernachweis' or proof of German ancestry, which the 'Young German Order', the core of the *Volksnationale*, demanded of its members, represented an insurmountable barrier for liberalism of any kind. It also proved impossible to reconcile the anti-capitalist stance of the Young Germans, for example, with the ideals embodied by the DDP.

The flight of the DDP into co-operation with the Young Germans was a flight from liberalism. It failed, as did the DVP's attempts to create a middle-class coalition movement – whether on a constitutional basis, perhaps with the *Deutscher Nationalverein* (German National Association), founded in 1932, or with the right against the Republic. Both were attempted; both failed. The votes in favour of the Enabling Act – two of the five State Party deputies, the chairman Hermann Dietrich and Theodor Heuss, had wanted to vote against, but had endorsed the three-man majority – as well as the compulsory self-dissolution of the DDP on 28 June 1933 and the DVP on 4 July now only eliminated organizational shells, whose contents had long since perished.

Liberal Programmes and Political Practice

The Restriction of the Revolution and Constitutional Reorganization

With the revolutionary movement of November 1918, and the collapse of monarchic Germany, which had already been destroyed on a military level, Social Democracy assumed the role that liberalism had played in the revolution of 1848. Both had power thrust upon them by a revolution which was not of their making and which they had not wanted, and both attempted to transform the revolution into democratically legitimized reforms as quickly as possible. In neither case was there a consensus on the extent of the reforms and the means of achieving them, yet in 1848 and 1919, with the broad support of the population, it was the moderate forces which asserted themselves. They wanted to end the revolution as soon as possible by the election of a constituent National Assembly, to which all the fundamental decisions on the new order would be entrusted. The immediate appeal to the 'sovereign people' and their election decision was to bring the revolution to an end, and introduce parliamentary reform. A revolutionary dictatorship, even of only brief duration, would have been irreconcilable, both with liberalism's understanding of democracy in 1848, and with that of Social Democracy in 1918. Both parties were anyway too closely bound up with the existing order to be in a position to wish for a total political or social revolution. For 1848–9 and for 1918–19 it is therefore true to say that 'the basis' of the new order 'was not the revolution, but the continuity wrung from the revolution'.[35]

The unexpected victors, who had done almost nothing to achieve their victory, were moderate; ready to share the power which now passed to them, to administer it according to legal principles and to return it to the electorate as soon as they could. Such democratic behaviour did not necessarily preclude radical reform, but it did inevitably limit the scope for reform. At the same time, it paved the way for a broad co-operation, which transcended political groupings. In 1848 the liberals had moved into the centre of power as representatives of the popular movement, and had tried to agree a reform pact with the old monarchic powers. When in 1918 Social Democracy was handed the reins of state power, it too sought co-operation with forces from other political and social camps which were willing to reform. Agreements were reached with the military command (the Ebert–Groener Agreement of 10 November 1918) and with the employers' associations, which signed the *Zentralarbeitsgemeinschaft* agreement with the unions on 15 November. And in the parliaments, too, (majority) Social Democracy showed that it was prepared to continue the co-operation with the Centre Party and the Left Liberals, which had been put to the test during the war.[36]

These agreements and coalitions established the parameters within which the National Assembly was able to operate in its work on the constitution. This framework of action offered the liberal middle classes surprisingly great opportunities to influence the revolutionary transitional phase between the Kaiserreich and the Republic. It was made possible by the clear and unmistakable declaration of support for the new republican state which the emerging DDP made in its announcement of 16 November 1918, and again in its party programme of December 1919: 'After a horrific war, we are now experiencing the turmoil of a powerful revolution. A state system which seemed invincible has collapsed, almost without putting up a fight; the pillars of the old power have fallen. All that is dead and beyond salvation. No one will be able to bring it back to life.' Left Liberals therefore voiced their clear, though not unconditional support for the new Republic in their founding statement. Liberalism measured the value of the Republic above all in terms of its importance as a shield, which could be used, they hoped, to deflect the revolution. Just as in 1848 liberals had uncompromisingly defended the 'constitutional monarchy' as a bulwark against anarchy and chaos, in 1918 they expected a parliamentary republic to have the same effect:

> [Our] first principle holds that we must remain firmly within the republican form of state, to represent it in elections and to seek to defend the new state against reaction of any kind, but also that a National Assembly, which has been elected under all the necessary guarantees, must make the decision on the constitution. Our second principle is that it should not be possible for us to separate freedom from order, from legitimacy and from the political equality of all members of the state, and that we must fight all Bolshevist, reactionary or other terrors, whose victory would mean nothing less than terrible misery and the enmity of the entire civilized world, which is filled with thoughts of justice.[37]

In political practice, the war against the 'terror' from the right and the left which was announced in the statement was aimed overwhelmingly at the alleged threat of the 'Bolshevization' of Germany. The revolutionary government was willing to compromise, and was Social Democratic in the majority – the USPD representatives left the Council of People's Representatives as early as 28 December 1918. Yet just as the government paved the way for the reforming alliance of the Social Democratic workers' movement and the Left Liberal middle classes, which had not been possible in the Kaiserreich, the DDP stressed above all the limitations of this alliance. As an announcement from the executive committee said on 18 December 1918, the DDP had 'a mission above all *to prevent the emergence of a socialist majority*, which would pose the greatest threat, not only to our future, but also to our economic life'.[38] Even Friedrich Naumann, one of the keenest supporters of a Social Democratic–liberal bloc before the First World War, declared that one of the main tasks of German liberalism was to 'oppose Bolshevism with all its might, so that we do not end up with a Russian situation'. In January 1919 he responded to the call to found an 'anti-Bolshevik league'.[39]

The DVP also went into the National Assembly elections with a surprisingly wide range of election announcements.[40] There was, however, a clear reservation behind its demand for a 'truly democratic policy', which then became unmistakable after the adoption of the constitution, when the party publicly demanded the re-establishment of the Hohenzollern monarchy.[41] But otherwise the election announcements of both liberal successor organizations agreed on many points, including the creation of a strong central power, whilst retaining cultural federalism and the annexation of German Austria. In tax policy both parties spoke out in favour of the 'strictest registration of war gains'. On the issues of nationalization and worker-participation – particularly explosive issues for the liberals – the DVP even tried to overtake the DDP on the left in its election announcements. Whilst already at the beginning of December 1918, the DDP stated that reforms should be as limited as possible, the DVP declared that it was in favour of the 'transfer of appropriate branches of commerce to public control and ownership' and of the 'appropriate co-operation of workers and employees through their committees and their representatives' in the firms.

Such declarations of support were, however, quickly abandoned after the elections. They do not document a fundamental change in course for the liberals, but reflect the mood of departure of the revolutionary weeks, which also gripped liberal voting circles. Both parties reacted to it in different ways, despite the apparent similarities in their election announcements. There were two competing directions in the DDP. The one believed that the only chance of building up a democratic republic lay in co-operation with the SPD. The other regarded the Republic primarily as a means 'of creating peace and order', in the words of Robert Friedberg, co-founder of the DDP and former (after

23 September 1917) first Chairman of the National Liberal Party.[42] In the DVP, on the other hand, the new order was only accepted in order to be better able to fight it. 'The world must come to terms with the new conditions, it cannot negate them, they are here. We call this the law of the *fait accompli*', explained Eugen Leidig, the Professor of International Law, in a chapter on 'Liberalism and Democracy' in the *German People's Party's Political Education Course*. What appeared to be a '*fait accompli*', he said, could turn out to be 'something temporary' in the future. This was as true of the aims of the victorious powers as it was of the revolution: 'Now that this infringement of the law has occurred, the People's Party initially has no option in its programme' than to accept the sovereignty of the people alongside universal suffrage as 'a second democratic view'. In contrast to the DDP's concept of the state, the DVP would adhere to the principle 'that the one personality is more significant and worth more than the other'. This principle would also have to be guaranteed in the formulation of social obligations for the future. Already in the Kaiserreich, with reference above all to municipal development, Leidig found that National Liberalism had 'even adopted the ideas of socialism' and that the 'barriers between the individual and the common economy' had not been 'unshakeable' for a long time. But liberalism's core should not be touched, he said; at its centre was not the 'mass', not 'a general average mediocrity', but the achievement of the individual. 'Democracy hates geniuses. ... But liberalism longs for geniuses.'[43]

As inconsistent as the attitude of the DDP, and above all the DVP, was to the '*fait accompli*' of the revolutionary decline of monarchic Germany, both parties submitted to the new order. This secured important opportunities for liberalism to co-operate in the constitutional formation of the new order.[44] The DDP occupied key positions in the constitutional debates. The constitutional lawyer Hugo Preuß was appointed Permanent Secretary for Home Affairs in mid-November 1918 and charged with drafting a constitution. Conrad Haußmann, Vice President of the National Assembly elected on 19 January 1919, was awarded the important post of Chairman of the Constitutional Commission. The DDP provided five members of the twenty-eight-strong commission, including the Party Leader, Friedrich Naumann, and his successor (1924–30) Erich Koch-Weser, Lord Mayor of Kassel at the time of his appointment. The DVP sent its party whip Karl Rudolf Heinze and the constitutional and ecclesiastical lawyer, Wilhelm Kahl. As even Social Democratic and Centre Party deputies recognized, when the constitution was accepted on 31 July 1919 by 262 votes to 75, the DDP could rightly regard the constitutional compromise which had often been threatened by failure, as its own work. 'The constitution has been born of our spirit, created, represented and wrapped up by our best people.' And one of its leading members, Conrad Haußmann gave it its name: the Weimar Constitution.[45]

The Constitution's structural shortcomings have often been criticized. The fact that its weaknesses could be exploited against the republican order, however, should not be blamed on the creators of the Constitution alone. 'Our sick age cannot be cured with a new constitution', one of its creators, the DDP deputy Koch-Weser, said as early as February 1919 to those whose expectations of a constitution were too great. And the Social Democrat Friedrich Stampfer later rightly stressed that the new Constitution had given 'the people two chances': 'It could elect a workable Reichstag and a workable National President.'[46] The fact that these two chances were not better exploited was not the fault of the creators of the Constitution. They devised a constitution which, given the political majorities, was necessarily a compromise, but the opportunity remained to develop it. This was also true of the responses to the three main issues which were wrestled over in the debates: the reorganization of the states and their relationship to the Reich; the distribution of authority between the central institutions of the state – the Reichstag, the National President and the national government; and the social organization of the Republic.

The profound territorial reorganization of the Reich envisaged by Preuß would have meant the dissolution of Prussia. He was unable to push this through, even in his own party. The DDP did demand a strong national power, but the positions adopted on Preuß's draft ranged from agreement to outright rejection of the 'fanatical unitarian features' which the Württemberg democrat Payer thought he could perceive in it. The traditions and interests of the individual states finally won the day. Thus, the legacies which the Weimar Republic was forced to take over from the Kaiserreich also included territorial organization, and therefore the overwhelming dominance of Prussia. None the less, the DDP and the DVP played an important role in strengthening central authority. The increase in the significance of the Reich, which had already coloured the development of the political ruling order in the Kaiserreich, could therefore be continued, despite the continued existence of the states.[47]

The legacy of the nineteenth century also weighed heavily on the institutional structure which the Constitution created. The revolution had decided the form of state, but even amongst Left Liberals, there were few convinced republicans. Yet whilst the Left Liberal 'rational republicans' became the architects of the Weimar state, the DVP's attitude to the new state continued to be mixed; for many it remained a 'Republic with reservations' (Bracher). In the final vote in the National Assembly the DVP refused to vote for the Constitution, and in its party programme of October 1919 it countered the Republic with a declaration of support for 'the empire' as the 'most appropriate form of state' for Germany 'given its history and type'. At the same time, however, it declared its support for co-operation 'within the current form of state'. Consequently, during the Kapp–Lüttwitz Putsch of March 1920, when militant right-wing circles attempted to seize government power, the DVP leadership wavered between 'disloyal behaviour' to the legitimate government and 'half-loyal behaviour' to the putschists. Only the failure of the putsch forced the DVP to adopt an unambiguous position. They 'managed to pull off the trick of simultaneously [distancing themselves] from the putsch and from the general strike' against the putsch, by expressing unconditional loyalty to the Constitution. Stresemann clearly voiced this reluctant, gradual acceptance of the Republic to his party's central committee:

> I now feel as though a theoretical effect of the Kapp Putsch is that we ourselves have taken one step too far in the direction of formal democracy; our proclamation of the sacred nature of the Constitution, in the form of an unconditional declaration of support for the existing order, might easily distort the impression amongst the public that what has happened has come about against our wishes and desires, and that the ideal of our lives lies in ruins.[48]

The monarchic ideal could not be revived, but it burdened the young Republic, for it lived on in the construct of the National President as a 'substitute monarch'. He had the right to dissolve

the Reichstag and to call a plebiscite on laws which he did not
want to sign; he was responsible for forming the government,
and Article 48 equipped him with a 'dictatorial power', which
Gerhard Anschütz, one of the few jurists who supported the
Republic, had called a 'deformalization of the exceptional law',
against which he voiced 'weighty reservations from the point of
view of the *rechtsstaatlich* principle'.[49] The democratic liberal
creators of the Constitution, on the other hand, wanted a strong
National President. 'What we expect', explained Koch-Weser for
the DDP in the National Assembly, 'is a man who stands on a
high vantage point, who steps down only when the hour of
danger has arrived and intervenes with strong words in the
conflicts of opinion'.

The 'historical handicaps of German parliamentarianism'
(E. Fraenkel) were made manifest in the powerful 'substitute
Kaiser', determined by plebiscite. Similar handicaps also ran
through the liberal perceptions of the political order: there were
reservations regarding the parties and the 'omnipotence of
parliament' (C. Haußmann); regarding the state's position 'above
the parties' and the 'pre-eminence of the executive' (L. Albertin),
even in the parliamentary system of government. If prominent
DVP members equated 'parliamentary rule' with 'party rule'
(K. R. Heinze), which they rejected outright, Left Liberals perceived the National President above all as the guardian of the
constitution. Yet they did not create the balance of power which
had been hoped for, but the often criticized 'dualistic birth
defects of the Weimar Republic': an 'ambivalent power structure
between the parliamentary and the presidential system', which
finally made it possible for the presidential state 'parallel consti-
tion' (Bracher) to overcome the parliamentary democracy in the
concluding phase of the Republic.[50]

On the subject of social organization, the National Assembly
also created a 'constitution without decisions' (O. Kirchheimer).
Successful attempts were made, however, to include in the
Weimar Constitution the idea that the state should address
'thoughts of social security'. Ernst Fraenkel rightly regards this as
Germany's 'significant and lasting contribution' to the development of 'Western democracy'. Its wide-ranging list of Basic
Rights shattered the traditional liberal canon, though the list was
not clearly defined. Indeed, it was little more than a 'stringing
together of the most varied demands, a series of socialist, liberal,

religious and conservative standards' (R. Rürup). As unclear and fragmentary as the aims of the list of Basic Rights were – the DNVP deputy Clemens von Delbrück called it a 'cornucopia', which would be 'tipped out indiscriminately over many population groups' – it did not actually obstruct anything, and it brought into focus those areas which could be developed at a later stage. Quite how was left to the future. The DDP and the DVP had played an important role in this outcome, which reflected the political majorities in the National Assembly, but which dashed the hopes of many people who had put their faith in a new future. As we have seen, the German liberalism of the nineteenth century had certainly been prepared for the idea of the protection of the individual on the part of a social state, and the first programmatic statements of the liberal successor parties had encompassed aims for wide-ranging social reforms. In the revolutionary transitional period, however, the fear that nationalization would lead to 'Bolshevization' began to dominate, and the 'peace of understanding between capitalism and socialism' propagated by Naumann failed. Article 165 of the Constitution envisaged factory committees and economic committees and the possibility of legislation on nationalization. But DDP members overwhelmingly hoped that it would be possible to bury the nationalization plans, with these 'clichés in paragraphs', as Carl Petersen (DDP Chairman 1919–24) described them, and the DVP rejected them outright. The DVP was the purest representative of the principles of economic liberalism.

The constitutional discussions had brought the DDP and the DVP closer together. This was also true of their social ideas. As this internal liberal understanding grew, the relations between Social Democracy and that part of liberalism which was willing for reform, and loyal to the Republic, grew correspondingly strained.[51] Only the future could decide on the viability of the Social Democratic–liberal part of the Weimar Coalition. It soon became a matter of the viability of the democratic Republic itself, on whose creation middle-class liberals, and above all the DDP, had exerted such a considerable influence.

Political and Social Models

German liberalism had always encompassed a wide range of socio-political ideas. As society became more complex, the variety of liberal models also grew, and organized liberalism experienced corresponding difficulties in bringing together the divergent interests of its clientele in a clear, broad programme, which would appeal to large sections of the population. In the Weimar Republic this blurring of the liberal contours climaxed in a variety of interests which had no strong integrative core. Both liberal successor parties ended up as little more than a 'federation of interest groups',[52] which did not succeed in reconciling their different aims. Nor could they, for the material interests of the employers, who were particularly influential in both parties, and the interests of the 'old' and 'new' *Mittelstand* and the workers' wing, were too varied or contradictory to form a workable basis for the programme and practice of liberal politics. Weimar liberals were familiar with this situation from the Kaiserreich, and they reacted to it in the usual manner. Once again, they tried to use the central values of the 'state' and the 'nation' to form bonds which would transcend the conflicts of interest and align party policies to a generally recognized goal. In both parties, intensive discussions began on these central values which would, it was hoped, create an identity and resolve the conflicts of interests. Yet these values meant different things to different people. Divisions from pre-war liberalism were continued, and now emerged more clearly than ever.

In its 'Principles' of October 1919, the DVP had still abstained from an open declaration of support for the National Liberal tradition in which it rightly placed itself. Under the impact of the revolution, however, even this programme, which aimed for the 'reconciliation of liberal and social ideas' and promised something to almost every social group, was held together only by the reference to the 'national idea of the state' and 'the people as a whole', the appeal to the 'essence of Germany' and 'love for the Fatherland'. The need to search for party consensus in the central values of the 'state' and the 'nation', which allegedly transcended parties, grew in line with the increasing influence of pressure groups, which turned the DVP into a 'party of company lawyers' (L. Döhn) and gradually adapted it to the new state, which it had initially accepted only with grave reservations. When Stresemann, its outstanding leading figure, was appointed Foreign Minister (August 1923 to his death on 3 October 1929) and rose to become one of the leading representatives of the Weimar Republic, the DVP was forced to underpin its policies and party unity in a way which 'transcended parties'. In doing so, it fell back on the 'indestructible ideals of national and liberal thinking and desires', as was stated in a DVP declaration of 1927, which commemorated the foundation of the National Liberal Party eighty years before. The degree to which the DVP hoped to find guiding values for the present and the future in the past are shown in the speeches on principles which were made before the DVP Central Committee on 25 May 1925 and published under the title 'German Liberalism'.[53] They also highlight the different definitions of these basic values in the party.

In the main speech, the Reichstag deputy Otto Most described a picture of decline which was permeated by caricatures of anti-democratic thought.[54] He referred to 'the death of politics' and 'the death of parliamentary activity', 'the battle for the feeding trough' and 'idle gossip', 'courting the favour of the voters' and the supremacy of 'the interests of the purse' (p. 5f.). Otto Most traced the wrong turns he thought he could perceive back to the radical changes which came with the 'second *Reichsgründung*. At that time, he said, 'economic issues' had become 'an end in themselves', and the 'true misery of the party system' began, when 'the strong internal bonds, the internal sense of community which helps one overcome all other conflicts' (p. 10) had dissolved. Once central liberal ideas had been realized in the legal and constitutional state, liberalism could only find an ideological basis as the 'representative of the *national idea of power*' (p. 15) which would be viable even 'if opinions diverge on individual practical questions' (p. 9). A liberalism for which the 'state as such' stands 'at the centre of thinking and political activity' (p. 17), Most declared to tumultuous applause, would also be able to take up the '*völkisch*' and the 'social idea', without betraying the innermost core of liberalism: the belief in the 'freedom of the individual'. Just as this freedom of the individual and the nation-state had once been pushed through against a society based on the system of estates, and against absolutism, he said, the '*salvation of the nation*' now had to be pushed through against the threatened '*dictatorship of the masses ... by means of the salvation of the individual*' (p. 20f.).

This fixation on the 'state as such', as the ideology of a 'national liberalism' which was searching for the key to the great successes of the past, always implied criticism of the present-day state too. But the extent of the criticism varied greatly. This is also reflected in the speeches of May 1925. If Most had held up the timeless ideological bases of liberalism as a counter-image to the present day, Wilhelm Kahl drew from it the practical application for the attitude of the DVP to the Weimar Republic: he was against the 'overloading of the democratic principle', and in favour of counteracting the 'supremacy of the masses, which debases or destroys the value of the individual' (p. 24). There was no commitment to a particular form of state, but assent in principle to a monarchy 'which stands above the parties', but which could also 'not be re-established ... by means of putsches'. He was in favour of a revision of the Constitution, but did not seek to 'reduce respect for the Constitution altogether. Nevertheless, it has created a solid, legal basis for the first time since the revolution's infringement of the law. It is our liberal duty to work together on its healthy *further development*, and to extract from it the right things which are needed to save the Fatherland and to rebuild it' (p. 26).

Whilst Kahl left a great deal up in the air, Stresemann adopted a clearer position in his concluding speech. He referred to a 'sacred duty *to collaborate in the work on the state as it is*' (p. 30), and called upon his party to combine its basic stance on the 'state' and the 'nation' with a 'search for the diagonal line between the different interests' (p. 31) which were ready for compromise.

All the speeches met with great applause, although their emphasis on the parliamentary Republic and its constitution differed widely. This lack of clarity was typical of the socio-political models which in the DVP ranged from reluctant acceptance of the democratic state as an evil which had been determined by the situation, and which should be corrected as soon as possible, to assent on principle to the Weimar Republic. In 1922 at the latest, after much deliberation, Stresemann finally came down in favour of a resolute defence of the Republic when he supported the 'law to protect the Republic' in the wake of the murder of Foreign Minister Rathenau. The issue had ceased to be 'theoretical republicans on this side, theoretical monarchists on the other!' It was now a 'conflict between assent to the state or destruction of the state'.[55] Stresemann later never denied the fact that he did not ascribe an 'eternal value' to all articles of the Constitution, but he always praised 'this Constitution, with all its weaknesses' as the only 'bond holding the German nation together'. He was only prepared to allow revisions 'within the republican form of state'.[56]

Only with difficulty could Stresemann persuade the conflicting interest groups in his party to agree to his course of a realistic revision of internal and external policies; a course determined by a readiness to reach an understanding. 'There are busy people at work in the party', he complained in 1929, who were seeking to place 'the leadership of the party in the hands of certain representatives of economic interests.' For these people, 'general politics is apparently only an appendix to the representation of interests', which 'far outweigh political issues of state'.[57]

Stresemann's death resulted in the loss of the strongest counter-weight to the heavy industrial right-wing of the DVP, whose 'liberalism had long since been reduced to the economic principle of private capitalism' (H. Booms). The political attempts, which began as early as the end of 1929, to bring together these influential forces, no longer set their sights on the 'stabilization of the hated Weimar system', but at exploiting the crisis of the Republic to engineer a 'fundamental and radical change in social and political circumstances'.[58] Under Eduard Dingeldey, who took over as party leader in 1930, following the brief interlude under Ernst Scholz (1929–30), the DVP finally adopted new 'objectives', as the 'shift of the fronts to the right' (L. E. Jones) was also expressed in the party programme. The DVP now adapted to form a coalition movement which sought to replace the parliamentary Republic with an authoritarian regime.[59]

The 'idea of the national community' described in the DVP's election handbook of 1924 as a core aim, which could only be achieved 'on the constitutional path',[60] continued to be regarded as the 'highest law' (p. 41) in the party's 'objectives'. Yet the language of the 1931 programme became a slave to anti-republican jargon. The Weimar state was denounced as an 'enforced state', placed 'in chains' by 'state socialism': an 'economically Utopian enforced system which would lead to the financial impoverishment of the entire nation' (p. 42). The DVP was now no longer willing or able to continue the attempt to use the model of the strong nation-state to bridge its internal conflicts. Demands from industrial circles to abolish the social laws were now clearly manifest in the programme, and were only thinly veiled by the praise of individual and professional 'independence', which would also be of use to the *Mittelstand* and the workers; the party was against all 'state control' which had arisen as a result of the 'penetration of socialist thought into the German legislation and administration' and in favour of 'greater flexibility in wages policy' and employment law (p. 46ff.).

Whilst demands such as these and the call for measures to be taken against 'an exaggerated parliamentarianism' could certainly be linked with liberal traditions, the cultural political sections of the programme went as far as the unveiled rejection of core elements of liberal thought. The demand for *'protection by the state from the current un-German activity, which is destroying the moral fibre of the nation, and from anti-culture, filth and trash in broadcasting, the theatre and film'* (p. 50), could no longer be reconciled with traditional liberal principles. This corruption of liberalism seems to have been taken furthest in the *Reichsgemeinschaft junger Volksparteiler* (National Community of People's Party Youth). In a statement of 5 August 1931, the secretary submitted a list of measures which reads like an anticipation of National Socialist policy: 'the liquidation of the Locarno and League of Nations policies' with which Stresemann had led Germany out of international isolation, 'the destruction of all free thinkers [all forces that would destroy the state], the purging of German art of filth and trash etc.'; the immediate dissolution of the KPD and the arrest of its leaders, 'radical measures' against the SPD, which would 'later' also have to be 'completely destroyed'; 'the depoliticization' of the unions, the suspension of all 'Marxist civil servants who hold high office', state control and new 'German' editors for the 'Berlin *Asphaltpresse*', amongst others.[61]

Demands such as these, which helped prepare the ground for the National Socialist dictatorship, did not determine the party course, however. In 1931 the party leader lamented the 'moral confusion' (p. 35) of the NSDAP in his programmatic speech. But during the concluding phase of the Republic, the DVP, which in 1925 had still regarded itself as the 'guardian of the liberal tradition',[62] openly abandoned its liberal models. From 1930 onwards, references to the National Liberal tradition, which it had only continued to a limited degree anyway, were heard less and less frequently in public statements: the liberal legacy was exhausted in the *Deutsche Volkspartei*. It declined even before the National Socialists eliminated its organizational shell in 1933. It put up no resistance: the DVP had no liberal values left to defend.

The *Deutsche Demokratische Partei* (DDP), which regarded itself as Left Liberalism's successor, also sought to focus the great variety of opinions and the interests of its members and voters in the central values of the 'state' and the 'nation'. It, too, encompassed a wide range of basic stances; a range which was probably even wider than that of the DVP. ' "Rational democrats" and "national democrats", convinced democrats and rational republicans, pacifists and imperialists of Wilhelmine stamp – there was a wide range of opinions which the party hoped to bridge with its assent to the constitution and the state and the representation of the interests of the state, oriented to the good of the whole.'[63] But in contrast to the DVP, the DDP's principles did not refer to a 'timeless' concept of the state and the nation, which could also be employed as a weapon against the Weimar Republic. The DDP saw itself rather as a republican constitutional party, whose desires for reform were not to destroy Weimar democracy, but to safeguard its continued existence.[64] Although in 1919 the republican constitution may initially have only represented a refuge from the feared 'Bolshevist chaos' for the DDP and for many of those who were 'democrats out of fear or opportunism' (Marie Elisabeth Lüders), it quickly developed to form the main bastion of the Protestant middle classes who were loyal to the Republic. Wilhelm Mommsen's summary in his list of Left Liberal achievements published in 1928, reflects this assent to the Weimar Republic, and the DDP's hope that it would be able to find a viable unifying adhesive force in the democratically fulfilled guiding values of the 'state' and the 'nation':

The republic as a form of state is secure today, as far as anyone can judge, and it is the duty of German republicans to provide it with the only content which can give the form any value. We know that we still have a lot to do in this respect, and we too recognize that every standstill is a step back. The permanent existence of the democratic Republic is not decided by its opponents, but by the supporters of the republican democratic state themselves. ... Whilst every German has the right to a say in the fate of the nation and the state, he also has a duty to exercise this right in consciousness of his responsibility to the whole. This thinking, which focuses on the state and the nation, must be supplemented by a genuinely social attitude, which will overcome all class-based attitudes, and which regards every citizen of the state above all as a German national comrade, ignoring all political and social conflicts. If it succeeds in arousing this feeling amongst all strata of the German people and strengthening it, then not only the democratic republican form, but also democratic republican thinking will be indestructible.[65]

One of the central problems which ultimately caused Weimar Left Liberalism to fail, was the fact that its guiding values were almost indistinguishable from those of the right-wing opponents of the Republic. For they too referred to the 'national community', though the democrats defined it differently, as their understanding of the terms 'nation' and 'national politics' shows. In their programme of 1919 they had protested against the Versailles 'diktat of power', which was bitterly condemned even by the convinced pacifists in their ranks. As late as 1921, a majority of the parliamentary party had rejected the 'London payment plan' which, under pressure of ultimata from the allied victors, had begun the German 'policy of appeasement'. But the DDP then managed to adopt a realistic position: it agreed with Stresemann's policies in the hope of being able to combine understanding and revision. 'Overcoming Versailles' formed the common basis of all foreign political attitudes in the DDP, but individually their aims for revision were very different. The merger with Austria to form a 'Greater Germany' was a distant aim for most liberals. Many hoped (as did sections of the Social Democrats) that German colonial acquisitions could be regained, and many advocated a programme of national expansion which vacillated between Central European and Pan-European ideas, which dreamed of a 'mission of German technology, economy and culture' (Hermann Höpker-Aschoff) and did not even shy away from formulas such as Gertrud Bäumer's 'Volk ohne Raum' (nation without territory). Despite all its similarities with the nationalism of the right, however, the democratic nationalism of the DDP was clearly different.[66] Its idea of the nation was not fixed and absolute, and was discussed in the context of the Weimar Constitution; it spoke of the 'Volksganze' and the 'Volksgemeinschaft' (national community), but did not adopt a position against the alleged 'enemy within'. It was not racist or anti-Semitic; it was revisionist, but not aggressively chauvinistic; it sought peaceful equilibrium, and sometimes even extended to pacifism.

At the end of the day, however, democratic nationalism was unable to distinguish itself clearly enough from the integral nationalism of the right. The transitions between the two were fluid, and towards the end of the Weimar Republic, when the flood of dissatisfied voters also pushed the DDP to the right, the frontiers became even more porous. The Left Liberal remnants in the German State Party then resorted to making national demands under the slogan 'active foreign policy', though they were not able seriously to compete with the radicalism of the right. When in 1931 the State Party declared that simultaneous membership of the *Deutsche Friedensgesellschaft* (German Peace Association) and the State Party was irreconcilable, the emptiness of democratic nationalism was once again made clear: there was no room for pacifists in the party now.[67]

The DDP also failed in its hopes for the reconciliation of the Left Liberal middle classes and the Social Democratic workers' movement. Anton Erkelenz, representative of the employees' wing in the party, moved over to the SPD; his personal response to the failure to push through the programme of 'social capitalism' in the DDP, with which the party had entered into the Weimar Republic.

> For 12 years we in the Democratic Party have fought for the middle classes and for the interests of a middle class, which, unfortunately, hardly exists; the so-called middle classes for whom we wanted to work, in that we opposed Social Democracy, unfortunately exist only amongst a thin layer of educated people, while the real middle classes are at least as inclined to the class struggle as the Social Democratic workers are.[68]

In order to prevent the material conflicts of interest from breaking out of its unifying formula 'as a party of the state and the constitution', the DDP was forced to allow conflicting opinions and votes on issues of economic and social policy. This is true, for example, of the problem of fighting inflation, which significantly affected the middle-class electorate in particular; the DDP adopted no clear position in the revaluation debate. It behaved similarly in other important areas, including the Law on Works Councils, the expropriation of princes' property and arbitration in wages disputes.

The Left Liberals were forced into a kind of 'programmatic passivity' (W. Schneider) on matters of social and economic policy. Despite several attempts, the DDP did not succeed in devising a social and economic programme, which would have adapted the corresponding passages in the party programme of 1919 to general and internal party developments. In October 1928 a party committee was entrusted with this task, but a year later only a private draft by the committee chairman Gustav Stolper was placed before the party conference.[69] It was filled with the conviction that *'capitalism and only capitalism is in a position to create a maximum of material riches and therefore the fundamental precondition for the greatest possible well-being of each individual'* (p. 27). Just as this message could hardly win workers over to the DDP at a time when unemployment in the unions had reached around 13 per cent, and more than 40 per cent in some towns,[70] the commercial middle class was unlikely to acquire a taste for Stolper's acceptance of the cartel and the monopoly. Stolper concluded his draft with twelve basic principles on the 'philosophy of democracy', which once again show that the DDP could only hope to conceal the conflicts of interest in its ranks by means of 'philosophical abstractions' (pp. 34–43, 36):

1. Democracy believes in the possibility of reconciling social and economic interests in the free state. . . .
2. Democracy believes that the fates of the classes are linked.
3. Democracy rejects the class struggle as a demand. . . .
4. Democracy also therefore rejects the dictatorship of the state and the dictatorship of a single class over the economy. . . .
5. The prerequisite for democracy, as the only possible system which can lead to a free society, is the economic and social freedom of the individual. . . .
6. Democracy therefore demands private property as the condition and basis of its existence, without which the freedom of the individual cannot exist. . . .
7. Democracy implies society's obligation to help bring about the highest possible degree of economic development. . . .
8. Democracy also means, however, the obligation of society to summon up all its power in the direct fight against social deprivation, wherever it is revealed. . . .
9. Democracy will not tolerate mass poverty, it has at its disposal all the means necessary to eliminate mass poverty. . . .

10. Democracy therefore assents to the state as the executor of its social wishes. . . .
11. The basis of democracy [is not to be found] in an anonymous mass, but in an association of independently thinking, freely responsible and freely acting individuals, which in turn makes strong leadership necessary.
12. And above all: democracy believes in the free individual, not in the state machine.

Stolper's draft was celebrated at the party conference with 'thunderous applause for the speaker' (p. 44), but it was not adopted as a guideline for party policy. Competing ideas continued to exist. They ranged from the employees' committee's hopes for the state control of the economy, with the prioritization of social policy, to the rejection of the *'Großwirtschaft'* by its middle-class opponents and to the ideas of the staunch supporters of a market economy which was as free of the state as possible.

Despite the apparent futility of the DDP's proposals of democratic doctrine as a solution for core economic and social problems, these suggestions were republican declarations of belief, not programmes for an authoritarian restructuring of the Weimar economy and its society. This is also true of the DDP's plans to reform the political order. In the words of their election slogan of 1928, they wanted to move 'from the incomplete to the complete republic' with a reform policy which was inherent in the system and which did not seek to destroy the system.[71] Above all, they demanded the reform of the electoral system, which would push back the splinter parties (including a '3 per cent clause' as a hurdle for entry into the Reichstag). They also sought a reform of the Reich, which envisaged a decentralized unified state.[72]

As the Left Liberals in the Reich declined to the point of insignificance during the concluding phase of the Republic, their enthusiasm for reform increased, until it was no longer confined to the limits of the Weimar state order. Ideas were now voiced on abolishing the parliamentary system in the states, which would further reinforce the position of the National President and limit the role of the parliamentary parties. The fact that the majority of Left Liberals viewed the 'party state' with scepticism and gave only limited assent to the parliamentary system of government, was shown once more during the state crisis. Yet even these plans, which could not be transformed into a new programme before 1933, were not aimed at the dictatorial overthrow of the Republic. They were looking for a 'new, reformed type of democracy': a 'parliamentarianism which had been reformed from head to toe', as Reinhold Maier wrote on 15 January 1933. Even where Left Liberals considered an 'authoritative government' (H. Höpker-Aschoff, 1931) or dictatorial forms of rule, they did so only in the context of a search for a tolerable way out of a situation which Left Liberals were powerless to change politically, and which they believed could no longer be tackled using the means available in the parliamentary Republic. 'If we cannot find a strong leadership or government authority, then we must come to terms with a dictatorship. If it comes in the form of Brüning, it is tolerable because this dictatorship would not be led by an adventurer', declared Höpker-Aschoff in August 1931 to the State Party committee. And exactly a year later, the Reichstag deputy Wilhelm Külz noted after the elections of July 1932, in which the NSDAP had become the strongest party in the Reichstag:

> The electoral battle has been fought. The German nation has before it a dreadful and cruel result.... In objective political terms, the outcome of the election is so dreadful because it shows that the current election will be the last normal Reichstag election for some time. The so-called nation of thinkers and poets is rushing, with flags held high, towards the dictatorship and towards a time which will be ploughed through by terrible revolutionary currents. ... If one looks at these things simply and soberly, the fact is that more than half of the German nation has declared its opposition to the current state, yet it is not saying what kind of state it favours. Organic development of any kind is therefore impossible for the time being. I would regard the fact that the present government is quite openly moving over to dictatorship as the least of the many evils we should fear.[73]

Even in the final phase of the progressive dissolution of the Republic, what Meinecke had written in 1926 remained true for the State Party: he had regarded the parliamentary system as by no means the 'inevitable consequence of a democratic republic. Our desire for reform is therefore to be clearly distinguished from the desire for reform of those who respect the external form of the Republic for the time being, but who wish to fill it internally with the spirit and the institutions of the old class-based and authoritarian state.'[74] Or, we might add, who wanted to transform it by apparently legal means into a dictatorship. When this threatened to occur, Meinecke named the 'four foundations of the Weimar Constitution' which, despite all reforms to counter the 'degeneration of parliaments and parties', 'should not be touched: the republic, democracy, parliament and the parties'.[75] When in 1932–3 his hopes were dashed that the National President might break the desire for a dictatorship on the behalf of the enemies of the Republic, he was left with nothing but an appeal to the electorate:

> The consequences of the elections of 5 March [1933] must be that the workers, and the middle classes too, express their desire to reject a fascist dictatorship so vociferously that there can be no thoughts of even an apparently legal elimination of our constitutional bases and inner freedom. If everyone does his duty, we can certainly hope that the majority will reject it in this way.[76]

His hopes were unfounded. And liberalism had nothing left but hope. There was no longer any support for its values amongst the German public.

The profound insecurity of Protestantism, the ideological centre of liberalism, had also played a role here. Since the shock of the lost war and the collapse of the monarchy, liberal theology had also lost its power of conviction. It was, its opponents maintained, a 'theology without crises' and for that reason it could find no responses to the crises of the 1920s.[77] This was bound to weaken the political power of resistance of liberal models.

Liberals in the Parliaments

There was a remarkable discrepancy between election results and the influence of both liberal parties in Reich politics. Although after 1920 the DDP was only ever in sixth or seventh position in terms of the number of seats it held, it participated in thirteen of the fifteen Reich governments between February 1919 and May 1932, holding important ministerial posts, before

declining to a splinter party in 1932. The DVP, always the fifth
or sixth strongest parliamentary party before 1932, held office
in eleven of the twelve governments between June 1920, when
it first entered a government, and 1 June 1932, when the presidential cabinet of Franz von Papen was appointed. In addition to
the foreign ministry, which Stresemann headed from August
1923 until his death in 1929, its members also sometimes held
further important ministerial posts in the ministries of the interior, economics and finance.[78]

Both parties were able to acquire this strong position because,
together or alone, they held key positions in the four coalition
models which enabled governments to be formed at Reich level:
the 'Weimar Coalition', made up of the SPD, the Centre Party
and the DDP (1919–20, 1921–2); the 'Grand Coalition' of the
SPD, the Centre Party, the DDP and the DVP (1923, 1928–30);
a coalition of the 'middle-class centre', composed of the Centre
Party, the DDP and the DVP (1920, 1922, 1923–4, 1926); and its
expansion by the DNVP to form a *Bürgerblock* (1925, 1927). The
DDP and the DVP also participated in Brüning's presidential
cabinet (1930–2). All coalition models suffered a permanent political dilemma: no coalition was able to agree on issues of both
domestic and foreign policy. The 'Grand Coalition' and the
'Weimar Coalition' were able to pursue a common foreign political
line, but in central domestic policy, defended differing, sometimes
contradictory positions. The reverse was true in the *Bürgerblock*,
while the coalition of the 'middle-class centre parties', utterly
dependent on tolerance, since it was a minority cabinet (see Table
16), required the votes of other parliamentary parties on issues of
domestic and foreign policy. This situation forced the Reich
governments to work with changing majorities – 'a process which
was anything but suitable for effecting the lasting stability of the
parliamentary system'.[79] This dilemma of coalition politics was
further intensified because none of the parties seemed able or
willing to exercise party or coalition discipline in the government
they carried. The German parties of the Kaiserreich had not been
able to practise the rules of the parliamentary system of government, and in the short era of the Weimar Republic they found
their way at best to a flawed understanding of the parliamentary
system. This contributed to the fact that the government and
opposition parties of the Reichstag did not oppose each other as
blocs. Even the government party in each case entirely or

partially adopted the role of the opposition in individual votes. This meant that the parliamentary majority could change suddenly, and the governments were subject to the interventions of the National President. The negative consequences of this politics of changing majorities were certainly recognized by contemporaries. 'What we have today is a coalition of ministers, not a coalition of parties. There are no government parties at all, there are only opposition parties. The fact that it has come to this is a greater threat to the democratic system than ministers and parliamentarians can conceive.' Stolper's (DDP) diagnosis of 1929 broadly coincides with Stresemann's verdict, also voiced in 1929.

The *Deutsche Volkspartei* has been represented in the Reich cabinet for almost six years. This has brought an end to the bright and cheerful opposition, to that lack of responsibility, which found it so easy to devise programmes which it had no need to implement itself. The in many respects more fortunate *Deutschnationale Partei* knew how to turn that to its advantage. Some party secretaries find it rather pleasant to stand in opposition to the state. It then becomes possible to ally oneself with the 'Stahlhelm' hardliners again; one can allow 'the national idea to shine before the nation' once more; one can once again make threatening speeches which are empty, but which are seized upon by the people with delight. Dissatisfaction in the party is reinforced by the fact that we are in a government with the Social Democrats. The Right refers to Social Democracy with the phrase 'traitor to the country', as if one could dare to say that of a party which in percentage terms probably lost most people in the World War, and on which we have had to rely in the votes in the East against Poland and in the West against the separatists. Whether and how far these sentiments reflect social links with the German national side, I do not wish to speculate. In the long term, the party will be able to tolerate a centre cabinet at the most. But many people's longings are pushing it to the right. Everyone assents to the Grand Coalition on principle, and most people are trying hard to prevent it.[80]

Stresemann aptly described a fundamental problem of government policy: both liberal parties had only limited room for manoeuvre on a domestic political level. Although from the

beginning the DDP was clearly open to co-operation with the
SPD, when the model of 'social capitalism' lost its validity in
the DDP, its ability to determine the course of domestic politics
with Social Democracy (and the Centre Party) diminished
accordingly.[81] The election results would certainly have allowed
a reform pact of this kind, for in 1919–20 and from December
1924 to September 1930, a government of the 'Weimar Coalition'
would have enjoyed an absolute majority of mandates, and as late
as 1930–2 the figure was approximately 43 per cent of votes (see
Table 15).[82] The DDP alone should not be blamed for the fact
that the opportunity to create a democratic basis for the Republic
was not exploited, but its failure to lead its special interest groups
onto such a course of action was certainly instrumental in it.

A policy of co-operation with the SPD on domestic policy was
always out of the question for the DVP. When in 1923 it entered
a 'grand coalition' which included Social Democracy for the first
time, it regarded it only as an emergency solution to find a way
out of the Ruhr conflict. 'The tactical alliance with Social Democracy', the DVP stressed in its *Election Handbook of 1924*, has *'never
changed* the party's basic attitude to the *battle against Social
Democracy at all'*.[83] Its domestic political aims relegated the DVP
to a coalition of the 'middle class centre', which never had a
parliamentary majority, however, or to the *Bürgerblock*, including
the DNVP, with which Stresemann's foreign policy could not
have been realized. Given the interests of the parties, there was
only one way out: Reich politics was 'dissected into a series of
individual conflicts, which at the same time reflect the lack of unifying force of the Weimar form of parliamentarianism'. Changing
alliances emerged, of which the 'foreign political Reichstag majority [was] ... the most enduring'.[84] Together with the DDP, the
Centre Party and the DVP, it also encompassed Social Democracy. On this basis, Stresemann was able to pursue foreign policies
of which Locarno and the German entry into the League of
Nations represent important stages. They are two of the great
achievements of the parties which were capable of sustaining
the Republic, and they should not be underestimated in all the
criticism of Weimar parliamentarianism. The unconditional
supremacy of foreign policy suited both liberal parties, for it
could be adapted to their socio-political models, in which the
'national state' and its return to the fold of the great powers was
unambiguously of paramount importance.

On issues of domestic politics there were no similar models which could legitimize internal party alliances and permanent alliances beyond party boundaries. Only a 'system of makeshift substitutes' was found, as the many split votes and positions, even in the most important areas, testify: they include the Law on Works Councils, tax reforms, the flag decree, princes' compensation, revaluation legislation, youth protection, defence policy, financial policy and arbitration. This policy did not preclude achievements such as the great social welfare legislation of 1927. Nevertheless it only made 'changing minorities and shifting alliances' possible.[85]

It was this very unstable openness which gave the parties of the middle-class liberal centre opportunities for influence which exceeded the significance of the number of seats they held. This in turn seemed to remove from the DDP and the DVP the need to commit themselves to a clear domestic political programme. In doing so, they would have had not only to deal with their internal conflicts of interests, thereby endangering party unity, but they would also have decreased their opportunities of forming alliances. In the elections of 1932, however, both parties paid the 'price' for this parliamentary openness without the resolution of conflicts in their own ranks: they could hardly find any voters any more who still supported their policy of encouraging integration by forgetting certain issues.

In comparison to the situation during the Kaiserreich, the responsibilities and areas of authority of the Reichstag and the national government had increased significantly, and the political importance of the states had decreased correspondingly. But the states did not become insignificant by any means. Research has so far been patchy on the policies pursued by the DDP and the DVP and their opportunities for political action in the *state parliaments*. Analyses of 'Weimar liberalism' usually ignore this sphere, despite the fact that the DDP and the DVP were better able to assert themselves in the state parliaments than in the Reichstag, and were able to do so for a longer period of time, though ultimately liberalism declined in the states, too (see Table 15). We will outline these developments using the examples of Prussia, Saxony and Hamburg.

Prussia, which in the Kaiserreich had been the strongest bulwark against the trend towards democratization, became the model of democratic stability in the Weimar Republic.[86] There were eighteen Reich governments before Hitler's first chancellorship, but only seven in Prussia, including three minority cabinets, compared with thirteen at Reich level. Before the *Preußenschlag* of 20 July 1932, when Chancellor von Papen removed the Prussian government with the help of the national army, there were members of the DDP in every cabinet. And with the exception of a brief interlude in 1921, when the Centre Party and the DDP formed a minority government, from the second cabinet onwards (25 March 1919), Prussia was always governed by the parliamentary parties of the 'Weimar Coalition' under the leadership of the SPD, supplemented by the DVP to form the 'Grand Coalition' between 1921 and 1925.

A series of factors contributed to this stability, which was achieved despite the fact that even in Prussia the parties of the 'Weimar Coalition', and above all the DDP, were forced to accept heavy losses of votes (see Table 15). Fewer people voted, which favoured the democratic parties in the concluding phase of the Republic. Most importantly, however, unlike the national constitution, the Prussian constitution exerted great pressure on the parliamentary parties to form coalitions which would be able to reach compromises. For Prussia lacked a head of state who could come to parliament's aid in an emergency and enforce decisions that the parliamentarians shied away from making. Although in Prussia, too, the parliamentary parties did not see themselves as henchmen of their government, they did seem to be more disciplined than the government party in the Reichstag. In the Prussian Parliament, therefore, the politics of changing majorities remained 'rather the exception'.[87] The influence of the government parties, the SPD, the Centre and the DDP on the distribution of civil servant posts also had a positive effect on government stability. It united the coalition parties amongst themselves and with the new state order, for which it created loyal civil servants. In contrast to the Reich, Prussian civil servants were prohibited from joining the NSDAP. The success of this policy is shown by the wave of sackings which took place in 1933–4: all provincial governors, thirty-two of the thirty-four government presidents and almost half of all senior civil servants employed before 1932 were replaced by the National Socialists.[88]

The Weimar Coalition parties and the DVP too – which voted for the Prussian constitution in 1920 and assented to the Republic at an earlier stage and more decisively than it did at Reich level – undoubtedly made Prussia a strong base of parliamentary democracy. But whether Prussian parliamentarianism can be understood as a 'historical alternative' to Reich parliamentarianism[89] is debatable. For the conflict-ridden major decisions on foreign and domestic policy had to be reached at Reich level, and not in Prussia. This relieved the pressure on the middle-class centre parties of the DDP and the DVP in the states. They were able to shift some of their internal conflicts of interest onto the Reich parties. The increase in liberalism's ability to compromise was one of the prerequisites for Prussia's political stability. But even here voters deprived the parties which were loyal to the Constitution of their majority in 1932.

Saxony, the industrial centre and traditional stronghold of Social Democracy, represents the opposite pole to the Prussian post-war development.[90] In 1919, majority Social Democracy rejected a possible co-operation in government with the DDP, and even when it nevertheless came about in October, it was only a stopgap coalition, which lost the majority in the elections of 1920, falling from 64.5 to 36 per cent. The big winners of the middle-class parties were the DNVP (which rose from 14.3 to 21 per cent) and the DVP (3.9 to 18.6 per cent) (see also Table 15). The socialist governments which then followed – the SPD first formed a coalition with the USPD, and from 1923 onwards with the KPD – led into a series of crises which climaxed in the intervention of the central authority in 1923. At the beginning of 1924, a 'Grand Coalition' was formed by the SPD, the DDP and the DVP – the Centre Party was not a significant force in Protestant Saxony – yet the preceding turmoil had torn open the political gulfs between the parties of the workers and the middle classes to the point where it was hardly possible to bridge them again. The SPD split in the internal party 'Saxon conflict'. The Old Social Democrats retired and withered away to a mere sect, and Social Democracy abandoned political power. For it rejected a coalition with the middle-class parties and they, in turn, no longer wanted to make a pact with the SPD. The result was a 'parody of parliamentarianism',[91] which was brought about by parties which were incapable of reaching compromises, and which were not prepared to enter a Social Democratic–liberal coalition, without which the democratic Republic clearly could not be sustained.

In the city-state of Hamburg, developments differed again.[92] After 1919 the SPD and the DDP formed the government core, which in 1925 was expanded by the addition of the DVP to form the Protestant 'Grand Coalition' (the Centre Party never won more than 1.6 per cent of the votes). Not until the September elections of 1931 did it lose its majority, though thanks to the Hamburg constitution and a national emergency decree, it was able to remain in power until March 1933. The conditions for a resilient Social Democratic–liberal coalition were particularly favourable in Hamburg. Even before the First World War, Social Democratic workers had politically and culturally come to identify with Hamburg society to a considerable degree. But equally significant was the fact that after the turn of the century, a Left Liberal organization had emerged in Hamburg, which campaigned for universal equal suffrage in the states and for sociopolitical reforms, including a labour exchange with equal representation on the part of employers and employees, for impartiality on the part of the state authorities in employment disputes, and for the building of cheap housing, etc. This social liberal wing influenced the Hamburg DDP after the war, and even those circles which adhered to a more traditional form of liberalism were clearly convinced that Social Democracy should not be excluded from government authority. Even in the concluding phase of the Republic, Hamburg liberals did not abandon this position, which was shared by some members of the DVP.

Although in Hamburg, too, the Social Democrats, the DDP and the DVP lost large numbers of votes in the elections between 1919 and 1932, they were able to prevent the decline of the middle-class liberal centre. In 1932, with 11.2 per cent of votes, the Hamburg DDP achieved by far the best result of all DDP state associations (see Table 15). This successful stabilization of the parliamentary democracy was made possible by a concerted policy of state intervention. All circles agreed that the port as the economic base should enjoy priority in state aid, but they also advocated a number of other things: most importantly, housing projects, the construction of public baths and parks, the expansion and reform of educational facilities, increases in social provision for state workers and welfare services.

The Hamburg DDP, which put up the first mayor, Carl Petersen, between 1924 and 1930, supported this state interventionist policy of social reform as a matter of conviction. It therefore also turned decisively against Brüning's deflation policy and against all plans for a right-wing middle-class coalition movement. However, it could not prevent the DDP's transformation into the State Party, any more than it could prevent the spread of Reich policy onto the Hamburg situation during the global recession. Despite the anti-Social-Democratic course which the DVP adopted in 1931, which sometimes brought it close to the NSDAP, it was possible to retain a viable Social Democratic–liberal senate in Hamburg. This was only possible because the democratic parties here did not shy away from assuming political responsibility even in difficult times, and because they firmly assented to the parliamentary system. Developments in the Reich finally destroyed the 'island of peculiarity' as Peter Stubmann, the state chairman of the DDP called Hamburg in 1926.[93]

One of the reasons that social liberal policies functioned better in Hamburg than in most other German states was its 'municipal socialist' tradition. In the Kaiserreich a social liberalism developed in the towns (cf. Chapter 4, pp. 218–28), which in the city state of Hamburg provided favourable conditions for a Social Democratic–Left Liberal reform coalition in the post-war period. As yet we know little about the development of *municipal liberalism* in the Weimar era. The democratization of suffrage regulations in 1919 destroyed the main bastion which the middle classes had used to exclude Social Democracy from municipal institutions. But even without this barrier, the political parties were still apparently less successful at penetrating the municipalities than they were at state or Reich level, and the frontiers between the middle-class groupings continued to be more permeable.[94]

As a rule, links between municipal politics and Reich politics continued to grow closer, as the growing influence of lord mayors in the Reich, for example, would suggest. A series of lord mayors sat in the National Assembly and in the Reichstag, in central governments and other national institutions. A large proportion of them were members of the DDP, and a smaller proportion came from the DVP. These liberals seem to have been better at asserting themselves as administrative experts than their parties were, for the increasing emaciation of liberalism also occurred in the municipal election committees.[95]

Liberals Before and After 1933: Taking Stock and the Outlook for the Future

The 'unique decline' of liberalism (S. Neumann) brought with it the decline of the foundations of the Weimar Republic. For the parliamentary democracy was built on the historical alliance which seemed to succeed in 1919 in the reform coalition between Social Democracy and Left Liberalism, between workers and the middle classes. With the decline of Left Liberalism, this alliance, and with it the basis of the Weimar state, therefore also inevitably declined.

To establish this is not an attempt to blame the failure of the first German democracy on the liberals and on the DDP in particular. Certainly, their 'relativistic thinking' undermined their ability to assert themselves and to promote the Republic. But even in retrospect, it is difficult to see how the collapse of the liberal parties might have been avoided.[96] Some historians believe that they have discovered the reason for the failure of liberal politics in two shortcomings in particular: in liberalism's ambivalent attitude towards the parliamentary republic; and in its reluctance to represent material interests openly and resolutely, and thereby to create a dependable basis for its policies. But judgements such as these fail to recognize the strength of the historical traditions upon which Weimar liberalism was based, and its limited room for manoeuvre in the extraordinarily difficult socio-political situation after the First World War.

Historically, the German liberals had not been prepared for an unqualified declaration of support for the parliamentary party state. It is for this very reason that their significant achievements after 1919 include the transformation of parliamentary ideas into political practice – although they had many reservations on this issue. Ridding themselves of these reservations would have required testing the viability of the parliamentary system over a long period of time, and learning the rules of the game. The parliamentary system and its defenders were never given the opportunity to do this. Instead, they had to try to overcome the difficult legacy of monarchic Germany with the means of the parliamentary party state, at a time whose crises many, including members of middle-class liberal circles, experienced as the 'end of the middle-class era'. This mood of crisis affected the liberals more than any other major political camp. For liberalism was particularly closely

associated with the German nation-state, and at the same time with
the values of 'Western civilization'. For this reason, it was hit
hardest by the 'demonstrative break with the pre-war world, its
values and trends'.[97]

'Liberal' was a word which already in the Weimar Republic
was loaded with negative connotations in public usage. Finally,
after 1933, it was placed firmly in the repertoire of political
denunciation. The disparagement of 'liberal' and 'liberalism'
occurred after the First World War, not only in anti-democratic
thinking, but even amongst those who were seeking new bases
for a democratic future. Adult education, which expanded enormously in the Weimar Republic, provides an eloquent example of
this. Filled with the conviction that they would be able to participate in the creation of a new Germany, many 'adult educators' in
the pre-war years adopted a perspective of decline in which
liberalism was also included. Thus prepared, in 1933 many
people took over with depressing ease the National Socialist myth
which denounced the Weimar 'system' as the work of a Jewish-
infiltrated Marxism and liberalism. In their secret reports on the
'mood of the nation', SS departments described almost all opponents of National Socialist policies at home and abroad under the
headings 'liberalism' and 'liberalist'. 'The liberalist concepts of
freedom, tolerance, progress, peace and co-operation between
nations' the report for 1938 said, 'were now used as battle cries
against National Socialism by all opponents, from Communists to
reactionaries.' The report continued,

> At the time of the report, the supporters and promoters of
> liberalism are increasingly revealed as our ideological oppo-
> nents, freemasons, political churches and Jews. There are close
> links with emigration of every kind. All means are used to
> organize a great propaganda, so that links may be formed with
> opponents who remain in Germany, and a liberalist front can
> be created in Germany too.[98]

In National Socialist Germany liberalism was one of the collective
terms used to describe opponents of the 'new Germany'. Yet
already during the Weimar Republic, anyone who declared his
support for liberalism had been accused of being responsible for
the decline of the old Germany and the misery of the present.
'No party here can call itself liberal today', wrote Heinrich

Herkner in 1925, 'liberal remains a pudendum which requires at least a national or social fig leaf.' Before 1914 Germany had been regarded abroad as the 'refuge of all illiberal currents'; 1918 now signified,

> the fall of the aristocracy, but by no means the rebirth of liberalism. Not only the working class, but other strata of our nation also regarded a planned economy and a soviet system as a rising star which promised salvation. And when the 'liberal' victor states and their satellites betrayed liberalism to Wilson's Fourteen Points in the Treaty of Versailles, liberalism was seen as an idol which had been wrecked and destroyed once and for all.

German liberalism as the victim of liberal Western democracy, which betrayed its ideals in Versailles – this German self-image was bound to weaken German liberalism, which Herkner wanted to change with programmes of social reform, and liberalism's ability to assert itself. In a similar way, Leopold von Wiese sought to strengthen liberal values. Oswald Spengler's maxim in his widely-read work *Preußentum und Sozialismus* (Prussianness and Socialism) (1920) was 'liberalism is a matter for rogues'. Von Wiese countered this with, 'the word liberalism contains within it the entire great hope of the modern age'. But his appeal to find a way out of the troubles of the time, which was based on fundamental rational, liberal and socialist values, lacked any concrete perspective of action.[99] That was inevitable. The liberals were denied the recourse to material interests as a basis for a policy of social reform, since the middle classes disintegrated into many mutually competing interest groups.

The state and constitutional adhesive force, with which the DDP and the DVP attempted to bring together this variety of interests, was seriously undermined in the global recession. In the concluding phase of the Republic, even liberals sought authoritarian ways out of the crisis of state and society. But they were lost from the start, since they were not able to slay the prophets of 'radical reform' on their own battlefield. Liberal thinking had always aimed for tolerance and for convincing people by means of rational argument. The liberal language of the Weimar Republic, the period of the decline of German liberalism, showed that it was still committed to this fundamental position. To a greater extent than all other political alignments, liberals used open formulations, and refused to issue dogmatic orders or demand obedience.[100] In an atmosphere of crisis which demanded the adoption of extreme positions, they seemed to offer ever fewer people a perspective of the future.

The post-war history of the liberal parties and the sociopolitical behaviour of the middle classes seems to point to the sober conclusion that the liberal parties did take part in the deliberalization of the middle-class centre, but it was not caused by them. In fact the reverse was true: the liberal parties declined because the liberal middle classes turned away from the liberal models; their power of conviction decreased as the crisis of state and society grew. The 'suicide of liberalism' (Bracher) was the suicide of the liberal middle classes, which necessarily brought with it the death of the liberal parties.[101] When the National Socialists eliminated the DDP and the DVP in 1933, they were destroying a liberalism which its former clientele had already abandoned. There was therefore no question of an organized liberal resistance to National Socialist rule; liberalism was too discredited to still be able to offer hopes of the future which would have made the risk to life and limb worthwhile. Theodor Heuss's description in July 1933 of the 'end of the parties' was particularly applicable to the liberals: 'Their tactical ability to change was undone, strategic planning had become impossible. So they decided to capitulate in lacklustre resignation, intimidated and morally weakened, and despairing of a meaningful opportunity to undertake further political activity. That is the fact of the matter. One should see it as it is.'[102]

The behaviour of liberals during the National Socialist dictatorship has hardly been researched at all. Even the most recent introductions to resistance research do not mention liberals.[103] As far as can be judged from the mostly unprofitable memoirs and biographies after 1933, the well-known Weimar liberals retired from politics when the *Gleichschaltung* of the press denied them public opportunities for action. We do not yet know whether this stance can be appropriately described as 'inner emigration', or whether many of them resisted the 'intellectual assimilation' to National Socialism, or even whether it is true to say that 'after its political failure, German liberalism represented an intellectual force which made it difficult for the National Socialists to push through their claim to totality and to some extent made it impossible', as Werner Jochmann would have it. Exact studies, above all biographical studies, are necessary to ensure that we do not simply assume that liberalism resisted the abasement of the individual intellectually, just because the protection of the individual had always been part of the core of liberal doctrine.[104]

Only very few liberals seem finally to have decided to undertake active resistance. Those who did had probably had a certain distance from the party core already before 1933, and had demanded more energetic social liberal policies. This was true of the members of a resistance group based in Hamburg, to which up to sixty Left Liberals and Social Democrats belonged throughout the Reich. They rejected violent resistance, hoping instead for a military coup. They made preparations for the 'day after' the coup, for which they had prepared a blueprint for a new order: it included safeguarding the principle of the state founded on the rule of law; socio-political reforms, to which economic policy would be subordinated; the peaceful co-operation of the European nations, especially France and Germany; and, last but not least, the gradual implementation of political self-government in order to 'gradually, by degrees, accustom the nation to free and responsible co-operation in the government, and thus to develop *the* state of political maturity step by step, which was erroneously assumed to be present in the leap from the Kaiserreich to the Weimar constitution'.[105] This scepticism towards the Germans' immediate capacity for democracy was shared by most 'middle-class' resistance groups, and was very often applied to the parliamentary party state too, which was blamed for the failure in development during the Weimar Republic. Few liberals seem to have pleaded so decisively for a return to the parliamentary constitution as the former DDP politician Ludwig Bergsträsser did in a memorandum of 1942.[106]

Many former liberal party members were forced into exile by the National Socialist dictatorship.[107] Of the sixty-six emigrants so far recorded from the ranks of the DDP, including four women, thirty-nine (59 per cent) were of the Jewish faith. Others came from Jewish families and were therefore subjected to the National Socialist terror, which finally culminated in genocide. Amongst the fourteen DVP members who emigrated (including one woman), two were Jewish and at least a further four had Jewish ancestors. These figures reflect the great significance of the Jewish middle classes for the liberal parties of the Weimar Republic. It had led their anti-Semitic opponents to denigrate the DDP in particular as a 'party of Jews'.

Very few of those who returned to Germany from enforced exile in 1945 returned to politics (DDP: 6; DVP: 3). Only three of them joined one of the liberal successor organizations in the Western (one) or the Soviet (two) occupied zones – a sign that even amongst former members of liberal parties, liberalism was no longer automatically regarded as a force with which a party could be formed. Liberalism as a political model, with the dignity of the individual at its centre, did regain its power of conviction during the sorry experiences of the National Socialist regime of injustice. But support for basic liberal values did not necessarily mean joining a party which called itself liberal after 1945.

6 The Rebirth of Liberalism?
A Brief Summary of Liberalism and Politics in West Germany after 1945

The *Freie Demokratische Partei* (Free Democratic Party, FDP), regards itself as the only liberal party in the Federal Republic of Germany. It believes that it, and it alone, continues the historical traditions of German liberalism. This claim to the liberal heritage is justified only if we are examining personal and ideological lines of continuity between the two liberal parties of the Weimar Republic and the new parties which were founded under various titles after 1945, and which merged in the three western zones to form the FDP on 11–12 December 1948. The FDP's claim to sole representation cannot be justified, on the other hand, if we are analysing the extent to which social views and state institutions in the Federal Republic have been influenced by liberal models, or the parties which have represented them.

The Federal Republic is the first state in German history in which the majority of the population has learned to accept liberalism as an ensemble of political, social and cultural values, and whose institutions are committed to liberal standards. A considerable part in these achievements has been played by the parties – but not only by the parties, and certainly not one party alone, or even one in particular. With the realization of basic liberal values in the Federal Republic, the research field of 'liberalism' has expanded enormously. Even for earlier periods it was certainly never confined to the parties and their policies alone. Liberalism as a blend of social models and as a political movement is older than the parties, and ever since the first parties were formed, liberalism has always transcended party liberalism. However, those who wanted to implement liberal ideas in the state and society in the Weimar Republic had always to rely on the liberal parties. It was only with the Federal Republic that it became true to say that 'liberalism is not really the stuff of a political party. It makes as much sense to talk of a "liberal society" and of a "liberal state" as it does to talk of a "liberal party"'.[1] Ralf Dahrendorf's words were born of his disappointment in the policies of his FDP, which could not be led from its 'depths' to the 'Olympus of Liberalism' by its intellectual mentors.[2] Nevertheless, they are views which suggest why a history of German liberalism cannot lead into a description of the FDP. The FDP is part of that history, certainly, but it is the liberal history of achievements in the Federal Republic and its limitations, and not the history of the FDP, which establishes the parameters of a history of German liberalism after 1945. This seductively difficult task can only be outlined in broad terms here.

The fact that a stable parliamentary democracy, anchored in basic liberal values, would emerge from the ruins of National Socialist Germany could certainly not have been foreseen in the early days of the Federal Republic.[3] A considerable number of the factors which had brought about the collapse of the Weimar Republic weighed even more heavily on German society after the Second World War. Then there were the additional burdens of the division of the state, the loss of large territories, huge numbers of refugees and people expelled from their homes, post-war poverty and the statute of occupation. But in retrospect, it is also possible to identify burdens which had now been lifted. The most important of these include the fact that a renewed flight from the problems of the present into a transfigured national past, or into radical visions of the future was prevented. The National Socialist dictatorship lay like a barrier before German history, which clearly could not now be used as part of an armoury against 'Western civilization'. The totality of the defeat which, in contrast to the situation after the First World War, turned Germany into an occupied country, limited its opportunities to shape its future, which, in turn, relieved it of a further burden. In West Germany the experiences of the

Sovietization of the Eastern Zone, and of Eastern Europe in particular, and West Germany's rapid Western integration, gave rise to a basic anti-Communist consensus, which united society across political divisions, and which excluded the KPD. The political stabilization of the Federal Republic was safeguarded by dynamic economic growth after 1952. Yet the 'economic miracle' did not automatically lead into the 'political miracle' of demo-cratization (H.-P. Schwarz). Institutional development and the parties also played a significant role in it.

The parties which emerged in the states after 1945 took up the lines of tradition which had been broken in 1933. But what was more important was the desire for programmatic and social reform. In comparison to the Weimar Republic, three factors characterize developments after 1945. Firstly, the licensing policies of the allies made it impossible for extreme right-wing parties to be founded, and even later their popularity was only shortlived. Secondly, a stable three-party system was formed from the mid-1950s onwards. This did not change again until the end of the 1970s and the beginning of the 1980s, when the FDP left several state parliaments, and when a fourth party, the Green Party, was established at all election levels, from the municipal to the federal. Thirdly, the CDU represented a new kind of party, which transcended confessional camps. It encom-passed 'conservative Catholic and reforming Catholic positions, as well as liberal–conservative or moderate German national views in the Protestant sphere'. In the elections it won votes from all social strata.[4] In several different ways, this new party seriously restricted the chances of development of the liberal parties which were reformed after 1945. It penetrated the middle-class Protestant milieu of traditional liberalism and its programmes incorporated many liberal positions.

Whilst in 1919 liberals had played a major role in determining basic decisions on the political order, with the exception of Württemberg–Baden, they were unable to do the same in the founding phase of the Federal Republic. They therefore rejected the draft constitutions in five states. Only the KPD showed its dissatisfaction more frequently (on eleven occasions). Just when liberal guiding principles, such as that of the state founded on the rule of law and the Basic Rights, had been anchored more securely than ever before on a constitutional basis, work on the creation of the constitution, which had always been the domain of the liberals in the past, was now transferred to the other parties. For the number and success of their motions make it clear that it was the CDU and the SPD which determined the constitutional debates in the states and in the Parliamentary Council.[5] The fact that a prominent liberal, Theodor Heuss, became the first Federal President, conceals the subordinate or, in the Parliamentary Council in particular, mediating role with which the FDP had to be content.

The FDP was best able to acquire a profile of its own in the constitutional political crossroads of the early years on matters concerning the future economic order. It was not able fully to implement its guiding principle of a 'property-ownership which would create a culture' (Heuss), since the possibility of the 'nationalization' of 'land, natural resources and the means of production' was allowed by the constitution (paragraph 15). But the FDP played a major role in blocking constitutional regulations which were aimed against the misuse of property. This stance was in keeping with its social profile and self-image. 'The FDP of the first hours was middle-class and close to the economy.'[6] That was certainly true of the 220 people (10 per cent) of a total of 2138 members of the constituent assemblies, who represented the FDP in the western zones between 1946 and 1952. Few statistical data exist for the state associations. The independent professions, the traditional recruitment pool of liberal parliamentarians, were equally well represented amongst FDP deputies as they were in the CDU parliamentary parties (13–15 per cent, and 13 per cent legal professions).

The FDP tried to stress its credentials as a strictly national party with 'an anti-socialist platform' (T. Rütten) to counter the CDU's image as a new coalition party which transcended milieux. Yet this orientation could only be pushed through after 1947, when in the formerly Left Liberal strongholds of the south west or the Hansa towns, the first liberal state parties to be re-established lost their organizational lead over the liberal organizations in North Rhine Westphalia, Hesse and Lower Saxony which had stronger National Liberal traditions. They believed that 'the only option for liberals which has any promise of a future' was to win over those 'circles of the population which were not bound to a particular milieu, and not represented by political Catholicism or the parties of the workers' movement' by adopting a 'strong anti-socialist message and not least a national slogan' (D. Hein). The

foundation of the FDP in December 1948 prevented a revival of
the liberal two-party tradition, but until the 1960s, the FDP remained a 'cartel of state parties' (W. Stephan), whose merger in
1948 began with the 'open dissent' on the future path to be
adopted. It was clear that the right wing of the party had become
the majority and that the development of a 'coalition movement
of anti-socialist forces' (Hein) was predetermined. The choice
of the name 'Free Democratic Party' could not prevent this.
It expressed the doubts of the founders of the party as to

> whether the word 'liberalism' means anything to this genera-
> tion, or rather, whether the word 'liberalism', which incorpo-
> rates part of the historical life of the nineteenth century, can be
> made useful again, and whether perhaps it burdens our time
> with memories of an era when some 'liberals' acted in a battle
> against religiousness, or of an era when no path led from
> 'Manchester liberalism' to an independent social policy.[7]

In spite of liberal self-doubts of this kind, the readiness of the
large parties to break free of the well-worn tracks in the German
party landscape seems to have had least effect in the FDP.
Indeed, in comparison to pre-1933 liberalism, its programmatic
spectrum in the pre-history and the early years of the Federal
Republic was even more reduced to the poles of the 'nation' and
'economic freedom'. As a 'middle-class' party, the CDU was more
successful than the FDP in its attempts to link these liberal
traditional values with ideas on socio-political reform. In terms of
their careers, the FDP's parliamentary representatives in the
constituent assemblies were more firmly rooted in the past than
their CDU, and above all SPD, counterparts. FDP parliamentarians had the highest average age (57.7 years) and disproportionately high numbers of them had undergone their political
socialization during the Kaiserreich (66.7 per cent) and the First
World War (33.3 per cent).[8] In terms of its deputies, therefore,
the FDP was a party of old people. This adherence to tradition
could certainly initially prove to be a strength. That was true of
the rapid and successful re-establishment of above all the south
west German associations as 'parties of the liberal milieu' (Hein).
In the long term, however, these links with the liberal tradition – which were now also perceived to be even closer than
before – proved to be a weakness in the FDP's competition for

the middle-class vote with the more changeable and 'younger' CDU, and even with the SPD. This was partly to blame for the loss of prestige which led, even in its traditional strongholds, to the FDP's decline to the 5 per cent mark of the minimum level of existence for a political party, and at times (Hamburg 1978–87, Bremen after 1983), even below that.

The FDP's decisively liberal economic course was not repaid in votes, for it failed to reap the benefits of the successful 'risk of liberal economic reforms' (Schwarz). The FDP's image was that of a 'party of the free market economy'.[9] The great economic and socio-political guiding principle of the Federal Republic, however, was the 'social market economy'. This idea embodied a hope which surpassed all other competing guiding principles in its political social unifying force: the advantages of a liberal economic order, built on secure individual property-ownership and on responsibility for oneself, were to be combined with the 'the social state's aim for social justice and social security' (H. Lampert). The early liberal vision of the 'classless society of citizens' was given a new up-to-date form in the promises of the 'social market economy', which was created by liberals from the circle of ordo-liberalism, as the neo-liberals who were close to the *Ordo* year-book were called. Yet it was the CDU which translated this new basic principle into political action and programmatic language. It adopted this 'felicitous linguistic construction' (W. Röpke) in its programme of 1949 ('Düsseldorfer Leitsätze', 'Düsseldorf Guiding Principles'). Voters regarded Ludwig Erhard as its political creator. Erhard had been appointed as Director of the Frankfurt economic administration in the Bizone in 1948 at the suggestion of the FDP, but then joined the CDU.

It was the CDU and not the FDP which took up the neo-liberal desire for reform. The 'ideal of so-called economic liberalism, namely the free market economy' should 'certainly not form [part] of the primary objective of intellectual and political liberalism', Wilhelm Röpke, one of the most important neo-liberal thinkers, tried to impress upon liberals in 1947. He regarded a 'peace settlement' between 'non-socialist liberals' and 'liberal socialists' as the more possible,

the more prepared a liberal is to emphasize the grave errors of an economic liberalism, which represented the idea of the market economy in a form which has proved to be so

312LIBERALISM IN GERMANY

intolerable today. . . . A peace agreement of this kind should be
made more easy on both sides by the understanding that liberals
and liberal socialists share so many intellectual ancestors, and
that they have both helped to construct a world which is
collapsing today, and which is carrying away things that both of
them hold dear as it does. But this has created a situation in
which not only the liberals and 'liberal' socialists, but all the
others who declare their support for the heritage of secular
liberalism, although not necessarily for the name itself, are
forced together to form a united front.

The newly coined 'social market economy', which was taken up
by the CDU, is one of these efforts to create a peace settlement
between liberals and social reformers. West German party
liberalism, on the other hand, adopted a stance which the neo-
liberal Alexander Rüstow characterized as 'paleoliberalism'.[10]

In terms of national politics, too, the early FDP looked for
support in the past and even in that which would only disappear
at a painfully slow rate.[11] For this reason, it was subject to the
greatest domestic political burdens in its German policy. It was
here of all areas that, as early as the mid-fifties, the first independent approaches were made which would ultimately build a
bridge to the SPD, which made possible the *neue Ostpolitik* of the
social liberal coalition (1969), and which are continued today,
even after the break-up of the 1982 coalition. The national political perspectives of the FDP encompassed many contradictory
views before this reorientation. It regarded itself as the 'party of
reunification' (Rütten), which as late as 1947 had tried to found a
pan-German party, and as early as 1956 had resumed pan-
German talks with the *Liberal-Demokratische Partei* (Liberal Democratic Party) of the GDR. Yet at the same time, the FDP accepted
the essence of Adenauer's policy of western integration, although
it had considerable reservations on individual issues (the *Bindungs-
klauseln* in the German Treaty of 1952 and the Saar Statute of
1954), and it resolutely advocated the Federal Republic's
integration into Europe, which it regarded as the prerequisite
for a viable free market economy and for German reunification.

In spite of all its openness in the search for ways to achieve
reunification, the Federal Republic's integration into the west took
precedence in the FDP. However, the nationalist vocabulary
employed by a large number of FDP politicians helped open the

party up to the right. The state associations of North Rhine Westphalia, Hesse and Lower Saxony in particular suffered under these circumstances, and were in danger of being 'swamped by not only former Nazis' (Rütten). Many a new FDP member 'still vibrated with pure, as yet undampened, enthusiasm for National Socialism', as one party secretary reported.[12] This development peaked in 1952 at the party conference at Bad Ems, where Marie Elisabeth Lüders warned against the revival of the 'Harzburg front', with which the national right had made the National Socialists socially acceptable in 1931. The 'German Programme' of the FDP right was allowing the 'border to right-wing radicalism to [become] fluid'. Those who were making their presence felt were 'no longer liberals, but German nationalists who had been shaken by two catastrophes, and who were not afraid of borrowing vocabulary from NS propaganda' (R. Zundel). However, this radicalization triggered a counter-movement in the FDP, which published its 'Liberal Manifesto' in November 1952. In the attempt to fend off an opening to the right, which was threatening to get out of control for the first time in the short history of the FDP, the counter-forces used the concept of liberalism to provide a theoretical basis for its central position between the CDU and the SPD.[13]

In 1953 the extreme swing to the right was halted. But even afterwards, it continued to cause great problems for the FDP, as it tried to open itself up to new things. This is true, for example, of its position on German military traditions. The reform concept of the 'state citizen in uniform' was overwhelmingly rejected in the FDP. Erich Mende spoke of the 'type of permanently distrustful soldier'. On several occasions he also demanded that the Iron Cross be reinstated as a war decoration. It 'should not be regarded as a provocation today (1953), any more than it was 140 years ago, be it with or without the small, almost invisible swastika'.[14]

In retrospect, the early FDP accomplished a considerable degree of integration, which was good for the young democracy, which was still not firmly established. For by absorbing nationalist forces, it helped to prevent the rise of extreme right-wing parties. Yet the FDP could only survive the pressure of this integration because the liberal party unity created in 1948 provided a sufficiently strong liberal–democratic counterweight within the party. Only when the nationalist legacy had been 'digested' from the German past, could the internal liberalization of the FDP begin. This process was accelerated in 1956, when the FDP left the federal government in which it had participated as one of Adenauer's coalition partners since the foundation of the Federal Republic. During its period in opposition, for which it had not been prepared, the FDP was forced to clarify its 'diffuse understanding of liberalism and its roles', which had not been enough to turn it into 'an independent partner with a clear profile'.[15] In the great decisions of the period of reconstruction, it had never developed beyond the role of a corrective to the CDU and the SPD. It was these two major parties which, together with the allies, had decided on the degree of liberalism to be incorporated into the institutional reorganization of the state and society. This was not only due to the smaller number of seats held by the FDP, which restricted its participation in parliamentary decisions. Above all, it lacked the power of innovation. The restricted liberal legacy from which the FDP sought to shape its future, hampered any chance of a policy of liberal innovation and represented a barrier which would have to be crossed before the Liberal Party could find a point of contact with the growing liberalism of the Federal Republic.

The extent of the liberalization of society in the Adenauer era remains a controversial subject, despite the numerous studies on the development of 'political culture' in the Federal Republic.[16] In 1953 the American journalist Theodore H. White wrote, 'Germany has now been divided into tiny compartments in every German heart: part of every German heart belongs to the Germany of today; part belongs to the old Germany; and a tiny little part still belongs to Hitler. We will have to wait and see who wins.' And as long as Konrad Adenauer led the government authoritatively – in 1957 Karl Loewenstein voiced his concerns about the 'demo-authoritarian' Bonn 'regime', which would 'choke... the democratic process' – doubts remained as to whether the democratic stability was 'merely temporary mimicry or a permanent change in behaviour'. This 'insecurity was part of the Janus face of the Adenauer era'.[17]

In 1965, only two years after Adenauer's forced resignation, the critical observer Ralf Dahrendorf wrote in his famous assessment of German history,

For the outside observer, especially one who has visited Germany several times over the last few decades, no change is more striking than the change in people's values. Discipline, love of order, obsequiousness, cleanliness, diligence, punctiliousness and all the other virtues which many Germans still ascribe to themselves in an echo of the memory of faded glory, have already given way to a much looser set of values and attitudes, in which economic success, a large income, holidays and a new car play a far greater role than the former virtues. Young people in particular possess only little of the acclaimed and vilified respect for authority and few of the disciplined virtues which their parents are said to have had. An extremely individualized world of values has emerged, which puts the happiness experienced by the individual above that of everyone else, and which is gradually and increasingly losing sight of the so-called 'whole'. Perhaps some people still feel a certain emptiness in that spot where, in days gone by, and even today in the other Germany, the collective idea brought and still brings people under its spell, but this emptiness is rapidly being filled with the direct enjoyment of life.

Dahrendorf then used this 'credit side of the account' to offer a prognosis for West German society; 'Those who have become accustomed to the individual's pleasures in life are unlikely candidates for totalitarian organization'. For this reason, the 'chances of liberal democracy ... have never [been] as great in German society as they are in the Federal Republic'.[18]

Surveys substantiate this view. Whilst in the days of the foundation of the Federal Republic and the period of reconstruction, they confirmed the enduring strength of authoritarian views, by the end of the Adenauer era 'all available data would suggest that the citizens of the Federal Republic regard democracy as the most useful form of communal life'.[19] The climate of reform which began to change society from the 1960s onwards can only be understood in the light of this new, positive attitude towards democratic values. It proved to be too much for many members of the Federal Republic's founder generation. It was then, as they said and still say today, that the safe road to an ordered democracy seemed to lose its way. There are many reasons for the social mood of departure symbolized by the student movement. The Vietnam War began to shatter the American model for many people, above all for the young. Radical democratic and anti-capitalist theories and anti-colonialism encountered enthusiastic support, and the legitimacy of the political and social conditions in the Federal Republic were called into question. Finally, in the 1970s, terrorism and the reactions to it threatened the liberalism which had been achieved. Yet these challenges served to reveal liberalism's strength. The 'participatory revolution' (M. Kaase) which began in the mid-1970s, initially placed the political system under great pressure, but in the long term it increased its 'democratic vitality' (D. Thränhardt).[20] Even the economic crises which followed the 'oil crisis' of 1973–4 and high unemployment have not caused the citizens of the Federal Republic to deviate from the guiding principles of the 'democratic state' and 'social liberalism'. Comparative surveys show that these values remain as steadfast in the face of economic problems in the Federal Republic as they are in neighbouring European Community states.[21] In a favourable economy, with which the first German democracy was not blessed, the Federal Republic has learned democracy. Yet since the 1960s, the second republic has no longer been a democracy of a booming economy. It is more likely that the Federal Republic's internal stability is anchored in the liberalness of its society. How has political liberalism reacted to this liberal success story? How has it accompanied and influenced these developments?

After neo-liberalism asserted itself in the CDU against the concept of a planned economy, the autonomy of the market was pushed through, despite many reservations, as the cornerstone of the economic constitution of the Federal Republic. In the 1950s, the 'social founding compromise of the Federal Republic' (L. Niethammer) was made good with a number of laws which began to provide the content for the model of the 'social market economy'.[22] The FDP had not wanted the compromise in the form which was achieved. It was unable to prevent it, but it did succeed in applying correctives, sometimes important ones, above all in the Industrial Constitution Law of 1952. The socio-political reforms were pushed through by social policy-makers from the CDU and the SPD. There was no *Bürgerblock* here, although the CDU/CSU government party always formed coalitions with middle-class parties until 1966 (FDP: 1949–56 and 1961–6; *Deutsche Partei* or German Party, 1949–61; *Bund der Heimatvertriebenen und Entrechteten*, or 'Association of Those who have been Expelled from Their Homeland and Deprived of

Their Rights' 1953–6). In the pensions reform of 1957, too, the government and the opposition did not oppose each other as blocs. This ground-breaking reform was extensively determined by the CDU, yet its outcome represented 'a kind of central position', which the FDP had unanimously rejected.[23]

The SPD began to replace its ideas on the planned economy with the Keynesian concept of global management as early as the 1950s, and underpinned its development into a popular party with the Godesberg Programme of 1959. The FDP, in contrast, remained until '1965 – and to some extent even later – entirely wedded to the categories of *Bürgerblock* thinking'.[24] This had been pushed through in the party after 1950, when the 'period of the *Bürgerblock* coalitions' (Kaack) began in the states. In Baden–Württemberg a coalition was formed with the SPD under Minister President Reinhold Maier, but FDP right-wingers left this aberration with the reproach that the liberals of Baden–Württemberg were being led by 'demi-Marxists'.[25] Only after the FDP of North Rhine Westphalia had made possible a Social Democratic–liberal state government in 1956, which triggered the break-up of the government coalition with the CDU in Bonn, did a lengthy process of reorientation begin, amidst vehement internal conflicts, as the FDP sought to find points of contact with the changed political and social conditions.

The Berlin Programme of 1957 was the FDP's first attempt to develop a profile as the 'third force' which had adopted a 'middle course' between the CDU and the SPD. Yet quite what was specifically liberal about FDP liberalism continued to remain unclear. The 'protection of the individual's freedom to undertake responsible action' demanded in the programme, was indistinguishable from the policies of the CDU or the SPD. Assisted by the end of the Adenauer era, the FDP increased its demands to the CDU, once again its coalition partner (1961–6), yet fell back on its role as 'a middle-class party with a corrective function to the CDU/CSU'.[26] There were not yet any prospects of an openness to the other two large parties, when in 1966 the 'Grand Coalition' between the CDU/CSU and the SPD was formed. Only now could the FDP, whose very existence was threatened by plans for a change in suffrage regulations, find its way to programmatic reform and the replacement of personnel. The Freiburg Theses of 1971 represent the programmatic peak of this development.[27]

It was a 'modernization in stages' (Vorländer), in which the FDP withdrew from the 'alliance of immobility' (Dahrendorf), which it had been part of itself. Urged on by a reform group which had a platform in the journal *liberal*, and which encountered wide support in the Federal Republic's media, the FDP entered the great debates of the period: on the emergency laws, penal and educational reform, Germany and *Ostpolitik*. Though its contact with the student movement and the extra-parliamentary opposition was shortlived, accompanied by vehement internal disputes and by a change in its membership, the FDP acquired an 'image of modernity' (R. Zülch) which was carefully reinforced. 'Symbols of advancement and progress' should, the Federal Whip advised in 1967, be adopted 'in all spheres of socio-political activity.'[28]

The Freiburg Theses were the strongest symbol of the new FDP. It was with this programme, which tested the very limits of compromise within the FDP, that the party finally made good the social founding compromise of the Federal Republic of the 1950s, and adapted itself to the social change in values of the 1960s. The FDP was probably only innovative in terms of the *'neue Ostpolitik'*, which it had prepared, and for which it shared responsibility in the Brandt–Scheel government. Otherwise, what Dahrendorf wrote on the secular history of citizens' rights is true: the 'social underpinning of formal rights – and thereby the actual fulfillment of citizens' rights – is above all the work of socialist parties. Many liberals took part in this; many others accepted the result only when it was in place. The Freiburg Programme of the FDP is an example of this.'[29] The openness symbolized by the Freiburg Programme is part of the climate of reform which made the social–liberal coalition possible, and which attempted to translate it into politics. The greatest part was played here by the SPD. It was the SPD, too, which made more efforts than any other party to conduct talks with the extra-parliamentary forces of reform, and to integrate their ideas and their members into its party.

The great significance of the SPD in reform discussions and reform policy was instrumental in the fact that, even during the social–liberal coalition (1969–82), the FDP failed to develop its own liberal profile. 'Liberal', as surveys from 1972 and 1976 show, was firmly associated with the FDP and almost always positively evaluated. Yet interviewees could never actually come up with anything 'concrete' to say about the party. The FDP was regarded as the party which decides which of the large parties will govern.[30] It was unable to shake off this role of majority maker and corrective in its coalition with the SPD or in its coalitions with the CDU/CSU. When the government alliance with the CDU/CSU was renewed in 1982, this role once again formed the core of its programme. It was, its election statement of 1983 said,

> an independent liberal force of the centre, which represents a counterweight to a conservatism which hinders progress, and to a socialism which neglects freedom, self-determination and responsibility for oneself. The F.D.P. is equidistant from both. For this reason, the F.D.P. bears a particular responsibility for the reform of German politics. On the one hand, liberalism is necessarily a philosophy of change, of reform; on the other hand, only the F.D.P. can ensure the continuity which is necessary in change. The liberals are the element of balance and assessment in our party system. They prevent it from swinging to extremes and ensure the stability of democratic development, while, if necessary, facilitating democratic change.

The 'Liberal Manifesto' of 1985 also stressed the increasing significance of the 'liberals' position of watchmen', given the growing spheres of state responsibility.[31]

Fortunately, the historian does not have to predict whether and how the FDP will in the future be able to combine its chosen office of watchman with the aim of not only understanding social change, but actively helping to shape it. The now firmly established four-party system will make the liberal middle path striven for even more difficult than it has been already.[32] A retrospective look at the liberal tradition will be of little use here. For the core of liberal ideals, the citizen of the state, which has been realized to a greater degree in the Federal Republic than ever before in a German state, is supported by all the parties. And outside this core area, a glance at the political liberalism of the past offers an image of lavish variety, contradictory change and – certainly by the early twentieth century – the extinguishing of its power of innovation. The history of liberalism cannot tell us what 'a thoroughly liberal force' should look like today, which Ralf Dahrendorf can only envisage in the form of a 'third party'.[33] But it does highlight the way in which a state is threatened when the meaning and the influence of liberal parties keeps decreasing, because society is losing its liberality. In the Federal Republic over the last three decades, it has been possible to see for the first time in German history that the two need not necessarily be linked.

Notes

Preface

1. R. Dahrendorf, *Die Chancen der Krise* (Stuttgart, 1983), p. 37.

Chapter 1. Early Liberalism and 'Middle-Class Society'

1. Heffter, *Selbstverwaltung*, p. 161.
2. L. Gall, 'Liberalismus und "bürgerliche Gesellschaft"', in L. Gall (ed.), *Liberalismus*, p. 168.
3. *Die Entstehung der politischen Strömungen in Deutschland 1770–1815* (Kronberg, 1978), p. 396.
4. See J. Garber's Afterword in the new edition of 1978 (cf. note 3); for a collection of source material, see Garber (ed.), *Revolutionäre Vernunft* (Kronberg, 1974); for a survey of the literature, see E. Fehrenbach, *Vom Ancien Régime zum Wiener Kongreß* (Munich, 1981), pp. 153ff.
5. R. Vierhaus, 'Liberalismus', in *Geschichtliche Grundbegriffe*, vol. 3 (Stuttgart, 1982), pp. 741–85.
6. Cf. R. Vierhaus, 'Politisches Bewußtsein in Deutschland vor 1798', in H. Berding and H.-P. Ullmann (eds), *Deutschland zwischen Revolution und Restauration* (Königstein, 1981), pp. 161–83.
7. Cited by Valjavec, p. 398f. (Schlözer); Garber (ed.), p. 131f. (Villaume), pp. 137–42 (Hennings).
8. Gall, p. 162; B. Vogel, *Allgemeine Gewerbefreiheit* (Göttingen, 1983), p. 36; K.-G. Faber, 'Strukturprobleme des deutschen

Liberalismus im 19. Jahrhundert', *Der Staat*, 14 (1975), pp. 201–27, 211f.; K. v. Raumer and M. Botzenhart, *Deutsche Geschichte im 19. Jh. Deutschland um 1800* (Wiesbaden, 1980), p. 11.

9. Gerth, *Intelligenz*, p. 72; B. Vogel, 'Beamtenkonservatismus', in D. Stegmann *et al.* (eds), *Deutscher Konservatismus im 19. und 20. Jh., 3. Festschrift F. Fischer* (Bonn, 1983), p. 6; see also R. Vierhaus, 'Liberalismus, Beamtenstand und konstitutionelles System', in Schieder (ed.), *Liberalismus*, pp. 39–54.

10. Cited by Vogel, *Gewerbefreiheit*, pp. 125 (Altenstein), 109 (Kunth).

11. Ibid., p. 226.

12. R. Koselleck, 'Staat und Gesellschaft in Preußen 1815–1849', in W. Conze (ed.), *Staat und Gesellschaft im deutschen Vormärz 1815–1848* (Stuttgart, 1983³), p. 108. The seminal work on the subject is Koselleck, *Preußen*.

13. *Badische Geschichte* (Stuttgart, 1979), p. 26 (L. Gall). For a discussion of 'privy councillor liberalism', see also F. Schnabel, *Deutsche Geschichte im 19. Jh.*, vol. 2 (Freiburg, 1933, Munich, 1987), p. 199f.

14. *Badische Geschichte*, p. 30 (Gall). For details of the criticism of the civil service, see W. Bleek, *Von der Kameralausbildung zum Juristenprivileg* (Berlin, 1972); Lee (on Baden).

15. Heffter, p. 168.

16. Cf. Winter, *Frühliberalismus*.

17. T. Nipperdey, *Deutsche Geschichte 1800–1866* (Munich, 1983), p. 287.

18. Cf. P. Wende, *Radikalismus im Vormärz* (Frankfurt, 1975).

19. C .T. Welcker, 'Staatsverfassung', in *Staats-Lexikon*, vol. 15 (Altona, 1843), p. 82, also in L. Gall and R. Koch (eds), *Der europäische Liberalismus im 19. Jh.*, vol. 2 (Frankfurt, 1981), p. 68; K. H. L. Pölitz, *Die Staatswissenschaften im Lichte unserer Zeit* (Leipzig, 1827), cited by H. Brandt (ed.), *Restauration und Frühliberalismus 1814–1840* (Darmstadt, 1979), p. 176f. K. von Rotteck, 'Constitution', in *Staats-Lexikon*, vol. 3 (1836), p. 767.

20. Cited in *Badische Geschichte*, p. 24 (Gall).

21. Heffter, p. 174.

22. H. Brandt, 'Urrechte und Bürgerrechte im politischen System vor 1848', in G. Birtsch (ed.), *Grund- und Freiheitsrechte im Wandel von Gesellschaft und Geschichte* (Göttingen, 1981), p. 474.

23. Cited by R. Schöttle, *Politische Freiheit für die deutsche Nation. C. T. Welckers politische Theorie* (Baden-Baden 1985), pp. 84–8.
24. The seminal work on the subject is T. Nipperdey, *Gesellschaft, Kultur, Theorie* (Göttingen, 1976), pp. 174–205.
25. Rotteck (1836); Hansemann (1830), cited in Brandt (ed.), pp. 392–94, 257.
26. Cf. H. Croon, 'Das Vordringen der politischen Parteien im Bereich der kommunalen Selbstverwaltung', in Croon *et al.* (eds), *Kommunale Selbstverwaltung im Zeitalter der Industrialisierung* (Stuttgart, 1971), p. 21f.; K. Obermann, 'Zur Genesis der bürgerlichen Klasse in Deutschland von der Julirevolution 1830 bis zu Beginn der 40er Jahre des 19. Jh.', *Jahrbuch für Geschichte* 16 (1977), pp. 53–5.
27. Dahlmann, *Die Politik auf den Grund und das Maß der gegebenen Zustände zurückgeführt (1835)* (Berlin, 1924), p. 200; extract in Brandt (ed.), p. 377ff.
28. R. Rürup, *Emanzipation und Antisemitismus* (Göttingen, 1975), p. 4.
29. See Boldt for details.
30. Kosellek, *Reform*, pp. 266, 234.
31. Ibid., pp. 254ff., 259.
32. Under 'Liberal, Liberalismus', in *Staats-Lexikon*, vol. 9 (1840).
33. The most detailed survey is to be found in P.M. Ehrle, *Volksvertretung im Vormärz*, 2 vols (Frankfurt, 1979). Brief information is given by V. Press, 'Landstände des 18. und Parlamente des 19. Jhs.', in Berding and Ullmann (eds), pp. 133–57.
34. Dahlmann, *Politik*, pp. 127, 137; L. Gall, B. Constant (Wiesbaden, 1963), p. 234. For the various ideas on representation, see especially Brandt, *Repräsentation*.
35. Dahlmann, *Politik*, p. 155; the Rotteck quotation is also to be found in the extract in Brandt (ed.), *Frühliberalismus*, p. 158.
36. Zachariae, *Vierzig Bücher vom Staat*, vol. 3 (1839²), cited by Brandt (ed.), *Frühliberalismus*, p. 344; Pfizer, *Liberal*; see especially L. Gall, 'Das Problem der parlamentarischen Opposition im deutschen Frühliberalismus' (1968), in G. Ritter (ed.), *Parteien vor 1918*, pp. 192–207.
37. Cf. R. Muhs, 'Freiheit und Elend', in Birtsch (ed.), p. 492ff. For the Dahlmann quotation, see Birtsch, *Politik*, p. 137.
38. Gall, 'Liberalismus und "bürgerliche Gesellschaft"', in Gall (ed.), *Liberalismus*, pp. 163–86, 176. See especially Sedatis,

Liberalismus; R. Koch, ' "Industriesystem" oder "bürgerliche Gesellschaft" ', in *GWU 1978*, pp. 605–28; and the relevant chapters in Schieder (ed.), *Liberalismus*.

39. Sedatis, p. 42 (Schulz); Brandt (ed.), *Frühliberalismus*, p. 388 (Rotteck's article, 'Census'); C. von Rotteck, *Lehrbuch des Vernunftrechts und der Staatswissenschaften*, vol. 4 (1835; reprinted Aalen, 1964), p. 178.

40. R. Walther, 'Wirtschaftlicher Liberalismus', in *Geschichtliche Grundbegriffe*, vol. 3, pp. 787–815. For German Smith supporters' attitude to the state, see M. E. Vopelius, *Die altliberalen Ökonomen und die Reformzeit* (Hamburg, 1968).

41. E. Angermann, 'K. Mathy als Sozial- und Wirtschaftspolitiker (1842–48)', in *ZGO* (1955), pp. 499–622, 538f.

42. H. J. Teuteberg, 'Die Ansichten des bayerischen Altliberalen C. T. Kleinschrod (1789–1869) über Industriestaat und Soziale Frage im Vormärz', in H. Dollinger *et al.* (eds), *Weltpolitik, Europagedanke, Regionalismus, Festschrift H. Gollwitzer* (Münster, 1982), pp. 219–46, 222, 234.

43. See 'Eigentum' in *Staatslexikon*, 2nd suppl. vol. (1846), cited by Gall and Koch (eds), vol. 4, p. 51.

44. Preußen und Frankreich (1984(2)); extracts in Brandt (ed.), *Frühliberalimsus*, p. 261ff. Concerning what follows, including further literary references, see E. Fehrenbach, 'Rheinischer Liberalismus und gesellschaftliche Verfassung', in Schieder (ed.), *Liberalismus*, pp. 272–94, from which all the quotations which follow are also taken (pp. 283–5).

45. Rotteck, *Lehrbuch*, vol. 4, p. 185f.

46. Cf. chapters by K. Düwell and H.-W. Hahn in Schieder (ed.), *Liberalismus*, pp. 239–71, 294–311.

47. Cf. L. Gall, 'Liberalismus und Nationalstaat', in H. Berding *et al.* (eds), *Vom Staat des Ancien Régime zum modernen Parteienstaat* (Munich, 1978), p. 2. *Festschrift T. Schieder*, pp. 287–300, quotations: p. 292; P. Wentzcke and W. Klötzer (eds), *Deutscher Liberalismus im Vormärz* (Göttingen, 1959), p. 262f. (Gagern).

48. *Politik*, p. 140.

49. Ibid., p. 53.

50. Rotteck, *Lehrbuch*, vol. I, p. 299; Welcker, 'Geschlechtsverhältnisse', in *Staats-Lexikon*, vol. 6 (1838), p. 640f.

51. Cf. A. Lorenz, *Das deutsche Familienbild in der Malerei des 19. Jahrhunderts* (Darmstadt, 1985), p. 138ff.

52. Cf. Obenaus; survey in H. Kramer, *Fraktionsbindungen in den deutschen Volksvertretungen 1819–1848* (Berlin, 1968).
53. Wentzcke and Klötzer (eds), pp. 313, 335f. For an excellent case study, see E. Illner, *Bürgerliche Organisierung in Elberfeld 1775–1850* (Neustadt a.d. Aisch, 1982).
54. The statistics which follow are taken from C. Foerster, *Der Preß- und Vaterlandsverein von 1832/33* (Trier, 1982).
55. Wolfram Sieman, in his *The German Revolution of 1848–49* (London: Macmillan, 1998), defines 'rough music' punishment campaigns as 'an old-fashioned vent for pent-up aggression. Gathering in front of the houses of unpopular people, a crowd would begin shouting, whistling, making noises, smashing windows and hurling insults and obscenities' (p. 175).
56. See also I. Cervelli, 'Deutsche Liberale im Vormärz', in Schieder (ed.), pp. 312–40 (includes literature on the subject).
57. Concerning what follows, see D. Düding, *Organisierter gesellschaftlicher Nationalismus in Deutschland 1808–1847* (Munich, 1984).
58. R. von Thadden, 'Protestantismus und Liberalismus zur Zeit des Hambacher Festes 1832', in Schieder (ed.), p. 103. The quotation which follows is from R. Haym, *Aus meinem Leben* (Berlin, 1902), p. 167.
59. Croon, p. 21ff.
60. For an introduction to the subject, see J. Sperber, *Popular Catholicism in 19th Century Germany* (Princeton, 1984). Cf. Heffter, p. 180ff.; R. Koch, 'Staat oder Gemeinde? Zu einem politischen Zielkonflikt in der bürgerlichen Bewegung des 19. Jh.', in *HZ*, 236 (1983), pp. 73–96.

Chapter 2. Liberal Politics in the Revolution of 1848–9

1. *Denkwürdigkeiten zur Geschichte der Badischen Revolution* (Heidelberg, 1851), p. 110f. The best new general account of the revolution is provided by Siemann, *Revolution*. For the changing image of the revolution in international history since 1948, see the chapters in D. Langewiesche (ed.), *Die deutsche Revolution von 1848/49* (Darmstadt, 1983); for a discussion of the German revolution in the context of the European revolutionary process, see Langewiesche, *Europa zwischen*

Restauration und Revolution 1815–1849 (Munich, 1993³); an introduction to the available literature on the subject is given there and in Siemann.

2. E. R. Huber (ed.), *Dokumente zur deutschen Verfassungsgeschichte*, vol. I (Stuttgart, 1978³), p. 330.
3. Ibid., pp. 352–9.
4. Siemann, p. 84; Botzenhart, *Parlamentarismus*, p. 132.
5. Botzenhart, p. 117.
6. For the text of the Heidelberg Declaration of 5 March 1848, see Huber (ed.), vol. I, pp. 326–8.
7. *Verhandlungen des Deutschen Parlaments*, part I (Frankfurt, 1848), pp. 5–7; also printed in Huber (ed.), vol. I, pp. 332–4.
8. *Verhandlungen*, part I, pp. 65f., 75, 64f., 83f.
9. Huber (ed.), vol. I, p. 335.
10. Verhandlungen, part I, p. 72.
11. Ibid., part 2, p. 52.
12. On this and what follows, see also D. Langewiesche, *Republik, Konstitutionelle Monarchie und 'soziale Frage'*. The fundamental problems of the German revolution are discussed in Langewiesche (ed.), *Revolution*.
13. Neumüller, *Liberalismus*.
14. *Verhandlungen*, part 2, p. 221.
15. Letter of 26 March 1848 in J. Hansen (ed.), *Rheinische Briefe und Akten zur Geschichte der politischen Bewegung 1830–1850*, vol. II/i (Bonn, 1942), p. 649.
16. B. Immendörffer (ed.), *Zwei Wiener Mädchentagebücher aus dem Jahre 1848/49* (Vienna, 1927), pp. 70, 89. For the Vienna revolution, see W. Häusler, *Von der Massenarmut zur Arbeiterbewegung* (Vienna, 1979).
17. B. Mann (ed.), *Heilbronner Berichte aus der deutschen Nationalversammlung 1848/49* (Heilbronn, 1974), p. 57f.
18. Concerning what follows, see Botzenhart, who provides the best information on the as yet insufficiently researched *Landtage*. For Prussia, see Grünthal, *Parlamentarismus*.
19. Ibid., p. 313.
20. *Stenographischer Bericht über die Verhandlungen der deutschen Nationalversammlung zu Frankfurt a.M.*, ed. F. Wigard, vol. 1 (Frankfurt, 1848), p. 356. For the quotations from this debate which follow, see pp. 429 (Jordan), 460 (Venedy), 409 (Simon), 410 (Welcker), 521f. (Gagern).

21. H. von Beseler (ed.), 'Aus G. Beselers Frankfurter Briefen 1848/49', *Deutsche Revue*, 37 (1912/1), p. 236.
22. Ibid., p. 238.
23. For details, see Botzenhart, p. 163ff; the controversial scholarly interpretations are discussed in D. Langewiesche, 'Die Anfänge der deutschen Parteien. Partei, Fraktion und Verein in der Revolution von 1848/49', *Geschichte und Gesellschaft*, 4 (1978), p. 336f.
24. A. Rapp (ed.), *Briefwechsel zwischen D. Strauß und Fr. Th. Vischer*, vol. I (Stuttgart, 1952), p. 225f.
25. R. Hübner (ed.), *Aktenstücke und Aufzeichnungen zur Geschichte der Frankfurter Nationalversammlung aus dem Nachlaß von J. G. Droysen (1924)* (Osnabrück, 1967), p. 435.
26. R. Haym, *Die deutsche Nationalversammlung von den Septemberereignissen bis zur Kaiserwahl. Ein weiterer Parteibericht* (Berlin, 1849), p. 294f.; *Stenographischer Bericht*, vol. 7, p. 5303 (Gagern).
27. Ibid., vol. 9, p. 6405 (Welcker), p. 6411 (Gagern).
28. Cf. Siemann, p. 204. A comprehensive examination of the Campaign for the Imperial Constitution is long overdue in revolution research.
29. *Stenographischer Bericht*, vol. 9, pp. 6697, 6710 (L. Simon); vol. 8, p. 6320 (Raveaux).
30. Cf. Botzenhart, p. 315ff.; Siemann, p. 90ff.; Langewiesche, Partei, p. 339ff.; Sources: W. Boldt, *Die Anfänge des deutschen Parteiwesens* (Paderborn, 1971).
31. Langewiesche, *Liberalismus*, p. 121f.; see also Siemann, Table 12, p. 107.
32. R. Weber (ed.), *Revolutionsbriefe 1848/49* (Frankfurt, 1973), pp. 138, 135 (Virchow); 'Vaterländische Blätter für Baden', 17 January 1849 (Häusser).
33. Ibid., supplement of 28 March 1849; differentiated for Baden, see G. Richter, 'Revolution und Gegenrevolution in Baden 1849', *ZGO*, 119 (1971); Botzenhart, p. 709ff.
34. Haym, *Nationalversammlung*, p. 6; *Die Waage. Deutsche Reichstagsschau von J. Venedey* (Frankfurt, 1848), no. 3, pp. 4ff., 20.
35. H. Gebhardt, *Revolution und liberale Bewegung* (Bremen, 1974), p. 143ff.
36. A. Duckwitz, *Denkwürdigkeiten aus meinem öffentlichen Leben, 1841–1866* (Bremen, 1877), p. 309ff., Häusser, p. 265.

37. *Die Linke in Frankfurt und ihr Märzverein* (Stuttgart, 1848), p. 10; Haym, *Nationalversammlung*, p. 137.
38. Langewiesche, *Partei*, p. 354; cf. J. P. Eichmeier, 'Anfänge liberaler Parteibildung 1847–1854', Dissertation, Göttingen, 1968; Gebhardt.
39. Eichmeier, V.
40. Beseler, *Briefe*, p. 368; Haym, *Nationalversammlung*, p. 3. For national politics, see G. Wollstein, *Das 'Großdeutschland' der Paulskirche* (Düsseldorf, 1977) and the study which is thematically narrow, but which presents the basic issues accurately, by H.-G. Kraume, *Außenpolitik 1848* (Düsseldorf, 1979) (on Limburg).
41. H. Rosenberg (ed.), *Ausgewählter Briefwechsel R. Hayms* (Osnabrück, 1967), p. 52.
42. Wollstein, p. 306.
43. Verhandlungen, part 1, p. 3.
44. W. Siemann, 'Wirtschaftsliberalismus 1848/49 zwischen Sozialverpflichtung und Konkurrenzprinzip', in H. Rabe *et al.* (eds), *Festgabe E. W. Zeeden* (Münster, 1976), pp. 407–32. For the free traders and protective tariff supporters, see H. Best, *Interessenpolitik und nationale Integration 1848/49* (Göttingen, 1980); for a collection of source material, see H. Scholler (ed.), *Die Grundrechtsdiskussion in der Paulskirche* (Darmstadt², 1982); J.-D. Kühne, *Die Reichsverfassung der Paulskirche* (Frankfurt, 1985).
45. *Stenographischer Bericht*, vol. 1, p. 433; vol. 2, p. 1334 (Beseler).
46. M. Isler (ed.), *G. Riessers gesammelte Werke*, vol. 1 (Frankfurt, 1867), p. 574.

Chapter 3. Liberalism between the Revolution and the *Reichsgründung*

1. Cf. Siemann, pp. 218–22; Botzenhart, pp. 407ff., 717ff., 767ff.; E. R. Huber, *Deutsche Verfassungsgeschichte seit 1789*, vol. 2 (Stuttgart, 1964), p. 894ff.; Huber (ed.), vol. 1, p. 534ff.
2. Charlotte Duncker's letter of 27 June 1849, in M. Duncker, *Politischer Briefwechsel*, ed. J. Schultze (Stuttgart, 1923; reprinted 1967), p. 19.
3. In the words of the liberal 'Württembergische Zeitung' of 27 June 1849, cited in Langewiesche, *Liberalismus und*

Demokratie, p. 198; the quotation which follows is also taken from this source.

4. *J. G. Droysen Briefwechsel*, ed. R. Hübner, vol. 2 (Stuttgart, 1929; reprinted 1967), p. 35. Concerning what follows, see the excellent study by W. Hardtwig, 'Von Preußens Aufgabe in Deutschland zu Deutschlands Aufgabe in der Welt. Liberalismus und borussianisches Geschichtsbild zwischen Revolution und Imperialismus', *HZ*, 231 (1980), pp. 265–324.

5. H. v. Treitschke, *Briefe*, ed. H. Cornicelius, vol. 1 (Leipzig, 1912), p. 261 (19 November 1854).

6. Ibid., p. 453 (24 January 1858), pp. 221, 228 (1854); Droysen, *Briefwechsel*, vol. 2, p. 102 (13 May 1852), p. 188 (29 October 1853), p. 263 (2 June 1854). For theses on the subject of 'the middle classes and the war', see C. Dipper, 'Über die Unfähigkeit zum Frieden. Deutschlands bürgerliche Bewegung und der Krieg, 1830–1914', in *Frieden in Geschichte und Gegenwart* (Düsseldorf, 1985), pp. 92–110.

7. Hardtwig, Aufgabe, p. 316.

8. Droysen, *Briefwechsel*, vol. 2, p. 300 (18 February 1854).

9. Ibid., p. 188 (29. October 1853); Beseler quotation: Duncker, *Briefwechsel*, p. 54.

10. Droysen, *Briefwechsel*, vol. 2, pp. 318, 339, 299.

11. Treitschke, *Briefe*, vol. 1, p. 352.

12. A. L. Rochau, *Grundsätze der Realpolitik*, ed. H.-U. Wehler (Berlin, 1972). All quotations are from this reprint; page numbers in brackets in text.

13. Concerning what follows, including further literature, see H.-H. Brandt, *Der österreichischer Neoabsolutismus. Staatsfinanzen und Politik 1848–1860*, 2 vols (Göttingen, 1978); a brief outline is to be found in H. Matis, 'Sozioökonomische Aspekte des Liberalismus in Österreich 1848–1918', in *Sozialgeschichte heute, 2. Festschrift H. Rosenberg*, ed. H.-U. Wehler (Göttingen, 1974), p. 234ff., Eder, *Liberalismus*, p. 124ff.; Winter, *Frühliberalismus*, p. 231ff.; Winter, *Revolution, Neoabsolutismus und Liberalismus in der Donaumonarchie* (Vienna, 1969); Franz, *Liberalismus*.

14. H.-H. Brandt, vol. 1, p. 260.

15. Nipperdey, *Geschichte*, p. 681. Concerning what follows, see Huber, *Verfassungsgeschichte*, vol. 3 (Stuttgart, 1970²); Heffter, p. 327ff.; Grünthal; J. Cervelli, *Liberalismo e conservatismo in Prussia 1850–1858* (Bologna, 1983).

16. W. Siemann, *'Deutschlands Ruhe, Sicherheit und Ordnung.' Die Anfänge der politischen Polizei 1806–1866* (Tübingen, 1985); Siemann (ed.), *Der 'Polizeiverein deutscher Staaten. Eine Dokumentation zur Überwachung der Öffentlichkeit nach der Revolution von 1848/49* (Tübingen, 1983).

17. G. Beseler to Duncker, 2 February 1855, in Duncker, *Briefwechsel*, p. 66.

18. The texts of the constitutions and the most important laws of the reactionary era are reproduced in Huber (ed.), vol. 1, p. 484ff.

19. *Kölnische Zeitung* of 3 August 1849, cited by Grünthal, p. 145. The quotation which follows is also from this source.

20. All figures, ibid., pp. 341ff. (for 1852); 415ff. (for 1855); 391ff. (parliamentary parties); Heffter, p. 330.

21. In addition to Grünthal, see especially Sperber, *Catholicism*, and H. Hömig, *Rheinische Katholiken und Liberale in den Auseinandersetzungen um die preußische Verfassung unter bes. Berücksichtigung der Kölner* Presse (Cologne, 1971).

22. Cited by Grünthal, p. 440; for election data for the provinces and large towns, see ibid., p. 438.

23. Ibid., p. 462.

24. *Briefwechsel R. Hayms*, p. 157 (7 July 1858).

25. *Das Großherzogtum Baden zwischen Revolution und Restauration 1849–1851. Die Deutsche Frage und die Ereignisse in Baden im Spiegel der Briefe und Aktenstücke aus dem Nachlaß des preußischen Diplomaten K. F. v. Savigny*, ed. W. Real (Stuttgart, 1983), p. 576. Concerning what follows, see Gall, *Regierende Partei*, p. 58ff. The quotation which follows: ibid.

26. Ibid., p. 61, note 8.

27. Heffter, ch. 6, provides the best information; for Gneist: p. 372ff.

28. Gall, *Regierende Partei*, p. 92.

29. Cited ibid., p. 112.

30. Cited ibid., note 51.

31. Ibid., p. 71.

32. Concerning what follows, see Langewiesche, *Liberalismus*, ch. C; the figures are taken from the tables, pp. 73 and 225.

33. Ibid., p. 247.

34. Cited ibid., p. 245.

35. Ibid., p. 281.

36. Compare with the scant, contradictory literature on the Rhenish liberalism of the fifties: B.-C. Padtberg, *Liberale Einflußmöglichkeiten in Köln nach der 48er Revolution*, in K. Düwell and W. Köllmann (eds), *Rheinland-Westfalen im Industriezeitalter*, vol. 1 (Wuppertal, 1983), p. 224–32.

37. Droysen, *Briefwechsel*, p. 200f.

38. Cited in *Handbuch der bayerischen Geschichte*, ed. M. Spindler, vol. 4/1 (Munich, 1974), p. 245. With the exception of Heffter, p. 404ff, the 'new era' outside Prussia is usually only fleetingly mentioned in the surveys. Nipperdey, *Geschichte*, pp. 699–704 is brief but informative.

39. Gall, *Regierende Partei*, p. 184; Gall's work is seminal for Baden; there is a brief survey in *Badische Geschichte*, p. 70ff.

40. See R. Rürup, 'Die Emanzipation der Juden in Baden', in Rürup, *Emanzipation*, pp. 37ff., 74.

41. Concerning what follows, see K.-J. Matz, *Pauperismus und Bevölkerung* (Stuttgart, 1980), p. 148ff.; Gall, *Regierende Partei*, pp. 177, 292ff.; for trade reform, see Sedatis, pp. 103f., 216 (note 188).

42. Ibid., p. 104.

43. Gall, *Liberalismus als regierende Partei*, p. 118.

44. *Preußische Jahrbücher 1858/2*, p. 454, cited by L. Haupts, 'Die liberale Regierung in Preußen in der Zeit der "Neuen Ära"', in *Historische Zeitschrift*, 227 (1978), pp. 45–85; for an important article, see S. Bahne, 'Vor dem Konflikt. Die Altliberalen in der Regentschaftsperiode der "Neuen Ära"', in U. Engelhardt *et al.* (eds) *Soziale Bewegung und politische Verfassung* (Stuttgart, 1976), pp. 154–96.

45. Reproduced in H. Fenske (ed.), *Der Weg zur Reichsgründung 1850–1870* (Darmstadt, 1972), pp. 133–6.

46. As K. Mathy wrote to Duncker on 24 November 1858, in Duncker, *Briefwechsel*, p. 79; the Duncker quotation: Haym, *Briefwechsel*, p. 160 (10 November 1858).

47. Droysen, *Briefwechsel*, vol. 2, p. 603 (8 June 1859).

48. Short interpretations are to be found in Nipperdey, *Geschichte*, p. 693ff.; H. Lutz, *Zwischen Habsburg und Preußen, Deutschland 1815–1866* (Berlin, 1985), p. 410ff.; L. Gall, *Europa auf dem Weg in die Moderne 1850–1890* (Munich, 1984).

49. Droysen, *Briefwechsel*, vol. 2, p. 601 (8 June 1859); Duncker, *Briefwechsel*, p. 188f. (Haym, 16 July 1859).

50. Bennigsen on 7 February 1861, in Oncken, R.v. Bennigsen, vol. 1, pp. 495; cf. H. v. Sybel (22 February 1860) in J. Heyderhoff and P. Wentzcke (eds), *Deutscher Liberalismus im Zeitalter Bismarcks*, vol. 1 (Bonn, 1925), p. 48; Baumgarten quotation (22 May 1859); ibid., p. 39.
51. All historical surveys address the subject: Huber, *Verfassungsgeschichte*, vol. 3, p. 449ff. is particularly detailed.
52. Nipperdey, *Geschichte*, p. 705. For this and a more exact examination of what follows, see Huber, *Verfassungsgeschichte*, vol. 3, p. 378ff.
53. Heyderhoff and Wentzcke (eds), *Liberalismus I*, p. 170 (6 September 1863).
54. Both are acknowledged in all descriptions of the era. For more details, see W. Real, *Der deutsche Reformverein* (Lübeck, 1966). For examinations of the *Nationalverein*, with literature: Eisfeld, *Parteien*; Offermann, *Arbeiterbewegung*. Na'aman, *Der deutsche Nationalverein* appeared after this manuscript had been completed.
55. Cf. Langewiesche, *Liberalismus*, p. 296ff.
56. According to Oncken, vol. 1, p. 577; *J. v. Miquels Reden*, ed. W. Schultze and F. Thimme, vol. 1 (Halle, 1911), p. 2 (4 September 1860). For the *Nationalverein* programme of 1859 and others, see H. Böhme (ed.), *Die Reichsgründung* (Munich, 1967), p. 101f.
57. Oncken, vol. 1, p. 647f. (9 November 1864).
58. All surveys discuss the constitutional conflict. There is a brief and astute appreciation in Nipperdey, *Geschichte*, pp. 749–68; there is a thorough analysis in Huber, *Verfassungsgeschichte*, vol. 3, ch. VI; E. N. Anderson, *The Social and Political Conflict in Prussia, 1858–1864* (Lincoln, 1954) is also important; for a collection of source material, see J. Schlumbohm (ed.), *Der Verfassungskonflikt in Preußen 1862–1866* (Göttingen, 1970).
59. Reproduced in Fenske (ed.), *Weg*, pp. 212–14; on the Progress Party, see especially Winkler, *Preußischer Liberalismus*; Gugel, *Aufstieg*.
60. Cited by Huber, *Verfassungsgeschichte*, vol. 3, p. 299; Heyderhoff and Wentzcke (eds), *Liberalismus I*, p. 102 (Sybel to Baumgarten, 21 June 1862).
61. Nipperdey, *Geschichte*, p. 758.
62. Heyderhoff and Wentzcke (eds), *Liberalismus I*, p. 120f. (Haym to Sybel, 17 December 1862).

63. Reproduced, for example, by Fenske (ed.), *Weg*, pp. 276–9; the King's response is cited by Huber, *Verfassungsgeschichte*, vol. 3, p. 317.

64. L. Parisius, *Die Deutsche Fortschrittspartei 1861–1878* (Berlin, 1879), p. 13.

65. Heyderhoff and Wentzcke (eds), *Liberalismus I*, p. 151f. (Baumgarten, 22 May 1863), p. 152f. (Sybel, 26 May 1863).

66. According to the important, though biased book by Gugel, p. 212 (quotation).

67. Extract in Schlumbohm (ed.), *Verfassungskonflikt*, pp. 45–9.

68. Cf. H.-W. Hahn, *Geschichte des Deutschen Zollvereins* (Göttingen, 1984), p. 165ff.

69. Cf. Langewiesche, *Liberalismus*, p. 424ff.

70. Cf. Parent, *Verfassungskonflikt*; Anderson, *Conflict*, p. 278ff.; Hess, *Parlament*; Parisius, p. 13.

71. *Rheinische Zeitung*, 2 April 1863, cited by Parent, p. 124. Concerning what follows, see also Parent, with the example of Cologne.

72. Anderson, p. 343f.

73. Heyderhoff and Wentzcke (eds), *Liberalismus I*, p. 161f. (12/14 July 1863); Sybel, ibid., p. 156 (17 June 1863); K. Twesten, ibid., p. 159, and Hoverbeck, cf. L. Parisius, *L. v. Hoverbeck*, vol. II/2 (Berlin, 1900), p. 1f.

74. Cited in Fenske (ed.), *Weg*, p. 189; Oncken, vol. I, p. 648. Cf. W. Bussmann, *Zur Geschichte des deutschen Liberalismus im 19. Jh.* (Darmstadt, 1969), p. 19.

75. All surveys deal with the subject. For detailed information, see Huber, *Verfassungsgeschichte*, vol. 3, p. 449ff.

76. Heyderhoff and Wentzcke (eds), *Liberalismus I*, p. 184 (A. Lammers, 22 November 1863); for the National Association announcement, see Oncken, vol. I, p. 625f.

77. Twesten's speech, extract in Fenske (ed.), *Weg*, pp. 288–90; Bunsen quotation: Heyderhoff and Wentzcke (eds), *Liberalismus I*, p. 187 (27 November 1863).

78. For a detailed examination of the subsequent stance of Prussian liberals and democrats before 1866, see Winkler (Waldeck quotations; ibid., p. 44f.). For Bavaria, see T. Schieder, *Die kleindeutsche Partei in Bayern in ihren Kämpfen um die nationale Einheit 1863–1871* (Munich, 1936); for Baden: Gall, *Regierende Partei*; for Württemberg: Langewiesche, *Liberalismus*.

79. Cf. ibid. for Baden: Weber, *Demokraten*; for Hesse, Frankfurt and Nassau, see N. M. Hope, *The Alternative to German Unification* (Wiesbaden, 1973).
80. Cited in Langewiesche, *Liberalismus*, pp. 416, 411 (Pfau).
81. Heyderhoff and Wentzcke (eds), *Liberalismus I*, p. 314 (Baumgarten 23 June 1866), p. 254 (Mommsen, 28 September 1865), p. 286f. (Haym, 16 May 1886); see also the Haym letters in Haym, *Briefwechsel*, p. 246ff.; Treitsche quotation: Treitschke, *Briefe*, vol. 2, p. 357 (22 November 1864); Droysen in Droysen, *Briefwechsel*, vol. 2, p. 876 (14 October 1866).
82. Pollmann, *Parlamentarismus*, p. 35.
83. Haym, *Briefwechsel*, p. 253 (30 June 1866).
84. K.-G. Faber, 'Realpolitik als Ideologie. Die Bedeutung des Jahres 1866 für das politische Denken in Deutschland', in *Historische Zeitschrift*, 203 (1966) pp. 1–45. The best introduction to source material is provided by K.-G. Faber, *Die nationalpolitische Publizistik Deutschlands 1866–1871*, 2 vols (Düsseldorf, 1963).
85. All quotations (page numbers in parentheses in text) are taken from the new edition, ed. A. M. Birke (Frankfurt, 1974). A fair appreciation of the work is to be found in Sell, *Tragödie*, pp. 222–4. Droysen, *Briefwechsel*, vol. 2 pp. 872 (2 August 1866).
86. Pollmann, p. 186. Pollmann provides the best information on the work of the Federal Parliament. There are no more recent larger studies on the liberal parties in the North German Confederation. For a general analysis, see J. J. Sheehan, *German Liberalism in the Nineteenth Century* (Chicago/London, 1978). See also Schwab, *Nationalliberale Partei 1864–80*; White, The Splintered Party; Nipperdey, *Organisation*; J. F. Harris, A Study in the Theory and Practice of German Liberalism: *E. Lasker 1829–84* (Lanham, 1984).
87. The programme is reproduced, for example, in Fenske (ed.), *Weg*, pp. 372–6; Oncken quotation: Oncken, vol. 2, p. 80. For the liberal suffrage debate in general, see W. Gagel, *Die Wahlrechtsfrage in der Geschichte der deutschen liberalen Parteien 1848–1918* (Düsseldorf, 1958).
88. Oncken, vol. 2, p. 11; Sell, p. 226, speaks of their capitulation.
89. Oncken, vol. 2, p. 59.
90. Concerning what follows, see Pollmann's seminal work (pp. 139–257); he also gives references to earlier literature.

91. Miquel, *Reden*, vol. 1, p. 226f. (23 March 1867).
92. See Pollmann, p. 186; for the votes, see ibid., p. 178ff.; Waldeck's speech in Parisius, *Fortschrittspartei*, p. 22.
93. Pollmann, pp. 515, 513f.; Wehrenpfennig: Heyderhoff and Wentzcke (eds), *Liberalismus I*, p. 391 (16 October 1867).
94. Heyderhoff and Wentzcke (eds), *Liberalismus I*, p. 421 (4 June 1868); Miquel quotations: Miquel, *Reden*, vol. 1, p. 301 (16 June 1868), p. 211 (9 March 1867), p. 396 (21 December 1869).
95. Oncken, vol. 2, pp. 211f., 203 (Bennigsen quotation); Miquel, *Reden*, vol. 1, p. 396 (21 December 1869); cf. W. Bußmann, 'Bismarck: Seine Helfer und seine Gegner', in T. Schieder and E. Deuerlein (eds), *Reichsgründung 1870/710* (Stuttgart, 1970), pp. 119–47.
96. An initial survey, with comprehensive bibliographical details, is provided by K. Tenfelde, 'Die Entfaltung des Vereinswesens während der Industriellen Revolution in Deutschland 1850–1873', in Dann (ed.), *Vereinswesen*, pp. 55–114.
97. Miquel, *Reden*, vol. I, pp. 49, 145–51 (Waterloo Celebration); for the other celebrations and the Fleet Association, see Anderson, p. 335ff.; Parent; P. U. Hohendahl, *Literarische Kultur im Zeitalter des Liberalismus 1830–1870* (Munich, 1985), p. 198ff.
98. D. Bellmann, 'Der Liberalismus im Seekreis 1860–70', in G. Zang (ed.), *Provinzialisierung einer Region* (Frankfurt, 1978), p. 193ff., quotations: pp. 214, 263 (note 236).
99. Cf. V. Hentschel, *Die deutschen Freihändler und der volkswirtschaftliche Kongreß 1858–1885* (Stuttgart, 1975); Offermann, pp. 169–71, 177 (professions of National Association members); for professions of Congress participants, see G. Stalmann, *Der Kongreß deutscher Volkswirte* (Düsseldorf, 1926), p. 96.
100. Speech of 3 January 1863, cited by Eisfeld, p. 44.
101. Aldenhoff, *Schulze-Delitzsch*, p. 241. For the views expressed in the *Deutsches Staats-Wörterbuch*, ed. J. C. Bluntschli and K. Brater (1857/67), see Faßbender-Ilge, *Liberalismus*, p. 233ff.
102. All figures: ibid., pp. 162–70; cf. Aldenhoff's contribution in Holl *et al.* (eds), *Liberalismus*, pp. 57–69.
103. All quotations from J. Prince-Smith, '*Die sogennante Arbeiterfrage (1864)*', in O. Michaelis (ed.), *Gesammelte Schriften*, vol.

I (Berlin, 1877), pp. 26–42, cited by Hentschel, pp. 110–16. For Lassalle – the 'iron law of wages' was formulated in his famous 'Offenes Antwortschreiben' – see S. Na'aman, *Lassalle* (Hanover, 1970).

104. Quotations from: Miquel, *Reden*, vol. 1, pp. 173, 166, 154, 199–209 (speech of 9 February 1867).

105. Reichstag speech on the law on workers' coalitions, 14 October 1867, quoted by Fenske (ed.), *Weg*, pp. 380–2.

106. Concerning what follows, with literature, see W. Conze and D. Groh, *Die Arbeiterbewegung in der nationalen Bewegung* (Stuttgart, 1966); J. Kocka, *Lohnarbeit und Klassenbildung. Arbeiter und Arbeiterbewegung in Deutschland 1800–1875* (Berlin, 1983); Offermann, *Arbeiterbewegung*.

107. U. Engelhardt, 'Gewerkschaftliches Organisationsverhalten in der ersten Industrialisierungsphase', in W. Conze and U. Engelhardt (eds), *Arbeiter im Industrialisierungsprozeß* (Stuttgart, 1979), p. 399f.

108. 'Liberalismus oder Sozialdemokratie? Ein Vergleich der britischen und deutschen politischen Arbeiterbewegung 1850–1875', in J. Kocka (ed.), *Europäische Arbeiterbewegung im 19. Jahrhundert* (Göttingen, 1983), pp. 129–66 (includes literature). See also the excellent study by C. Eisenberg, *Deutsche und englische Gewerkschaften* (Göttingen, 1986).

109. Concerning what follows, in addition to the literature already mentioned, see the articles on the individual parties in *Lexikon zur Parteigeschichte*.

110. A comprehensive list of specialist literature on Württemberg and Saxony is presented in D. Langewiesche, 'Zur Frühgeschichte der deutschen Arbeiterbewegung', in *Archiv für Sozialgeschichte*, 15 (1975) pp. 301–21. The figures which follow are taken from Langewiesche, *Liberalismus*, pp. 344, 352ff.; for the social structure of the Württemberg parties, for which the most accurate figures are available, see ibid., pp. 370ff., 225.

111. Concerning what follows, see above all Sperber's study, which also contains important insights for the liberals, and Hess, *Parlament*; Eisfeld; Nipperdey, *Organisation*.

112. Sperber, p. 138ff. Election data in E. Anderson, *The Social and Political Conflict in Prussia 1858–1864* (Lincoln, 1954), p. 413; Gagel, pp. 177–9; Hess, p. 54.

113. For Württemberg, see the tables in Langewiesche, *Liberalismus*, p. 225. Other figures from Sperber, pp. 132–7; Gugel, p. 61f. For Bavaria, see C. Stache, *Bürgerlicher Liberalismus und katholischer Konservatismus in Bayern 1867–71* (Frankfurt, 1981).

114. B. Ehrenfeuchter, 'Politische Willensbildung in Niedersachsen zur Zeit des Kaiserreiches', Dissertation, Göttingen, 1951, p. 25ff.

Chapter 4. The Nation-State, Industrial Society and *Weltpolitik*: Liberals in the German Kaiserreich

1. In place of a long list of literary references, we refer the reader to Ploetz's survey of political, economic, social and cultural developments: *Das deutsche Kaiserreich*, ed. D. Langewiesche (Freiburg, 1984) (includes secondary literature). See also Huber, *Verfassungsgeschichte*, vols 3 and 4, which is more detailed and broader in terms of subject matter than its title would suggest.

2. G. *Freytag and Herzog E. von Coburg im Briefwechsel 1853–1893*, ed. E. Tempeltey (Leipzig, 1904), p. 248 (20 June 1871); Heyderhoff and Wentzcke (eds), *Liberalismus I*, p. 494 (Sybel).

3. R. M. Lepsius, 'Parteisystem und Sozialstruktur: zum Problem der Demokratisierung der deutschen Gesellschaft', in Ritter, *Parteien vor 1918*, pp. 56–80, remains stimulating.

4. In 1871 the elections were held under conditions which were too irregular to serve as a starting point. Unless otherwise stated, all population and social data are taken from G. Hohorst *et al.*, *Sozialgeschichtliches Arbeitsbuch* (Munich, 1975); all election data from G. A. Ritter and M. Niehuss, *Wahlgeschichtliches Arbeitsbuch* (Munich, 1980). For the history of the parties and the most important literature, see Ritter, *Parteien 1830–1914*.

5. Lepsius is seminal on this most frequently tested analysis of the socialist milieu.

6. One of the earliest (1928), and as yet best, election studies attempted to establish voter migration, but only for the Weimar Republic: see J. Schauff, *Das Wahlverhalten der deutschen Katholiken im Kaiserreich und in der Weimarer Republik*, ed. R. Morsey (Mainz 1975[2]). An attempt which was restricted to

the local level and which highlighted the problems was undertaken by O. Büsch, 'Gedanken und Thesen zur Wählerbewegung in Deutschland', in Busch *et al.* (eds) *Wählerbewegungen in der deutschen Geschichte* (Berlin, 1978), pp. 125–69. The most recent studies are S. Suval, *Electoral Politics in Wilhelmine Germany* (Chapel Hill, 1985); J. Sperber, *The Kaiser's Voters. Electors and Elections in Imperial Germany* (Cambridge, UK, 1997).

7. In addition to the works by G. A. Ritter referred to in note 4, see B. Vogel *et al.*, *Wahlen in Deutschland* (Berlin, 1971).

8. See especially Gagel; cf. Wegner, *T. Barth*, p. 131.

9. J. Sheehan, 'Liberalism and the City in 19th Century Germany', *Past and Present*, 51 (1971), pp. 116–37; ch. 3.

10. Fenske, *Strukturprobleme*, p. 64f.; figures are taken from Ritter and Niehuss, pp. 38–42, 104–16, 121–7.

11. J. H. Knoll, *Führungsauslese in Liberalismus und Demokratie* (Stuttgart, 1957), p. 174 (1884–1912).

12. See also the early (1912), but still stimulating sketch by Emil Lederer in Lederer, *Kapitalismus, Klassenstruktur und Probleme der Demokratie in Deutschland 1910–1940* ed. J, Kocka (Göttingen, 1976), pp. 33–50; Rosenberg, *Depression*.

13. The professional composition of the Reichstag parliamentary parties is, however, not as accurately known as the exact figures in the tables given here would suggest. Laborious source studies would often be required to ascertain whether the profession given in each case was also in fact practised. R. Köhne (*Nationalliberale und Koalitionsrecht*, Frankfurt, 1977) has checked all the information on the National Liberal Reichstag parties after 1890; his findings often deviate considerably from earlier findings. Further clues to the social profile of liberal Reichstag parties, with differentiations in Left Liberalism are to be found in Wegner, p. 99; Müller-Plantenberg, *Freisinn*, p. 105ff.; Nipperdey, *Organisation*; Sheehan, *Liberalismus*, p. 190ff.; Jaeger, *Unternehmer in der deutschen Politik 1890–1918* (Bonn, 1967), p. 50ff.; Molt, *Reichstag*, includes a great deal of data.

14. E. Fehrenbach, *Wandlungen des deutschen Kaisergedankens 1871–1918* (Munich, 1969); for Bavaria see W. K. Blessing, *Staat und Kirche in der Gesellschaft* (Göttingen, 1982).

15. König's quotation: *Das Tagebuch J. Hölders 1877–1880. Zum Zerfall des politischen Liberalismus in Württemberg und im*

Deutschen Reich, ed. D. Langewiesche (Stuttgart, 1977), p. 162. See also p. 92.

16. Concerning what follows, see Table 5 and especially the data in Jaeger, *Unternehmer*, p. 50ff.; see also Sheehan, *Liberalismus*, p. 195f. regarding Badenese, Bavarian and Württemberg Chambers of Deputies during the early decades. See Ritter and Niehuss for the changes in seats and votes.

17. Jaeger, pp. 74–6; for the elections, see D. Thränhardt, *Wahlen und politische Strukturen in Bayern 1848–1953* (Düsseldorf, 1973).

18. White demonstrates this for the Hessian National Liberals. For figures, see T. Klein, 'Reichstagswahlen und -abgeordnete der Provinz Sachsen und Anhalt 1867–1918', in *Festschrift für F. v. Zahn*, ed. W. Schlesinger, vol. I (Cologne, 1980), pp. 65–141, 135.

19. *Krisenherde des Kaiserreichs* was the title of an important collection of Kaiserreich studies by H.-U. Wehler (Göttingen, 1970/1979²).

20. For the period before 1871, see Langewiesche, *Liberalismus und Demokratie*. Research on the history of the Württemberg parties during the Kaiserreich has been patchy and unbalanced. We know little about the liberals, and have more detailed information on the democrats only for the period after 1890. Cf. Simon, *Demokraten*; J. C. Hunt, *The People's Party in Württemberg and Southern Germany 1890–1914* (Stuttgart, 1975); D. Blackbourn, *Class, Religion and Local Politics in Wilhelmine Germany. The Centre Party in Württemberg before 1914* (Wiesbaden, 1980). What follows is taken from the introduction to *das Tagebuch J. Hölders*, ed. Langewiesche.

21. Nipperdey's *Organisation* is seminal. Most studies of individual liberal parties or politicians also include reference to organization. White is particularly informative on the National Liberals, especially on Hesse. There are no comparable studies for other individual states. Schwab, *Aufstieg*, is very detailed for the period up to 1880.

22. See Simon, *Demokraten*, p. 12ff.; White, p. 43f.

23. Nipperdey, *Organisation*, p. 87.

24. *Ritter und Niehuss*, pp. 41, 69, 78, 90.

25. White, p. 136ff.; cf. H.-J. Puhle, *Agrarische Interessenpolitik und preußischer Konservatismus im wilhelminischen Reich 1893–1914* (Bonn, 1975²), p. 193ff.

26. Concerning what follows, see Nipperdey, *Organisation*, 92ff.; W. Link, 'Der Nationalverein für das liberale Deutschland', *Politische Vierteljahresschrift*, 5 (1964), pp. 422–44. After 1912 neither the Association of Young Liberals nor the right-wing response to it (founded in 1912), the *Altnationalliberaler Reichsverband*, were formally regarded as National Liberal Party organisations. See also K.-P. Reiß's edition, *Von Bassermann zu Stresemann. Die Sitzungen des nationalliberalen Zentralvorstands 1912–1917* (Düsseldorf, 1967), which reproduces the party statutes of 1892, 1905 and 1912.

27. Nipperdey, *Organisation*, p. 100. For the figures which follow: ibid., p. 101ff.; for Baden, see Thiel, *Großblockpolitik*, p. 234ff.

28. Nipperdey, *Organisation*, p. 104. See p. 161ff for the liberal unions. Data from S. Suval, *Electoral Politics in Wilhelmine Germany* (Chapel Hill, 1985), p. 125 (local associations); Nipperdey, pp. 103–5; Thiel, pp. 244, 273, 275–82 (for Baden).

29. Thränhardt, p. 85f.

30. What follows is taken from Nipperdey, *Organisation*, p. 176ff.; I. Steinbrecher, 'Liberale Parteiorganisation unter bes. Berücksichtigung des Linksliberalismus 1871–1893', Dissertation, Cologne, 1960; Seeber, *Bebel und Bismarck*; Elm, *Fortschritt und Reaktion*; Müller-Plantenberg; Wegner; I. S. Lorenz and E. Richter, *Der entschiedene Liberalismus in Wilhelminischer Zeit 1871–1906* (Husum, 1981); A. Rubinstein, *Die Deutsch-Freisinnige Partei 1884–1893* (Berlin, 1935); Düding, *Der Nationalsoziale Verein*; see also the articles in *Lexikon zur Parteiengeschichte*.

31. N. Schloßmacher, *Düsseldorf im Bismarckreich. Politik und Wahlen, Parteien und Vereine* (Düsseldorf, 1985), p. 74ff. One of the few studies to examine liberal party development at local level is I. Fischer, *Industrialisierung, sozialer Konflikt und politische Willensbildung in der Stadtgemeinde* (Augsburg, 1977) (for Augsburg).

32. For the programme, see G. Seeber, 'DFP', in *Lexikon zur Parteigeschichte*, vol. 1, p. 640; for Hoverbeck, including numerous sources, see Parisius, 2 parts/3 vols, 1897–1900.

33. In the words of Nipperdey, *Organisation*, p. 219.

34. Cf. B. Greven-Aschoff, *Die bürgerliche Frauenbewegung in Deutschland 1894–1933* (Göttingen, 1981), pp. 125–47; U. Frevert, *Frauen-Geschichte* (Frankfurt, 1986), pp. 104–28.

35. According to Jaeger, *Unternehmer*, pp. 112, 122.
36. The most important association studies, in so far as they are relevant to liberals are: S. Mielke, *Der Hansa-Bund für Gewerbe, Handel und Industrie 1909–1914* (Göttingen, 1976); H.-P. Ullmann, *Der Bund der Industriellen* (Göttingen, 1976); Puhle, *Interessenpolitik*; D. Stegmann, *Die Erben Bismarcks. Parteien und Verbände in der Spätphase des Wilhelminischen Deutschlands* (Cologne, 1970); H. Kaelble, *Industrielle Interessenpolitik in der Wilhelminischen Gesellschaft. Centralverband deutscher Industrieller 1895–1914* (Berlin, 1967); T. Nipperdey, 'Interessenverbände und Parteien in Deutschland vor dem Ersten Weltkrieg', in H.-U. Wehler (ed.), *Moderne deutsche Sozialgeschichte* (Cologne, 1966/Königstein, 1981⁶), pp. 369–88.
37. Kaelble, pp. 120ff., 225.
38. Ullmann, p. 145.
39. Puhle, pp. 189ff., 193ff.; for the *Deutscher Bauernbund*, see G. Müller and H. Schwab, in *Lexikon zur Parteiengeschichte*, vol. 2, pp. 31–41.
40. All figures from Mielke.
41. The best source for what follows is K. Saul, *Staat, Industrie und Arbeiterbewegung im Kaiserreich* (Düsseldorf, 1974), especially p. 98ff.; for the social–liberal union movement, see also H.-G. Fleck, in E. Matthias and K. Schönhoven (eds), *Solidarität und Menschenwürde* (Bonn, 1984), pp. 83–106; I. Fischer, pp. 293–320, uses the example of Augsburg.
42. See R. vom Bruch, 'Bürgerliche Sozialreform im deutschen Kaiserreich', in vom Bruch (ed.), *'Weder Kommunismus noch Kapitalismus'*, pp. 61–179 (also gives specialist literature).
43. U. Ratz, *Sozialreform und Arbeiterschaft* (Berlin, 1980), p. 57.
44. See H. Dräger, *Die Gesellschaft für Verbreitung von Volksbildung* (Stuttgart, 1975); as a case study, D. Kramer, *'Volksbildung' in der Industriegemeinde* (Rüsselsheim, 1975); D. Langewiesche, 'Arbeiterbildung in Deutschland und Österreich', in W. Conze and U. Engelhardt (eds), *Arbeiter im Industrialisierungsprozeß* (Stuttgart, 1979), pp. 439–64; vom Bruch (ed.), p. 114ff.; H. Heitzer, *Der Volksverein für das katholische Deutschland im Kaiserreich 1890–1918* (Mainz, 1979).
45. Ritter and Niehuss, p. 167; *Politisches Handbuch der Nationalliberalen Partei* (for 1907), p. 831ff.; R. Vierhaus, 'Bildung', in *Geschichtliche Grundbegriffe*, vol. 1 (Stuttgart, 1972), p. 523ff.; D. Langewiesche, 'Bildungsbürgertum und Liberalismus im

342 NOTES

19. Jh.', in J. Kocka and H.-U. Wehler (eds), *Bildungsbürgertum im 19. Jh.*, vol. II (Stuttgart, 1988).
46. Dräger, p. 79.
47. D. Langewiesche and K. Schönhoven, 'Arbeiterbibliotheken und Arbeiterlektüre im Wilhelminischen Deutschland', *Archiv für Sozialgeschichte*, 16 (1976), pp. 134–204, 151.
48. Cf. G. Kratzsch, *Kunstwart und Dürerbund* (Göttingen, 1969); W. R. Krabbe, *Gesellschaftsveränderung durch Lebensreform* (Göttingen, 1974).
49. Figures for the *Evangelischer Bund* are taken from an unpublished *Examensarbeit* by Armin Müller. His doctoral dissertation on the *Bund* is forthcoming. For the national mass associations, see especially R. Chickering, *We Men Who Feel Most German* (London, 1984), p. 202ff.
50. *Erinnerungen von L. F. Seyffardt* (Leipzig, 1900).
51. L. Parisius, *Die Deutsche Fortschrittspartei 1861–1878* (Berlin, 1879), pp. 55, 37 (1873); M. Weber, 'Parlament und Regierung im neugeordneten Deutschland (1918)', in *M. Weber Gesamtausgabe*, part I, 15, ed. W. J. Mommsen and G. Hübinger (Tübingen, 1984), p. 441.
52. J. Jolly, *Der Reichstag und die Parteien* (Berlin, 1880), p. 109; see L. Bamberger, 'Die Sezession (1880)', in Bamberger, *Politische Schriften 1879–1892 (Gesammelte Schriften*, vol. V) (Berlin, 1897), pp. 39–134, 53; M. Philippson, *M. von Forckenbeck* (Leipzig, 1898), p. 256ff.
53. W. Cahn (ed.), *Aus E. Laskers Nachlaß* (Berlin, 1902), p. 52f., the following quotations are on pp. 51, 59; for Lasker, see the biographical studies by A. Lauf (Göttingen, 1984) and J. H. Harris (Lanham, 1984). The most detailed information (though frequently with biased judgements) on the internal expansion of the Reich and the federal states is given by Huber, *Verfassungsgeschichte*, vol. 4.
54. Jolly, *Reichstag*, p. 23.
55. See the provisional conclusion (with literature) in: W. J. Mommsen, 'Die Verfassung des Deutschen Reichs von 1871 als dilatorischer Herrschaftskompromiß', in O. Pflanze and E. Müller-Luckner (eds), *Innenpolitische Probleme des Bismarck-Reichs* (Munich, 1983), 195–216.
56. Weber, *Parlament*, pp. 442–4; Duncker, *Briefwechsel*, p. 463 (H. Baumgarten, 8 December 1870).

57. Haym, *Briefwechsel*, p. 325; Hölder, *Das Tagebuch J. Hölders*, pp. 242 (10 April 1880), 248 (29 April 1880). For Bismarck's policies after the *Reichsgründung*, see especially L. Gall, *Bismarck* (Berlin, 1980), pp. 459ff., 526ff.
58. See Oncken, vol. 2, p. 292ff.; *R. von Bennigsens Reden*, vol. I, ed. W. Schultze and F. Thimme (Halle, 1911), p. 322ff.; for an analysis of the justice laws, see A. Laufs, *E. Lasker* (Göttingen, 1984), p. 99ff.; Stürmer, *Regierung*, p. 62ff gives a rather dramatic depiction of the Press Law as an indication of the decline of liberalism; see also the more informative E. Naujoks, *Die parlamentarische Entstehung des Reichspressegesetzes in der Bismarckzeit (1848/74)* (Düsseldorf, 1975). See also J. Ziekursch, *Politische Geschichte des neuen Deutschen Kaiserreichs*, vol. 2 (Frankfurt, 1927), p. 257ff.
59. Oncken, vol. 2, pp. 295, 247.
60. Cited by L. Parisius, *Deutschlands politische Parteien*, pp. 180f., 191; for the Military Law, see Gall, *Bismarck*, p. 532ff. (quotation: p. 521); Ziekursch, p. 294ff. (quotation); Stürmer, p. 118ff. adopts the view of the Progress Party, combined with his own inclination to dramatize.
61. Bennigsen, *Reden*, vol. I, p. 300ff.; Oncken, vol. 2, p. 261ff., quotation, p. 255; see also the letters in Heyderhoff and Wentzcke (eds), 2 vols (1926/reprinted Osnabrück, 1970), p. 99ff.
62. Rosenberg, *Große Depression*, is still the seminal work; a more recent economic historical viewpoint is offered in K. E. Born, *Wirtschafts- und Sozialgeschichte des Deutschen Kaiserreichs 1867/71–1914* (Stuttgart, 1985), p. 107ff.; see Gall, *Bismarck*, p. 526ff, for the political change in course in general; H.-E. Matthes discusses the liberals in 'Die Spaltung der Nationalliberalen Partei und die Entwicklung des Linksliberalismus 1878–1893', Dissertation, Kiel, 1953; cf. Sheehan, *Liberalism*, p. 181ff.; H. A. Winkler, 'Vom linken zum rechten Nationalismus. Der deutsche Liberalismus in der Krise von 1878/79', *Geschichte und Gesellschaft*, 4 (1978), pp. 5–28.
63. Cahn, *Laskers Nachlaß*, p. 95; Rosenberg, p. 29.
64. See Gall's assessment, *Bismarck*, p. 535f.; O. Pflanze, '"Sammlungspolitik" 1875–1886. Kritische Bemerkungen zu einem Modell', in Pflanze (ed.), pp. 155–93.

NOTES

65. Cahn, *Laskers Nachlaß*, p. 117f.; the quotation which follows is on p. 119.
66. Lucius von Ballhausen, *Bismarck-Erinnerungen* (Stuttgart, 1921[4]), p. 131; for the negotiations see especially Matthes, p. 49ff.; see also Gall, p. 554ff.
67. Miquel, *Reden*, vol. 2, p. 345 (22 November 1890); cf. Herzfeld, *Miquel*, p. 23f. On the other hand, the Left Liberal C. Funck noted in his diary that Miquel's appointment was 'regarded by all sides' as the first significant 'triumph of parlamentarianism': *Lebenserinnerungen* (Frankfurt, 1921), p. 13.
68. Oncken, vol. 2, p. 302.
69. See Matthes, p. 104ff. (includes literature and sources); see also the informative newly accessible source: *Das Tagebuch J. Hölders*. W. Gerloff, *Die Finanz- und Zollpolitik des Deutschen Reiches* (Jena, 1913), p. 124ff., remains seminal on tax and customs reform.
70. *Die politischen Reden des Fürsten Bismarck*, ed. by H. Kohl, vol. 8 (Stuttgart, 1893), p. 137ff.; for details, see Gall, *Bismarck*, p. 585ff.
71. Parisius, *Fortschrittspartei*, p. 38; Windhorst quotation cited by Matthes, p. 122 (9 July 1879).
72. Heyderhoff and Wentzcke (eds), vol. 2, p. 251 (H. Blum to Lasker 10 July 1879); Weber, *Parlament*, p. 441; Cahn, *Laskers Nachlaß*, p. 133.
73. Lucius von Ballhausen, p. 160.
74. Heyderhoff und Wentzcke (eds), vol. 2, p. 210 (Rickert, 15 July 1878), p. 290f. (Stauffenberg, 28 January 1880); Lorenz, p. 93.
75. Bennigsen, *Reden*, vol. 2, pp. 87, 84 (19 September 1880); cf. Oncken, vol. 2, p. 430ff.
76. Jolly, *Reichstag*, pp. 157ff, 168ff.
77. L. Bamberger, 'Die Sezession', in Bamberger, *Gesammelte Schriften*, vol. V (Berlin, 1897), pp. 118, 128, 131, 134. Cf. S. Zucker, L. Bamberger (Pittsburgh, 1975).
78. Heyderhoff and Wentzcke (eds), vol. 2, p. 378f. (29 March 1881).
79. See U. Engelhardt, *Bildungsbürgertum* (Stuttgart, 1986).
80. For the subject covered by this chapter as a whole in the European context, see *Handbuch der Kirchengeschichte*, vol. VI, ed. H. Jedin (Freiburg, 1971/85); M. Greschat, *Das Zeitalter*

der Industrialisierung. Das Christentum vor der Moderne (Stuttgart, 1980); H. Maier, *Revolution und Kirche* (Munich, 1959), etc.; for a brief discussion of Germany see K. Kupisch, *Kirchengeschichte*, vol. V (Stuttgart, 1975); Blessing, *Staat und Kirche*, is a stimulating study for Bavaria.

81. *Politisches Handbuch der Nationalliberalen Partei* (1907); Treitschke, *Briefe*, vol. 2, p. 331 (10 June 1864), p. 333f. (28 June 1864); Droysen, *Briefwechsel*, vol. 2, p. 300 (12 December 1854).

82. Bennigsen, *Reden*, vol. 2, pp. 283–99 (16 January 1873); Miquel, *Reden*, vol. 2, p. 212 (23 April 1874); Cahn, *Laskers Nachlaß*, p. 73.

83. The election announcement is in *Parisius, Deutschlands politische Parteien*, pp. 150–2; for the significance of the *Kulturkampf* for Reich politics and the liberal parties, see, for example, Gall, *Bismarck*, p. 477ff.; G. Schmidt, 'Die Nationalliberalen – eine regierungsfähige Partei?', and R. Morsey, 'Die deutschen Katholiken und der Nationalstaat zwischen Kulturkampf und Erstem Weltkrieg', both in Ritter (ed.), *Parteien vor 1918*, pp. 208–23, 270–98. There is a broad analysis of the *Kulturkampf* in the Reich and in the individual states in Huber, *Verfassungsgeschichte*, vol. 4, pp. 645–831. For Austria, see Franz, *Liberalismus*, p. 405ff.

84. See, with varying individual evaluations, L. Gall, 'Die partei- und sozialgeschichtliche Problematik des badischen Kulturkampfes', *ZGO*, p. 113 (1965), pp. 151–96; Becker, *Staat*; Zang (ed.), p. 307ff; on Bavaria, Stache.

85. See G. Korff, 'Kulturkampf und Volksfrömmigkeit', *Geschichte und Gesellschaft*, special issue 11 (1986), pp. 137–51; Sperber, p. 207ff.

86. Parisius, *Deutschlands politische Parteien*, p. 201.

87. Cahn, *Laskers Nachlaß*, p. 87.

88. Parisius, *Hoverbeck*, vol. II/2 (1900), p. 298f.; L. Bamberger, 'Der staatserhaltende Beruf der Hölle (1892)', in Bamberger, *Gesammelte Schriften*, vol. I (Berlin, 1889), pp. 361–86; Zucker, p. 96f.

89. Heyderhoff and Wentzcke (eds), vol. 2, p. 249 (29 June 1879).

90. In 1899–1904 and 1907–11 there were approximately 33 per cent Catholics in the Bavarian Liberal Association: see A. Knapp, 'Das Zentrum in Bayern 1893–1912', Dissertation, Munich, 1973, p. 39.

91. W. Beyschlag, *Der Friedenschluß zwischen Deutschland und Rom* (Leipzig, 1890), p. 22; cf. R. Wittram, *Das Nationale als europäisches Problem* (Göttingen, 1954), p. 134ff.

92. Heffter, p. 580.

93. Sperber, p. 236 (includes an analysis of members and of the relationship between religiousness and liberalism); for the relationship between liberals and Old Catholics, see Thränhardt, *Bayern*, p. 75; regarding Munich and Allgäu as centres of Old Catholicism, Schloßmacher, Düsseldorf, pp. 79–82.

94. H. Gruber SJ, 'Liberalismus', in Wetzer and Welte's *Kirchenlexikon oder Enzyklopädie der katholischen Theologie und ihrer Hilfswissenschaften*, vol. 7 (Freiburg, 1891), cols 1898–944, p. 1912f.

95. Philippson, p. 391f.; the reason given was that he had belonged to the state court for church affairs. The court was established in 1873, its sphere of duties restricted in 1882, and dissolved in 1886.

96. Workers and the workers' movement are two of the best researched aspects of the Kaiserreich. A comprehensive account of the state of research is given by K. Tenfelde (ed.), *Arbeiter und Arbeiterbewegung im Vergleich (Historische Zeitschrift)*, special issue 15 (Munich, 1986); see also the short and readable K. Schönhoven, 'Arbeiter und Arbeiterbewegung in der Gesellschaft des Kaiserreichs', in Ploetz, *Das deutsche Kaiserreich*, pp. 150–8.

97. All quotations are from *Zehn Jahre Deutscher Kämpfe* (Berlin, 1913), pp. 93–170. This collection of political writings of the day was first published in 1874. The third edition appeared in 1897.

98. Cf. Langewiesche, *Arbeiterbildung*.

99. The most informative work on the part played by the liberals in the enactment of all anti-socialist laws is W. Pack, *Das parlamentarische Ringen um das Sozialistengesetz Bismarcks 1878–1890* (Düsseldorf, 1961); Gall, *Bismarck*, p. 564ff., is brief, but places the subject in the overall political context; it is portrayed as part of a political drama in the struggle between 'absolutism' and 'parliamentarianism' by Stürmer, Reichstag, pp. 216ff, 241ff.

100. Bennigsen, *Reden*, vol. 1, pp. 384, 393; Philippson, p. 299; *Großherzog Friedrich I von Baden und die Reichspolitik 1871–1907*, ed. W. Fuchs, vol. 1 (Stuttgart, 1968), p. 281.

101. Bennigsen, *Reden*, vol. I, p. 413f.; *Das Tagebuch J. Hölders*, p. 119 (29 July 1878).
102. Lorenz, pp. 133, 141ff.; see also Pack, p. 147ff. The Centre Party vote was also split. After 1884 Left Liberals again voted unanimously against an extension.
103. See K. E. Born, *Staat und Sozialpolitik seit Bismarcks Sturz* (Wiesbaden, 1957), p. 135ff.
104. Hentschel, *Freihändler*, p. 284.
105. Treitschke, *Kämpfe*, pp. 160, 106; for the liberal co-operative idea, see especially Aldenhoff, *Schulze-Delitzsch*.
106. Concerning what follows, see especially the chapters by J. Reulecke and R. vom Bruch in vom Bruch (ed.), pp. 21–59, 61–179. (includes all specialist literature).
107. Heyderhoff and Wentzcke (eds), vol. 2, p. 57f. (11 August 1872).
108. 'Warum betreiben wir die soziale Reform?' (*Schriften der Gesellschaft für soziale Reform*), part 11 (1903), p. 27), cited by vom Bruch, p. 132.
109. Lorenz, pp. 141, 133.
110. See W. Mommsen (ed.), *Deutsche Parteiprogramme* (Munich, 1960), pp. 160–3 (DVP), 173–6 (FVP); for the DVP see also Simon, *Demokraten*, pp. 38–41; Hunt, *People's Party*, pp. 111–25; K. Gerteis and L. Sonnemann (Frankfurt, 1970); E. Engelberg, 'Das Verhältnis zwischen kleinbürgerlicher Demokratie und Sozialdemokratie in den 80er Jahren des 19. Jh.', in Pflanze (ed.), pp. 25–46; Seeber, pp. 148–59.
111. Lorenz, p. 90; for the quotation which follows see p. 137. For the attitude of the liberal parties to social legislation, see Born, *Staat und Sozialpolitik*, and O. Quandt, *Die Anfänge der Bismarckschen Sozialgesetzgebung und die Haltung der Parteien* (Berlin, 1938/reprinted 1965), and Matthes, pp. 185–202; Rubinstein, pp. 96–100.
112. L. Bamberger, 'Die Invasion der Sozialistischen Ideen', in Bamberger *et al.*, *Gegen den Staatssocialismus* (Berlin, 1884), p. 26.
113. Bamberger, *Sezession*, pp. 131–3.
114. Bamberger, *Invasion*, pp. 13, 19, 22, 24.
115. T. Barth, 'Die charakteristischen Züge des heutigen Staatssocialismus', in Bamberger *et al.*, pp. 31–44, 33, 40; cf. Wegner, ch. II.

116. Bennigsen, *Reden*, vol. 2, pp. 104–24: speech at the National Liberal Party conference for Saxony (9 October 1881), p. 116.
117. Miquel, *Reden*, vol. 3, pp. 247–57, 253 (20 May 1889).
118. Ibid., pp. 171 (21 June 1886), 244 (1 April 1889), 231 (20 January 88).
119. Ibid., pp. 171; 292f. (unions).
120. Parisius, *Fortschrittspartei*, p. 47.
121. The best brief survey with secondary literature is J. Reulecke, *Geschichte der Urbanisierung in Deutschland* (Frankfurt, 1985).
122. The most important exception is Sheehan, *Liberalism and the City*, pp. 116–37. This essay was unfortunately not included in his liberalism book.
123. Concerning what follows, see: Reulecke, 'Urbanisierung' (includes figures); Krabbe, 'Kommunalpolitik' (for Dortmund and Münster, but with general surveys); Krabbe, 'Munizipalsozialismus und Interventionsstaat', in *Geschichte in Wiss. u. Unterricht 1979*, pp. 265–83. The quotation which follows is from p. 276.
124. Krabbe, *Kommunalpolitik*, p. 93. The programme is reproduced in Adickes and Beutler, *Die sozialen Aufgaben der deutschen Städte* (Leipzig, 1903), pp. 88–90. Further programmes, including that of the People's Party, in A. Damaschke, *Aufgaben der Gemeindepolitik* (Jena, 1901⁴), p. 213ff. Concerning what follows, see especially the article 'Kommunalpolitik der politischen Parteien', in *Handwörterbuch der Kommunalwissenschaft*, vol. 3 (Jena, 1924), pp. 1–35. For Social Democracy, see D. Rebentisch, in *Archiv für Sozialgeschichte*, 25 (1985), pp. 1–78. For Preuß, see S. Grassmann, *H. Preuß und die Selbstverwaltung* (Lübeck, 1965).
125. Heffter, p. 616.
126. All figures from Philippson.
127. Herzfeld, Miquel, vol. 1, p. 526ff.; he also covers what follows; for the Elberfeld System, see Reulecke, *Urbanisierung*, p. 65f.
128. Miquel, *Reden*, vol. 3 (1913), p. 299f. Similarly Miquel's successor: see Adickes, *Aufgaben*, p. 65ff.
129. *Handwörterbuch der Kommunalwissenschaft*, vol. 3, p. 19.
130. Concerning what follows, see especially the excellent studies by H. Croon; in particular, *Vordringen*, pp. 15–58; Krabbe,

'Kommunalpolitik', p. 103ff. (from which the figures for Dortmund and Münster are taken). J. Rolling, Frankfurt (see Table 14); W. Hofmann, *Die Bielefelder Stadtverordneten* (Lübeck, 1964); Hofmann, 'Preußische Stadtverordnetenversammlungen als Repräsentativ-Organe', in J. Reulecke (ed.), *Die deutsche Stadt im Industriezeitalter* (Wuppertal, 1978), pp. 31–56; Sheehan, *City; Schriften des Vereins für Socialpolitik*, vols 117–120 (Leipzig, 1905–9) is a contemporary work, which includes a great deal of material; references to literature and a survey of municipal law and suffrage regulations can be found in *Deutsche Verwaltungsgeschichte*, ed. K. G. A. Jeserich *et al.*, vol. III (Stuttgart, 1985)

131. W. Hofmann, 'Die Entwicklung der kommunalen Selbstverwaltung 1848–1918', in *Handbuch der Kommunalen Wissenschaft und Praxis*, vol. I (Berlin, 1981), p. 83.

132. Hoffmann, 'Repräsentativ-Organe', p. 50; figures are taken from Croon, *Vordringen*, p. 41, Hamburg: Eckardt (see Table 8), p. 37 (1903/4).

133. *Handwörterbuch der Kommunalwissenschaft*, vol. 3, p. 20. The quotation is also from this source.

134. Krabbe, 'Kommunalpolitik', pp. 138–47.

135. Miquel, *Reden*, vol. 3, p. 98f.

136. See especially Croon, *Vordringen*; Croon, 'Die Stadtvertretungen in Krefeld und Bochum im 19. Jh.', in *Festgabe F. Hartung* (Berlin, 1958), pp. 289–306; Croon, *Auswirkungen*; Krabbe, 'Kommunalplitik', pp. 150–74; Rolling on the subject of Frankfurt; the *Schriften des Vereins für Socialpolitik*, vols 117–118, 120/I–III are also informative.

137. *Handwörterbuch der Kommunalwissenschaft*, vol. 3, p. 24; cf. p. 25 on the liberal parliamentary party in Krefeld.

138. Krabbe, 'Kommunalpolitik', p. 157ff.

139. See Rolling, p. 175ff.

140. See L. Niethammer, *Umständliche Erläuterung der seelischen Störung eines Communalbaumeisters in Preußens größtem Industriedorf oder: Die Unfähigkeit zur Stadtentwicklung* (Frankfurt, 1979); H. Reif, 'Arbeiter und Unternehmer in Städten des westlichen Ruhrgebiets 1850–1930. Räumliche Aspekte einer Klassenbeziehung', in J. Kocka (ed.), *Arbeiter und Bürger* (Munich, 1986), pp. 151–81.

141. Cited by R. Morsey, 'Die deutschen Katholiken und der Nationalstaat zwischen Kulturkampf und Erstem Weltk-

rieg', in Ritter (ed.), *Parteien vor 1918*, pp. 270–98, 281; see especially W. Loth, *Katholiken im Kaiserreich* (Düsseldorf, 1984)

142. Cited by Lorenz, p. 136f.; for what follows, see J. C. G. Röhl, *Deutschland ohne Bismarck. Die Regierungskrise im Zweiten Kaiserreich 1890–1900* (Tübingen, 1969), p. 74ff.; Matthes, p. 267ff.

143. Mommsen (ed.), *Parteiprogramme*, pp. 159–60, 157.

144. Cited by Gall, *Bismarck*, pp. 674, 677 (Bamberger); for the cartel, see ibid., pp. 672–83; Oncken, *Bennigsen*, vol. 2, pp. 509–54; Herzfeld, *Miquel*, vol. 2, pp. 93–151.

145. Miquel, *Reden*, vol. 2, pp. 170–83; Bennigsen, *Reden*, vol. 2, pp. 187–201.

146. Miquel, *Reden*, vol. 2, pp. 262–80; Heyderhoff and Wentzcke (eds), vol. 2, p. 429 (Bamberger 25 February 1887).

147. Herzfeld, *Miquel*, vol. 2, p. 104; W. J. Mommsen, 'Die latente Krise des Wilhelminischen Reiches', in *Militärgeschichtliche Mitteilungen 1974/I*, pp. 7–128.

148. Mommsen, *Weber* is seminal on the subject; Weber quotation: p. 145.

149. *Erinnerungen von Seyffardt*, p. 595. For this and what follows, see also J. J. Sheehan, 'Deutscher Liberalismus im postliberalen Zeitalter 1890–1914', *Geschichte und Gesellschaft*, 4 (1978), pp. 29–48.

150. M. Weber, 'Der Nationalstaat und die Volkswirtschaftspolitik (1895)', in Weber, *Gesammelte Politische Schriften*, ed. J. Winckelmann (Tübingen, 1971³), pp. 2–25, 23; Miquel, *Reden*, vol. 3, pp. 262–80, 276 (2 February 1890).

151. See especially Hardtwig, *Preußens Aufgabe*, pp. 265–324.

152. *Politisches Handbuch der Nationalliberalen Partei* (Berlin, 1908); pp. 772, 775. A survey and introduction to the current state of research is to be found in H. Gründer, *Geschichte der deutschen Kolonien* (Paderborn, 1985), pp. 63–78 (stance of the parties on colonial policy), quotation p. 65; G. Schöllgen, *Das Zeitalter des Imperialismus* (Munich, 1986). Concerning what follows, see especially W. J. Mommsen, 'Wandlungen der liberalen Idee im Zeitalter des Liberalismus', in Holl and List (eds), *Imperialistischer Staat*, pp. 109–47.

153. *Politisches Handbuch*, pp. 595, 585.

154. For a brief survey and the most important literature, see K. Holl, 'Krieg und Frieden und die liberalen Parteien', in

Holl and List (eds), pp. 72–88; Mommsen, 'Wandlungen', pp. 109–47.

155. K. Helfferich, *G. von Siemens* (Berlin, 1923), pp. 184f., 187.

156. F. Mehring, *Gesammelte Schriften*, vol. 14 (Berlin, 1965), pp. 214; the Richter quotation is from his Reichstag speech of December 1899 (p. 3358f.).

157. Concerning what follows, see Mommsen, *Weber und die deutsche Politik*; Mommsen, 'Wandlungen', quotation p. 123; Theiner, *Liberalismus* (includes older literature); readers in a hurry should consult Theiner, 'F. Naumann und der soziale Liberalismus im Kaiserreich', in Holl and Trautmann (eds), *Sozialer Liberalismus* (Göttingen, 1986), pp. 72–83.

158. Mommsen, *Weber*, pp. 52; Theiner, *Naumann*, p. 74f; T. Barth, *Neue Aufgaben des Liberalismus* (Berlin, 1904).

159. Eschenberg, *Kaiserreich*, is still the seminal work; cf. Theiner, *Liberalismus*, pp. 169–94; B. Heckart, *From Bassermann to Bebel. The Grand Bloc's Quest for Reform in the Kaiserreich 1900–1914* (New Haven, 1974), pp. 44–87; P.-C. Witt, *Die Finanzpolitik des Deutschen Reiches 1903–1913* (Lübeck, 1970), pp. 152–316.

160. On the subject of these hopes, see, for example, W. Kulemann, *Der Zusammenschluß der Liberalen* (Dresden, 1905); A. Blaustein, *Von der Uneinigkeit der Liberalen bei den Reichstagswahlen 1867–1910* (Munich, 1911).

161. Concerning what follows, see Grosser, *Konstitutionalismus*, pp. 60–75; Eschenburg, pp. 132–75; M. Rauh, *Die Parlamentarisierung des Deutschen Reiches* (Düsseldorf, 1977), pp. 156–86 (a distastefully arrogant book with important observations which the author brings together in his thesis of the 'quiet introduction of the parliamentary system'.); Gilg, *Erneuerung*.

162. *Aus C. Haußmanns politischer Arbeit* (Frankfurt, 1923), p. 15.

163. Cited by Theiner, *Liberalismus*, p. 194.

164. Concerning what follows, see Thiel, *Großblockpolitik*, quotation p. 128; Heckart, pp. 91–121.

165. *Politisches Handbuch*, pp. 901, 347. See, generally, Greven-Aschoff, pp. 125–31; Theiner, *Liberalismus*, p. 201; Elm, p. 249 (World War); the programme is reproduced in Mommsen (ed.), *Parteiprogramme*, pp. 173–6.

166. A. Faust, *Arbeitsmarktpolitik im Deutschen Kaiserreich* (Stuttgart, 1986), pp. 180–4.

167. L. Nelson *et al.*, *Was ist Liberal?* (Munich, 1910), pp. 73, 61; Link, *Nationalverein*, pp. 422–44, 423 (foundation appeal).
168. On this subject and on what follows, see Theiner, *Liberalismus*, pp. 195–217 (the quotation which follows, p. 211), Thiel; see also Heckart, pp. 186–287; Mielke, pp. 121 86; Reiß's edition, pp. 22–30; J. Bertram, *Die Wahlen zum Deutschen Reichstag 1912* (Düsseldorf, 1964); Stegmann, chs IV–IX; Eschenburg, pp. 258–74; Rauh, p. 172ff.
169. F. Meinecke, *Werke*, vol. 2 (Darmstadt, 1979[4]), p. 249; H. Fenske (ed.), *Unter Wilhelm II. 1890–1918* (Darmstadt, 1982), p. 368 (Bethmann Hollweg).
170. For a general discussion, see F. Fischer, *Griff nach der Weltmacht. Die Kriegszielpolitik des kaiserlichen Deutschland 1914/18* (Düsseldorf, 1961; special edition 1967) for a brief survey of the controversial research issues, see G. Schöllgen, '"Fischer-Kontroverse" und Kontinuitätsproblem', in A. Hillgruber and J. Düllfer (eds), *Ploetz – Geschichte der Weltkriege* (Freiburg, 1981), pp. 163–77. For National Liberal politics during the war, see: Thieme, *Liberalismus*; Grosser, *Vom monarchischen Konstitutionalismus*, part II; Reiß's edition; E. Matthias and R. Morsey's edition, *Der Interfraktionelle Ausschuß 1917/18*, 2 vols (Düsseldorf, 1959). The quotation is taken from J. Reimann, *E. Müller-Meinigen sen. und der Linksliberalismus in seiner Zeit* (Munich, 1968), p. 162.
171. Cited by Thieme, p. 77.
172. Cited by Theiner, *Liberalismus*, pp. 230, 234; Grosser, p. 114 (Stresemann, 3 September 1916).
173. For Left Liberal war aims and reform policies, see Theiner and Grosser, and especially Gottschalk, *Linksliberale*, pp. 13–56; Reimann, pp. 157–216; Simon, *Demokraten*, pp. 145–86; Elm, pp. 236–60; Mommsen, *Weber*, pp. 185–304; cf. also D. Krüger, *Die Nationalökonomen im wilhelminischen Deutschland* (Göttingen, 1983), chs IX–X.
174. Reproduced in: Fenske (ed.), *Unter Wilhelm II*, pp. 487–92. For the July crisis and the IFA, see Matthias and Morsey's edition and Grosser: *U. Bermbach, Vorformen parlamentarischer Kabinettsbildung in Deutschland* (Cologne, 1967), and Rauh, ch. C.
175. K. v. Beyme, *Die parlamentarischen Regierungssysteme in Europa* (Munich, 1973[2]), pp. 258–62, 260 (the Haußmann quotation of 1908); see Rauh, p. 363ff. on 'crypto-parliamentarianism'.

**Chapter 4. The Deliberalization of the 'Middle-class Centre':
The Decline of Political Liberalism in the
Weimar Republic**

1. The best access to the controversial interpretations of Weimar research is provided by E. Kolb, *Die Weimarer Republik*
   (Munich, 1984). Kolb also provides an introduction to the
   seminal literature, which I will not list individually, but to
   which I am indebted.
2. U. Heinemann, *Die verdrängte Niederlage, Politische Öffentlichkeit und Kriegsschuldfrage in der Weimarer Republik* (Göttingen,
   1983).
3. Cf. Weisbrod, *Schwerindustrie*, p. 333ff. The current state of
   research is outlined in G. D. Feldmann (ed.), *Die Nachwirkungen der Inflation auf die deutsche Geschichte 1924–1933* (Munich,
   1985); W. Abelshauser (ed.), *Die Weimarer Republik als Wohlfahrtsstaat* (Stuttgart, 1987).
4. A. Dix, *Die deutschen Reichstagswahlen 1871–1930 und die
   Wandlungen der Volksgliederung* (Tübingen, 1930), p. 30;
   K. D. Bracher *et al.*, *Die nationalsozialistische Machtergreifung*
   (Cologne, 1966/Berlin, 1974), p. 200; T. Geiger, 'Panik im
   Mittelstand', in *Die Arbeit* (Berlin, 1930), pp. 637–54.
5. K. D. Bracher, 'Demokratie und Machtvakuum: Zum Problem des Parteienstaats in der Auflösung der Weimarer
   Republik', in K. D. Erdmann and H. Schulze (eds), *Weimar.
   Selbstpreisgabe einer Demokratie* (Düsseldorf, 1980), pp. 109–34,
   117.
6. H. Kuhn, 'Das geistige Gesicht der Weimarer Zeit (1961)', in
   M. Stürmer (ed.), *Die Weimarer Republik* (Königstein, 1980),
   pp. 214–23, 223.
7. See E. Fromm, *Arbeiter und Angestellte am Vorabend des Dritten
   Reiches*, ed. W. Bonß (Frankfurt, 1980) (the survey was carried
   out in 1929–30). See also Frevert, *Frauen-Geschichte*, pp. 180–
   99. For population trends, see P. Marschalck, *Bevölkerungs-
   geschichte Deutschlands im 19. u. 20. Jh.* (Frankfurt, 1984). Concerning what follows, see D. Petzina *et al.*, *Sozialgeschichtliches
   Arbeitsbuch*, vol. III (Munich, 1978) (includes literature).
8. Kuhn, p. 216f; Kolb, pp. 91–106 provides a survey.
9. J. Herff, *Reactionary Modernism: Technology, Culture and Politics
   in Weimar and the Third Reich* (Cambridge, MA, 1984); P. Gay,
   Die Republik der Außenseiter. Geist und Kultur der Weimarer Zeit

354   NOTES

(Frankfurt, 1970/1987²); for the effect of 'mass culture' on the social milieux, see D. Langewiesche, 'Politik – Gesellschaft – Kultur', *Archiv für Sozialgeschichte*, 22 (1982), pp. 359–402.

10. See G. A. Ritter, 'Kontinuität und Umformung des deutschen Parteiensystems 1918–1920', in Ritter, *Arbeiterbewegung, Parteien und Parlamentarismus* (Göttingen, 1976), pp. 116–57. Neuman, *Parteien* (quotation, p. 27) remains unsurpassed as a general survey. An excellent overall description is also provided in: M. R. Lepsius, 'From Fragmented Party Democracy to Government by Emergency Decree and National Socialist Takeover: Germany', in J. J. Linz and A. Stepan (eds), *The Breakdown of Democratic Regimes: Europe* (Baltimore, 1978), pp. 34–79. The liberal parties of the Weimar Republic have been better researched than those of the Kaiserreich. For brief surveys (with literature), see: L. Albertin and J. C. Heß, in Vorländer (ed.), *Verfall*, pp. 57–89, 91–116. The most important examinations of the period as a whole, or of individual phases, are: Frye, *Democrats*; Stephan, *Aufstieg* (from the viewpoint of the DDP General Secretary); Schustereit, *Linksliberalismus*; Albertin, *Liberalismus*; Schneider, *Demokratische Partei*; Optiz, *Sozialliberalismus* (with problematic opinions); Pois, *Democrats*. For the final phase, see E. Matthias and R. Morsey, 'Die Deutsche Staatspartei', and H. Booms, 'Die Deutsche Volkspartei', in Matthias and Morsey (eds), *Parteien*, pp. 31–97, 533–9. For the DVP, see especially Hartenstein, *Anfänge*; Döhn, *Politik*, and the Stresemann literature. For Stresemann's party politics, see especially Turner, *Stresemann*. Briefer but informative outlines of the small, shortlived liberal groupings are to be found in *Lexikon zur Parteiengeschichte*, 4 vols; for the DVP: W. Ruge, vol. 2, pp. 413–46, for the DDP: W. Fritzsch, vol. I, pp. 574–622. L. E. Jones has produced a series of important essays, including: 'The Dissolution of the Bourgeois Party System in the Weimar Republic', in R. Bessel and E. J. Feuchtwanger (eds), *Social Change and Political Development in Weimar Germany* (London, 1981), pp. 268–88; his other studies are referred to in Jones, 'In the Shadow of Inflation: German Liberalism and the Legitimacy Crisis of the Weimar Party System, 1924–30', in Feldman (ed.), *Nachwirkungen*, pp. 21–41.

11. The announcement is reproduced in A. Erkelenz (ed.), *Zehn Jahre deutsche Republik* (Berlin, 1928), p. 25f.; the best

information on the *Gründungsphase* is provided by Albertin, *Liberalismus und Demokratie*.

12. Turner, *Stresemann*, p. 37; Albertin, p. 60 (Gothein). Concerning what follows, see the works referred to in note 1 and also E. Portner, 'Der Ansatz zur demokratischen Massenpartei im deutschen Linksliberalismus', *Vierteljahreshefte für Zeitgeschichte*, 13 (1965), pp. 150–61; *Linksliberalismus in der Weimarer Republik*. *Die Führungsgremien der Deutschen Demokratischen Partei und der Deutschen Staatspartei 1918–1933*, K. Wegner and L. Albertin's edn (Düsseldorf, 1980).

13. Simon, *Demokraten*, p. 218; Hartenstein, p. 278; K. D. Bracher, *Die Auflösung der Weimarer Republik* (Villingen, 1955/1971⁵), p. 78.

14. Hartenstein, p. 251; Albertin, p. 155ff. agrees and differentiates further; see also Neumann's verdict of 1932 or Dix (1930); see all works cited in note 1.

15. H. Kühr, *Parteien und Wahlen im Stadt- und Landkreis Essen in der Zeit der Weimarer Republik* (Düsseldorf, 1973), p. 96f.; Hartenstein, p. 251; R. Giersch *et al.*, 'Verband der Deutschen Gewerkvereine', in *Lexikon zur Parteiengeschichte*, vol. 3, pp. 211–17, 211.

16. J. C. Heß, 'Die Desintegration des Liberalismus in der Weimarer Republik', in Vorländer (ed.), pp. 91–116, 95; see also Winkler, *Mittelstand*, pp. 121–39.

17. J. Falter *et al.*, *Wahlen und Abstimmungen in der Weimarer Republik* (Munich, 1986), especially chs 2–4.

18. This is unfortunately also true of the tables which indicate movements between parties from election to election. An important critique is to be found in Sperber, *The Kaiser's Voters*.

19. Ibid., p. 146.

20. Ibid., pp. 83–5. Addressed in more detail by G. Bremme, *Die politische Rolle der Frau in Deutschland* (Göttingen, 1956), Table IV, pp. 243–52.

21. Dix, p. 3.

22. Fritzsch, *DDP*, p. 576; Ruge, *DVP*, p. 428; Frye, p. 94f.

23. Bremme, p. 124, Table 39; Greven-Aschoff, p. 159ff.; Simon, *Demokraten*, p. 215.

24. Priamus, *Angestellte*, pp. 153–9; Döhn, pp. 132–9 (also on the break between the DVP and the DHV 1932); L. E. Jones, 'The Crisis of White-Collar Interest Politics: Deutschnationaler Handlungsgehilfen-Verband and Deutsche Volkspartei in

the World Economic Crisis', in H. Mommsen *et al.* (eds), *Industrielles System und politische Entwicklung in der Weimarer Republik* (Düsseldorf, 1974), pp. 811–23.
25. Möller, *Parlamentarismus*, pp. 254–310·

Percentage of Civil Servants in Prussian Landtage

	1919	1921	1924	1928	1932
DDP	38.4	34.5	48.1	37.9	
DVP	57	43	46.5	50	
Centre	43.1	38.3	37	37.8	32.8
DNVP	40	32	25.8	26.8	29.1
SPD	9.5	18.4	19.4	19.6	19.2
NSDAP					16.8
Landtag	27.7	29.7	28.2	26.7	22.5

In 1932 the DDP won only two seats altogether, the DVP seven. For the Reichstag see A. Borell, *Die soziologische Gliederung des Reichsparlaments als Spiegelung der politischen und ökonomischen Konstellationen* (Gießen 1933), pp. 44–66; for the DVP Reichstag parliamentary party: Dohn, p. 348; for the DDP parliamentary party: Schnieder, p. 51.
26. W. Runge, *Politik und Beamtentum im Parteienstaat* (Stuttgart, 1965), pp. 200–4.
27. Cited by Turner, *Stresemann*, p. 239, and L. Albertin, 'Faktoren eines Arrangements zwischen industriellem und politischem System in der Weimarer Republik 1919–1928', in Mommsen *et al.* (eds), pp. 658–74, 671 (DDP-executive meeting 21 June 1927); for a report on this meeting, see *Linksliberalismus*, p. 429f. Concerning what follows, see especially Döhn (on the DVP), Schneider DDP and Weisbrod, *Schwerindustrie*.
28. Cited by Schneider, p. 236. For Erkelenz, see especially R. W. Brantz and A. Erkelenz, 'The Hirsch–Duncker Trade Unions and the German Democratic Party', Dissertation, Ohio State University, Columbus, 1973 (University Microfilms, Ann Arbor, no. 74–125).
29. Schneider, pp. 69ff., 230ff.; *Linksliberalismus*, XXXVIff.; C. Hohberg, 'Hansa-Bund', in *Lexikon zur Parteiengeschichte*, vol. 3, 91–108.

30. Döhn, pp. 79, 111–29.
31. S. Neumann, p. 99. For corporate trends, see especially C. E. Maier, *Recasting Bourgeois Europe* (Princeton, NJ, 1975).
32. Dix, p. 27; cf. Döhn, p. 372ff.; Schneider, p. 237ff.; Eksteins, *Limits*; B. Sösemann, 'Periode des Übergangs oder "Ende des Systems"? Liberale Publizistik im Weimar der Präsidialkabinette', in T. Koebner (ed.), *Weimars Ende, Prognosen und Diagnosen in der deutschen Literatur und politischen Publizistik 1930–1933* (Frankfurt, 1982), pp. 143–81.
33. See Jones, *Shadow*, p. 34ff.; Döhn, p. 284ff.; K. Rohe, *Das Reichsbanner Schwarz Rot Gold* (Düsseldorf, 1966); Schneider, p. 246ff.
34. Matthias and Morsey, *Staatspartei*, p. 37. Concerning what follows, see L. E. Jones, 'Bestrebungen zur Bildung einer neuen Mittelpartei', *Vierteljahreshefte für Zeitgeschichte*, 25 (1977), pp. 265–304; Scheider, p. 293ff.; W. Fritzsch, 'Radikal-Demokratische Partei', in *Lexikon zur Parteiengeschichte*, vol. 3, pp. 608–13; J. Kohn and K. Rüss, 'Deutscher Nationalverein', ibid., vol. 2, pp. 216–20; Booms, *DVP*; for Württemberg see T. Schnabel, *Württemberg zwischen Weimar und Bonn 1928–1945/46* (Stuttgart, 1986), p. 73ff.
35. R. Rürup, *Probleme der Revolution in Deutschland 1918/19* (Wiesbaden, 1968), p. 5. The best introduction to revolution research is provided by Kolb, *Weimarer Republik*.
36. See also Kolb, *Weimarer Republik* (includes literature); a good overall survey is provided in Kolb (ed.), *Vom Kaiserreich zur Weimarer Republik* (Cologne, 1972).
37. Announcement of 1918, in O. Nuschke, 'Wie die DDP wurde, was sie leistete und was sie ist', in Erkelenz (ed.), *Zehn Jahre Republik*, pp. 24–41, 25f.; the party programme of 1919 in: W. Mommsen (ed.), *Parteiprogramme*, pp. 508–14.
38. Nuschke, p. 31 (italics as orginal).
39. Theiner, *Liberalismus*, p. 284.
40. See Albertin, *Liberalismus und Demokratie*, pp. 72–4 (the following quotations are also taken from this source).
41. See Turner, *Stresemann*, p. 50ff.
42. Cited by Albertin, *Liberalismus und Demokratie*, p. 87f.
43. E. Leidig, *Liberalismus und Demokratie* (Berlin, 1919²), quotations from pp. 10–14.
44. Concerning what follows, see especially Albertin, *Liberalismus und Demokratie*, p. 265ff.; E. Portner, *Verfassungspolitik*.

45. Portner, p. 51, quotation: p. 50.

46. R. Rürup, 'Entstehung und Grundlagen der Weimarer Verfassung', in Kolb (ed.), *Vom Kaiserreich*, pp. 218–43, 240 (Koch-Weser); F. Stampfer, *Die vierzehn Jahre der Ersten Deutschen Republik (1936)* (Hamburg, 1953³), p. 137, cited by Portner, p. 253.

47. For the stance of the DDP and the DVP, see especially Portner, pp. 93–115; the seminal work on the subject is G. Schulz, *Zwischen Demokratie und Diktatur. Verfassungspolitik und Reichsreform in der Weimarer Republik*, vol. I (Berlin, 1963).

48. Hartenstein, *DVP*, pp. 149–93 (on the Kapp Putsch), all quotations, including the Stresemann quotation, pp. 192–4; for the DVP's monarchism see pp. 107–20; Bracher, *Demokratie und Machtvakuum*, p. 123; for the DVP programme of 1919, see Mommsen (ed.), *Parteiprogramme*, pp. 519–31; quotations are on p. 520f.

49. G. Anschütz, *Die Verfassung des Deutschen Reichs vom 11. August 1919*, 3rd revision (Berlin, 1930), p. 247; for his political models, see H. Döring, *Der Weimarer Kreis. Studien zum politischen Bewußtsein verfassungstreuer Hochschullehrer in der Weimarer Republik* (Meisenheim, 1975).

50. Bracher, *Demokratie und Machtvakuum*, quotations on p. 117; Portner, p. 141 (Koch-Weser); E. Fraenkel, 'Historische Vorbelastungen des deutschen Parlamentarismus (1960)', in Fraenkel, *Deutschland und die westlichen Demokratien* (Stuttgart, 1964²), pp. 13–31; Albertin, *Liberalismus und Demokratie*, pp. 269, 273 (Haußmann in the constitutional commission, 5 April 1919), p. 276 (Heinze); for Max Weber's ideas and participation in the constitutional discussions, see Mommsen, *Weber*, pp. 356–445.

51. See especially Albertin, *Liberalismus und Demokratie*, pp. 293–308, 306: Delbrück quotation; O. Kirchheimer, 'Weimar – und was dann? (1930)', in Kirchheimer, *Politik und Verfassung* (Frankfurt, 1964), pp. 9–56, quotation on p. 52; Fraenkel, *Deutschland*, p. 33; Rürüp, *Weimarer Verfassung*, p. 238; Theiner, *Liberalismus*, p. 293 (Naumann); Portner, p. 189 (Petersen), pp. 180–93: on the DDP and the DVP. For an analysis of the constitution, see also H. A. Winkler, *Von der Revolution zur Stabilisierung. Arbeiter und Arbeiterbewegung in der Weimarer Republik 1918–1924*, pp. 227–42.

52. As Booms (p. 524) says of the DVP. The heterogeneity of the DDP is stressed by J. C. Heß, 'Überlegungen zum Demokratie- und Staatsverständnis des Weimarer Liberalismus', in H. Boockmann *et al.* (eds), *Geschichte und Gegenwart* (Neumünster, 1980), pp. 289–311; Heß, 'Desintegration'.
53. *Deutscher Liberalismus, Reden der Reichstagsabgeordneten Oberbürgermeister Dr. Most, Geheimrat Prof. D. Dr Kahl, Reichsminister Dr. Stresemann* (Berlin, 1925); all quotations are taken from this source (page numbers in parentheses in text; italics as original). The 'Principles' of 1919 and the declaration of 1927 are to be found in Mommsen (ed.), *Parteiprogramme*, pp. 519–31, 531f. Concerning what follows, see especially Döhn, *Politik*, quotation on p. 129; Döhn, 'Wirtschafts- und Sozialpolitik der DDP und der DVP', in Holl *et al.* (eds) *Liberalismus*, pp. 84–109; Holl, 'Zur Funktion der sozialökonomischen Entwicklung in Deutschland für den Liberalismus von Weimar', in J. Garber and H. Schmitt (eds), *Die bürgerliche Gesellschaft zwischen Demokratie und Diktatur* (Marburg, 1985), pp. 146–92; Heß, *Desintegration*.
54. See K. Sontheimer, *Antidemokratisches Denken in der Weimarer Republik* (Munich, 1968[2]); F. Stern, *Das Scheitern illiberaler Politik* (Berlin, 1974; English edition, 1972), pp. 212–28. Koebner (ed.), *Weimars Ende*.
55. Stresemann, *Reden und Schriften*, vol. II (Dresden, 1926), p. 10.
56. Speech to the *Verein Deutscher Studenten* (Association of German Students) of 6 July 1926, ibid., pp. 262–302, 293f. For an assessment of Stresemann, see Döhn, *Politik*, pp. 378–95; Turner, *Stresemann*.
57. G. Stresemann, *Vermächtnis*, ed. H. Bernard, vol. III (Berlin, 1932), p. 441.
58. According to B. Weisbrod, *Schwerindustrie*, p. 499, in contrast to H. A. Turner, *Faschismus und Kapitalismus in Deutschland* (Göttingen, 1972), p. 132f; Booms, *DVP*, p. 525.
59. L. E. Jones, *Sammlung*, p. 303; the following quotations (page numbers in parentheses in text; italics as original) are taken from *Kampf und Politik der Deutschen Volkspartei. Rede des Parteiführers Dingeldey in der Sitzung des Zentralvorstandes der DVP am 19. April 1931. Kampfziele der D. V. P.*, (Berlin, 1931). See especially Döhn, *Politik*, pp. 208–34.

60. *Wahlhandbuch 1924*, ed. Reichsgeschäftsstelle der DVP (Berlin, 1924), p. 162.

61. Reproduced in Döhn, *Politik*, pp. 437–9; see p. 228 for the internal party response.

62. *Deutscher Liberalismus*, p. 3.

63. Heß, 'Überlegungen', p. 290. Concerning what follows, see above all the detailed studies by Schneider, *DDP*, and Heß, '*Das ganze Deutschland*'.

64. See J. C. Heß in the works already cited. His essays ('Überlegungen', 'Desintegration') provide the best brief surveys of the DDP, and contain fair appraisals.

65. W. Mommsen, 'Wie die Deutsche Republik wurde', in A. Erkelenz (ed.), *Zehn Jahre*, pp. 1–15, 15. M. E. Lüders, 'Was uns gefehlt hat', *Das Demokratische Deutschland*, 3 (1921), p. 221. For an example of a DDP state association to which Lüders' dictum does not apply, see U. Büttner, *Vereinigte Liberale und Deutsche Demokraten in Hamburg 1906–1930* (Hamburg, 1980; first published in *Zs. f. Hamb. Geschichte*, 63 (1977)); Büttner, *Politische Gerechtigkeit und sozialer Geist. Hamburg in der Zeit der Weimarer Republik* (Hamburg, 1986).

66. Here I follow Heß, '*Das ganze Deutschland*'; H. Höpker-Aschoff, 'Nach Osten', in *Der Demokrat*, 11 (1930), p. 29, cited by Schneider, *DDP*, p. 208; G. Bäumer, *Grundlagen demokratischer Politik* (Karlsruhe, 1928), p. 68, cited by Schneider, p. 206; cf. especially W. Huber and G. Bäumer (Augsburg, 1970). For foreign policy in general, see P. Krüger, *Die Außenpolitik der Republik von Weimar* (Darmstadt, 1985).

67. See K. Holl, 'Pazifismus oder liberaler Neu-Imperialismus? Zur Rolle der Pazifisten in der DDP 1918–1930', in J. Radkau and I. Geiss (eds), *Imperialismus im 20. Jh.* (Munich, 1976), pp. 171–95; Matthias and Morsey, *Staatspartei*, p. 39.

68. Erkelenz, in a letter of 2 August 1930, cited by Heß, '*Das ganze Deutschland*', p. 319, note 9; concerning what follows in general, see Theiner, *Liberalismus*, ch. VII; Döhn, *Wirtschafts- und Sozialpolitik*; Schneider, *DDP*, pp. 57–62, 163–200; Jones, *Shadow*; Schustereit, *Linksliberalismus*.

69. G. Stolper, *Die wirtschaftlich-soziale Weltanschauung der Demokratie* (1929). All quotations (page numbers in text; italics as original) are taken from this source. Concerning what follows, see Schneider, *DDP*, pp. 163–75, quotation on p. 164;

Heß, 'Wandlungen', pp. 55–63; *Linksliberalismus*, K. Wegner's edition, p. 498ff.

70. D. Petzina, 'Arbeitslosigkeit in der Weimarer Republik', in Abelshauser (ed.), *Wohlfahrtsstaat*, pp. 239–59, 240, 246: for example, Chemnitz 41.5 per cent, Kiel 40.4 per cent, Duisburg-Hamborn 49.6 per cent.
71. It is important to stress this, as Heß, Schneider *et al.* do, in opposition to Opitz (*Sozialliberalismus*). Quotation from Heß, 'Wandlungen', p. 64.
72. Schneider, *DDP*, pp. 141–60.
73. Reproduced in Matthias and Morsey, *Staatspartei*, pp. 85f. (Külz), pp. 73–5 (Höpker-Aschoff); Heß, 'Wandlungen', p. 71 (Maier).
74. Meinecke, *Werke*, vol. II, p. 411 (italics as orginal).
75. Ibid., p. 474 (12 October 1932).
76. Ibid., p. 481f. (22 February 1933) (italics as original).
77. R. J. Zwi Werblowsky, 'Die Krise der liberalen Theologie', in Thadden (cd.), pp. 147–54, 153; see H.-G. Geyer, 'Die dialektische Theologie und die Krise des Liberalismus', in ibid., pp. 155–70; F. W. Graf, 'Kulturprotestantismus', *Archiv für Begriffsgeschichte*, 28 (1984), pp. 214–68, 249ff.
78. For a list of the governments, see, for example, Ploetz, *Weimarer Republik*, ed. G. Schulz (Freiburg, 1987), pp. 209–18; Falter *et al.*, *Wahlen*, p. 45. For a survey of what follows, see Kolb, *Weimarer Republik*, pp. 71–91; M. Stürmer, *Koalition*; Stürmer, 'Koalitionen und Oppositionen: Bedingungen parlamentarischer Instabilität (1967)', in Stürmer, *Die Weimarer Republik* (Königstein, 1980), pp. 237–53; Fenske, *Strukturprobleme*, ch. VIII.
79. Kolb, *Weimarer Republik*, p. 73.
80. Stresemann, *Vermächtnis*, vol. III, p. 436; also cited in the useful collection of source material by W. Michalka and G. Niethart (eds), *Die ungeliebte Republik* (Munich, 1980), p. 255f.; Kolb, *Weimarer Republik*, p. 73 (Stolper).
81. For details, see Schustereit, *Linksliberalismus*.
82. I have added together Centre Party and BVP mandates, which seemed permissible on the basis of the rapprochement they reached in 1925. Cf. K. Schönhoven, *Die Bayerische Volkspartei 1924–1932* (Düsseldorf, 1972).
83. *Wahlhandbuch, 1924* (DVP), p. 161.
84. Stürmer, *Koalitionen*, p. 240.

85. Ibid., p. 244. For the issues which were voted on, see Schneider, *DDP*, *passim*.
86. For details of what follows, see H. Möller, *Parlamentarismus* (includes all specialist literature).
87. Ibid., p. 529.
88. See Runge, p. 240f.; for a relativization of these figures, see H. Mommsen, *Beamtenpolitik im Dritten Reich* (Stuttgart, 1966), p. 59.
89. As Möller says, p. 597.
90. There is a brief and informative survey in Fenske, *Strukturprobleme*, pp. 124–34; H. A. Winkler, *Der Schein der Normalität. Arbeiter und Arbeiterbewegung in der Weimarer Republik 1924 bis 1930* (Bonn, 1985), pp. 195–202, 327–33; for election results see Falter *et al.*, p. 108.
91. Winkler, p. 329.
92. See Büttner, *Vereinigte Liberale*; Büttner, *Politische Gerechtigkeit*; Büttner, *Hamburg in der Staats- und Wirtschaftskrise 1928–1931* (Hamburg, 1982); Büttner and W. Jochmann, *Hamburg auf dem Weg ins Dritte Reich* (Hamburg, 1983).
93. Cited by Büttner, *Vereinigte Liberale*, vol. I: for Baden and Württemberg, two liberal strongholds, see H. Fenske, *Der liberale Südwesten* (Stuttgart, 1981), ch. IX; Schnabel, *Württemberg*; Simon, *Demokraten*; Rothmund and Wiehn (eds), *FDP/DVP in Baden–Württemberg*.
94. For a case study, see P. Steinborn, *Grundlagen und Grundzüge Münchener Kommunalpolitik in den Jahren der Weimarer Republik* (Munich, 1968).
95. See W. Hofmann, *Zwischen Rathaus und Reichskanzlei. Die Oberbürgermeister in der Kommunal- und Staatspolitik des Deutschen Reiches 1890–1933* (Stuttgart, 1974); figures are given there for the changes in seats. Schnabel, pp. 49–57, pp. 90–104, pp. 187–204, is informative on the municipal level generally.
96. See J. C. Heß, 'Gab es eine Alternative? Zum Scheitern des Liberalismus in der Weimarer Republik', in *HZ*, p. 223 (1976), pp. 638–54; positions adopted in recent research are described in more detail there and in Wegner, *Linksliberalismus*. All quotations are from Neumann, pp. 49, 52, 54.
97. See K. D. Bracher, *Die Krise Europas 1917–1975* (Berlin, 1982²), quotations on pp. 92, 94.

98. H. Boberach (ed.), *Meldungen aus dem Reich*, vol. II (1939; reprinted Berlin, 1984), p. 64f.; D. Langewiesche, 'Erwachsenenbildung', in Langewiesche and H.-E. Tenorth (eds), *Handbuch der deutschen Bildungsgeschichte*, vol. V (Munich, 1988).

99. H. Herkneer, 'Sozialpolitischer Liberalismus', in *Die Wirtschaftswissenschaft nach dem Kriege*, vol. I (Munich, 1925), pp. 33–52, 3, 38; L. v. Wiese, 'Gibt es noch Liberalismus?', in ibid., pp. 15–29, 17.

100. S. Ertel, 'Liberale und autoritäre Denkstile', in R. v. Thadden (ed.), *Krise*, pp. 234–55.

101. Bracher, *Demokratie und Machtvakuum*, p. 134.

102. Cited by Matthias and Morsey, *Staatspartei*, p. 97.

103. See, for example, K.-J. Müller (ed.), *Der deutsche Widerstand 1933–1945* (Paderborn, 1986); J. Schmädeke and P. Steinbach (eds), *Der Widerstand gegen den Nationalsozialismus* (Munich, 1985). Concerning what follows, see above all the exhibition catalogue: H. R. Sassin, *Widerstand*.

104. W. Jochmann, 'Der deutsche Liberalismus', in V. Thadden (ed.), pp. 115–28, 125f. The lack of resilience of liberal ideas is stressed by H. Mommsen, 'Der lange Schatten der untergehenden Republik'. I would like to thank Hans Mommsen for letting me read this unpublished essay, which deals with individual liberals. Many thanks to Peter Steinbach, too, for drawing my attention to useful pointers. For the development of the liberal journal *'Die Hilfe'* after 1933 and the life of G. Bäumer, see W. Hubner. Heuss is dealt with in W. Wiedner, *T. Heuss* (Düsseldorf, 1973); M. Eksteins, *T. Heuss und die Weimarer Republik* (Stuttgart, 1969); J. C. Heß, *T. Heuss vor 1933* (Stuttgart, 1973). Autobiographies of liberals include: W. Stephan, *Acht Jahrzehnte erlebtes Deutschland* (Düsseldorf, 1983); E. Lemmer, *Manches war doch anders* (Frankfurt, 1968); T. Stolper, *Ein Leben in Brennpunkten unserer Zeit* (Tübingen, 1960); E. Schiffer, *Ein Leben für den Liberalismus* (Berlin, 1951).

105. W. Benz, 'Eine liberale Widerstandsgruppe und ihre Ziele', in *VfZ*, 29 (1981), pp. 437–71, 452, 461 (Hans Robinsohn's memorandum of 1939).

106. Unpublished, referred to by Mommsen, *Schatten*, p. 22.

107. All statistics are from: *Biographisches Handbuch der deutschsprachigen Emigration nach 1933*, 3 vols (Munich, 1980). The

figures given in the index had to be corrected for the DVP, since membership of organizations before 1919 or after 1945 were taken together and indiscriminately listed under 'Deutsche Volkspartei (DVP)'.

Chapter 6. The Rebirth of Liberalism? A Brief Summary of Liberalism and Politics in West Germany after 1945

1. R. Dahrendorf, *Fragmente eines neuen Liberalismus* (Stuttgart, 1987), p. 237.
2. R. Dahrendorf, *Die Chancen der Krise. Über die Zukunft des Liberalismus* (Stuttgart, 1983), p. 40.
3. For recent surveys of a readable length and with references to the most important general and specialist works, see: D. Thränhardt, *Bundesrepublik* (1945–86); R. Morsey, *Die Bundesrepublik Deutschland* (Munich, 1987) (1945–69); quotations: H.-P. Schwarz, *Die Ära Adenauer, 1957–1963* (Stuttgart, 1983), pp. 347, 333.
4. Thränhardt (in the Appendix) gives the most accessible figures for the Bundestag and Landtag elections and for Bavaria, including municipal elections.
5. From F. R. Pfetsch, *Verfassungspolitik*, pp. 133–73; Pfetsch, 'Die Gründergeneration der Bundesrepublik', in *Polit. Vierteljahresschrift*, 27 (1986), pp. 237–51. Concerning what follows, see E. H. M. Lange, *Politischer Liberalismus in der Bundesrepublik* (Göttingen, 1980), pp. 48–91, 63 (Heuss quotation).
6. Pfetsch, 'Gründergeneration', p. 247. The statistics which follow are given there and in Pfetsch, *Verfassungspolitik*. The seminal work on the development of the state associations until the foundation of the FDP, is: Hein, *Milieupartei* (includes the most important specialist literature). The following appeared at the same time or soon afterwards: Rütten, *Liberalismus* (includes the LDP of the *Ostzone*); K. Schröder, *Die FDP in der britischen Besatzungszone, 1946–1948* (Düsseldorf, 1985); G. Serfas, *'Lieber Freiheit ohne Einheit als Einheit ohne Freiheit'. Der Neubeginn der Demokratischen Volkspartei in Württemberg–Baden 1945/46* (Heidelberg, 1986).

7. Cited by J. Dittberner, 'Die Freie Demokratische Partei', in R. Stöss (ed.), *Parteien-Handbuch*, vol. II (Opladen, 1984), pp. 1311–81; Hein, pp. 351–53, Rütten, p. 69.

8. Pfetsch, *Verfassungspolitik*, p. 141ff. (age of political socialization: 18–24 years).

9. H. Vorländer, 'Der Soziale Liberalismus der F.D.P.', in Holl *et al.* (eds), *Liberalismus*, pp. 190–226, 197. Concerning what follows, see Ambrosius, *Marktwirtschaft*; W. Abelshauser, *Wirtschaftsgeschichte der Bundesrepublik 1945–1980* (Frankfurt, 1983), p. 71ff.; H.-P. Schwarz, *Die Ära Adenauer, 1949–1957* (Stuttgart, 1981), p. 84.

10. W. Röpke, *Das Kulturideal des Liberalismus* (Frankfurt, 1947), p. 25f.; H. O. Lenel, 'A. Rüstows wirtschafts- und sozialpolitische Konzeption', in *Ordo. Jahrbuch für die Ordnung von Wirtschaft und Gesellschaft*, 37 (1986), pp. 48–58; H. Lampert, in *Staatslexikon*, vol. I (Freiburg, 1985[7]), p. 971; cited by Morsey, p. 41.

11. Concerning what follows, see Rütten, Chapters 2 and 4; S. J. Glatzeder, *Deutschlandpolitik*, cf. P. Bender, *Neue Ostpolitik* (Munich, 1960). For the LDPD, including sources and literature, see B. Itzerott, in: H. Weber (ed.), *Parteiensystem zwischen Demokratie und Volksdemokratie* (Cologne, 1982), pp. 179–213.

12. Quotations are from Rütten, p. 229.

13. Ibid., p. 247; R. Zundel, *Erben*, p. 53. See J. M. Gutscher, *Entwicklung*. The FDP programmes are reproduced in P. Juling, *Programmatische Entwicklung der FDP 1946–1969* (Meisenheim, 1977); see also H. Kaack, *Die F.D.P.*; there is a selection in G.R. Baum and P. Juling, *Auf und Ab der Liberalen von 1848 bis heute* (Gerlingen, 1983), selection begins with 1832.

14. Cited by Rütten, p. 211, and D. Wagner, *FDP*, p. 154.

15. Kaack, pp. 18, 20.

16. The most important works, based on opinion poll research, are given in O. W. Gabriel, 'Demokratiezufriedenheit und demokratische Einstellungen in der Bundesrepublik Deutschland', in *Aus Politik und Zeitgeschichte*, B22 (1987), pp. 32–45. M. and S. Greiffenhagen, *Vaterland*, includes a comprehensive bibliography and an extensive summary of survey results.

17. Schwarz, *Adenauer 1957–63*, pp. 333, 326 (White); K. Lowenstein, *Verfassungslehre* (Tübingen, 1959; English, 1957), p. 93.

18. Dahrendorf, *Gesellschaft*, pp. 471f.

19. Gabriel, p. 35.
20. Thränhardt, *Bundesrepublik*, p. 173; M. Kaase, 'Partizipatorische Revolution – Ende der Parteien?', in: J. Raschke (ed.), *Bürger und Parteien* (Opladen, 1982), pp. 173–89.
21. See Gabriel, p. 37.
22. L. Niethammer, 'Entscheidungen für den Westen – Die Gewerkschaften im Nachkriegsdeutschland', in H. O. Vetter (ed.), *Aus der Geschichte lernen – die Zukunft gestalten* (Cologne, 1980), pp. 224–34 (Niethammer's phrase refers to the codetermination law of 1951). Concerning what follows, see H. G. Hockerts, 'Bürgerliche Sozialreform nach 1945', in vom Bruch (ed.), pp. 245–73 (contains exhaustive literary references).
23. H. G. Hockerts, *Entscheidungen*, p. 421.
24. H. Kaack, 'Die Liberalen', in R. Löwenthal and H.-P. Schwarz (eds), *Die zweite Republik. 25 Jahre Bundesrepublik Deutschland – eine Bilanz* (Stuttgart, 1974), pp. 408–32, 410.
25. Cited by Kaack, *F.D.P.*, p. 17.
26. Ibid., p. 28.
27. K.-H. Flach *et al.* (eds), *Die Freiburger Thesen der Liberalen* (Hamburg, 1972). Concerning what follows, see Vorländer, *Sozialer Liberalismus*, pp. 202–26 and the relevant chapters in Vorländer (ed.), *Verfall*, pp. 215–92; K. Sontheimer (ed.), *Möglichkeiten und Grenzen liberaler Politik* (Düsseldorf, 1975); and Albertin (ed.), *Politischer Liberalismus, passim*. For an angry retrospective view by an insider who moved over to the SPD in 1982, see: G. Verheugen, *Der Ausverkauf: Macht und Verfall der FDP* (Reinbek, 1984).
28. Cited by Vorländer, *Sozialer Liberalismus*, pp. 206, 202, 203 (Dahrendorf); R. Zülch, *Von der FDP zur F.D.P.* (Bonn, 1972), p. 42. The influential articles by Flach, for whom the office of FDP General Secretary was created in 1971, are collected in: K.-H. Flach, *Mehr Freiheit für mehr Menschen* (Baden-Baden, 1979); Flach, *Liberaler aus Leidenschaft* (Munich, 1974).
29. Dahrendorf, *Chancen*, p. 210.
30. H. D. Klingemann, 'Der Wandel des Bildes der FDP in der Bevölkerung', in Albertin (ed.), pp. 125–50, 131.
31. Baum and Juling, p. 164 (1983); *Zukunftschance Freiheit. Liberales Manifest für eine Gesellschaft im Umbruch* (1985), p. 6.
32. For the most recent study on the relationship between values and voting behaviour in the Bundestag elections of 1987, see:

R.-O. Schultze, 'Die Bundestagswahl 1987 – eine Bestätigung des Wandels', in *Aus Politik und Zeitgeschichte*, B12 (1987), pp. 3–17; P. Gluchowski, 'Lebensstile und Wandel der Wählerschaft in der Bundesrepublik Deutschland', in ibid., pp. 18–32; U. Feist and H. Krieger, 'Alte und neue Scheidelinien des politischen Verhaltens', in: ibid., pp. 33–47.

33. Dahrendorf, *Chancen*, pp. 225.

Select Bibliography

The following bibliography focuses on the more recent studies of the subject, which also provide access to older works. Periodical articles, contributions to collections and source materials are cited only in the notes. For a survey of the most important specialist literature and sources, and of the numerous bibliographies which, with a few exceptions, are not listed here, see: J. C. Heß and E. van Steensel van der Aa, *Bibliographie zum Deutschen Liberalismus* (Göttingen, 1981).

General Analyses

vom Bruch, R. (ed.), *'Weder Kommunismus noch Kapitalismus': Bürgerliche Sozialreform in Deutschland bis zur Ära Adenauer* (Munich, 1985).

Dahrendorf, R., *Gesellschaft und Demokratie in Deutschland* (Munich, 1965, 1985); published in English as *Society and Democracy in Germany* (New York: W. W. Norton, 1979).

Fenske, H., *Strukturprobleme der deutschen Parteiengeschichte* (Frankfurt, 1974).

Fenske., H., *Der liberale Südwesten: Freiheitliche und demokratische Traditionen in Baden und Württemberg, 1790–1933* (Stuttgart, 1981).

Gall, L. (ed.), *Liberalismus* (Cologne, 1976), includes a bibliography on international developments.

Gall, L. and Langewiesche, D. (eds), *Liberalismus und Region. Zur Geschichte des deutschen Liberalismus im 19. Jahrhundert* (Munich, 1995) (*Historische Zeitschrift*, Supplement 19).

Geschichte des deutschen Liberalismus (Cologne, 1966).

Heffter, H., *Die deutsche Selbstverwaltung im 19. Jh.* (Stuttgart, 1969, 2nd edn).

Holl, K. *et al.* (eds), *Sozialer Liberalismus* (Göttingen, 1986).

Jarausch, Konrad H. and Jones, Larry Eugene (eds), *In Search of a Liberal Germany: Studies in the History of German Liberalism from 1789 to the Present* (New York, Oxford, Munich, 1990).

Klotzbach, K., *Das Eliteproblem im politischen Liberalismus* (Cologne, 1966).

Krieger, L., *The German Idea of Freedom* (Boston, MA, 1957).

Langewiesche, D., 'The Nature of German Liberalism', in *Modern Germany Reconsidered, 1870–1945*, ed. Gordon Martell (London, New York, 1992), pp. 96–116.

Lexikon zur Parteiengeschichte, 4 vols, ed. D. Fricke *et al.* (Leipzig, 1983–6).

Nipperdey, T., *Die Organisation der deutschen Parteien vor 1918* (Düsseldorf, 1961).

Ritter, G. A., *Die deutschen Parteien, 1830–1914* (Göttingen, 1985).

Ritter, T. (ed.), *Die deutschen Parteien vor 1918* (Cologne, 1973).

Rothmund, P. and E. R. Wiehn (eds), *Die F. D. P./DVP in Baden-Württemäberg und ihre Geschichte* (Stuttgart, 1979).

Schieder, T., *Staat und Gesellschaft im Wandel unserer Zeit* (Munich, 1958, 1970).

Sell, F. C., *Die Tragödie des deutschen Liberalismus* (Stuttgart, 1953; 2nd edn Baden-Baden, 1981).

Sheehan, James, *German Liberalism in the Nineteenth Century* (Chicago, London: Humanities Press, 1978; 2nd cdn 1995).

Snell, J. L., *The Democratic Movement in Germany, 1789–1914* (Chapel Hill, NC, 1976).

Vorländer, H. (ed.), *Verfall oder Renaissance des Liberalismus? Beiträge zum deutschen und internationalen Liberalismus* (Munich, 1987).

Winkler, H. A., *Liberalismus und Antiliberalismus. Studien zur politischen Sozialgeschichte des 19. u. 20. Jahrhunderts* (Göttingen, 1979).

From the Beginnings to the Reichsgründung

Aldenhoff, R., *Schultze-Delitzsch* (Baden-Baden, 1984).

Bazillion, R. J., *Modernizing Germany: Karl Biedermann's Career in the Kingdom of Saxony, 1835–1901* (New York, Zurich, 1989).

Boldt, H., *Deutsche Staatslehre im Vormärz* (Düsseldorf, 1975).

Botzenhart, M., *Deutscher Parlamentarismus in der Revolutionszeit, 1848–1850* (Düsseldorf, 1977).

Brandt, H., *Landständische Repräsentation im deutschen Vormärz* (Neuwied, 1968).

Dann, O. (ed.), *Vereinswesen und bürgerliche Gesellschaft in Deutschland* (Munich, 1984).

Eder, K., *Der Liberalismus in Alt-Österreich* (Vienna, 1955).

Eisfeld, G., *Die Entstehung der liberalen Parteien in Deutschland* (Hanover, 1969).

Faßbender-Ilge, M. H., *Liberalismus – Wissenschaft Realpolitik; Untersuchung des 'Deutschen Staats-Wörterbuchs' von J. C. Bluntschli und K. Brater als Beitrag zur Liberalismusgeschichte zwischen 48er Revolution und Reichsgründung* (Frankfurt, 1981).

Franz, G., *Liberalismus. Die deutschliberale Bewegung in der habsburgischen Monarchie* (Munich, 1955).

Gall, L., *Der Liberalismus als regierende Partei.: Das Großherzogtum Baden zwischen Restauration und Reichsgründung* (Wiesbaden, 1968).

Gerth, H. H., *Bürgerliche Intelligenz um 1800* (Göttingen, 1976).

Grünthal, G., *Parlamentarismus in Preußen 1848/49–1857/58* (Düsseldorf, 1982).

Gugel, M., *Industrieller Aufstieg und bürgerliche Herrschaft. Sozioökonomische Interessen und politische Ziele des liberalen Bürgertums in Preußen zur Zeit des Verfassungskonflikts 1857–67* (Cologne, 1975).

Herzog, D., *Religious Politics in Pre-Revolutionary Germany: Conflicts over Ethnicity, Sexuality and Gender in Baden, 1809–1849* (1991).

Hess, A., *Das Parlament, das Bismarck widerstrebte* (Cologne, 1964).

John, M., 'Liberalism and Society in Germany, 1850–1880: The Case of Hanover', *English Historical Review*, **102** (1987), pp. 579–98.

Koselleck, R., *Preußen zwischen Reform und Revolution* (Stuttgart, 1967; 4th edn 1987).

Langewiesche, D., *Liberalismus und Demokratie in Württemberg zwischen Revolution und Reichsgründung* (Düsseldorf, 1974).

Lee, L. E., *The Politics of Harmony: Civil Service, Liberalism, and Social Reform in Baden, 1800–1850* (Newark, 1986).

Na'aman, S., *Der deutsche Nationalverein* (Düsseldorf, 1987).

Neumüller, M., *Liberalismus und Revolution* (Düsseldorf, 1973).

Nipperdey, Thomas, *Germany from Napoleon to Bismarck, 1800–1866*, trans. Daniel Nolan (Princeton NJ, 1996).

Obenaus, H., *Anfänge des Parlamentarismus in Preußen bis 1848* (Düsseldorf, 1984).

Offermann, T., *Arbeiterbewegung und liberales Bürgertum in Deutschland, 1850–1863* (Bonn, 1979).

Oncken, H., *R. v. Bennigsen*, 2 vols (Stuttgart, 1910).

Padtberg, B.-C., *Rheinischer Liberalismus in Köln während der politischen Reaktion in Preußen nach 1848/49* (Cologne, 1985).

Parent, T., *'Passiver Widerstand' im preußischen Verfassungskonflikt. Die Kölner Abgeordnetenfeste* (Cologne, 1982).

Pollmann, K. E., *Parlamentarismus im Norddeutschen Bund, 1867–1870* (Düsseldorf, 1985).

Rohr, D. G., *The Origins of Social Liberalism in Germany* (Chicago, 1963).

Rosenberg, H., *Politische Denkströmungen im deutschen Vormärz* (Göttingen, 1972).

Schieder, W. (ed.), *Liberalismus in der Gesellschaft des deutschen Vormärz* (Göttingen, 1983).

Schwab, H., *Aufstieg und Niedergang der Nationalliberalen Partei, 1864–80*, 2 vols (Habil.-Schrift, Jena, 1968).

Sedatis, H., *Liberalismus und Handwerk in Süddeutschland* (Stuttgart, 1979).

Siemann, W., *Die deutsche Revolution von 1848/49* (Frankfurt, 1985).

Valjavec, F., *Die Entstehung der politischen Strömungen in Deutschland 1770–1815* (1951; Kronberg, 1978).

Walker, M., *German Home Towns, 1648–1871* (Ithaca, NY, 1971).

Weber, R., *Kleinbürgerliche Demokraten in der deutschen Einheitsbewegung, 1863–1866* (Berlin, 1962).

Winkler, H. A., *Preußischer Liberalismus und deutscher Nationalstaat* (Tübingen, 1964).

Winter, E., *Frühliberalismus in der Donaumonarchie* (Berlin, 1968).

The Kaiserreich, 1871–1918

Becker, J., *Liberaler Staat und Kirche in der Ära von Reichsgründung und Kulturkampf. Geschichte und Strukturen ihres Verhältnisses in Baden, 1860–1876* (Mainz, 1973).

Berghahn, Volker R., *Germany, 1871–1914: Economy, Culture and Politics* (Providence, RI, 1993).

Düding, D., *Der Nationalsoziale Verein, 1896–1903: Der gescheiterte Versuch einer parteipolitischen Synthese von Nationalismus, Sozialismus und Liberalismus* (Munich, 1972).

Elm, L., *Zwischen Fortschritt und Reaktion: Geschichte der Parteien der liberalen Bourgeoisie in Deutschland, 1893–1918* (Berlin, 1968).

Eschenburg, T., *Das Kaiserreich am Scheideweg: Bassermann, Bülow und der Block* (Berlin, 1929).

Gilg, P., *Die Erneuerung des demokratischen Denkens im Wilhelminischen Deutschland* (Wiesbaden, 1965).

Grosser, D., *Vom monarchischen Konstitutionalismus zur parlamentarischen Demokratie* (The Hague, 1970).

Heckart, B., *From Bassermann to Bebel: The Grand Bloc's Quest for Reform in the Kaiserreich, 1900–1914* (New Haven, CT, 1974).

Herzfeld, H., *J. v. Miquel*, 2 vols (Detmold, 1938).

Holl, K. and List, G. (eds), *Liberalismus und imperialistischer Staat* (Göttingen, 1975).

Krabbe, W. R., *Kommunalpolitik und Industrialisierung* (Stuttgart, 1985).

Lorenz, I. S. and Richter, E., *Der entschiedene Liberalismus in Wilhelminischer Zeit, 1871–1906* (Husum, 1981).

Matthes, H.-E., 'Die Spaltung der Nationalliberalen Partei und die Entwicklung des Linksliberalismus bis zur Auflösung der Deutsch-Freisinnigen Partei, 1878–1893', dissertation, Kiel University, 1953.

Molt, P., *Der Reichstag vor der improvisierten Revolution* (Cologne, 1963).

Mommsen, W. J., *Max Weber und die deutsche Politik, 1890–1920* (Tübingen, 1974²).

Mommsen, W. J., *Imperial Germany, 1867–1918: Politics, Culture and Society in an Authoritarian State*, trans. Richard Deveson (London and New York, 1995).

Müller-Plantenberg, U., 'Der Freisinn nach Bismarcks Sturz', dissertation, Berlin University, (1971).

Rosenberg, H., *Große Depression und Bismarckzeit* (Berlin, 1967).

Seeber, G., *Zwischen Bebel und Bismarck: Zur Geschichte des Linksliberalismus in Deutschland, 1871–1893* (Berlin, 1965).

Simon, K., *Die württembergischen Demokraten. Ihre Stellung und Arbeit im Parteien- und Verfassungssystem in Württemberg und im Deutschen Reich, 1890–1920* (Stuttgart, 1969).

Stürmer, M., *Regierung und Reichstag im Bismarckstaat, 1871–1880* (Düsseldorf, 1974).

Struve, W., *Elites against Democracy: Leadership Ideals in Bourgeois Political Thought in Germany, 1890–1933* (Princeton, NJ, 1973).

Theiner, P., *Sozialer Liberalismus und deutsche Weltpolitik: F. Naumann im Wilhelminischen Deutschland* (Baden-Baden, 1983).

Thiel J., *Die Großblockpolitik der Nationalliberalen Partei Badens, 1905–1914* (Stuttgart, 1976).

Thieme, H., *Nationaler Liberalismus in der Krise: Die nationalliberale Fraktion des Preußischen Abgeordnetenhauses 1914–1918* (Boppard, 1963).

Ullmann, H.-P., *Der Bund der Industriellen* (Göttingen, 1976).

Vascik, G., 'Rural Politics and Sugar in Germany: A Comparative Study of the National Liberal Party in Hanover and Prussian Saxony, 1871–1914', PhD dissertation, University of Michigan (1988).

Wegner, K., T. *Barth und die freisinnige Vereinigung* (Tübingen, 1968).

White, D. S., *The Splintered Party: National Liberalism in Hessen and the Reich, 1867–1918* (Cambridge, MA, 1976).

Zang, G. (ed.), *Provinzialisierung einer Region* (Frankfurt, 1978).

The Weimar Republic and the National Socialist State

Albertin, L., *Liberalismus und Demokratie am Anfang der Weimarer Republik* (Düsseldorf, 1972).

Döhn, L., *Politik und Interesse. Die Interessenstruktur der Deutschen Volkspartei* (Meisenheim, 1976).

Eksteins, M., *The Limits of Reason: The German Democratic Press and the Collapse of Weimar Democracy* (Oxford, 1975).

Frye, B. B., *Liberal Democrats in the Weimar Republic: The History of the German Democratic Party and the German State Party* (Carbondale, IL, 1985).

Gottschalck, R., 'Der Linksliberalismus zwischen Kaiserreich und Weimarer Republik: von der Julikrise 1917 bis zum Bruch der Weimarer Koalition um 1919', dissertation, Tübingen University (1969).

Hartenstein, W., *Die Anfänge der Deutschen Volkspartei, 1918–1920* (Düsseldorf, 1962).

Heß, J. C., *'Das ganze Deutschland soll es sein': Demokratischer Nationalismus in der Weimarer Republik am Beispiel der Deutschen Demokratischen Partei* (Stuttgart, 1978).

Holl, K. (ed.), *Wirtschaftskrise und liberale Demokratie: Das Ende der Weimarer Republik und die gegenwärtige Situation* (Göttingen, 1987).

Jones, L., *German Liberalism and the Dissolution of the Weimar Party System, 1918–1933* (Chapel Hill, NC, 1988).

Matthias, R., and Morsey, E. (eds), *Das Ende der Parteien 1933* (Düsseldorf, 1966).

Möller, H., *Parlamentarismus in Preußen, 1919–1932* (Düsseldorf, 1985).

Neumann, S., *Die Parteien der Weimarer Republik* (Stuttgart, 4th edn, 1977).

Opitz, R., *Der deutsche Sozialliberalismus, 1917–1933* (Cologne, 1973).

Peterson, W. F., *The Berlin Liberal Press in Exile: A History of the 'Pariser Tageblatt – Pariser Tageszeitung', 1833–1940* (Tübingen, 1987).

Pois, R. A., *The Bourgeois Democrats of Weimar Germany* (Philadelphia, 1976).

Portner, E., *Die Verfassungspolitik der Liberalen, 1919* (Bonn, 1973).

Priamus, H.-J., *Angestellte und Demokratie: Die nationalliberale Angestelltenbewegung in der Weimarer Republik* (Stuttgart, 1980).

Sassin, H. R., *Widerstand, Verfolgung und Emigration Liberaler, 1933–1945* (Bonn, 1983).

Schneider, W., *Die Deutsche Demokratische Partei in der Weimarer Republik, 1924–1930* (Munich, 1978).

Schustereit, H., *Linksliberalismus und Sozialdemokratie in der Weimarer Republik* (Düsseldorf, 1975).

Stephan, W., *Aufstieg und Verfall des Linksliberalismus. Geschichte der Deutschen Demokratischen Partei* (Göttingen, 1973).

Stürmer, M., *Koalition und Opposition in der Weimarer Republik, 1924–1928* (Düsseldorf, 1967).

v. Thadden, R. (ed.), *Die Krise des Liberalismus zwischen den Weltkriegen* (Göttingen, 1978).

Thimme, R., *Stresemann und die DVP* (Lübeck, 1961).

Turner, H. A., *Stresemann – Republikaner aus Vernunft* (Berlin, 1968).

Weisbrod, W., *Schwerindustrie in der Weimarer Republik* (Wuppertal, 1978).

Winkler, H. A., *Mittelstand, Demokratie und Nationalsozialismus. Die politische Entwicklung von Handwerk und Kleinhandel in der Weimarer Republik* (Cologne, 1977).

The Post-War Period and the Federal Republic

Albertin, L. (ed.), *Politischer Liberalismus in der Bundesrepublik* (Göttingen, 1980).

Ambrosius, G., *Die Durchsetzung der sozialen Marktwirtschaft in Westdeutschland, 1945–1949* (Stuttgart, 1977).

Glatzeder, S. J., *Die Deutschlandpolitik der FDP in der Ära Adenauer* (Baden-Baden, 1980).

Greiffenhagen, M. and S., *Ein schwieriges Vaterland* (Munich, 2nd edn 1979).

Gutscher, J. M., *Die Entwicklung der F. D. P. von ihren Anfängen bis 1961* (Meisenheim, 2nd edn 1984).

Hein D., *Zwischen liberaler Milieupartei und nationaler Sammlungsbewegung, 1945–49* (Düsseldorf, 1985).

Hockerts, H. G., *Sozialpolitische Entscheidungen im Nachkriegsdeutschland* (Stuttgart, 1980).

Kaack, H., *Die FDP* (Meisenheim, 3rd edn 1979).

Kaack, H., *Geschichte u. Struktur des deutschen Parteiensystems* (Opladen, 1971).

Kaack, H., and Roth, R. (eds), *Handbuch des deutschen Parteiensystems*, 2 vols, (Opladen, 1980).

Koerfer, D., *Die F. D. P. in der Identitätskrise: Die Jahre 1965–1969 im Spiegel der Zeitschrift 'liberal'* (Stuttgart, 1981).

Krippendorff, E., *Die Liberaldemokratische Partei Deutschlands in der sowjetischen Besatzungszone, 1945–48* (Düsseldorf, 1961).

Niclauß, K., *Demokratiegründung in Westdeutschland* (Munich, 1974).

Pfetsch, F. R., *Verfassungspolitik der Nachkriegszeit* (Darrnstadt, 1985).

Rütten, T., *Der deutsche Liberalismus, 1945–1955* (Baden-Baden, 1984).

Thränhardt, D., *Geschichte der Bundesrepublik Deutschland* (Frankfurt, 1986).

Wagner, D., *FDP und Wiederbewaffnung* (Boppard, 1978).

Wulff, M., *Die neoliberale Wirtschaftsordnung* (Tübingen, 1976).

Zülch, R., *Von der FDP zur F.D.P.* (Bonn, 1972).

Zundel, R., *Die Erben des Liberalismus* (Freudenstadt, 1971).

Index

Adenauer, Konrad, 312, 314, 315
Agrarian League (*Bund der Landwirte, BdL*), 143, 157, 171–2, 174, 177
Albrecht, Wilhelm Eduard, 29
Alsace Lorraine, 122, 244
Alsace Progress Party (*Elsässische Fortschrittspartei*), 221, 223–4, 225
Altenstein, Karl von, 7
Anschütz, Gerhard, 278
anti-socialism, 157, 194, 206–10, 231, 233, 309
association, freedom of, 11, 31
associations, pressure groups and organisations, 11, 23–7, 47–51, 102–20, 128–83, 204, 229
  Imperial Association Law (1908), 239
  in municipalities, 218–28
  and social reform, 212–13
  in the Weimar Republic, 252, 259–69, 280
  workers' associations, 178
  see also under names of associations
Auerswald, Rudolf von, 66
Augsburger Hof parliamentary party, 39–41, 42, 44
Austria, 14, 61, 113
  associations in, 26
  Austrian Reichstag (Vienna), 38

Catholicism in, 201
civil servants in, 68
Congress of Vienna, 8, 11, 63
and the German Confederation, 82
and the German nation-state, 44, 52, 58, 95, 113, 122
and Italy, 80–1
liberalism in, 9, 25, 63–4
and Prussia, 58, 62, 81–2, 89, 93, 100, 112, 190
reform in, 9, 30, 82
revolution in (1848), 36–7, 39
and the Treaty of Olmütz, 58

Baden,
democrats in, 93, 112
Grand Bloc in, 231
and the *Kulturkampf*, 120, 202
liberal politics in, 8, 67–70, 120, 128, 138, 147, 159–61
the 'new era' in, 76–8, 95
revolution in, 34, 67
Baden-Württemberg, 317
Ballhausen, Lucius von, 195
Bamberger, Ludwig, 197–8, 203, 212, 214–15, 228, 232, 233
Barth, Theodor, 162, 216, 221
Basic Rights, 11–12, 29, 51, 53–4, 65, 71–3, 278–9, 308
Bassermann, Ernst, 178, 210, 241, 244
Bassermann, Friedrich Daniel, 29

375

liberalism (*continued*)
'Gotha party', 57
in the Kaiserreich, 121–249
and the *Kulturkampf*, 199–206
the 'liberal era', 183–99, 232
milieu, 182–3, 269, 279–91, 310
municipal liberalism, xiv, xviii,
218–28
and the nation-state, 95–101,
108–9, 133, 135–6, 183,
185, 189, 206, 219, 229,
234–5, 269
and the parliamentary system,
16, 65, 98–9, 185, 194,
196–7, 231
professional composition of
liberal parties, 139–56
and recession, 190–1, 195–6
and reform, 183–4
Rhenish liberalism, 12, 15,
20–1, 23, 25
and social democracy, 231, 234
and socialism, 206–18
social liberalism, xiii–xiv
social model, 16–23, 77, 234–6
social profile of, 23–7
and social reform, 179–80, 243
in the Weimar Republic,
250–305
in the Wilhelmine era, 228–45
and workers, 178–9
see also under middle classes; *see
also* under names of liberal
parties
Lieber, Ernst, 230
Liebig, Freiherr Justus von, 158
Liebknecht, Wilhelm, 113
Loewenstein, Karl, 314
Lower Saxony, 309
Lüders, Marie Elisabeth, 285, 313

Maier, Reinhold, 290, 317
Malmö Armistice, 52
Manchester liberalism, 18
Manteuffel, Otto Theodor von,
67, 78
March ministries, 28, 33, 38
Masurians, 122
Mathy, Karl, 19

Maximilian, Prince of Baden, 248
Maximilian II of Bavaria, 76
Mayer, Carl, 156
Mecklenburg-Schwerin, 138
Mehring, Franz, 238
Meinecke, Friedrich, 245, 290–1
Mende, Erich, 313
Merck, Ernst von, 54
Metternich, Prince Clemens
Lothar Wenzel, 63
Mevissen, Gustav, 20
middle classes, the, xv, xviii–xix,
58
and associations, 47–51, 105,
117
commercial middle class, 26, 71,
74–5, 88, 167
diversification of, 195–6
educated middle class, 24, 26,
75, 88, 196, 199–200, 211,
256
and liberalism, 1–27, 53, 62–3,
235
lower middle classes, 24
in municipalities, 219, 228
in the Weimar Republic, 256,
259–60, 264, 279–91,
300–1
Miquel, Johannes, 98, 100, 101,
232–3, 236
and associations, 83, 103
and Bismarck, 188
as mayor of Frankfurt, 222–3,
226–7
as mayor of Osnabrück, 222
as Prussian Finance Minister,
192, 223
and workers, 107–8
Mittermaier, Karl, 53
Mohl, Robert von, 16
Moltke, Helmuth Graf von, 189
Mommsen, Wilhelm, 237, 285
Most, Otto, 281
municipalities, 138, 145–53,
218–28
legal reforms in, 184
municipal civil servants, 145
municipal liberalism, 219–28,
299

INDEX 385